W: Manly

Montreal

21 May 1862

STATE OF NEW YORK.

No. 225.

IN ASSEMBLY,

FEBRUARY, 27, 1860.

Introduced on notice by Mr. Flagler; read twice, and referred to a select committee; reported favorably from said committee, and committed to the committee of the whole; considered and amended in said committee, ordered printed as amended, forthwith, and made the special order for Monday, February 27th, at 7 o'clock, P. M.

An Act in relation to the Transportation of Freight on the several Railroads of this State.

The People of the State of New York, represented in Senate and Assembly, do enact as follows:

SECTION 1. Every railroad corporation in this state, which now is, or hereafter shall be engaged in the transportation or carriage of property, except where steam shall not be used for such transportation, is hereby required to make up a full and complete arrangement and classification, in the order from highest to lowest, as each railroad corporation for itself shall rate the relative value of transportation of all and singular, the property usually carried by it, upon the whole, or any portion of the line of its railroads, and shall designate the several grades and orders of such arrangement and classification, as class first, class second, third, fourth, &c., and no article shall appear in more than one classification; such arrangement and classification shall also contain a full and complete specification of the rates and prices, respectively, at which such railroad corporation will transport each article, or class of articles of property, (the transportation upon which is rated at the same value respectively,) which rate and price for transportation shall be specified as a sum certain per ton per mile; which rate and price of transportation shall apply as well to a lesser or fractional part of a ton, as to a greater quantity than one ton (except as herein provided), to be transported upon the whole lines of its railroad.

In case of any article, or class of articles of property, which usually have been transported by railroad by the car load, barrel, package, or other known quantity, and not by the ton, then such specifications may be made up in other respects, as aforesaid, by the car load, barrel, package, or other known quantity, specifying the rate per mile at which the same shall respectively be transported by the car load, barrel, package, or other known quantity as aforesaid.

Every such railroad corporation shall, at all times, take, receive, transport, load, unload, handle and deliver all way freight, and all property, from any station upon the line of its railroad, to any other station upon the line of its railroad, and from either terminus of such railroad, to a way station, or station on the line thereof, which it may transport ordinarily, over the whole line of its railroad, or to any part thereof; and it shall transport each and all said way freight, and each and every item and article of said property transported upon its said railroad, at the same rate per ton per mile as that mentioned in said arrangement and classification, and specifications, and at the same rate per ton per mile, upon a portion of its said railroad, as upon the whole line thereof. Except as herein provided, it shall not be lawful to charge or collect, for the transportation of such way freight, more than the following rates in addition to the rate per ton per mile charged on freight passing over the whole line thereof, to wit: For any distance not exceeding ten miles, one hundred and fifty per centum per ton per mile of the aforesaid published through rates; for any distance more than ten, not exceeding twenty miles, one hundred per centum; for any distance more than twenty, not exceeding thirty miles, seventy-five per centum; for any distance more than thirty, not exceeding fifty miles, fifty per centum; for any distance more than fifty, not exceeding one hundred miles, twenty-five per centum; and for any distance more than one hundred, and less than one hundred and fifty miles, fifteen per centum; for any distance more than one hundred and fifty, and less than two hundred miles, ten per centum; and for any distance more than two hundred, and less than three hundred miles, five per centum; conditioned that the rates on way freight shall, in the pursuance of the aforesaid provisions, be so adjusted, that in no case shall a greater sum, in the aggregate, be charged or collected for a shorter than a longer distance, and provided, also, that the whole charge per ton on way freight, shall in no case exceed the whole charge per ton on the through freight.

When any item or article of property shall be transported upon any such railroad, and the same shall not be mentioned in the arrangement, classification and specifications herein required to be made by the railroad upon which the same is transported, the same shall be transported, at the lowest rate per ton per mile, as aforesaid, mentioned in said arrangement, classification and specification aforesaid.

No article, or class of articles of property, according to the arrangement and classification herein named, shall be charged a price for transportation per ton per mile, greater than triple the rate imposed upon the lowest article or class of articles named in said arrangement and classification. Fresh meats and fresh fish, transported between the months of May and November, inclusive, ores, mineral coal, milk, garden vegetables and fruit, shall be excepted from the provisions of this act.

Every lot and quantity of property, although the same shall consist of two or more items, articles, tons, bales, barrels, parcels, or other known quantity, being of the same classification and arrangement as aforesaid, offered for transportation at one time, or named upon one bill of lading, ticket, or other method of designating the property intended for transportation, for one owner or owners, shall be considered one lot and quantity, for the purpose of ascertaining the rates, and aggregate price, at which the same shall be transported, received, loaded, unloaded, handled and delivered.

Any fractional part of a mile which such property respectively shall be transported, when the same shall be transported more than one mile, shall be considered as a whole mile, in ascertaining the price of transportation of said property respectively; but no railroad shall be compelled to transport any article for a less compensation in the aggregate than twenty-five cents.

No railroad corporation of this State shall give to any station upon its line, or either terminus of its railroad, any precedence or preference over any other station upon its said railroad, in the use of its facilities for the receiving, transporting, handling or delivering of any property which may be transported upon either the whole or part of its railroad, and, as near as may be, shall receive, transport and handle all property which it transports upon the whole or any part of its railroad, in the order of priority of tender or receipt, (at any station upon its line,) of such property, for the purpose of having the same transported to any other station upon its railroad.

A plainly printed or written copy of the arrangement, classification and specifiation of prices for transportation, receiving, loading, unloading, handling and delivering, which shall be in force at the time, shall be signed by the president, vice-president, general freight agent or superintendent of such railroad, and shall at all times, be kept posted in a conspicuous place in each and every freight house, station house and depot of such railroad corporation, or used by it in connection with its railroad, which copies respectively shall, at all times during business hours, be subject to inspection without hindrance. A copy of such arrangement, classification and specification aforesaid, signed as aforesaid, by the president, vice-president or general agent of such railroad, and which shall be duly acknowledged before, and certified by some officer authorized to take the acknowledgment of deeds, shall be filed with the auditor in the canal department at Albany, within three days after the adoption, or the making of the same, or the making any amendment, change or modification of the same, which copy, or a transcript thereof, and of the certificate of the acknowledgment thereof, certified with the time of the filing thereof, by the said auditor, shall be legal evidence in any court, civil or criminal, in this state, of the said arrangement, classification, specification, and the contents thereof; that the same was made by such railroad corporation, and of the filing, and the time of filing thereof. Such arrangement, classification and specification, respectively, shall in all cases, remain unchanged for at least five days after the adoption and filing as aforesaid, of the same, and the pro rata price for the transportation of any article, or class of articles aforesaid, shall in no case be changed at any alteration of any such arrangement, classification or specification, more than thirty per cent from the lowest price aforesaid, as to said article or class of articles, respectively, in that current year. Nor shall such railroad corporation collect or receive either a less or greater sum or consideration in payment for receiving, transporting, loading, unloading, handling and delivering, than that which shall appear to be due by computations from the arrangement, classification and specfications aforesaid, in force at the time being.

§ 2. No railroad corporation shall, directly or indirectly, permit any other person or persons, corporation or corporations, to carry, transport or forward, over the whole, or any part of its railroad, any property for less rates or prices respectively, than those which the said railroad corporation itself would be entitled to receive for the receiving, loading, transporting, unloading, handling and delivering according to the provisions of this act; but the provisions of this act shall not be so constructed as to prevent express companies from charging a commission in addition to tariffs for the time being, established under and by virtue of this act.

§ 3. No railroad corporation shall, directly or indirectly, pay back any portion of the aggregate sums respectively, so, as aforesaid, to be charged by it, for the receiving, loading, transporting, unloading, handling, and delivering, of property as aforesaid, or make any rebate or deduction therefrom, but shall, in all cases, keep and retain each and all sums received by it for said receiving, loading, transporting, unloading, handling and delivering any property as aforesaid.

§ 4. No railroad corporation shall, directly or indirectly, or by or through any officer or servant thereof, combine with, or make any agreement with any other person or persons, corporation or corporations, for the receiving, loading, transporting, unloading, handling or delivering any property transported on any other railroad, vessel or line of carriage, in the course of that transportation, for any less sum or price than the aggregate of the price which, according to the arrangement, classification and specification aforesaid, the said railroad would be entitled to receive if the property was carried only on its own railroad, added to the local tariffs, ordinary rates and charges for the transportation and forwarding of the same kinds of property respectively, at the time being, over the other railroads, and by vessels or other lines of transportation, respectively, over or upon which the same is carried, as aforesaid, when the same is carried only on these other railroads, vessels, or other lines of transportation or carriage alone respectively. No railroad corporation of this state shall, pursuant to any such combination or agreement, or in furtherance thereof, charge or receive a less sum or price for the carriage, transportation, receiving, loading, unloading, handling and delivering of any property which shall, in the course of that transportation, have been carried over or upon any other railroad, vessel, or line of carriage or transportation than the aggregate of the price which, according to the arrangement, classification and specifications aforesaid, the said railroad would be entitled to receive if such property was only transported over its railroad, added to the local tariffs and ordinary rates and charges for the carriage, transportation and forwarding of the same kind of property respectively, for the time being, over or upon the other railroads, vessels, or lines of carriage or transportation respectively, on which the same is carried, when the same is only transported on such other railroads, vessels or lines of carriage or transportation alone, respectively. Any railroad corporation which shall deliver at any point any property carried upon its railroad, which shall, in the course of that carriage or transportation, have been carried on any other railroad, vessel or line of carriage or transportation, and which shall charge or receive on such delivery a less sum for receiving, loading, transporting, unloading, handling and delivering of the same than the aggregate of the price and sum it would as aforesaid be entitled to receive according to said arrangement, classification and specification, and the aggregate of the local tariffs and ordinary rates and charges for the carriage, transportation and forwarding of the same over or upon such other railroad, vessels, and other lines of carriage or transportation, respectively, over or upon which the same shall have been carried or transported as aforesaid, respectively, where the same is only carried or transported on such other railroads, vessels, or lines of carriage or transportation respectively alone, shall be held prima facie to have violated this section and this act.

§ 5. Each and every director, officer, agent, or servant, of every railroad corporation who shall be guilty of a violation of any part of this act, or of aiding or abetting therein, shall be deemed guilty of a misdemeanor, and on conviction thereof, shall be punished by fine of not less than two hundred and fifty dollars, nor more than one thousand dollars, or imprisonment, as now provided by law, or both.

§ 6. This act shall apply to each and all railroad corporations now incorporated, or hereafter to be organized or incorporated under any law of this state, except the Long Island railroad, and all other railroads now constructed, or that shall hereafter be constructed on Long Island.

§ 7. This act shall take effect on the first day of April, one thousand eight hundred and sixty.

§ 8. All acts and parts of acts inconsistent with this act, or any part thereof, are, to that extent, hereby repealed.

SPEECH

OF

HON. LUCIUS ROBINSON,

OF CHEMUNG,

ON THE

PRO RATA BILL,

IN ASSEMBLY, FEB. 27, 1860.

ALBANY:
COMSTOCK & CASSIDY, PRINTERS,
1860.

SPEECH.

In Assembly, Feb. 27, 1860.

Mr. Chairman :—

The bill which was the first-born of the Select Committee, was ushered into the world, as will be remembered, with a flourish of trumpets. Its perfections were wonderful. No amendment was to be allowed. No "shears" were to come near it. Not a letter to be changed. What has become of this child of so much promise? Why, sir, we have to-day seen it consigned to the grave, and by its own parents. It is a clear case of infanticide. A coroner's inquest should be held. Short and troubled was the life of the deceased; speedily was it hurried to the tomb and laid in its last resting place.

"So fades a summer cloud away;
So sinks the gale when storms are o'er;
So gently shuts the eye of day;
So dies the wave along the shore."

And now, sir, having paid the funeral honors due to the distinguished dead, let us look at its successor, provided we can keep it before us unchanged long enough for that purpose. If you examine it you will at once be struck with its family likeness to the deceased. If you look very closely, you will find that there has been another crime committed—that the grave has been robbed, and that it is the corpse which was supposed to have been buried this morning which has been brought back to us dressed in disguise to make it less offensive. All that has been done to the bill (dropping the figure) amounts to nothing but a recorded confession that its principals are wrong and cannot be carried out without the grossest injustice.

It appears by the last official report, that there are within the bounds of this State, 2,398 miles of railways, which have cost, in the aggregate, $149,262,311. They have added countless millions to the wealth of the State, and they contribute daily to the prosperity and comfort of the people. We have also 812 miles of canals, which have been constructed at an immense expenditure from the public treasury. No State, no nation in the world, can exhibit more magnificent results springing from the spirit of commercial enterprise. The bill before us, if enacted into a law, must affect very seriously, for good or for evil, all these vast interests. In discussing its merits, I trust this House will put aside all the selfish interests of canal forwarders, of "Clinton Leagues," and railway managers; that it will rise above all excitements and prejudices, and will take its stand on the high and broad ground of those eternal principles of truth, justice and honor, by which the action of a great State should ever be governed. In the light of such principles I shall endeavor to examine the provisions of this bill.

I have not offered a single amendment to the bill, and have advocated but one of those proposed by others. The reason why I have abstained from all attempts to improve the bill, is, that it appears to me incapable of being brought into any tolerable form by any series of amendments. The first section contained, as originally reported, 132 lines, and covered five pages. The other sections covered four more pages. And such a complicated labrynth of words has never yet been seen upon our statues, and I trust never will be.

I make these remarks with the more freedom, because I am informed that the bill came from outside, and was not prepared by the Select Committee, or by any member of this House. Without such information, it was sufficiently apparent that the mind which gave us the compact and well written report made by the Chairman of that Committee, the gentleman from Niagara, had nothing to do with weaving this entangled web, which seems to have neither beginning, end or middle.

But, sir, objectionable as the bill is in point of form, that is as nothing compared with the unsound and odious principles which lie buried beneath its flood of verbiage. It proposes a violent and sweeping interference with the business of all the railroads in the State. It proposes to wrest from them franchises solemnly guarantied to them by law, to invade all their station houses and depots, to abolish all their freight regulations, and to establish for them an inflexible and iron pro rata rule, such as the experience of all time upon every avenue of commerce has shown to be unsound, impracticable and unjust.

The ground upon which the Legislature is asked to do this great violence, appears at first sight very plausible. It is, that higher prices are frequently charged for way freights than for through freights, for short distances than for long ones. This naturally strikes every mind not familiar with the course of trade as being unequal and wrong. And I have no doubt that most of the petitions presented here have been signed under that first impression. When I received and read the "Clinton League" documents which were so profusely scattered over the State, presenting only this aspect of the question, and before I had time for examination, I frankly admit that if one of these petitions had been presented to me, I might and probably should have signed it.

One or two illustrations will best serve to remove that impression and show the fallacy of this pro rata rule. Take, for instance, the New York and Erie Road; it starts from Dunkirk with a train of cars as long as one locomotive can draw and all completely filled, and carrying, say 200 tons of freight at $5 per ton. It moves on to New York without any stoppage or interruption, except for the usual supplies of wood and water, and when it has arrived at its destination it will receive $1000 for the freight earned by the trip. Charge against this the wages of the men employed, the cost of fuel, the wear and tear and all other expenses, reaching say $750; and the balance, $250, will be clear profits. Take now a train for way freight, starting from Dunkirk with only three or four cars partly filled, and stopping at every station along the whole line of 450 miles and picking up here and there half-loaded cars, and finally arriving at New York with perhaps the same number of cars as the through train, but not more than one-half the quantity of freight, say 100 tons, and even charging the same price per ton as upon the through train, there would be but $500 received. Supposing the expenses of the way train to be the same as of the through train (and the proof shows that they would be far more,) it will be seen at a glance that whereas there was a profit of $250 upon the through train there is a loss of the same amount upon the way train.

My friend, Mr. Diven, late Senator from my district, who is very familiar with this whole subject, and especially with the operations of the Reading road, has kindly sent me a statement, which I beg leave to read as further illustrating the same position:

The Reading Railroad is 100 miles in length. A locomotive draws 100 four-wheel cars, carrying five tons each, from Pottsville to Richmond, the whole length of the road. Experience has shown that coal carried in this way will pay a fair profit at one cent per ton per mile. This load pays $500 drawn through. Now if you start frem Pottsville with five car loads, and stop every five miles and load five cars at each stop, you reach Richmond with a full load, and at one cent per ton per mile on a load gathered in this way, you receive $250; and every railroad operator can see that it will cost more to earn $250 in this way than $500 on the through load.

These illustrations might be continued to any extent. They show I believe with entire fairness the distinction between through and way freights—the absolute necessity which the laws of trade enforce, of charging more in proportion upon way than upon through freights. They show too why this always has been done and always must be done if the carrying trade be conducted upon sound business principles. Moreover if we look into the evidence given before the select committee, we find that several of the ablest and most experienced men connected with railroad management in the whole country were examined, and all concur in the statement that it is impossible to do a way business at the same rates as a through business, because it is far more expensive. Every man of common sense must see that it would be as improper to require it as to compel a merchant to sell his goods at retail for the same price as at wholesale.

Let us look a little farther into the practical working of this pro rata principle. The original bill provided that all freights should be carried at a sum certain per ton per mile, and the same rate to apply as well to a lesser as to a greater quantity. There was also to be allowed at the rate of 40 cents per ton (in the elegant language of this bill) "for receiving, loading, unloading, handling, delivering and doing the other things aforesaid." Suppose then you wish to send a barrel of flour from Dunkirk on the Erie road a distance of five miles. A half dime would seem a small sum to charge for that service, and a barrel of flour being about the tenth part of a ton, there would be four cents "for receiving, loading, and unloading, handling, delivering and doing the other things aforesaid," making altogether nine cents—a very moderate charge, truly. But pro rate it to New York, and it would amount to $4,50, frequently more than the flour would be worth. Extend the principle over a line of road a thousand miles in length, say from Chicago to New York, and the freight would amount to $10 per barrel or $100 per ton. If you do not like to pro rate up in this way, suppose we pro rate down. Start a barrel of flour from Chicago to New York at $1 per barrel, which is more than the usual charge. It would make the rate for 10 miles one cent, 5 miles half a cent, and one mile one mill. To such ridiculous and absurd results does this principle lead.

The author of the bill, whoever he may have been, was obliged himself to violate the principle of it as its friends have been to-day, and to save it from these ludicrous results provided that an arbitrary sum of twenty-five cents should be paid for carrying any distance. But this does not affect the principle, it only shows a consciousness that it is unsound.

The majority report of the Select Committee refers with an air of triumph to the fact that several roads running in connection pro rate with each other. But in every instance adduced in the report it was through freight, carried over the entire length of all the roads, and in such cases it makes no difference whether the prices charged are a sum in gross or at so much per mile. The result would be the same either way. It therefore proves nothing.

The friends of this bill recoiled with horror from the proposition to apply it to the canals. They gave as an excuse that competition would regulate the prices on the canals, and so it will, but not on the pro rata principle, which is thus proved to be wrong. It was proven before the committee, and not denied, that in May last freight was carried by canal from New York to Buffalo, 514 miles, for 10 cents per 100 lbs., while from New York to Rochester, 415 miles, 12 cents per 100 pounds was charged. At pro rata it should have been $8\frac{4}{100}$ cents per 100 pounds, or one-third less than was charged to Buffalo. In July, from New York to Syracuse, 8 cents per 100 pounds was charged for 316 miles, while from Syracuse to Manlius, 10 miles, 8 cents per 100 lbs. At pro rata, the rate between Syracuse and Manlius would have been 3 mills per 100 pounds, instead of 8 cents. So to Rome, 125 miles, 10 cents per 100 pounds, and from New York to Syracuse, 316 miles, 8 cents per 100 pounds. At pro rata, from Albany to Rome it should have been $3\frac{27}{100}$ cents per 100 pounds. At the same time, from Albany to Utica, 100 miles, 10 cents per 100 pounds was paid, and from New York to Detroit 12 cents per 100 pounds. A pro rata would be, from Albany to Utica, $1\frac{96}{100}$ cents per 100 pounds, or less than one-quarter the price charged.

I will not detain the committee by multiplying facts and instances which are so well known and to which there is no exception. Upon no road, upon no river, upon no canal in the whole country has this iron pro rata rule ever been applied to way freights. All rules and all analogies are against it. The same postage stamp required to carry a letter one mile will carry it a thousand miles. Express charges vary but little on account of distances. The freights are but a trifle higher from New York to Liverpool than from New York to Charleston. The great rival lines of railroads engaged in ardent competition with ours are free and untrameled. Why then should we step in to aid those lines by putting handcuffs and straight-jackets upon our own roads? Why should we thus interfere with the natural course of trade, and intermeddle in a business which will be much better managed by those who are engaged in it and understand it, than it can possibly be by the Legislature?

Sir, the gentleman from Herkimer, who advocates this violent interference with the transportation business referred in terms of admiration to the late Michael Hoffman —a name never to be pronounced by me but in terms of respect and veneration. I would like to ask my friend from Herkimer, what that wise and faithful statesman would have said to such a proposition as this. Often have I wished during this debate that the "Grey Eagle of Herkimer," as we used to delight to call him, might have been spared to rise in his place here and blast with the lightning of his great intellect a scheme so full of mischief as the one before us. But, sir, though dead, he yet speaks and shall be heard. I will read from a speech delivered by him upon this floor in the Constitutional Convention of 1846. He was referring, as will be seen, to the subject of levying tolls upon transportation, but his remarks will apply with equal force to the violent and lawless interference proposed in this bill:

Some effort has been made to tax the railroads on their transportations, as if the company paid this class of taxes and not the persons who consumed the articles transported. The Legislature have made some progress in this Spanish-Bourbon legislation of pensioning the government on trade and travel. We would make internal improvements and cheapen transportation, and tax the transportation to make it dear. If we attempt to extend and fix this system of taxes on transportation, if we pursue the course of taxing transportation on roads not made at the expense of the State, we shall make the government a real highwayman—odious and an oppressor. Such a course may, like any other abuse answer for a time; but it must fail from surrounding circumstances. Trade, travel and transportation will be driven from us, and our industry must languish for want of the rewards which untaxed transportation and trade can alone secure to labor.

I never can consent that the current expenses of the State, and all its great expenditures, should be charged on the right of way, which the sovereign should hold, not as property for revenue, but in trust for the million—to promote travel, transportation and commerce. To the extent that the State makes advances and incurs a reasonable risk in making a road or canal, the State, from the tolls, should fully indemnify itself for those expenses and that risk. But when a citizen, at his own expense, makes the road or canal, I can think of no worse or more oppressive course than the Bourbon one which we have commenced of taxing the transportation on it for the benefit of the State.

If the policy of levying tolls upon transportation deserved to be characterized as a Spanish-Bourbon policy, how much more does this pro rata scheme deserve that epithet? For the tolls there is a show of reason. There is at least the excuse that they will bring some revenue into an exhausted and empty treasury, and, as Hoffman declares, the State should indemnify itself for its expenses. But the pro rata measure does not offer even that poor apology. It will be a violent and mischievous interference with trade and transportation, which may produce a little temporary benefit to a few canal forwarders, but to no one else, either government or people, and must ultimately end in disaster to all parties. What good can it do? Will it lower the rates of freight for our own citizens? The complaint is not that the charges upon us are too high, but those upon our neighbors are too low. The proof shows conclusively that the rates for way freights, upon the roads in this State, are lower than upon almost any roads in the country. If by passing this act we break up the through business we shall compel the roads to raise our own freights in order to support themselves at all. Will the people thank us for that?

In defiance of the evidence, the advocates of the measure contend that it can be enforced, and our roads still keep their business—that the rates on this business can be increased without losing it. They tell us that New York has a plateau which is the natural track of commerce; they point us to the heavy grades at the South, and the cold winters at the North; and by a series of easy and pleasing deductions they arrive at a logical demonstration that the rival lines cannot compete with us, and that the trade must continue to pass over our plateau. They are like certain learned writers who proved only a few years ago that railroads could never carry freight at all, and that steamships could not cross the Atlantic, and that all who differed from them in these opinions were very ignorant people. The speculations were all good; the logic perfect, but the misfortune was that the event would never agree with the prediction. Even while the demonstration that these things could not be done, was going on, the things actually were done.

So it is with our friends. Their reasoning is good, their conclusions most gratifying, but the actual event falsifies all. They build us a pleasant house to dwell in; but it is founded upon the sand and the storm sweeps it away. Whilst we are listening to the proof that those rival roads cannot compete with ours, they actually are competing. Whilst we are being told that the grand trunk road is, up towards the North Pole, frozen up and incapable of carrying freight to New York as cheaply as our own roads, its trains are running but a few miles north of us, its agents are all over the west, and it is actually carrying freight from Chicago to Liverpool cheaper than our roads can carry it to New York. There has been expended upon it and other works in connection, to enable them to compete with us, more money than the Erie canal and our two great lines of railroad originally cost. The total amount of capital invested in works competing with us more or less for this western trade, in Canada and the States, is not less than $350,000,000. Our own railways have cost in the aggregate near $150,000,000. What mean these immense and almost incredible expenditures? Do gentlemen suppose that they are for no purpose? Has Canada, backed by the British government, expended nearly $100,000,000 for nothing? No; delude us with specious reasoning as you may, as to the impossibility of competition, the patent fact stands out in defiance of all logic. These tremendous interests are engaged in a desperate struggle. The New York roads are pressed on every side, and are put to their utmost energies to maintain themselves. In carrying at low rates they submit to a stern necessity. Who doubts that they would obtain higher prices if they could? Are we to be told that they wantonly throw away money? No; to compel them to charge higher is to compel them to abondon the business. To pass this law is to put chains upon their limbs at a time when they most require the free use of all their powers in this tremendous contest.

I will not detain the committee longer upon this branch of the subject. I have not deemed it necessary to reply at much length to arguments intended to prove that certain events could not happen when they are actually happening every day before our eyes.

There is another question of a most serious character, to which I now ask attention. Has the Legislature a constitutional right to pass this act, and can it do so without a violation of its faith and honor? This question has not hitherto been referred to, except in a very general way by the report of the select committee, which does not touch the real point involved.

I have already alluded to the fact that $150,000,000 have been invested in the railroads of this State, a sum sufficient to admonish us that we are dealing with immense interests and should proceed with caution. The Legislature has at all times encouraged the construction of these works, which have done so much to develop our wealth and revenues. The monies expended upon them belonged not to the State but to individuals, who were induced to advance their funds in consideration of certain rights and franchises granted by the State. One of those franchises was the right of each company to fix and regulate the rates of freight. It is an established rule of law that a charter to such a corporation is a contract between the government and the company. To take away or impair one of the franchises granted by such a charter would therefore be a clear violation of the Constitution, but for the clause which is usually inserted reserving the power "to alter, modify or repeal." Now what is the fair import and meaning of that formal provision inserted in all charters? Does it mean that the Legislature may, without a forfeiture of the charter, step in wantonly and take away the rights and franchises which it has granted to a company and render them worthless? This would be a monstrous doctrine. Although the State may have power so to act, good faith and common honesty forbid it. Let me call attention to the language of Chancellor Kent upon this subject:

2d Kent's Com., 372, 9th Ed,—306 old Ed.

General Railroad Act, Sec. 28, Sub. 9 and 10, Sec. 33.

The law gave the right to fix and regulate rates of freight. It gave authority to mortgage that franchise with the other property. Such mortgages have been given and money advanced upon them to the amount of many millions. And now it is proposed to step in and take away the right. Is not this a gross violation of faith? And here let me again quote another passage from the speech of Michael Hoffman, already referred to. "I have," said he "no desire to make a stalking horse of the public faith, but I wish to bring before the committee what is meant by a breach of public faith. In a moral point of view, and

and in its numerous consequences, it is in relation to the sovereign body what wilful and corrupt perjury is to the individual man. It is the maximum of human guilt."

I know not how this matter may appear to others; with my views of it I could not vote to violate the faith of the State, as I believe this bill does, without feeling this "maximum of human guilt" resting upon my conscience.

These remarks apply to all the railroads generally. But, sir, as to the longest of those roads, the New York and Erie, I take still stronger grounds, and insist that the passage of this bill will not be only a breach of public faith, but a direct and palpable infraction of the Constitution. Upon looking into the law upon this subject, I find that the Erie road stands upon grounds peculiar to itself, as a brief reference to its history, and the legislation in regard to it, will show.

It will be remembered by the older members of this House, that immediately after the completion of the Erie canal, the southern tier of counties complained that whilst they had been taxed for that work they were not benefitted but rather injured by it. With a view of doing justice to them the project of a State road was started as an offset for the canal, and the Legislature ordered a survey to be made and measures to be taken for the construction of such a road. While the matter was yet under discussion, public attention was directed to the then new mode of conveyance by railways, and the idea became prevalent that a railway had better take the place of the State road. Finally, in 1832, the New York and Erie Railroad Company was chartered, with the understanding from the onset that it was to receive aid from the State. It was chartered as a freight road. One of the powers given to it in express terms was to "fix, regulate and receive the tolls and charges" for transportation. I read from the 14th section of its charter.

The company was organized, and in 1836 the State in pursuance of the purpose all along entertained, advanced stock to aid in the construction of the road to the extent of $3,000,000. Subsequently the company entirely broke down, the work was suspended, and for several years there was little hope of its ever being completed. There were applications and a report in the Senate to adopt it as a State work. But finally, after great embarrassment and much negotiation, the company was reorganized under a law passed in 1845, and the work went on to completion. And I now wish to call particular attention to that law of 1845. It will be seen that it is not only in substance but even in form a contract between the State and the company. The language is: "If the New York and Erie Railroad Company," &c , then it shall be lawful for them to issue bonds which shall be mortgages, &c., a first lien, &c. There is no authority reserved to repeal or modify this act. On the contrary, it contains a section repealing all acts in conflict with it. Under this guaranty of the State, the mortgage bonds were issued, the $3,000,000 advanced upon them, and by the express terms of this law they became a first lien upon all the property and franchises of the road. One of these franchises was the right to fix and regulate its own freights, and I respectfully submit that you cannot interfere with that franchise without violating the constitutional provision that no law shall be passed impairing the obligations of contracts, and also violating the pledged faith of the State by trampling under foot the rights of the mortgagees of that road.

In view of these circumstances, I ask the members of this House to consider well whether we can pass this law and still act in accordance with the admonitions of the learned and pure minded Chancellor Kent? Will it exhibit that "extreme moderation and discretion" which he so earnestly and so wisely commends? Or will it exhibit that recklessness of public faith and constitutional obligations which will be the first step in a downward road of dishonor, where every succeeding step will become more easy and rapid ?

A few general remarks and I have done. The railroads have been arraigned here, as "grinding monopolies," making war upon the canals and the people. I do not stand here as their advocate or apologist. I have no interest in them or their management, other than such as every citizen has. I admit that these great corporations should be watched and strictly confined to their legitimate duties. I think it more than probable that in the rush and hurry of the heated competition in which they are engaged, they may have been at times too heedless of the rights of our citizens. But I do not believe that this has been the result of design, or of any intention to make war against the interests of a State upon which they depend for their very existence, and in whose honor and prosperity the managers feel as high a pride and as deep an interest as any of us. I have no doubt that there is some truth and a great deal of exaggeration in these charges hunted up and brought forward by the "Clinton League," for the purpose of making out a case against them. Doubtless most of these instances are accidental irregularities which will be corrected by public opinion, and free competition, a stronger power in commercial matters than legislative acts. The railroad corporations are not perfect any more than other human institutions, and we cannot make them so. If they make mistakes, the Legislature might make those which would be as bad or worse. Let us not take their affairs into our hands. Our success in the canal business has not been such as to encourage us to undertake the ruining of the railroads.

Why should we denounce them as grinding monopolies and charge them with oppression? They are not monopolies; they have no exclusive privileges. Every body may build a Railroad to compete with any other. There is entire freedom in this respect, and they are all in competition, more or less, with other roads. And how have they oppressed us? Has it been by pouring out their money like water until they have expended $150,000,000 to bring the markets of the world to our very doors? Has it been by carrying us and our merchandize from place to place with the speed of the wind and laying at our feet the tribute of all quarters of the globe? Has it been by carrying food to the consuming millions at rates so low that nearly all the companies are on the verge of bankruptcy and the Railroads are becoming paupers? Call you this oppression? And who, among us, ever knew that we were oppressed at all until the "Clinton League" told us so? But for the uncall-ed for obtrusion of this information, we should have lived on in blissful ignorance of what we were suffering.

Again, I ask, why the Railways are charged with oppression? Not because they charge us too much, but because they are kind to our neighbors and charge them too little. We propose to make it a criminal offence, and to inflict pains and penalties if they do not charge them higher and compel people to pay more for their bread. Is the great State of New York to make such an exhibition of herself? Is she to legislate with the mean and envious spirit "which pines and sickens at another's joy?"

But it is said that the effect of this is to depress the value of our lands and depopulate our State. Is there any truth in that assumption? Does anybody believe it? Will our farmers sell out and move a thousand miles farther west, because they can have their produce carried to the seaboard for a few cents less? No sir; it is all fiction. We have countervailing advantages which more than overbalance all this. The farmers of the west have much more difficulty and expense to reach their shipping points than we have. And if there is depression in the value of the land at the East, so is there at the West; and the railroads had nothing to do with it in either case. It is the natural result of the commercial revulsion of two years ago, and the failure of western crops, the effects of which are still felt everywhere.

It is said that the railroads are competing with the canals, and taking away their business. That is true to some extent. No one can deny it. The State built canals, and it authorized and encouraged the building of railroads along their banks. Competition was the natural and inevitable result. If the State was determined to avoid competition it should never have gone into the canal business, or else it should not have authorized the railroads. Having done both, and brought its competitors into the field, it is unfair and unmanly to rule them off by the power of law.

Legislate as much as we may, the trade will go where it can go quickest and cheapest. In doing so it obeyes the laws of trade, which are higher than any that we can make. Let us not forget that we live in a progressive and a fast age and country. Commercial enterprise is running its competing lines all over the globe. Railways are supplanting Canals, and the brain may even now be at work which is to invent some power to take the place of railways. We can no more stay these things than we can change the course of the planets. There is as has been well said "an inexorable logic of events" which it is as vain to resist as it is to contend with the Almighty.

The bill before us is, in my opinion, an attempt to reverse the wheels of time and make them roll backward. It is a bill to violate the laws of trade, to enact a manifest wrong, to do injustice to the railroads, and to sacrifice American to British enterprise, to drive away the trade and commerce of the State and of its great emporium. Worst of all, it is a bill to violate the faith of the State and the Constitution of the United States. These are my reasons for opposing it, I think they are sufficient.

OPPOSITION TO RESTRICTIONS UPON TRADE.

Remonstrance of the Business Men of New-York.

TO THE HON. THE LEGISLATURE OF THE STATE OF NEW-YORK:

Your Petitioners, merchants and business men of the City and County of New-York, remonstrate against the passage of bills now before your honorable body, providing for the regulation of Rail-Roads, and their Freight Tariffs. That one bill, commonly called the Pro Rata Freight Bill, is grounded on false principles of legislation, tyrannical in its provisions, and subversive of the best interests of this State. It provides that all the Rail-Roads in this State shall carry freight at the same rate per mile for a short distance that they charge for a long distance. This arbitrary interference with the natural laws of trade is justified by the friends of the bill on the ground that the producers of this State need protection from Western competition, and that the State Canals need protection from Rail-Road competition. Instead of obstructing our means of transport and communication with the great and growing West, the State should do every thing in its power to increase these facilities. Our commercial supremacy is not so secure for the future as we are prone to believe. We have active and vigilant rivals on every side, and they are exerting every effort to draw off our trade. The effect of the Special Tax proposed would be to enhance the prices of food brought from the West to the populations of our crowded cities and villages, while it would at the same time tend to diminish the employment, and reduce the compensation of labor. For these, and many other reasons that might be advanced, your remonstrants respectfully, but most earnestly urge the rejection of both bills.

Names and Places of Business.

ABBOTT, J., 94 Broadway.
Atwater & Co., Wm., 94 Chambers-street.
Andreæ, B., 75 Chambers-street.
Arthur, Geo. D., 146 Broadway.
Agnew & Sons, Wm., 284 and 286 Front-st.
Allen & Co., Joseph, 11 South-street.
Agnew, John T., 284 and 286 Front-street.
Adee, Geo. T., 40 Wall-street.
Arnold & Tournade, 50 Beaver-street.
Angell & Co., 158 Chambers-street.
Acker, Merrall & Co., 132 Chambers-st.
Andrews, Giles, Sanford & Co., 100 Chambers-street.

Names and Places of Business.

Abbott, Jno. M., 111 Chambers-street.
Allen, Julian, 130 Water-street.
Archer & Bull, 177 Water-street.
Asten, Harry, 120 Maiden Lane.
Allin, R. C., 15 Wall-street.
Anthony, Jno. W., 252 Broadway.
Agate, Joseph, 256 Broadway.
Amielon & Leavitt, 256 Broadway.
Adams & Hawthorne, 51 South-street.
Arnold & Co., L. L., 36 Liberty-street.
Adams, McKeenny & Co., 96 Liberty-st.
Adler & Rosenblatt, 95 and 97 Liberty-st.
Adler, Brother & Co. 93 Liberty-street.

Ackerman & Bro., B., 154 West-street.
Archer & Bro., 202 West-street.
Appleton & Co., D., 346 Broadway.
Adams, J. L, 108 and 110 Warren-street.
Adams, Seth, 166 Pearl-street.
Aspinwall, James S., 86 William-street.
Anthony, E., 308 Broadway.
Ashley, O. D., 52 Exchange Place.
Adee, Chas. T., 99 West 42d-street.
Adams, F. T., 84 Orchard-street.
Algernon & Jarvis, 192 and 194 Cherry-st.
Abeel & Co., Jno. H., 190 South-street.
Andarim, W. E., 322 Pearl-street.
Adams, J. Q., 95 Church-street.
Allen, Geo. C., 415 Broadway.
Allason, Wm., 396 Broadway.
Appleton, Daniel S., 346 Broadway.
Allaire, Anthony, 364 Broadway.
Aldrich, H. D.
Alfred, S. M., 13 Gold-street.
Arthur, M., 89 Gold-street.
Aldrich, T. C., 58 Beekman-street.
Armstrong, David, 254 Water-street.
Adee, Frederic, 114 Norfolk-street.
Acklande, Thos. R., 226 Greenwich-street.
Adams & Co., Jay L., 200 Greenwich-st.
Ackerman, James, 192 Pearl-street.
Alger, E. W., 16 Spruce-street.
Adams, Jno., 503 Greenwich-street.
Ackerman, James, 192 Pearl-street.
Agnew, T. R., 260 Greenwich-street.
Anthony, N. K., 39½ Exchange Place.
Ayres, Geo. E., 362 Broadway.

BAKER, G. W., 162 Broadway.
Beardsley, J. A., 18 Wall-street.
Busteed, N. W., 16 Wall-street.
Bryce & Co., William, 29 Chambers-street.
Brownson, Slocum & Hopkins, 45 Chambers-street.
Boorman, Johnston & Co., J.
Barney, A. H., 82 Broadway.
Barney, D. N., 82 Broadway.
Baldwin, A. P., 72 Broadway.
Brown, Chas. W., 11 Broadway.
Baker, Frank T., 23 Wall-street.
Barnly, J. W., 23 Wall-street.
Bayles, R., 126 Broadway.
Burroughs, Wm., Jr., 192 Broadway.
Bird & Co., Wm. E., 218 Front-street.
Bensel & Co.
Blake, E. J., 184 Broadway.
Bogert & Oakley, 89 Pearl-street.
Bean & Raymond, 97 Pearl-street.
Beach & Brumley, 9 Coenties Slip.
Brewer & Caldwell, 20 Old Slip.
Brundage & Co., J. H., 36 Burling Slip.
Brewer, H. O., 20 Old Slip.
Babcock, F. A., 69 Beaver-street.
Bellows & Co., Chas., 41 Beaver-street.
Brown, James, 7 Whitehall-street.
Burkhalter & Co., C., 188 and 190 Chambers-street.

Binns & Halsted, 145 Chambers-street.
Bruce & Co., A. T., 147 Chambers-street.
Baker & Bro., H. J., 142 Water-street.
Bull, Henry, 169 Water-street.
Beebe & Brother, 149 Front-street.
Blossom, Chas. W., 145 Front-street.
Banker, James H., 49 South-street.
Briggs, Austin A., 117 Maiden Lane.
Brown, E. B., 117 Maiden Lane.
Blodgett, A., 93 Maiden Lane.
Baldwin & Johnston, 63 Maiden Lane.
Boyd, Wm., 91 John-street.
Bunting, Wm., 104 John-street.
Blackwell & Co., R. M., 144 Front-street.
Barker, Jas. T., 148 Front-street.
Butler, W. R., 240 Water-street.
Bowen, Hilton R., 163 Maiden Lane.
Becar, Alfred, 187 Broadway.
Barry, Saml. F., 135 Broadway.
Barry, W. F., 135 Broadway.
Baker, D. P., 177 Broadway.
Brooks, Samuel, 181 Broadway.
Benedict, Hall & Co., 21 Park Row.
Baldwin & Starr, 23 Park Row.
Benkard & Hutton, 58 Broadway.
Barnes, H. W., 26½ Broadway.
Ball, Black & Co., 247 Broadway.
Babcock, D. M., 252 Broadway.
Bunn, Wm. C., 291 Washington-street.
Berry & Smith, 261 Washington-street.
Beatty & Mitchell, 231 Washington-street.
Burdett & Titus, 4 Jones Lane.
Bateman, Benj., 138 Maiden Lane.
Booraem, W. G., 59 Liberty-street.
Bolles, E. L., 32 Liberty-street.
Bertram & Co., G. V., 64 Liberty-street.
Bush, Gale & Robinson, 186 Greenwich-st.
Bart, E. N., 100 Liberty-street.
Breeden, A. H., 107 and 109 Liberty-st.
Blun, Nathan, 101 Liberty-street.
Benton & Co., J., 90 West-street.
Benton & Bro., 90 West-street.
Brush & Son, Platt, 160 West-street.
Browning & Hiscox, 164 West-street.
Besson, John, 184 West-street.
Butler & Co., Edwin T., 316 Broadway.
Bowen, Holmes & Co., 320 Broadway.
Brown & Co., E. J., 330 Broadway.
Bliss, E., 232 Jay-street, Brooklyn.
Byrne, John E., 332 Broadway.
Blydenburgh & Co., 85 Murray-street.
Bacon, L. B., 59 Murray-street.
Butler, Cecil, Rawson & Co., 11 Murray-st.
Browning, John H., Fourth Av. and 94th-st.
Browning, E. F., 326 and 328 Broadway.
Bevredge & Co., J., 121 Warren-street.
Bate & Co., Thos. H., 7 Warren-street.
Bainbridge, Bros. & Co., 47 Cliff-street.
Barton & Scott, 18 and 20 Cliff-street.
Bliven & Mead, 243 and 245 Pearl-street.
Benton, B. T., 20 Cliff-street.
Braman, Elias, 20 Cliff-street.
Blanchard, L. D., 26 Cliff-street.

Bussing, Crooker & Co., 32 Cliff-street.
Boswell, Jno. H., 189 Pearl-street.
Biggs, Wm. S., 113 Wall-street.
Black, Gramm & Co., 41 Beekman-street and 166 William-street.
Berlin & Jones, 134 William-street.
Barnet, H., 126 William-street.
Birch, Wm. M., 114 William-street.
Brinckerhoff, V. W., 88 William-street.
Belknap & Sons, E. S., 8 Gold-street.
Brown, A., 12 Gold-street.
Bowles, S. B., 12 Gold-street.
Boyd, John T., 45 William-street.
Breidenboh, Jr., J. H., 58 William-street.
Babcock, D. S., New-York.
Bach, A., 79 William-street.
Block, J., 83 William-street.
Bergmand, Althof, 54 Maiden Lane.
Baxter & Co., C. H. & A. T., 82 Maiden Lane.
Bosler & Dreyer, 90 and 92 Maiden Lane.
Britton, Jno. P., 96 Fulton-street.
Block, S., 154 Fulton-street.
Bidwell, N., 146 Fulton-street.
Brown, D. W., 130 Fulton-street.
Brown, A. S., 130 Fulton-street.
Beville, Jno., 126 Fulton-street.
Besson & Van Syckel, 39 South William-street.
Bloodgood, John.
Brooks, Geo., 46 Ferry-street.
Bailey, Lang & Co. H., 54 Cliff-street.
Baker, H., 23 South-street.
Beecher, Wm. A., 1 Hanover-street.
Bert, Jacob, 3 Hanover-street.
Brown & Blake, 323 Broadway.
Betts, T. B., 349 Broadway.
Bridge, Charles, 359 Broadway.
Bulpin, Gregson & Elliott, 361 Broadway.
Burr, Geo., 267 Broadway.
Bement, E., 40 Exchange Place.
Baker & Co., Anson, 47 Warren-street.
Burtis & Kirby, 75 Warren-street.
Buzby, Jno., 83 Warren-street.
Brockelmann, J. R., 16 Exchange Place.
Ballin & Sander, 24 Exchange Place.
Birney E. H., 69 Wall-street.
Brown, Bros. & Co.
Beach, Wm. H., 20 East 11th-street.
Benner & Deake, 113 Wall-street.
Burdick & Frisbie, 103 Wall-street.
Bowerman, Wm. D., 91 Wall-street.
Braynard, T. L., 81 Wall-street.
Braynard, S., 81 Wall-street.
Bronson, J. M., 388 Broadway.
Black, James, 399 Greenwich-street.
Barth, R. F., 388 Broadway.
Bissell, Champion, 257 Front-street.
Blackman, J. S., 259 Front-street.
Beards & Cummings, 279 and 281 Front-st.
Bird & Co., Wm. Edgar, 218 Front-street.
Bampton, F. W., 206 South-street.
Burr & Co., 114 South-street.
Bloomer & Macbeth, 24 and 26 Peck Slip.
Blachly, Simpson & Co., 36 Dey-street.
Benjamin John, E., 59 Dey-street.
Brown, Jr., & Co., Wm. A., 41 Dey-street.
Breed, J. B. & Co., 26 Cortlandt-street.
Burgoyne, Theo., 65 Liberty-street.
Bierwith, Leopold, Merchants' Exchange.
Barber, Palmer & Co., 207 Duane-street.
Booth, Peck & Barber, 141 Duane-street.
Briggs, James A., 25 William-street.
Beach & Co., H. C., 71 Pine-street.
Bristol, E. L., 413 Broadway.
Ballard, W. J. H., 364 Broadway.
Bartlett & Lesley, 426 Broadway.
Bailey & Southard, 27 Park Place.
Barnwall, W., 74 Beaver-street.
Brown, Francis, 83 Beaver-street.
Brown & Powers, 362 Broadway.
Bramhall, C., 442 Broadway.
Bogert, Ed. C., 49 William-street.
Beets, A. W., 43 Exchange Place.
Barclay & Livingston, 24 Beaver-street.
Burt, Edwin C., 27 Park Row.
Boyd, J. L., 70 Gold-street.
Bridgens, Wm. H., 189 William-street.
Brinckerhoff, J., 103 Fulton-street.
Botsford, Stephen, 78 West 48th-street.
Baldwin, C., 53 Gold-street.
Brass, J. D., 58 Beekman-street.
Burns, M. H., 58 Beekman-street.
Barrows & Scott, 124 Maiden Lane.
Brown, Jr., Henry, 5 Gold-street.
Booth, Alfred, 243 Water-street.
Burkhalter, S., 220 Greenwich-street.
Beckwith, B. L., 43 Pine-street.
Beale, Geo. W., 39 Pine-street.
Balmforth, C., 5 Pine-street.
Bininger, Andrew G., 12 Pine-street.
Ballin, M., 175 Pearl-street.
Brown, Elijah T., 40 Spruce-street.
Brooks & Co., James, 32 Spruce-street.
Brooks & Co., Geo. J., 8 Spruce-street.
Brimlow, Wm., 16 James Slip.
Booth, Wm. T., 132 King-street.
Bahan & Co., T. S., 675 Washington-street.
Bell, John, 330 West-street.
Bayles, J. C., 400 West-street.
Braine, Wm., 160 Pearl-street.
Barneys, W., 160 Pearl-street.
Blake, Wheelock & Co., 71 Gold-street.
Blodget, Brown & Co., 83 Beekman-street.
Bulkley, Bro. & Co., 67 Beekman-street.
Barnes & Sons, Edward, 18 Beekman-st.
Barry, James, 22 Beekman-street.
Brett & Son, J. G., 122 Beekman-street.
Baker, W. B., 23 Park Row.
Baldwin, H. M., 25 Park Row.
Braynard, T. L., 23 Boorman Place.
Brown, J. C.

CARTER, R. B., 120 William-street.
Clark, & Williamson, 1 Wall-street.
Clarkson, D., 34 Wall-street.

Christian, G. H., 18 Wall-street.
Canfield, A. W., Fifth Avenue and 38th-st.
Cooper, M., 112 Chambers-street.
Christie, George, 29 Chambers-street.
Coles, Nathaniel, 26 Broadway.
Crary, Geo. D., 31 Wall-street.
Curtis, Cyrus, 98 Broadway.
Clark, Frederick, 130 Broadway.
Cawley, J. F., 290 Front-street.
Crawford, T. R., 84 South-street.
Cromwell, Edward, 209 Front-street.
Clark, Albert, 15 Fifth Avenue.
Conant & Bolles, F. J., 204 Broadway.
Curley & Kirk, 233 Front-street.
Couillard, K., 107 South-street.
Crowell & Co., E., 42 Water-street and 6 Coenties Slip.
Churchman & Roberts, 40 Water-street.
Chauncey, Henry, 42 South-street.
Cooper, Wm. B., 70 South-street.
Corning, E. S., 84 South-street.
Caldwell, S. B., 20 Old Slip.
Collins, Geo., Jr., 93 Beaver-street.
Chazournes, F., 79 Cedar-street.
Cronkhite, C., 14 Beaver-street.
Cashman, M. H. & D., 5 Beaver-street.
Crocker & Co., H. C , 88 Beaver-street.
Church, Jno. B., 62 Beaver-street.
Carpenter, Joshua S., 26 Beaver-street.
Chemullin, J. B., 12 Broadway.
Cooper, M. H., 205 Broadway.
Clark & Banks, 204 Chambers-street.
Cary, Howard, Sanger & Co., 105 and 107 Chambers-street.
Curtis & Baker, 149 Chambers-street.
Comstock, Jno. D., 155 Chambers-street.
Cromwell, Wm. A., 157 Chambers-street.
Collins, Benjamin, 96 Broadway.
Cobb, March & Co., 62 Beaver-street.
Carters & Hawley, 41 Broad-street.
Cohen & Co., M. S., 124 Water-street.
Cooper & Co., 138 Front-street.
Clough, Lowe & Co., 164 Front-street.
Clack & Co., Thomas, 193 Front-street.
Crocker, Wood & Co., 52 South-street.
Clucas & Leeds, 119 Maiden Lane.
Christian & Son, A., 81 Maiden Lane.
Clark, Jr., Ezra, 145 Maiden Lane.
Cochran, Geo. W., 102 Broad-street.
Cooper, Edward, 17 Burling Slip.
Chase, E. S., 137 Broadway.
Caldwell & Co., John, 155 Broadway.
Clark, Emmons, 173 Broadway.
Carhart, J. B., 58 Broadway.
Carhart & Brother, 58 Broadway.
Chandler, Foster & Co., 52 Barclay-street.
Coe, Lucius, 52 Barclay-street.
Cumming, S. C. R., 58 Barclay-street.
Cohen & Co., H. M., 60 Barclay-street.
Carlton, James, 267 Barclay-street.
Cain & Co., J. H., 238 Fulton-street.
Copland, P. H., 56 South-street.
Cooley, M. A., 12 Dey-street.
Campbell & Beach, 98 Liberty-street.
Clapp, Jr., John, 30 Beekman-street.
Cohn & Hyman, 112 Liberty-street.
Cohen & Trishell, 121 Liberty-street.
Conteul, Noah, 119 Liberty-street.
Clark, Alfred H., 161 West-street.
Corwin, A. M., 326 Broadway.
Comstock, Wm. K., 320 Broadway.
Congreve & Son, Chas., 13 Cliff-street.
Campbell & Fitzpatrick, 177 Pearl-street.
Cornelis, F., 51 Cedar-street.
Crosby, Gillespie & Stanton, 186 William-street.
Cohen, S. L., 184 William-street.
Cullen, J. C., 138 William-street.
Coffin, Redington & Co., 88 William-st.
Chymau, George, 72 William-street.
Clarke, J. H., 209 West Fourteenth-street.
Cornell, A. N., 39 Wooster-street.
Clark, Green & Baker, 48 Maiden Lane.
Cavendy, Edward, 74 Maiden Lane.
Cleu, J. F., 90 Maiden Lane.
Craft, Jno., 88 Fulton-street.
Cottrill, W. H., 278 Pearl-street.
Castellanos, A. V., 31 Old Slip.
Crocker, Edmund, 239 Henry-street.
Choate, Joseph H., 147 Ninth-street.
Cockroft, J. H. V., 3 Hanover-street.
Conover, Stephen, 298 Broadway.
Conover, Stephen, Jr., 298 Broadway.
Congdon, Jno. G., 310 Broadway.
Cornish, C. L., 310 Broadway.
Cameron, Edwards & Co., 265 Broadway.
Cumming, Simpson & Armstrong, 279 Broadway.
Cohn, H., 301 Broadway.
Coffin, Robert, 313 Broadway.
Chambers, M. H., 391 Broadway.
Corey, E. Francis, Jr, 9½ Merchants' Exchange.
Cook, Geo. E., 89 Wall-street.
Carter, Samuel.
Clarke, J. W., 388 Broadway.
Crowell, Jno. E., 55 Avenue A.
Collins, D. M., 271 South-street.
Cromwell, Wm., 36 Dey-street.
Combes, R., 26 Cortlandt-street.
Chollar, J., 38 Cortlandt-street.
Cornell, Sidney, 36 Cortlandt-street.
Cornell, Thomas L., 36 Cortlandt-street.
Cornell, Samuel M., 36 Cortlandt-street.
Crawford, J. P. & H. L.
Conklin, B. R., 189 Reade-street.
Cammann & Co., 56 Wall-street.
Curran, Jno. P., 566 Broadway.
Casey, A. L., 413 Broadway.
Carroll, Herrick & Mead, 392 Broadway.
Church, S. G., 388 Broadway.
Coe, Geo. S., 126 Broadway.
Curtis, P. A., 364 Broadway.
Cornell & Amermau, 10 Park Place.
Cavan, W. R., 1 Park Place.
Couran, Thos., 31 North Moore-street.

Cook, James, 56 Gold-street.
Cobb, Nathaniel R., 27 William-street.
Clover & Glenton, 6 South William-st.
Cæsar & Pauli, 4 South William-street.
Cousinery & Co., F., 27 South William-st.
Chapin, George, 116 Maiden Lane.
Creamer, Robert, 11 Gold-street.
Combs, Daniel, 39 Peck Slip.
Christianson, N., 216 Greenwich-street.
Constantine, Thomas, 60 Pine-street.
Currier, J. W., 136 Sixth Avenue.
Cox & Wright, 4 and 6 Gold-street.
Coit, Jno. B., 50 Ferry-street.
Converse, W. P., Tyler & Co., 168 Pearl-st.
Clark, Alexander, 205 Sixth Avenue.
Conner & Sons, James, 29 Beekman-street.
Clarke, Wilson & Co., 81 Beekman-street.
Curtis, Joseph, 364 Broadway.
Curtis, Alfred L., 364 Broadway.
Commerford, Chas. C., 454 Broadway.
Cheesman, Oscar, 145 Duane-street.
Catlin, C. T., 25 William-street.

DAY, Henry, 12 Wall-street.
De Forest, Armstrong & Co. 80 and 82 Chambers-street.
Dayton & Gilder, 35 Chambers-street.
Dewitt, Chas. A., 82 Broadway.
De Angelis, Gideon, 33 Wall-street.
Dusenbery, Wm. Cox, 142 Broadway.
Drumgold, L., 177 South-street.
De Forest & Co., W. W., 82 South-street.
De Camp, R. L., 212 Front-street.
Decker, D. H., 55 Whitehall-street.
Dimon, F., 67 South-street.
Dodge, Wm. H., 59 Beaver-street.
Dibble, E. A., 9 Beaver-street.
Douglass, Geo. E., 19 Beaver-street.
De Rham, H. C., 24 Fifth Avenue.
Duer, Denning, 53 William-street.
Dinsmore, W. B., 59 Broadway.
Deuel & Co., 159 Chambers-street.
Dickie, H. P., 144 Chambers-street.
Deen, John L., 78 Water-street.
Durkee & Hough, 85 Water-street.
Dayton & Co., 186 Front-street.
Daters & Co., 161 Front-street.
Davis, Morris & Co., 87 Wall-street.
Dayton, J. O. & Co., 107 Front-street.
Deiser, Thos. R., 117 Maiden Lane.
Dibble & Bunce, 119 Maiden Lane.
Dickinson, Whittemore & Reed, 245, 247 and 249 Water-street.
De Witt & Bro., G., 109 John-street.
Durfee, S. L., 34 Broadway.
Dunning, A. A., 252 Broadway.
Dohrmann & Bernett, 273 Washington-st.
Dodge, Levi, 62 South-street.
Dammarell, James, 69 South-street.
Dennis & Co., Samuel, 71 Dey-street.
Darden, Geo., 96 Liberty-street.
Dittman, Isidor, 117 Liberty-street.
Doubleday & Beak, 49 Murray-street.
Dibblee, & Co., H. E., 25 Murray-street.
Dickinson, Ed. J., 51 Cliff-street.
Dodge, Wm. E., 19 and 21 Cliff-street.
Dutell, P., 51 Cedar-street.
Davison, Van Pelt & Crane, 50 William-st.
Doyle, J. E., 97 William-street.
Davids, Geo. W., 127 William-street.
Denny, Jr., Thos., 39 William-street.
Davis, Gilbert, cor. Pine and William-st.
Davis, Saml. C., cor. Pine and William-st.
Devoe, Jno. C., 350 Houston-street.
Dayton, Albert, 23 South-street.
Dunn, Joseph, 8 Old Slip.
Douglas, Benj., 314 Broadway.
Duryee, Jaques & Co., 326 Broadway.
Dieseldorff & Co., H. R., 395 Broadway.
Derby & Jackson, 119 Nassau-street.
Davis, W. H., 50 Exchange Place.
De Escoriaza, J. V. G., 10 Broadway.
Dow, Aug. F., 89 Wall-street.
Driggs & Co., M. S., 278 & 280 South-st.
Davis, Jas. L., 184 South-street.
DeGraff, L., 19 Jay-street.
Davidson & Lazarus, 26 Dey-street.
Duckworth & Hayn, 80 Dey-street.
Denison & Wyckoff, 82 and 84 Dey-street.
Demarest, G. W., 177 Reade-street.
Duncan & Son, John, 405 Broadway.
Dayton, Lyman & Co., 1082 Broadway.
Danforth, Sylvester & Co., 504 Broadway.
Dodd, M. W., 506 Broadway.
Dennis, Chas., Vice-President Atlantic Mutual Insurance Company.
Dronge, Clause, 206 William-street.
Dunham, Edward, 13 William-street.
De Salvo, F. G., 3 South William-street.
De Penmeret & Co., 9 South William-st.
Dutilh & Co., 23 South William-street.
Davis, G. L., 58 Beekman-street.
Danforth, J., 15 Gold-street.
Demyer, Henry M., 309 Pearl-street.
Dupignac, Jr., E. R., 8 Peck Slip.
Dunning, J., 227 Greenwich-street.
Dunniers, John A., 200 Greenwich-street.
De Mier, Juan C., 60 Pine-street.
Dike Brothers, 66 Pine-street.
Dike, H. A., 66 Pine-street.
Dillon & McDonagh, 299 Greenwich-st.
Dorr & Son, 339 Greenwich-street.
Drake, John J., 28 Spruce-street.
Dudley & Stafford, 69 Beekman-street.
Douglas Manuf. Co., 68 Beekman-street.
Davis, C. & J., 225 Fulton-street.
Dyer, H. Ballard, 25 Park Row.
Day, M. W., Beekman-street.
Dart & Co., James, 50 Exchange Place.
Duffey, J. P., 35 William-street.
Dean, R. E., 442 Broadway.
Dudley, M. & Penn, 97 Pearl-street.

EARLE, John K., 10 Beaver-street.
Egleston, Battell & Co., 166 South-street.
Ernst, Franklin, 193 Broadway.

Ely, Thomas, 25 Beaver-street.
Ely, James, 25 Beaver-street.
Ellis, Bennett & Co., 151 Chambers-street.
Ely, Dudley P., 140 Front-street.
Engs & Sons, P. W., 131 Front-street.
Evans, Henry G., 85 Maiden Lane.
Elliott, J., 93 John-street.
Esenwein, F., 171 Broadway.
Elliott & Co., H. G., 182 and 184 Greenwich-street.
Eckerson, Jacob, 165 West-street.
Eastman, Bigelow & Dayton, 332 Broadway.
Eager, J. & J., 34 Cliff-street.
Ellis, Robert H., 19 and 21 Merchant's Ex.
Ermand, W. G. Dey, 20 Exchange Place.
Elastic Cone Spring Co., 48 Exchange Pl.
Eastwood, C. W., 76 Reade-street.
Edmoston, S. S., 213 Duane-street.
Evans, Henry, Deposit, N. Y.
Edgerton, L., 292 Broadway.
Emery, G. W., 522 Broadway.
Edwards, A. W., 54 Gold-street.
Edmun & Bowly, 13 South William-st.
Ely, Eugene, 57 Gold-street.
Ember, W., 58 Beekman-street.
Earl & Bartholomew, 196 Greenwich-st.
Eberhard, A., 328 Greenwich-street.
Ely, Jr., Smith, 103 Gold-street.
Ely, Henry G., 31 Ferry-street.
Emmet, William J., 91 Beaver-street.

FALLS, M., 16 Broadway.
France, Richard, 61 Chambers-st.
Frothinghan & Baylis, 80 South-street.
Fish & Co., J. D., 105 South-street.
Fellows, Geo. A., 14 and 16 Beaver-st.
Faber, H. E., 36 Beaver-street.
Franchere, Gabriel, 12 Broadway.
Fleming & McKennee, 163 Chambers-st.
Faile, Williams & Co., 192 and 194 Chambers-street.
Fowler, F. R. & W. C., 142 Front-street.
Fatman & Cardoza, 166 Front-street.
Finch & Sons, R. R., 238 Water-street.
Farmer, Wm. G., 171 Broadway.
Foster, V. W., 52 Barclay-street.
Flye, W., 53 South-street.
Fox, Jno. W., 89 Liberty-street.
Fitch, Halsey, 111 Liberty-street.
Fowler, F. J. D., 85 West-street.
Farrington, G. B., 324 Broadway.
Foote, T. C., 334 Broadway.
Felt, David, 120 William-street.
Ferner & Bremshaer, 101 William-street.
Fleet & Co., O. S., 62 Maiden Lane.
Freeman, Ryer & Co., 23 Maiden Lane.
Freeman, A., 84 Fulton-street.
Fowler, S. L., 98 Fulton-street.
Fuller, E., 52 Cliff-street.
Frame, Joseph L., 237 West 28th-street.
Ferguson Brothers, 351 Broadway.
Foster, Henry, 267 Broadway.
French, George H., 313 Broadway.
Fordham, George W., 15 Merchants' Ex.
Fitch, George P., 20 Exchange Place.
Fall, Robert H., 69 Wall-street.
Fox, George S. 61 Wall-street.
Fitch, Harvey, 245 Front-street.
Frank & Co., Gustave, 222 Front-st.
Freeborn & Co., Wm. A., 254 South-st.
Field, C. A., 40 Peck Slip.
Fridenberg & Wolf, 29 Dey-street.
Foote, J. A., 64 Whitehall-street.
Foote & Co., 101 Pearl-street.
Fuller Brothers, 36 Warren-street.
Fink & Hencken, 191 and 193 Duane-st.
Foster, Abram K., 63 Pine-street.
Faye, Jas., 532 Broadway.
Fagan, Patrick, 544 Broadway.
Francis, Daniel G., 554 Broadway.
Francis, C. S., 554 Broadway.
Fawcett, F. & L., 70 Gold-street.
Fraser, Alexander, 13 Barclay-street.
Frobisher, H. W., 212 Greenwich-street.
Fuller, Walter, 209 Greenwich-street.
Fenner & Hardenbergh, 313 and 315 Greenwich-street.
Fawcett, Thomas, 70 Gold-street.
Foster, J. W., 80 Beekman-street.
Fellows, Hoffman & Co., 74 Beekman-st.
Fersenheim, H., 76 Beekman-street.
Fowler, M. V. B., 49 Wall-street.
Ford, A. L., 23 Park Row.
Fisher, N., 25 Park Row.
Fosdick, William R., 1 Beaver-street.

GARTHWAITE, Darcy & Co., 45 Chambers-street.
Graham, N. B., 110 Broadway.
Green & Co., Wm. L., 58 Water-street.
Gordon & Co., O. H., 155 Maiden Lane.
Gilman, Samuel, 91 Beaver-street.
Green, Jno. C., 10 Washington Square.
Goldschmidt, C. H., 38 Beaver-street.
Garhue & Davis, 121 Chambers-street.
Gerard, Wm., 106 Wall-street.
Gaynor, John, 561 Broadway.
Gilbert, John A., 23 Park Row.
Gould & Co., R. S., 267 Greenwich-street.
Guth & Brother, Jno., 68 Dey-street.
Goldstein & Lowenstein, 113 Liberty-st.
Garett, George, 22 Cedar-street.
Grapel, W., 51 Cedar-street.
Gespritz, 65 Maiden Lane,
Gaudelet & Gonvé, 97 William-street.
Gensler, Louis, 99 William-street.
Gunther & Sons, C. G., 46 Maiden Lane.
Greig, James, 112 Fulton-street.
Gaseier, Joseph, 128 Fulton-street.
Gomez, Wallis & Co., 29 South Wm-st.
Gilchrist & Son, 72 Water-street.
Grove & Co., William, 23 South-street.
Gourlie, McGee & Miller, 5 Hanover-st.
Gerety, Francis, 8 Old Slip.
Goulding, S. & J., 325 Broadway.

Gantz, John W., 353 Broadway.
Giddings & Hixon, 303 Broadway.
Gilbert, H. L., Metropolitan Hotel.
Greenleaf, E. B., 50 Exchange Place.
Gillespie, A. O., 137 Second Avenue.
Gray, William N., 114 West 34th-street.
Gall, Henry, 92 Sixth-street.
Gilman, George F., 98 Gold-street.
Griffard & Co., J. J., 20 Maiden Lane.
Goodwin & Cort, 258 Water-street.
Gasquoine, Samuel, 70½ Pine-street.
Godfrey & Sons, E., 34 Spruce-street.
Garnar, Thomas, 32 Spruce-street.
Gillespie & Studwell, 33 Spruce street.
Gray, James, 16 Spruce-street.
Getty, S. E., 108 Morton-street.
Goetze, A., 19 Spruce-street.
Gray Brothers, 69 Beekman-street.
Gunnison, A. C., 51 Exchange Place.
Gilman, A., 47 Exchange Place.
Gibson, Wood, 362 Broadway.
Gelston, Wm. J., 76 Wall-street.
Grant, R., 65 Pine-street.
Grayden, Swanwick & Co., 43 Park Place.

HASTINGS, Plimpton & Co., 51 Chambers-street.
Hay, Silas C., 82 Broadway.
Hollister, E. R.
Hoyt, Geo. A.
Hayward, Abner.
Hinrichs, C. F. A., 150 Broadway.
Haight & Ewens, 226 Front-street.
Harris, Chas. J., 244 Front-street.
Hoyt & Co., Thos., 258 and 260 Front-st.
Holcomb, C. M., 288 Front-street.
Hathaway, Francis, 80 South-stseet.
Hayden, Nath'l, 192 Broadway.
Hubbell, Harvey, 202 Broadway.
Hoyt, Wm. W., 201 Broadway.
Hewlett, C. Sidney, 109 South-street.
Holmes, J. M., 2 Coenties Slip.
Herrick & Son, J. B., 10 South-street.
Hopkins, S. W., 72 Beaver-street.
Hynard, M., 5th Ward Hotel.
Hull & Holt, 202 Chambers-street.
Hall, Wm., 176 Chambers-street.
Hanford & Co., E. H., 154 Chambers-st.
Hall, Dixon & Co., 149 Chambers-street.
Homans, Sheppard, 94 Broadway.
Hawley, Irad, 47 Fifth Avenue.
Hexisner, Wm., 112 Pearl-street.
Hoffman, Emanuel, 140 Water-street.
Hammill, Jas. P., 155 Water-street.
Hunter, & Co., Jas., 174 Front-street.
Holt & Sons, P., 188 Front-street.
Howell & Co., Wm. E., 167 Front-street.
Hussey, Wm. H., 115 Maiden Lane.
Hazard, J. H., 121 Maiden Lane.
Hammann, 264 Water-street.
Hall, Wm. H., 163 Maiden Lane.
Hodges, Henry, 187 Broadway.
Hitchcock, W. G., 187 Broadway.
Hegeman & Co., 161 Broadway.
Hurd, W. C., 183 Broadway.
Hersey, J. D. T., 187 Broadway.
Hoyt, F. S., 58 Barclay-street.
Halsey & Co., Jno. J., 257 Broadway.
Hyatt, Walter, 291 Washington-street.
Hopping & Co., A. D., 214 Washington-st.
Harris, L. M., Jr., 62 South-street.
Heath, Wynkoop & Co., 63 Liberty-st.
Howland, William, 34 Liberty-street.
Harral, Risley & Kitchin, 76 Barclay-st.
Haydock, Bobert, 101 Liberty-street.
Hardple, Emanuel.
Howell & Co., Wharton A., 97 Liberty-st.
Hyde, John H., 89 Liherty-street.
Hyman, Henry, 112 Liberty-street.
Hieghts & Joidor, 113 Liberty-street.
Hamm & Rosenheim, 111 Liberty-street.
Hedges & Powers, 51 Murray-street.
Hersh & Rice, 39 Murray-street.
Hooley & Co., Abraham, 35 Murray-st.
Hyne, C. H., 314 Broadway.
Hadden, W. A., 340 Broadway.
Haines, S., 117 Warren-street.
Haring, Wm., 177 West-street.
Holden, Hawley & Co., 11 and 13 Cliff-st.
Hammond, W. P., 12 Cedar-street.
Hendrickson & Shattuck, 22 Cedar-st.
Hure, Ernest, 189 Pearl-street.
Hopkins & Brother, F., 193 Pearl-street.
Hooper & Bartlett, 158 William-street.
Horn, Albert, 23 Lamartine Place.
Howard & Mather, 66 William-street.
Hermann & Bloomingdale, 93 William-st.
Hahln & Stieghtz, 95 William-street.
Hagar & Co., Wm., Jr., 38 Gold-street.
Hicks & Betts, 72 Maiden Lane.
Horsey, Jr., Joseph, 84 Maiden Lane.
Hewett, M. T., 112 Fulton-street.
Hearn, John, 29 South William-street.
Herckenrath, Schneider & Co., 21 South William-street.
Haydock, E. M., 278 Pearl-street.
Hurman, William N., 278 Pearl-street.
Hickcox, T. W., 280 Pearl-street.
Honser & Brother, Thomas, 38 Ferry-st.
Howes, Henry, 6 Coenties Slip.
Hull, George C., 2 Hanover-street.
Hamersley, John W., Bond-street.
Hoffman, William B., 24 East 18th-street.
Henderson, Alex., 326 Broadway.
Henderson, Thomas A., 326 Broadway.
Hazard & Browning, 326 Broadway.
Hayden, F. M., 337 Broadway.
Hart & Brother, B. J., 297 Broadway.
Humphrey, H. D., 26 Abingdon Square.
Hyde, A. G., 41 and 43 Warren-street.
Howell, Foster & Wilson, 65 Warren-st.
Hodges, George W., 42 Exchange Place.
Hassal, Alfred J., 63 Wall-street.
Husta, S.
Hicks, John J., 206 South-street.
Hubbard & Co., J. W., 179 South-street.

Hewins, M. K., 36 Peck Slip.
Holland, John F., Newark Av., Jer. City.
Hoppock & Co., 65 Dey-street.
Hazenfrau, Wm. H., 41 Montgomery-st.
Hurlbut, Van Volkenburgh & Co., 64 Reade-street.
Hoyt & Co., N. W., 187 Reade-street.
Halsey & Northrum, 191 Reade-street.
Hopke, E. F. & M., 307 Washington-st.
Hoyt & Brother, E. T., 159 Duane-street.
Hasseldick, Meyer & Brettman, 199 Duane street.
Hale, Frederick, 46 Beekman-street.
Hicks, Willet, 116 Maiden Lane.
Hill & Co., Thomas, 15 Gold-street.
Holcomb, Henry, 181 South-street.
Harral, Risley & Kitchen, 76 Barclay-st.
Hall, William H., 212 Greenwich-street.
Holmes, George W., 227 Greenwich-st.
Hopkins, Horace E., 89 Maiden Lane.
Hoe & Co., R., 29 and 31 Gold-street.
Hapgood, D. M., 36 Spruce-street.
Holcombe & Son, S. Q., 17 James Slip.
Hicks & Wells, 580 Washington-street.
Harriott & Son, Warren, 124 Charles-st.
Horton & Lewis, 352 West-street.
Henniston & Nichols, 289 Greenwich-st.
Hall & Co., Francis C., 282 Greenwich-st.
Herrick, W., 252 Greenwich-street.
Hampton, Adam, 60 Gold-street.
Hoyt, J. B., 28 Spruce-street.
Hill, William W., 83 Beekman-street.
Harmer, Hays & Co., 72 Beekman-street.
Hawkes, Clement, 74 Beekman-street.
Hard, Melvin, 44 Beekman-street.
Hart, J., 20 Beekman-street.
Hayes, William, 23 Park Row.
Hewitt & Co., 55 Exchange Place.
Hull, John W., 41 Exchange Place.
Hanford, Joseph F., 364 Broadway.
Hedge, George W., 442 Broadway.
Hoag, Harny, 75 Pine-street.
Hatch, W. T., 292 Broadway.
Hobe & Son, A. F., 484 Broadway.
Hunt, J., 430 Broadway.
Hunt, Tillinghast & Co., 15 Park Place.
Hurd & Giles, 13 Park Place.
Halsted, Haines & Co., 60 Murray-street.
Holmes, J., 88 Wall-street.
Howes, D. W., 29 Wall-street.

IRVING, Wheeler & Co., 43 Chambers-st.
Isham, S. & C. H., 91 Gold-street.
Isham, Wm. B., 93 Gold-street.
Iram, James H., 193 Broome-street.
Ingalls, T. C., 17 Beekman-street.

JANES, M., 82 Broadway.
Jones & Co., 242 Front-street.
Jackson & Co. W., 246 Front-street.
Jackson, John L., 193 Broadway.
Josephs, John, 157 South-street.
Jenkins, W. A., 69 Liberty-street.
James, Ely, 25 Beaver-street.
Johnston, James, 93 Maiden Lane.
Jennings Brothers, 5 Burling Slip.
Jordan, Geo. W., 53 South-street.
Jones & Smith, 89 Liberty-street.
Jacobsohn & Schleestein, 115 Liberty-st.
Johns & Crosby, 510 Broadway.
Jaudon, Peyton & Frank, 17 William-st.
Jackson, Jno., 8 South William-street.
Jordan, L., 11 Gold-street.
Jones, Wm. B., 8 Spruce-street.
Jessup, Cole & Co., 327 Greenwich-street.
Johnson & Bliss, 193 Washington-street.
Jordan, C., 23 Park Row.
Jennings, E., 454 Broadway.
Johnson, N., 332 Broadway.
Johnson, S. F., 332 Broadway.
Jones, J. D., 51 Wall-street.
Jenkins, J. C., 69 Liberty-street.
Jannist, Anderson & Co., 67 Pine-street.
Jennings, Wm., F., 566 Broadway.
Johnson, Wm. B., 406 Broadway.
Jenks, L., New-York.
Jones, R. C., 60 Cedar-street.
Japha, Samuel, 104 William-street.
Jaquays, A. W., 66 Maiden Lane.
Jones, Little & Buell, 139 Fulton-street.
Jenkins, E. F., 1 Hanover-street.
Jones & Hanabergh, 285 Broadway.
Jackson, Frank C., 155 South-street.

KINNILLY, W. A., 88 Chambers-street.
King, E. J., 62 Broadway.
Knapp, Shepherd, 33 Wall-street.
Ketchum, H. F., 67 South-street.
Kemeys, Wm., 69 Beaver-street.
Kennedy, Robert Lenox, 99 Fifth Avenue.
Keeler, W. M. & C. C., 145 Chambers-st.
Keeler, Wm. A., 109 Front-street.
Kissam & Keeler, 90 John-street.
Kingsland & Co., J. D., 104 and 106 John-st.
Kettell, Thos. P., 142 Fulton-street.
Kopp, O. H., 173 Broadway,
King, Mark J., 54 Broadway.
Ketcham, A. W., 752 Broadway.
Kerneys & Ross., 279 Washington-street.
Kaupe, E. & Cummings, 88 Liberty-street.
Kohas, L. & Bro., 91 Liberty-street.
Kinsey, John D., 212 West-street.
Kerr, L., 7 Gramercy Place.
King, John S.
Kellogg, L. E., 324 Broadway.
Korham, A., William-street.
Klauberg, Carl, 195 William-street.
Kendall, Arthur, 5 South William-street.
Knox, Alexander, 5 Pine-street.
King, David, 175 Pearl-street.
King, James G., 45 East 21st-street.
Kissam, R. A., 2 Jacob-street.
Keese & Pearsall, 101 Gold-street.
Kumbel & Son, Wm., 33 Ferry-street.
Kitchen, Montross & Wilcox, 360 B'way.
Kissam, G. A., 45 Cedar-street.

Kiggins & Kellogg, 125 William-street.
Kemkamp, L., 159 William-street.
Kittell & Klugerberg, 60 Maiden Lane.
Kaulbuch, & Co., 96 Fulton-street.
King, John, 326 Broadway.
Knight, R. H., 385 Broadway.
Ketchum, Son & Co., 40 Exchange Place.
Kirby, John W., 108 Broadway.
Kelbener, J. & Heller, 69 Warren-street.
Keep, Henry, 20 Exchange Place.
Kendall, Geo. W., 117 Wall-street.
Kruger, F. J., 117 Wall-street.
Kirtland, F. S., 388 Broadway.
Kempf, Roman, 215 West 38th-street.
Knapp, F. S., 4 Broad-street.
Kimball, T. C., 85 Dey-street.
Kingsbury, John A., 46 Cortlandt-street.
Kirkpatrick, R. F., 71 Pine-street.
Kirtland, Wm. H., 388 Broadway.
Kilner, James, 508 Broadway.
Knoedler, M., 366 Broadway.

LAMPORT, H. H., 45 Ninth-street.
Laurance, Jno. J., 264 Fourth-street.
Loder & Lockwood, 126 and 128 Chambers-street.
Leavitt, Toler & Co., 31 Chambers-street.
Lambert & Co., Edward, 55 Chambers-st.
Lansing, B. B., 72 Broadway.
Lansing, H. S., 72 Broadway.
Lewis, Wm. E., 164 Broadway.
Linington, S., 216 Front-street.
Leggett & Son, A., 205 Front-street.
Little, Chas. F., 200 Broadway.
Lersner, E., 201 Broadway.
Lewis, Arnold A., 42 Front-street.
Lynch, Thomas, 7 Cedar-street.
Lichtenstein, J. P., 161 Chambers-street.
Lester, Andrew, 103 Chambers-street.
Leavitt & Smith, 164 Front-street.
Lane & Co., Geo. W., 173 Front-street.
Lowber, Robert W., 61 Wall-street.
Lowerre, Wm. J., 117 Maiden Lane.
Levy, Henry, 49 Maiden Lane.
Lord, J. A., 87 John-street.
Lawrence & Sons, Henry, 80 John-street.
Le Roy & Co., Thos. Otis, 261 and 263 Water-street.
Lee, Robert B., 167 Broadway.
Lina & Co., 52 Broadway.
Lockwood, Jno. B.
Loeschigk, O., 227 West 31st-street.
Lee, Benj, F., 45 Liberty-street.
Lawrence & Co., L. S., 164 Nassau-street.
Leerburger & Rubens, 47 Dey-street.
Lynch, M. A. J., 4 Erie Building.
Lane, R. H., 205 Duane-street.
Ladd, E. H., 500 Broadway.
Ladd, T. C., 500 Broadway.
Lambert, F. L., 340 Broadway.
Lawson, J. D., 364 Broadway.
Lesher & Whitman, 8 Park Place.
Livingston, Crocheron & Co., 1 Park Place.
Leuzmann, Charles, 54 Cedar-street.
Lynch, Thomas, 7 Cedar-street.
Lawrence, J. M., 184 William-street.
Lawrence & Co., William-street.
Lippmann & Bro., M., 150 William-street.
Lindmark, M. N., 72 William-street.
Lazell, Marsh & Gardiner, 10 Gold-st.
Lane, Jr., Stephen, 127 William-street.
Lemon, S. H., 63 William-street.
La Mott, H., 128 Fulton-street.
Lavery, Samuel, 139 Fulton-street.
Lafraniere, Oliver, 280 Pearl-street.
Lunt, B. P. & G. D., 28 South-street.
Lamont, Chas. A., 159 Pearl-street.
Lane, Nathan, 69 Wall-street.
Lyon, J. F., 388 Broadway.
Leggett & Son, Abraham, 205 Front-st.
Lager, Jno., 44 Gold-street.
Ludlow, Patton & Co., 19 William-street.
Lindsay, Jr., G. R., 19 William-street.
Ludmann, C., 6 South William-street.
Livingston, Edward, 9 South William-st.
Lawrence, Giles & Co., 11 South Wm.-st.
Legien, H. L., 57 Gold-street.
Lowerre, Thos. H., 9 Gold-street.
Leverett & Co., Josiah S., 89 Maiden Lane.
Leupp & Co., Chas. M., 20 Ferry-street.
Lord, C., 16 Spruce street.
Lee, W. Creighton, 2 Jacob-street.
Lapham, H. G., 28 Ferry-street.
Ludlam, William, 126 Beekman-street.
Lewis & Co., Jno. W., 534 Washington-st.
Loveland & Welsh, 381 West-street.
Loring, Andrews & Co., 72 Gold-street.
Leggett, Reuben, 40 Spruce-street.
Lyon & Son, Wm. P., 29 Beekman-street.
Liebenroth & Co., A., 25 Beekman-street.
Laland & Crossjean, 70 Beekman-street.
Lefferts & Bro., M., 90 and 92 Beekman-st.
Lee, James, 49 Wall-street.
La Rue, Aaron, 364 Broadway.
Lindsley, Caleb F., 22 Broad-street.
Lee & Co., Wm. H., 314 and 316 Broadway.
Lyon, Geo. W., 336 Broadway,
Langdon, C. H., 336 Broadway.
Lazell, Stephen, 320 and 322 Broadway.

MacDONALD, C. H., 34 Wall-street.
Macy, F. W., 12 Wall-street.
Mulligan, Wm., 10 Wall-street.
Morrison, Hurd & Co., 35 Chambers-street.
Mygatts, Ingraham & Co., 43 Chambers-st.
McMeney, Robert, 61 Chambers-street.
Mann & Co., Edward J.
Marsh, T. B., 82 Broadway.
McKay, J., 82 Broadway.
Myers, Joseph S., 62 Broadway.
Murphy, Lawrence, 19 Wall-street.
Mills, E., 11 East 29th-street.
Maverick, B., 135 Grand-street.
Murray, Jr., Byron, 128 Broadway.
McCarthy, John, 183 Broadway.
Mills, Merritt & Co., 250 and 252 Front-st.

Manwaring, D. W., 248 Front-street.
Miller, H. R., 179 South-street.
Maxwell, John T. B., 77 South-street.
Morrison, John B., 204 Broadway.
McWhood, E., 142 Fulton-street.
Morris, J. C., 203 Broadway.
Messenger, W. H., 225 Front-street.
Meerds, C., 23 Old Slip.
Minturn, R. B., 78 South-street.
Meyer, James, 43 Beaver-street.
Mairet, Barber & Co., 49 Beaver-street.
Monaghan, P. 51 Beaver-street.
Molloy, D. O., 59 Beaver-street.
McKay & Cornelison, 84 Cedar-street.
Magraw, H., 9 Beaver-street.
McGuire, Jno., 25 Beaver-street.
McCormick, James, 29 Beaver-street.
McAtavey, Francis, 29 Beaver-street.
Muren & Bonner, 28 Broad-street.
Marchant, Jr., H., 48 Beaver-street.
Marchant, Henry, 48 Beaver-street.
McMullen, Thomas, 44 Beaver-street.
Motley, James M., 16 Broadway.
Mears, Charles E., 17 Murray-street.
Morse, E. W., Wall-street.
Mills & Co., John, 14 Broadway.
McLanahan, James X., 14 Broadway.
Magee, James, 14 Broadway.
Mott, R. W., 4 Broadway.
Mc Arthur, Josiah, 175 Chambers-street.
Morje & Wix, 154 Chambers-street.
Mitchell & Worcester, 146 Chambers-st.
McEwing & Snyder, 103 Chambers-street.
Morrison & Son, David, 111 Chambers-st.
McKim, T., 16 Broadway.
McMillan, Rob't H., 110 Broadway.
Mayher, John, 180 Broadway.
McLaughlin, John, 180 Front-street.
Macy's Sons, Josiah, 189 Front-street.
Meekan & Son, C. H., 97 Maiden Lane.
McKewan, John, 55 Maiden Lane.
Messenger, H., 161 Maiden Lane.
Moore, Alfred, 141 Broadway.
McDonald & Anchler, 183 Broadway.
Martens, F. W., 83 Wall-street.
Marx, Shultz & Co., 44 Barclay-street.
Mead, Hiram W., 58 Barclay-street.
Miller, S. B., 292 Washington-street.
Mackus & Co., Jos. P., 281 Washington-st.
Meyer & Fincke, 271 Washington-street.
Murray, D. C., 62 South-street.
Mallett, Peter, 62 South-street.
Macy & Jenkins, 67 Liberty-street.
McMichael, J., 56 Liberty-street.
Mease, Charles B., 34 Liberty-street.
Morgan, Jas. K., 192 Greenwich-street.
Mackin & Brother, 103 Liberty-street.
Meyers & Sondheim, 89 Liberty-street.
Martin, M. C., 107 Liberty-street.
Marston & Powers, 95 Beaver-street.
McClellan, Edward, 94 Gold-street.
Mahr, George, 193 William-street.
Mayer, Wm., 196 William-street.
Munroe, E. S., 17 William-street.
Mayer, J. & G.
Maghee, Thos. H.
Mila, George, 22 South William-street.
Moring, H. E., 16 South William-street.
Makas, Louis, 9 South William-street.
McFarlan, Henry, 17 South William-st.
Montgomery, J. P., 56 Beekman-street.
Maguire, Charles, 128 Maiden Lane.
Marshall, Wm. H., 5 Gold-street.
Miller, George, 210 Greenwich-street.
McClusky, James, 208 Greenwich-street.
Mowbray, John, 74 West-street.
Mirick Brothers, 16 Spruce-street.
Morrell, Jno. H., 129 Roosevelt-street.
Martin & Corey, 283 Greenwich-street.
Morrison, Jas. J., 318 Greenwich-street.
Mattison & Co., M., 36 Spruce-street.
Melvin & Danforth, 26 Spruce-street.
Mayer, Bernard, 80 Beekman-street.
Meriden, Cutlery Co., 45 Beekman-street.
Meyer, E., 17 Beekman-street.
Malford & Cary, 27 Spruce-street.
Merritt & Brown, 18 Beekman-street.
Mott, Jr., Wm. F., 16 Beekman-street.
Moseman, J. H., 120 Beekman-street.
Milne, Robert, 49 Wall-street.
Maas, M., 29 Park row.
Martin, R. M., 52 Exchange Place.
Montgomery, H., 27 Wall-street.
Moriarty, J. D., 442 Broadway.
Milford, Henry E., 458 Broadway.
Mears, John, 179 Pearl-street.
Murray, R., New-York.
Morrispat, Louis, 101 William-street.
Markz, B., 107 William-street.
Macy, Wm. H., 45 William-street.
Meinell, James, 207 West 14th-street.
Monash, H., 69 William-street.
Mann, A., 96 Maiden Lane.
Maloy, E. L., 98 Fulton-street.
Magnus Bros., 104 Fulton-street.
Monell, W. J., 127 Fulton-street.
Mann, Geo. C., 141 Fulton-street.
Mott, Jno. W., 36 South-street.
Millet, Wm. E., 329 Broadway.
Mountain, 353 Broadway.
Mellys, James T., 285 Broadway.
Morrell, Daniel, 29 Merchants' Exchange.
Meigs, Chas. A., 50 Exchange Place.
Maxwell, Lascelles E., 69 Wall-street.
Maxwell, Jno., 69 Wall-street.
Murray, Jno. W., 65 Wall-street.
Merrell, Wm. R., 61 Wall-street.
Marckwald, Jr., M. B.
Meade, Geo. N. F., 85 West 14th-street.
Moore, L. H., 212 Front-street.
Marsh, Hiram, 206 Front-street.
Mott & Son, Jno. G., 122 Beekman-street.
Miller, A. B., 271 South-street.
Miller & Conger, 271 South-street.
Monk, W. W., 205 South-street.
Mitchell, W. L., 162 South-street.

Mullender, J. G.
Meeker, J. C., 55 Dey-street.
Mecklem & Co., 287 Greenwich-street.
Myers, W. H. & F. R., 165 Duane-street.
MacBride, J. H., 298 Washington-street.
Merchant, John, 199 Chambers-street.
Miller & Carpenter, 8 Erie Building.
Montgomery, Wm., 65 Pine-street.
Maple, C., 53 Pine-street.
Magonigle, J. Henry, 404 Broadway.
Morris, M., 508 Broadway.
MacDonald, E., 522 Broadway.
Mount, Hall & Co., 49 Park Place.
Matthews, E. B., 1 Park Place.
Marsh & Co., T. W. & A., 153 West-street.
Mead & Co., W. A., 338 Broadway.
Martin, R. M., 52 Exchange Place.
Mullany, E. B., 41 Murray-street.

NORTH, Sherman & Co., 98 Chambers.
Nichols, C. E., 19 Wall-street.
Nessleye, J. H. H.
Newman & Co., W. H., 78 Pearl-street.
Newbold, C., 98 Broadway.
Nelson, R., 152 Broadway.
Noyes, R. S., St. Mark's Place.
Nichols, Burtnett & Co., 51 Maiden Lane.
Napier, Alexander D., 187 Broadway.
Nevers, Copland & McLaren, 187 Broadway.
Neilson & Anthony, 62 Liberty-street.
Newland, J. J., 96 Liberty-street.
Norton, H. L., 100 Liberty-street.
Nemburges & Co., L., 112 Liberty-street.
Noe, P. F., Wall-street.
Norton & Wood, 157 Duane-street.
Noble, Brown & Co., 125 and 127 Duane-st.
Newell & Beers, 34 Cedar-street.
Nicolay, A. H., 52 William-street.
Nagle, C., 74 Maiden Lane.
Nye, Ezra, 17 South-street.
Notman, P., 67 Wall-street.
Nevers, Wm. G., 101 Wall-street.
Nixon & Son, J. C., 173 William-street.
Nicholl, Jno., 183 William-street.
Neidig, Chas., 203 William-street.
Norris & Gregg, 62 and 64 Gold-street.
Nesbitt, Joseph, 74 Beekman-street.
Nagell, Geo., Beekman-street.

O'DONOGHUE & Sons, Jno., 239 Front.
Osborn, John, 45 Beaver-street.
O'Malley, D., 59 Beaver-street.
O'Toole, John, 21 Beaver-street.
Overton, James L., 174 Front-street.
O'Neill, David, 192 Front-street.
Onativia & Co., J. V., 47 South-street.
Oliver, Hannah & Co., 92 John-street.
Oppenheim & Co., J. M., 60 Broadway.
Opdyke, George, 36 & 38 Barclay-street.
Oliver, Marshall, 60 Barclay-street.
Oakes, Josiah, 22 Cedar-street.
Oaksmith & Co., 112 William-street.
Olmstead, Jno. A., 171 William-street.
Olyphant, G. Talbot, 23 William-street.
Ogden, M. C., 53 Cliff-street.
Oothout & Bro., Wm., 3 Cliff-street.
Olds, E. B., 332 Broadway.
Osborn, L. A., 92 Warren-street.
Ogden, Wm., 103 Water-street.
Ottinger & Goldstein, 35 Dey-street.
Oakley & Pendleton, 56 Pine-street.

PECK, Cyrus, 18 Wall-street.
Pinneo & Co., 76 Chambers-street.
Pays, Walter K., 31 Wall-street.
Pratt, Charles H., 85 South-street.
Power, J. N., 192 Broadway.
Platt, Cornelius, 210 Broadway.
Pryer & Co., James, 217 Front-street.
Pomeroy & Co., A. H., 4 South-street.
Pares, Francis, 828 Broadway.
Penfold & Schuyler, 178 Front-street.
Peck, Stoughton & Co., 191 Front-street.
Pyle, James, 345 Washington-street.
Pawling, L., 105 Front-street.
Peters, E. J., 53 South-street.
Peck, William T., 98 John-street.
Prosser & Son, Thomas, 28 Platt-street.
Perkins, G. Deming, 187 Broadway.
Poag, John, 171 Broadway.
Phelps, William H., 38 Broadway.
Pendexter, G. F., 252 Broadway.
Peck, Edwin, 254 Broadway.
Patten & Samson, 265 Washington-street.
Parker, Geo. C. & Bro., 259 Washington.
Peters, Wm. B., 156 South-street.
Peck & Samter, 117 Liberty-street.
Power, J. W., 192 Broadway.
Parmenter, H., 10 Cedar-street.
Phineas, Myer, 100 William-street.
Pfizer & Co., Charles, 90 William-street.
Pettit, S., 152 Fulton-street.
Pearson, Jr., Samuel, 150 Fulton-street.
Phillips, H., 126 Fulton-street.
Poppenhusen & Konig, 44 Cliff-street.
Potter, M. L., 28 South-street.
Phillips & Oakley, 3 Hanover-street.
Penney, T. W., 326 Broadway.
Porter & Co., A. D., 327 Broadway.
Perego & Son, 381 Broadway.
Peno, Chas. H., 61 Wall-street.
Paddock & Co., F. A., 83 Wall-street.
Prime & Woolsey, 213 Front-street.
Purdy, A. B., 194 West-street.
Poillon, John H., 68 Murray-street.
Platt, John R., 79 Murray-street.
Porteus & Co., James A., 65 Murray-st.
Prankard, F. T. & W. C., 59 Murray-st.
Pratt, Oakley & Co., 21 Murray-street.
Pike, Jr., Benj., 294 Broadway.
Partridge, Son & Co., William, 27 Cliff-st.
Phelps, Dodge & Co., 61 and 63 Cliff-st.
Park & Co., Rufus, 63 Dey-street.
Plunkett, A., 85 Liberty-street.
Perry, Jr., Geo. T., 29 Cortlandt-street.

Peck, Wm. B., 5 and 7 Stone-street.
Peck & Schuyler, 4 West-street.
Peters, H. N., 59 Reade-street.
Putzel & Stein, 5 Erie Building.
Peterson, A. A., 406 Broadway.
Pierce, Benj. H., 388 Broadway.
Partridge, Jr., Geo. S., 364 Broadway.
Price, Wm. M., 424 Broadway.
Peck & Co., 3 Park Place.
Peckell, J. W., 45 Gold-street.
Perry, W. C., 13 Gold-street.
Phillips & Lee, 177 William-street.
Paulus, G., 179 William-street.
Purdy, Jno. F., 17 William-street.
Pairsen, Wm. B., 22 New-street.
Phelan, M., 128 Maiden Lane.
Percy, Robt. P., 214 Greenwich-street.
Pechin & Goery, 29 Spruce-street.
Paten, Wm., & Noble, 42 Spruce-street.
Peck & Walton Manuf. Co., 85 Beekman-st.
Preble, J. Q., 28 Beekman-street.
Powell, R. B., 100 Beekman-street.
Petit, Joseph, 49 Wall-street.
Patterson Bros, 27 Park Row.
Place, J. K. & E. B., 30 Broad-street.

QUAAS, John, 203 William-street.
Quirk Bros., 98 Maiden Lane.

RANKEN, John, 10 Wall-street.
Rosenblatt & Brother, G., 78 Chambers.
Randall & Co., John, 66 Broadway.
Rowland, C. N. S., 142 Broadway.
Rood, E. H., 164 Broadway.
Rodman, R. W., 82 South-street.
Russell, Edwin C., 182 Chambers-street.
Rathbone, R. C., 108 Broadway.
Ripley, B., 162 and 164 Broadway.
Robb, Ralph, 180 Broadway.
Reed & Co., John A., 203 Broadway.
Rogers, John, 189 Broadway.
Rooney & Leutts, 81 Water-street.
Rich & Co., Josiah, 172 Front-street.
Renburgh & Bryan, 171 Front-street.
Rosenburg, A., Maiden Lane.
Roys, Harlow, 100 John-street.
Rose, Andrew, 129 Maiden Lane.
Rollhaus, P., 250 Water-street.
Richardson, F. E., 107 John-street.
Rider, John, 165 Broadway.
Reid & Townsend, 269 Washington-st.
Roe & Comstock, 197 Washington-street.
Rudderow, Jones & Co., 14 & 16 Liberty.
Reid, George W., 32 Liberty-street.
Ray Brothers, 8 Dey-street.
Randolph & Heady, 14 Dey-street.
Rose & Weil, 105 Liberty-street.
Runyan, Nelson, 95 Liberty-street.
Rothschild, Benham & Solomon, 91 Liberty-street.
Reynolds & Smith, 37 Murray-street.
Rogers, M. W., 292 Broadway.
Rutherford, Thos., 314 Broadway.
Russell Erwin Manuf. Co., 87 Beekman-st.
Recknagel & Co., 46 Cedar-street.
Richter, Chas. G., 86 Cedar-street.
Romaine, Wm. H., 21 Cedar-street.
Robinson, Jno., 148 William-street.
Raynor, Samuel, 118 William-street.
Robins & Son, G. S., 54 William-street.
Remsen, W., 51 William-street.
Roosevelt & Sons, 94 Maiden Lane.
Richmond, C. C., 150 Fulton-street.
Rogers & Raymond, 125 Fulton-street.
Russell, A. T., 137 Fulton-street.
Ripley, D. C., 70 Water-street.
Rosenbeüth & Cohn, 325 Broadway.
Rumrill & Co., A., 264 Broadway.
Rorbach & Manning, 9 Warren-street.
Robinson, B. H., 41 and 43 Warren-st.
Roe & Co., W. D., 59 Wall-street.
Ritter, Washington, 69 Wall-street.
Roome, A. P. M., 67 Wall-street.
Rese, John, Harlem.
Rose, John, 160 Mott-street.
Robbins, E. M., 70 Reade-street.
Riggs, H. E., 189 Reade-street.
Richardson, Francis, 470 Broadway.
Raymond & Co., 536 Broadway.
Rogers, Thomas, 189½ William-street.
Rio, W. J.
Robinson, J. F., 39 South William-street.
Rice, Thomas W., 41 Bowery.
Rutter, Wm., 6 Ferry-street.
Rogers, N. A., 111 Nassau-street.
Raymond, Geo. H., 364 West-street.
Rockwell & Co., J. S., 47 and 49 Ferry-st.
Redfield, J. S., 34 Beekman-street.
Reed, C. R., 359 Broadway.

SACKETT, E. W., 25 John-street.
Sibell, E. W., Brooklyn.
Swift, Seamen & Co., 122 Chambers-st.
Starr, J., 44 Chambers-street.
Scott & Co., John D., 37 Chambers-street.
Schanck & Downing, 45 Chambers-street.
Smith, W. M., 49 Chambers.street.
Shultz, Mayer, 113 Liberty-street.
Southwick, B., 107 and 109 Liberty-st.
Scott, Wisner & Co., 112 Pearl-street.
Swain, P. Harbeck, 77 Water-street.
Smith, Spelman & Co., 170 Front-street.
Schlegel, H., 184 Front-street.
Schiffer, S. & J., 194 Front-street.
Saugerties White Lead and Paint Company, 159 Front-street.
Sturges, Bennett & Co., 125 and 127 Front-street.
Snowhill, W. O., 121 and 123 Front-st.
Simes, Chase & Co., 66 South-street.
Smith & Son, W. H., 89 Maiden Lane.
Southmayd & Sons, Horace, 147 Maiden Lane.
Shepard, W. H., 208 Water-street.
Stamford Manuf. Co., 159 Maiden Lane.
Spies, A. W. & Co., 187 Broadway.
Salisbury, Henry, 171 Broadway.

Sewell, Robert, 15 Wall-street.
Seymour, R. M., 177 Broadway.
Saxton, M. F., 25 Park Row.
Schlesinger & Co., H., 50 Broadway.
Samuels, S. & G., 46 Broadway.
Smyth, B. S., 38 Broadway.
Shobelt, E. C.
Stryker, Jr., Samuel D.
Scott, John D., 37 Chambers-street.
Still & Co., J. W., 42 Barclay-street.
Strahlheim & Co., 44 Barclay-street.
Snediker & Co., Wm., 50 Barclay-street.
Sterratt & Co., 252 Broadway.
Shaw, W. B., 256 Broadway.
Sumner, Henry H., 256 Broadway.
Spring, L. Louis, 279 Washington-street.
Simmons & Elsworth, 257 Washington-st.
Schumsahl, Hinck & Co., 239 Washington-street.
Sloat, Jr., John D., 65 South-street.
Storms, Wm. J., 185 Washington-street.
Shaw, Alex. L., 183 Washington-street.
Stebbins, Gray & Co., 224 Fulton-street.
Shulman & Brothers, L., 105 Liberty-st.
Stern & Erdman, 110 Liberty-street.
Strouse & Brother, S. H., 121 Liberty-st.
Stewart, W. J., 157 South-street.
Stiles, Samuel, 1 Wall-street.
Shepard, W. H., 74 Broadway.
Stone, Doras L., 45 Wall-street.
Stansbury, Edward A., 108 Broadway.
Smith & Hanford, 249 Front-street.
Sniffin, Jr., John, 80 South-street.
Schreiner, O. H., 192 Broadway.
Sonthack, John, 196 Broadway.
Shepard, F. M, 201 Broadway.
Stewart, Robert K., 157 South-street.
Sturges & Co., 31 South-street.
Schedel, William J., 76 Pearl-street.
Scott & Ingraham, 76 Front-street.
Storey & Stevens, 12 Old Slip.
Sherman & Weeks, 11 Coenties Slip.
Stevens, Jr., J. M., 195 Water-street.
Sturges, Jonathan, 125 Front-street.
Spaulding, M. B., 240 Broadway.
Stephenson, George S., 49 South-street.
Straiton, Sanford & Co., 59 Beaver-street.
Secor, William H., 91 Beaver-street.
Shuttruff & Leopold, 21 Beaver-street.
Symington, James, 39 Beaver-street.
Schott, James, Jr., 42 Beaver-street.
Stevens, John A., 63 Bleecker-street.
Stewart & Co., Daniel, 46 Beaver-street.
Slipper & Goadby, 2 Broadway.
Solomon, A. H., 2 Broadway.
Stebbins, Hoyt & Co., 152 Chambers-st.
Stone, Starr & Co., 113 Chambers-street.
Schiels, L., 119 Chambers-street.
Straus, Branchi & Co., 155 Chambers-st.
Storm, S. F., 187 Broadway.
Sheffield & Co., 60 Broad-street.
Schafer & Benecke, 111 Liberty-street.
Suydam, Lambert & Co., 107 West-street.
Shaw & Bro., 152 West-street.
Sturgis, Shaw & Co. 74 and 76 Murray-st.
Swain, P. M., 296 Broadway.
Scudder & Co., H. G., 118 Warren-street.
Shook & Morgan, 112 Warren-street.
Seymour & Co., John F., 78 Warren-st.
Stafford, Candee & Co., 74 Warren-street.
Samson, C. B., 51 Cliff-street.
Shortridge, Howell & Co., 24 Cliff-street
Schmitt, Constantine, 10 Doyer-street.
Samuels, Samuel.
Stringer, H. E., 117 Wall-street.
Schmidt, Wm., 66 Washington-street.
Schiffer, Jno., 10 Doyer-street.
Steward, W. M., 157 South-street.
Seabury, Chas. B., 112 South-street.
Smith & Sons, A. E., 38 Peck Slip.
St. John, Burr, 308 Broadway.
Schroeder, J., 227 Seventh-street.
Schlicher, J., 519 Fourth-street.
Shaw, P. P., & Co., 31 and 33 Dey-street.
Small & Co., E., 63 Stone-street.
Smith, Phineas, 179 Reade-street.
St. John, Chas. W., 2 Erie Building.
Stanton, Henry, 17 William-street.
Stanton, Jr., John, 25 William-street.
Schlesinger & Son, 63 Pine-street.
Sloat, L. W., 63 Pine-street.
Strong, Wm. K., 50 and 52 Pine-street.
Sands & Co., 51 Pine-street.
Sniffen, J. L., 388 Broadway.
Scribner & Co., Grand-street.
Starr, Alfred A., 22 Vandam-street.
St. John, S. H., 526 Broadway.
Smith, Stephen Wm., 534 Broadway.
Smith, J. T., 344 Broadway.
Sloane, Geo., 593 Broadway.
Sloane, Wm., 593 Broadway.
Smith, Phineas, 418 Broadway.
Smith & Co., Ira, 370 Broadway.
Stone, Boorman & Bliss, 20 Park Place.
Spencer, W., 45 Park Place.
Scott & Son, Wm. H., 36 Murray-street.
Seguine, Wm., 860 Houston-street.
Sheffield & Co., J. B., 63 Beekman-street.
Studwell & Co., A., 181 William-street.
Spalings & Brother, 186½ William-street.
Schmidt, Frederick C., 3 South William-st.
Sand, C. H., 11 South William-street.
Stuart & Son, J. P., 15 South William-st.
Simonin, Aénédée H., 37 So. William-st.
Sullivan & Hyatt, 54 Beekman-street.
Speir, Francis, 54 Beekman-street.
Simmons & Co., D., 7 Gold-street.
Sears, H. P., 238 Greenwich-street.
Shiers, King & Co., 62 Pine-street.
Sweetser, Saml., 80 Pine-street.
Steele, M. M., 43 Pine-street.
Stratton & Co., 1 Pine-street.
Sherwood, W. E., 40 Spruce-street.
Smithson, Thos. B., 16 Spruce-street.
Simmons, Thos. S., 10 Ferry-street.
Stokes, Henry, 29 Cliff-street.

Smithson, Thos. B., 16 Spruce-street.
Smithson, Wm., 16 Spruce-street.
Sage, W. B., 10 Spruce-street.
Snyder & Sons, 236 South-street.
Stelzriede, 182 Christopher-street.
Sheldon, Elijah, 306 West-street.
Schoonmaker, Cyrus, 364 West-street.
Smith, Jas. O., & Sons, 81 Fulton-street.
Swasey & Co., E. R., 3 Ferry-street.
Sherman, Geo. S., 149 Broadway.
Sherwood, Wm., 40 Spruce-street.
Stout, Thomas H., 37 Spruce-street.
Stout, William, 37 Spruce-street.
Smith, Isaac, 139 West 21st-street.
Smith, David, 16 Cedar-street.
Sandwich, A. S.
Sanger, Joseph T., 22 Cedar-street.
Shattuck, W., 208 Broadway.
Shattuck, Albert G., 22 Cedar-street.
Stevens, B., 56 Cedar-street.
Schiefflin, Ph. & Lewis, 78 Cedar-street.
Smellie, James, 45 Cedar-street.
Smith & Bro., E. A., 180 William-street.
Sadlier & Co., D. & J., 164 William-st.
Sanford, J. T., 93 West-street.
Strasburger & Nuhn, 65 Maiden Lane.
Schaefer, A., 65 Maiden Lane.
Schundeberg, Julian, 87 William-street.
Satterthwaite Bros., 61 William-street.
Satterthwaite, T. B., 61 William-street.
Schenck, Jacob B., 96 Maiden Lane.
Selleck, J. N., 98 Fulton-street.
Smith, Wm., 110 Fulton-street.
Scott & Co., M. A., 152 Fulton-street.
Shendan, A. F., 150 Fulton-street.
Smith, J. F., 149 Hudson-street.
Scofield, W. H., 98 Hester-street.
Scranton, W. B., 82 Broad-street.
Sale & Co., Wm. A., 46 South-street.
Southmayd, Chas. F., 39 Ninth-street.
Starr, L. M., 4 Hanover-street.
Sprague, C. J., 117 Pearl-street.
Stone, S. R., 46 Exchange Place.
Samuels, A. S., 310 Broadway.
Sherman, T., 337 Broadway.
Schmidt, Henry, 337 Broadway.
Strang, Adriance & Co., 355 Broadway.
Solomon & Hart, 369 Broadway.
Stockbridge, Benj., 285 Broadway.
Stewart, O. L., 29 Wall-street.
Steele, Joseph L., 53 Warren-street.
Smith's Sons & Co., Isaac, 77 Warren-st.
Sartorius & Loewe, 81 Warren-street.
Slocum, Wm. S., 10 Merchants' Exchange.
Smith, R. Burnett, 44 Exchange Place.
Sherwood, W. E., 40 Spruce-street.
Smith, G. R., 28 Spruce-street.
Smith & Bros., E. A., 180 William-street.
Spear, Chas. R., 181 Water-street.
Sprague, Jas. J., 15 Beekman-street.
Steinecke, H. F., 46 Beekman-street.
Savery's Sons, John.
Sargant & Co., 85 Beekman-street.
Studwell, Jr., Joseph, 25 Park Row.
Stebbens & Co., W. A., 51 Exchange Pl.
Stanton & Riley, 43 Exchange Place.
Such, Geo.
Semrad, A., 438 Broadway.
Smith, J. A., 442 Broadway.
Smith & Lounsbery, 456 Broadway.
Smallwood, J. L., 10 Beaver-street.
Stephenson, Chas. F., 65 Beaver-street.

TAY, Charles H., 31 Cortland-street.
Todd, Charles H., 118 Chambers-street.
Thayer, C. P., 82 Broadway.
Todd, Charles P., 166 Broadway.
Terrett, H. N., 251 Front-street.
Trevor, Jr., J. B.
Ten Eyck, C. A., 67 South-street.
Tucker, Cooper & Co., 70 South-street.
Tyler & Co., Owen, 86 South-street.
Terry & Dellatorre, 106 South-street.
Thompson, Lyon & Co., 79 Pearl-street.
Thomae, George F., 82 South-street.
Truesdell & Co., 141 Pearl-street.
Thorley's Food for Cattle Depot, 21 Broadway.
Thompson, Elmor, 111 Chambers-street.
Travis, Wm., 110 Broadway.
Tims & Co., C. M., 164 Broadway.
Thompson, Jonathan, 47 South-street.
Tiers, Peter, 43 Maiden Lane.
Taylor, Charles, 212 Water-street.
Tracy, Irwin & Co., 234 and 235 Broadway.
Todd, Gilbert M., 254 Broadway.
Tryon & Co., E. W., 257 Broadway.
Terey & Co., 56 South-street.
Trask & Dearborn, 62 South-street.
Taylor, Brothers, 76 Wall-street.
Tilton, A. E., 25 and 27 Cedar-street.
Tracy, E., William-street.
Towt & Son, John W., 56 Beekman-st.
Thompson, A. R., 52 Beekman-street.
Tucker & Burrell, 104 Maiden Lane.
Tooker, S., 238 Greenwich-street.
Thompson, Allanby, 45 John-street.
Trapton, Wm. H., 85 Broad-street.
Tappan, John S., 63 William-street.
Tuttle, E. G., 246 and 247 South-street.
Turner, D. H., 118 King-street.
Terry Brothers, 83 Gold-street.
Tatham, C. B., 82 Beekman-street.
Tuttle & Bailey, 74 Beekman-street.
Tyler, Christopher, 36 Beekman-street.
Thomasius, Rich'd W., 16 Spring-street.
Todd, George W., 64 Dey-street.
Thompson & Nephew, 63 Pine-street.
Thurston & Sons, N., 554 Broadway.
Thorne, J. R., 6 Murray-street.
Tuske & Brother, P. H., 146 William-st.
Thalmessinger & Co., M., 76 William-st.
Tracy, George M., 87 William-street.
Thompson, Francis, 37 William-street.
Tilton, R. L., 152 Fulton-street.

Taylor, Henry H. & Brother, 58 Beekman-street.
Timson & Dater, 37 William-street.
Taylor, H. E., 278 Pearl-street.
Taylor & Co., F. C., 7 Old Slip.
Turner, David L., 52 South-street.
Teller, West & Co., 32 South-street.
Tripp, Ferris, 326 Broadway.
Taylor, Joseph S., 303 Broadway.
Trimble, Merritt, 86 Broad-street.
Trippe, Joseph E., 71 Warren-street.
Thoman, Wm. A., 65 Wall-street.
Townsend, Samuel, 61 Wall-street.
Townsend, Dwight, 102 Wall-street.
Tunkner, John, 98 Elm-street.
Talmage & Co., Daniel, 269 South and 60 Water-street.
Town, William, 228 Wooster-street.
Trowbridge, W. S., 340 Broadway.
Taylor, Wm., 334 Broadway.
Tappan, J. P., 26 Pine-street.
Tappan & Starbuck, 77 Water-street.
Titts & Webb, 122 Warren-street.
Tuthill, James M., 114 Warren-street.
Treadwell & Son, E., 104 Warren-street.
Townsend & Crain, 45 Murray-street.

UNDERHILL, Jr., Wm., 183 Water-st.
Underwood, H., 69 South-street.
Ullman, Blumenthal & Co., 24 Dey-st.
Underhill, L. & A., 297 Broadway.
Underhill, A. S., 69 Wall-street.
Underhill, F., 181 South-street.

VANDERLIP, John M., 18 Wall-street.
Valentine, Robert B., 10 Wall-street.
Van Nest & Co., Abm. R., 60 Warren-st.
Van Benschoten, J., 84 Chambers-street.
Vallette, J. C.
Van Valkenburgh, R., 6 John-street.
Valeno & Fassin, 40 Beaver-street.
Vanderpoel, A., 14 Broadway.
Voorhees, J. C., 112 Pearl-street.
Valentine, Willis & Co., 93 John-street.
Van Zandt, N. L., 135 Broadway.
Valentine, T., 243 Washington-street.
Varney, James C., 53 South-street.
Van Buskirk, Richard, 218 Greenwich-st.
Vanderbilt, Wm. S., 408 Broadway.
Vandervoort, R. J., 116 Fulton-street.
Van Benschoten, S., 15 Old Slip,
Van Benschoten, Chas. C., 15 Old Slip.
Vining, H. S., 31 Old Slip.
Van Harnen, Geo. W., 62 Pine-street.
Vanderhoef, S. S., 25 Ferry-street.
Valentine & Co., L. T., 45 Beekman-st.
Vernon Brothers, 23 Beekman-street.
Van Winkle, A. J., 9 Spruce-street.
Van Nest & Hayden, 79 Beekman-street.
Van Horn, C., 70 Beekman-street.
Van Wart & Co., Irving, 72 Beekman-st.
Van Saun, Isaac, 193 Washington-street.
Van Winkle, Albert, 205 West-street.
Van Ness & Emerson, 123 Warren-street.
Van Kleeck & Lewis, W. H., 120 Warren-street.

WARD, Albert, 18 Wall-street.
Wakeman & Co., J. P., 47 Chambers-street.
Wolfers, G. & Co., 75 Chambers-street.
Wells, Fargo & Co., 82 Broadway.
Wright, Chas., New-Rochelle.
Willis, Geo. W., 25 Wall-street.
Walcott, Jr., B. S., 45 Wall-street.
Westcott, Robt. F., 168 Broadway.
Woodhull & Co., 207 Front-street.
Wood, Jno. A., 142 Fulton-street.
Wood, Geo. W., 2 Dutch-street.
Wells & Provost, 215 Front-street.
Woodside, David, 163 South-street.
Walsh, Carver & Chase, 30 South-street.
Whitman Bro. & Co., 72 Beaver-street.
Woodruff & Robinson, 14 Coenties Slip.
Williams, F. B., 85 Pearl-street.
Westervelt, Jno. Z., 203 Front-street.
Wild, J., 62 Cedar-street.
Weldon, W., 37 Beaver-street.
Weekes, Geo., 37 Beaver-street.
Williams, J. M., 35 William-street.
Warner, John H., 51 Exchange Place.
Watt, James S., 39 Beaver-street.
Warner & Co., 159 Chambers-street.
Warford, Wm. K., 18 Broadway.
Watson, George, 196 Broadway.
Walker, R. R., 76 Water-street.
Williams, C. F., 161 Water-street.
Waring, Henry P., 164 Front-street.
Woods, Robt. L., 137 Front-street.
Whittemore, W. M., 91 Maiden Lane.
Wallach, A., 33 Maiden Lane.
Worthington, S., 141 Maiden Lane.
Weekes, Aug. F., 264 Water-street.
Watson & Meares, 34 Burling Slip.
Waldo, F. W., 135 Broadway.
Waldo, Jr., Horace, 135 Broadway.
Winant, D. D., Williamsburgh.
West, Caldwell & Co., 52 Broadway.
Watt, Dunning & Graham, 245 Broadway.
Whitmore, J., 47 South-street.
Walker, T. H.
Wiley, Alexander, 70 South-street.
White, Morris & Co., 25 Wall-street.
Walsh, H., 400 Greenwich-street.
Woolsey, Jno., 208 Front-street.
Woodhull, E. S., 207 Front-street.
Wollem, Chas. H., 47 Gold-street.
Walker, E., 47 Gold-street.
White & Co., Chas. T., 65 Beekman-st.
White, P. A., 102 Gold-street.
Whitmore, Geo. W., 177 William-street.
Wright & Campbell, 190 William-street.
Weston, Dortic & Co., 19 William-street.
Ward, Edward F., 6 South William-st.
West, George, 7 South William-street.
Wright & Mace, 58 Beekman-street.
Walsh & Plume, 60 Beekman-street.

Ward, A., 54 Beekman-street.
Warens, J. P., 46 Beekman-street.
Wilcox, S. L.
Walker, D., 126 Maiden Lane.
Wade, Jr., Ezekiel, 17 Peck Slip.
Wiggins, J., 75 Barclay-street.
Weeks, E., 210 Greenwich-street.
Wells, Sidney B., 27 Spruce-street.
Withers, R., 135 Second Avenue.
Williams, Wm., 16 Spruce-street.
Wight & Son, J., 232 South-street.
Walton, Elisha L., 534 Water-street.
Wetmore & Kirkland, 311 Greenwich-st.
Walker, F. R., 22 Spruce-street.
Warren, H. M., 20 Spruce-street.
Wells, Sidney A., 27 Spruce-street.
Weed, T., 83 Beekman-street.
Waefelaer, L., 74 Beekman-street.
Wemmell, Andrew A., 31 Park Row.
Wetherbee, Wm., 52 Exchange Place.
Winslow, Joseph, 64 Exchange Place.
Wells, Charles, 434 Broadway.
Wood, O. J., 444 Broadway.
Wright & Co., Wm. W., 252 Broadway.
Wilbur, Charles, 189 Washington-street.
Wakeman, Dimon & Co., 73 South-st.
Willis & Elsworth, 66 Liberty-street.
Warren, James K., 96 Liberty-street.
Weeks, F. S., 100 Liberty-street.
Way, D. H., 22 Cliff-street.
Wilkinson, F., 15 Murray-street.
Ward, O. D., 296 Broadway.
Ward, W. H., 296 Broadway.
Whitehead, W. H., 314 Broadway.
Ward, Elijah, 314 Broadway.
Willard, G., 94 Warren-street.
Weed, Jas. M., 86 Warren-street.
White, Chas., 65 East 12th-street.
Wilde, Wm. L, 388 Broadway.
Wygant & Hoyt, 68 Dey-street.
Wells & Co., Nelson, 81 Dey-street.
Wagner, Chas. K., 71 Cortlandt-street.
Willis, Wm. M., 36 Cortlandt-street.
Wiley, F., 78 Reade-street.
Wilkie & Co., 169 Reade-street.
Weeks, B. M., 194 Duane-street.
Wilbur & Price, 50 Pine-street.
Wilde, Jr., & Co., James, 388 Broadway.
Wilde, Joseph, 97 Livingston-street, Bk.
Willcox, Wm. H., 312 Broadway.
Winston, F. S., 94 Broadway.
Warner, Peck & Co., 376 Broadway.
Wing & Winans, 418 Broadway.
Wetherald & Young, 33 Park Place.
Wines, G. H., 1 Park Place.
Wallach, Willy, 131 William-street.
Whitney, E.
Windle & Co., 56 Maiden Lane.
Willard, Harvey & Co., 84 Maiden Lane.
Woodward, Pinckney & Clarke, 118 Fulton-street.
Williams, A. J., 210 Broadway.
Waters, E. G., 16 Wall-street.
Watts, C. C., 130 Fulton-street.
Ward, F. A., 29 South William-street.
Williams, Edward, 1½ Hanover-street.
Willets, Amos, 276 Pearl-street.
Winthrop, Francis B., 4 Hanover-street.
Wright & Co., Wm. P., 6 Hanover-street.
Westervelt & Son, James, 32 Old Slip.
Wickersham, Jno. B., 312 Broadway.
Woodruff, A. G., 326 Broadway.
Woodruff, David, 326 Broadway.
Williams, Geo. H., 353 Broadway.
Williams, Jno. H., 353 Broadway.
Wilson & Co., C., 297 Broadway.
Walton, J. M., 67 Warren-street.
Weed, Wm. C., 85 Warren-street.
Wilson, J. Y., 270 Washington-street.
Williamson, D. O., 28 Exchange Place.
Wood, Wm. H., 65 Wall-street.
White, Ezra, 61 Wall-street.
Whitmore, P. D., 117 Wall-street.
Wunderlich, Thomas, 117 Wall-street.
Wade, Edmund J., 101 Wall-street.
Wall, Wm. J. B., 42 Clinton Place.
Wilde, Jno. S., 36 Remson-street, Bk.
Wilde, Jno. T.

YOUNG, Davidson & Co., 262 and 264 Front-street.
Young, Arch. & Co., 314 Broadway.
Young, James, 314 Broadway.

ZELLMACHER, Wise & Co., 103 Chambers-street.
Ziegenbien, F. W., 400 Greenwich-street.
Zinsser & Marc, 197 William-street.
Zabriskie & Lumley, 225 Greenwich-st.
Zibley & Co., J. F., 13 Spruce-street.

Pro Rata Question.

READ AND CIRCULATE.

OPENING REMARKS

OF

JOHN THOMPSON, ESQ.,

ON BEHALF OF THE RAILROADS,

AGAINST

A PRO RATA LAW;

AND THE TESTIMONY OF

J. W. BROOKS, Esq.,

BEFORE THE

SELECT COMMITTEE OF THE ASSEMBLY;

ALSO, THE TESTIMONY OF

SOLOMON DRULLARD, ESQ.,

General Freight Agent New York Central Railroad

ALBANY:
WEED, PARSONS & COMPANY, PRINTERS.
1860.

SPEECH OF MR. THOMPSON,

Before the Select Committee of the Assembly.

Mr. THOMPSON said he had endeavored to demonstrate, by way of protest to these petitions, as follows:

It is plausibly urged that by the low rates charged from Chicago or other Western points to New York, the millers of Rochester or Oswego are *injured*, and that as they are compelled to buy grain in Michigan or Wisconsin, they cannot freight it to Rochester, flour it, barrel it and get it to New York as cheaply as the Millers at Chicago or Detroit. Might admit all that to be true, and would it therefore follow that the Rochester miller is the *final cause* of all railroads, that the natural course of trade, the products of agricultural, the prosperity and enterprise of all the Empires of the New World are to bend to the thrift of Rochester millers, and go through the hoppers of Rochester mills? It is a strange assumption that any business become unprofitable in our own state by the *nature of things*, should be protected and kept up by unjust discrimination against all that may come into competition, might be applied equally to our *mills* here, our *wool* growing. It ought never to be thought of in reference to the great staple of life, *bread*, and especially when for seven months the Rochester mills has canal at its door and for balance the markets of Portland and Boston, but thus *demonstrated* by way of protection to these petitions.

1. The fallacy of the assumption, that railroad companies have any *privileges* or exemptions from the burdens borne by other trading or mercantile interests of the state, but on the contrary they are subjected to all the burdens of taxation, on their real estate, rolling stock and capital, working our highways, their own rivals, building our school houses and thus aiding our educational interests, and bring the wealth of the states to be invested in their stocks and bonds to one hundred and fifty millions of dollars, penetrating remote districts, and enhancing fourfold the price of lands where they go, building up villages, equalizing the value of property, affording large districts a valuable market for wood, and contributing by these means as well as by the employment of labor to the wealth and prosperity of the whole state. Grand Trunk exempt from a long entire line. I endeavored to establish that it was the purpose of the state in former times to foster and encourage these public enterprises, by putting them on a *footing of equality* with other forms of *associated* wealth and private enterprise, giving only such *general* regulation to their modes of operation, as experience had demonstrated would work no injury to them, and at the same time give assurance that no abuses should be tolerated where the remedy laid within the purview of legislative correction.

That within these general principles Railroads were on the *same footing as individuals*, in the transaction of their business, being governed by the laws of trade, the law of demand and supply and by the *usages* of business, as it develops, and that these laws of *trade* like the principles of the common law are progressive and changeable; changing with the growth and development of the country which they intersect, with the character of the business and merchandise which employs them, and that no rule can or should be imposed by the Legislature to cripple their usefulness or destroy their income.

I endeavored further to show that *political and moral right* ought to back and fortify *naked powers* before it is exercised to interfere with the natural commerce of corporations, and that in this respect all they should and did stand upon the footing of individuals, being entitled to the same legal protection and the same legislative regard. That *commerce* made her *own laws*, and that any interference with these, within the limits and between the states of this confederacy, was contrary to the spirit of the constitution of the United States, in direct violation and usurpation of the powers of Congress over *commerce.* Operating as effectually and disastrously as the erection of a custom house at Dunkirk or Buffalo or Oswego or Albany, to *levy a duty on all western tonnage before it should be permitted* to pass their own borders.

That such a policy would inevitably destroy what it professed to *protect.* That such hasty ill-advised legislation to protect *class interest,* always recoiled upon the very interest it was designed to foster, and instead of giving each a fair chance in the race of honorable competition ruined both.

2. That the allegation, that our railroads unjustly discriminated between *citizens of our own state* and citizens of western states was *unfounded* and unjust, the same rates being demanded of *every one shipping from the same point*, and that any discrimination in prices of transportation have *relation simply to distances and not to persons*, and that in this respect the *way* business and the *through* business of our railroads were kept on separate footings, and carried on by the companies at different rates of expense.

That no person could complain living on the line of the road, while the business was done promptly, cheaply and more to his advantage than in any other mode. That the Company might be able to carry from more distant points, for the same or a less price per ton per mile.

That the idea of the same price per ton per mile, is as absurd as if applied to a New York city omnibus or railroad car, permitting 6d for the longest ride, and demanding a pro rata diminution for any shorter distance, or lighter weight.

That the way business of the road, resting on its own footing, and conducted on a separate basis, is to be considered and regulated, if at all, solely in reference to itself.

That it is neither increased nor diminished by the passage of western merchandise over the road. That its expense is regulated by what it costs, with a small ordinary profit, depending upon grade of the road, time employed in delivering and receiving freight, cost and consumption of fuel, freight houses to be built at the stations, labor to be employed along the line, most of these being items of cost, not necessarily entering into the cost of through transportation, in respect of which, most of it passes on the road, simply without reloading or handling—being loaded at Cleveland, or Toledo, or Chicago, or other western points, from whence it comes passing direct to New York, by the Erie, or to Albany on Central.

That way transportation could not, in the nature of things, be carried on as cheaply as that between distant points—and that to this rule there is no exemption.

That way freight on the ocean, in the coasting trade, on all our rivers, canals, and railroads, pays and must pay a higher rate for short distances than for longer ones.

That a locomotive carried usually 30 cars filled with through freight, with few stoppages, and no loss of time. While the same power on a way train, carried not to exceed 20 cars, and these only partly filled, with greater loss of time, and consumption of fuel, and expenses of handling.

And the only legitimate question before the committee is: Are the rates of freight too expensive, from any station, on the line of the road to New York?

That any other view of the case, is a prostitution of the road and its uses, to operate as a limitation and check to the free enterprise of the whole country and any part of it.

That there is no power in the Legislature, to *directly prohibit* the roads from carrying cars, coming on from other States; and that it is equally unjust to compel them to charge such prices, as to effectually exclude them from the roads—thus, doing that *indirectly*, which they have no power to do directly.

That it should be the wish and effort of enlightened statesmanship, to force through our State, and into its metropolis, these streams of western merchandise, and to aid our channels of communication, in diverting it from rival lines by a fostering Legislature, instead of so crippling our own roads, as to drive this trade away from us; for it is as absurd to suppose, that the human heart can carry on its pulsations, sending blood through all its channels to the extremities, as that New York, the mart of the State, can remain wealthy, or retain her influence and prestige, when these channels of trade are strangulated or dried up.

That cheap transportation on through lines, is benefit to producer and consumer, and merchant alike.

It costs a less price when delivered in the market, which is divided between production and consumption; each receiving a portion of that by the *regularity* of railroad transportation, merchants are enabled to do business with less capital, supporting their families, and employing labor, and increasing the growth and resources of the metropolis.

I had further endeavored to demonstrate the fallacy of the allegation, that the canals were thus deprived of their "legitimate traffic," as false *in principle* and unfounded in *fact*.

That the State is no more entitled to the carrying trade, as her legitimate and peculiar field of profit, than an individual or a corporation; and that she has the same right to embark in the manufacture of iron, or quarrying of stone, or raising of agricultural products, and they lay a tax on all these branches of business for her own protection, as to compel the railroad to charge rates so high, as to throw the business they now do into the hands of *forwarders* on the canals.

If the canals cannot be supported without the destruction of all private business that may interfere with them, they had better be *abandoned, and the sooner the better*.

That it is unfounded in fact, inasmuch as the bulk of freight now carried on the railroads would not pass the canals, if the railroads were unable to carry it. That all that part of it which consists of live stock, and dead hogs, which is made up of light, valuable or perishable materials, and which must get *rapidly* to market, would seek other rail lines in getting to seaboard; and that this trade once diverted, would never return to its former channels.

That if the through freight was abandoned, as it would be through the imposition of higher prices, the way freights would require to be *largely advanced* all along the line, to enable the roads to continue their business; and upon the Erie Road this would be a calamity without any relief, as there is no other means of communication, which would therefore depreciate the price of property all along the line, from the increased expenditure required to send it to market, and along the Central. While it might aid canal transportation a little in the summer, it could not affect freights in the *winter season*, when the canal is frozen. And that unless the State desires to attempt a confiscation of the railroads, and running them on its own account (a worse boon to her than the canals), she cannot justly interfere in the matter.

That a new and cheaper mode of transportation is never, in a wise government, burdened with the expenses of the old and inferior.

There could be no progress in civilization, no advances in political or social or commercial life, under such a barbarian rule. We, on the contrary, reward the inventor with a right to the exclusive use of his invention; but of what avail is his patent, if he must buy out all the old churns, scows and machinery his invenion is designed to supersede? And that on this principle, the river craft on the Hudson, and all the dock owners along its borders, might apply to the Legislature, to compel the Hudson River Railroad to pay the price of all property which this new mode of transportation has rendered unprofitable.

3. I also attempted to expose the fallacy of the allegation that the railroad was carrying *through* freight for less than they can afford.

1. Because the petitioners have and can have no knowledge on the subject.

2. Because it is safe usually to leave com-

panies to be governed by their own instincts and experience, they being better judges of this matter than any one else can be, and that the benevolence of these petitioners towards the stockholders and bondholders of these roads is altogether quixotic and misplaced.

That the allegation that this loss is made up by excessive way freights is not true, and if true would, in summer aid, and not injure the canal; and that it is equally unjust to the company to charge it as the reason of advanced rates on *winter* transportation, as

1. The canals do not thus conflict with them; and,

2. The actual cost of winter transportation is increased in about the same ratio. And that no person along the line was compelled to delay his shipments for winter transportation, and if so, he ought, in justice, to pay the necessarily increased cost.

4. I endeavored, moreover, to expose the folly that "parties all along the line had yielded equal "rights for the erection of railroads, and were "entitled as a consideration to be placed on the "footing of through freight." That as these lines had conferred benefits and benefits only on the country at large, no one had *yielded anything*, his land was increased in value; his products found a market, cities and villages and towns were increased and built up, and other certain places and taverns on the canal might suffer, it was only the same thing that happened to the old turnpike and some of its villages by the construction of the canal. They yielded nothing, the course of trade *retreated* and left them high and dry.

I endeavored, moreover, to demonstrate the absurdity of pro rata freight charges, having reference to long *lines and freights out of the State.*

That with efficient agencies, now employed in all western cities and the inducements at present offered, to bring it through our state it is only by continued struggle that our railroads retain it at all, and that the imposition of any new burden or charge upon it would send it off on rival lines, all equally anxious to divert it; and that once gone from us, as the course of trade is to carve its own channels deeper and deeper, we could offer under legislative resolutions no means for its recovery.

That there was no less than eight different lines of communication from the southwest, to the sea coast south of us, and two rival lines north of us, all in eager competition for this trade, which will bear no burdens it can avoid, but will seek such market as it can get at the cheapest.

That the products of Ohio, Indiana, Illinois, have natural and feasible outlets, through the Pennsylvania Central and the Baltimore and Ohio Rail Road, which are fostered and encouraged by the States; and run lines of vessels from those cities to New York, carrying up coal, and wood and lumber, and take freight back as ballast, or at nominal prices in return.

That produce, and pork and beef on the Ohio and at Chicago, goes either to the river for preparation, slaughter and packing, and so round by water to the seaboard, or down the lakes, and through the Grand Trunk Rail Road to Boston and Portland.

That Chicago has, in fact, opened a direct trade with Liverpool, sending one vessel, the Dean Richmond, *in* 1856; *in* 1857, 13 *vessels*, and in 1858, 40 *vessels.*

That Boston is on the wing, through all the northwest, soliciting and paying a premium on this freight. We sit here deliberating whether we shall not notify them we shall tax. I am half suspicious, the finger of Boston is on these petitions on your table. If they had paid ten thousand dollars for them, they are worth it all if they accomplish what they desire.

TESTIMONY OF J. W. BROOKS.

Mr. J. W. Brooks, President of the Michigan Central Railroad, then gave testimony as follows—Mr. Thompson conducting the examination:

Q. Where do you reside?

A. At Newton, near Boston.

Q. What is your business?

A. I am President of the Michigan Central Railroad Company.

Q. How long have you been in the railroad busness?

A. Something over 20 years—between 20 and 25 years.

Q. Will you state where your stations have been during that period—the points at which you have been located?

A. For the last 16 or 17 years I have been connected with the Michigan Central Railroad, and the roads running from it to Missouri; but my attention during that time has been confined to that line.

Q. You were President of that line during the time you spoke of?

A. I constructed the Michigan Central road, commencing in 1846, and was not President of the Company until some time after 1850—I do not recollect the year—perhaps it was 1853 or '54. Previous to that I was local manager at the west, and constructor.

Q. Are you acquainted with railroad transportation and the movement of freight and passengers on those western roads, through to the east, and the general course of business?

A. I am, as far as a person who had control of one of the long lines would be likely to have, sir.

Q. As a manager of a road I ask you this question: what is the difference in the cost of railroad transportation of through freight as compared with way freight?

A. Almost every road would present a somewhat new case. But there is no doubt that upon all roads it costs a good deal more to transport the local than the through freight. On some roads the difference in the two classes would be very much greater than on the others. There are so many causes that affect it more in some cases and less than in others, one can hardly fix a stated per cent difference. The cars in the one case do not run as full as in the other, nor do the trains take as many cars. The maximum number of cars of a full train is about thirty. The local train takes one or two on and picks others up on the route, as it picks up and drops cars on the route, the average will differ from station to station. I have generally supposed that more money could be made at two cents per mile per ton on long business, than at three cents on local. That must make a difference of 50 per cent. Some roads will make that figure smaller. There are cases where it might be larger. There is entering into that question a phase that is not always thought of. New business is generally long business. New business can be done somewhat cheaper than old business. If you will allow me to go into an explanation I will try to make myself understood in that regard. The fixed business, for which the road is built, has fairly charged upon it the whole expense of the operation of the road. The fixed business, which may be regarded as legitimately belonging to the line, is that which the public depends upon it to perform, and for which it was built. There are certain classes of expenses connected with the management, not incidental to the increase of business; as, if you please, the decay of the perishable materials connected with its structure. The roadway, the ties, the care of its bridges, its culverts, its drainage, ditches, the sliding of its banks, the wooden material connected with its rolling stock. The decay of that goes on as much in a smaller as in a larger business. There is a certain class of agencies connected with it, not influenced by the greater or less quantity of business. All the principal agents at the extremities of the line, these are not influenced in any appreciable degree by new business brought upon the line. I have generally supposed that perhaps nearly one-third of the expenses of railway management, was not increased by the increase of business. Therefore, I would say, that if the total cost of working the road or business was a cent a ton per mile (I state that not as representing the cost, but as a mere example), then new business could be done for two-thirds of a cent, and the other trade would not be affected by increased tonnage. It will follow from that that if new business is taken at the exact cost of the current business of the line, there is a profit incident to that business, which if you take the whole business at that cost, your line is worthless. In my own judgment I have always regarded that theory and have sought new business as the exigency of trade seemed to make it expedient. If we had current trade one way and empty cars the other, we would take freight at a very low rate, to fill up the empty cars. There are seasons of the year when our rolling stock is unemployed, that we would enter it upon any business at these low rates to make something out of it. The new business thus sought, not being legitimate business belonging to the road, and for which tho road was not constructed, has been almost always taken at rates which are near the cost of movement. It is that element which I have endeavored to describe, which generally rendered it desirable for long lines to seek distant business.

Q. You have stated the occasion of this difference; will you now state the cost of winter transportation on these Northern routes, the principal lines, the New York Central and the New York and Erie, as compared with the cost in summer.

A. We all know and feel that there is a good deal of difference between the winter and summer expense of working lines of railroads. There is generally very much more difference than appears in the monthly figures that make up the cost; the rigidity of the railway, caused by freezing, of course would wear out rails much more rapidly. They may be fresh in fall, and partially fresh in the spring, but they are not taken out until the wear of years completes their destruction, when they have to be taken out in the regular course of repairs; winters vary very much. Then in regard to the rails, I will cite an example in the Lowell Railroad. When the rails were first laid they were laid on stone, which made the track as rigid as if frozen; it was found that the rails and machinery wore out the iron, which was bolted on the stone sleepers; the rails wore out quickly by reason of the rigidity with which the track was laid; they took them up and inserted a wooden block between the rail and the tie, to give them an amount of elasticity which would relieve the rail from the rigidity. I suppose that state of things is incident to rails frozen up; but winters are different. Within a few years, I do not recollect the time, we had two successive winters during which I do not believe many roads in this climate made any money at all. We, almost all of us, did not find ourselves clear of the damage until the succeeding July or August; that is, our machinery went into the winter business in better repair than they were subsequently, until the following July or August; so that the expense of it remained until the fall business following. We were pretty busy on the Michigan Central in getting ready and repairing machinery, injured by the hard winter service. Then there are other winters which are far different. We never have a winter but what the track freezes, but there are winters when we are not troubled so much with snow, so that the operation of the road during the winter season varies in the difficulties that are attendant upon it with the severity of the season. I speak now of the latitude in which we are. North of New York it is very different. South of New York, where the climate is considerably changed, it might be still worse than it is here; though I do not know when we get down to the freezing point, how much additional influence it has upon it. Of course, in the south, this does not amount to anything as their winters are not severe.

Q. As the result of this action upon the rails, the wear and tear of machinery and the repair of track, what, in your judgment as a railroad expert, is the average difference in the cost of winter and summer transportation ?

A. I think I could only give it as a matter of judgment; I have never given the subject an accurate investigation.

Q. That is all we expect.

A. We, of course, are compelled to run smaller trains in the winter; we are liable to the difficulties of frosty stock, and we do less service with the same stock. I think few people would place it as low as one-third; I think I should place it at that figure; I think I could make more money at two cents in the summer than three in the winter. You can calculate, very nearly, what can be done in the summer; the winter has surrounding the business so many risks that trains have to be lighter, everything has to be handled more delicately, and necessarily greater destruction and damage ensues. The difficulty of estimating the damage is, that a great deal of the repairing is done during the ensuing season; but we know that the rails are hammered in the ends, and early in the spring we have to take out a multitude of rails; it is difficult to measure the damage in dollars and cents.

Q. I ask you, as a distinct question, what an advantage has the Southern over the Northern routes in the winter?

A. I do not see if you get south but what the Southern routes have an advantage exactly equal to the inconvenience and extra expenditure of the Northern lines, caused by their cold climate. Whatever measures the one, will measure the other; if we had not winters here we would be free from all this inconvenience and expense; they have a sort of advantage beyond that, which generally would not be estimated very high, but I think it is worth something; I should regard it, in long lines of competition, as an advantage; the current of their business is not disturbed by the exigencies of our line of service; therefore it is easy for them to take and retain business at certain prices the long traffic, that would be regarded as valuable in the carrying business against competing lines.

Q. In case of a stated published tariff by any of the roads, not variable for a month, and published throughout the east and west, what would be its effect on the through business?

A. I think that question almost every one can judge of; it is a sort of mixed commercial and carrier question; it may be said to be not very different from the case of certain merchants on one side of a street having their prices fixed and unchangeable, while on the other side they were not so restricted; I should think that the people on the other side would do the business for that month certainly; in the long traffic we all meet in the centres of trade—the western sources of business (I speak of centres as being those points where, from the number of railroads centering from the interior, make them common points), what we call common points, points from which we reach the seaboard markets. If any one of these several lines puts out its rates as fixed and unchangeable for a month, the others would certainly do the business, unless the rate was fixed at a point where no profit could be made; then I think the line having the fixed rate would do the business. I have had a little experience on that question in relation to the passenger business; I cannot recollect the year, but it was very soon after we opened our line to Chicago. The Michigan Southern line were entering into competition for the long traffic for passengers; we all had our offices in the sources for business along the west and northwest of Chicago; we thought we did wisely in playing a very conservative part in regard to cutting rates; we placed fixed rates, which we had agreed upon, in the hands of our agents, leaving them no discretionary power to go below them; we found, immediately after this arrangement was made and the price settled upon, the traffic began to lessen and divert; it grew out of small changes, sometimes cutting fifty cents under price for a passenger to New York, or if that did'nt answer the purpose, a dollar. We had a great deal of difficulty growing out of this changing of rates, and I finally gave orders to ask the price which was asked by the other route. From that time rates were steady; no advantage could be taken by reducing rates, because the other was changed at the same hour. That settled the question definitely.

Mr. CONKLING—This practice to which you refer, not only enables you to retain your share of the business, but it operates as a regulator of the rates?

A. It keeps the rates steady; there was not gain to be made; for if one man lowers, he knows his neighbor is ordered to lower at the same hour; so that it is a question only whether he will carry a passenger at a dollar loss, for of course he gets no more passengers than if he had adhered to the rates.

Q. You say, in regard to freight, that the road having the fixed tariff would lose the freight; why would it lose it?

A. What I said in regard to passengers, will apply to freight. I look upon these two as being affected by the same causes; but one in a greater degree than the other. I instanced the passenger question because it is one in which I had had experience. Passengers will not leave at once the line on which they have been accustomed to travel, because of a slight reduction of price on a competing line; but if the reduction is adhered to for a long time, they will gradually leave it for the line which has the less price. But with regard to freight, it makes very little difference with the owner of property, whether it is carried in a red car or a brown one, so that it gets to market in a stated reasonable time. There is not much difference in the time in which freight reaches the market on any of these lines. There is less than a day's travel in the distance of carriage, between the longest and the shortest one. The time on freight has little or nothing to do with it. While I know that the passengers would leave a line gradually, I have no doubt that freight would leave it *en masse* at once. I know when we had an arrangement which we could not change, and the other parties could change, we could not get any of the other parties' traffic, and they did get some of ours. You cannot get freight from a given point unless you transport it as cheap as any one else. There is another reason which affects passengers to a certain extent, so long as the passenger has business to do along the line, a half dollar nor even a dollar would change the passenger from one line to another; but freight has no such stopping necessity.

Q. In your judgment, as a railroad man, can the way and through business be done at the same rates practicably?

A. I have no doubt about its being impracticable. There may be a good many definitions of the word impracticable, but as it is generally understood the business could not be conducted with any profitable result; the two are widely different in their character. One of them, to be done at all, situated as these lines are, has got to be done under the same elasticity on one line which the other has, it would very much derange business to have that changed every day or every hour. I do not think there is any profit of the long business that amounts to much if you have got to connect it in any way with the local business. You have got to use the long business to make it profitable, to fill up the gaps as it were. You must rely upon the local business to a great extent as a steady business, running all the year pretty nearly equal as the business of the country runs.

Q. What effect would result, in your judgment, to the way freights if the through freights were abandoned?

A. On different roads it would bring about a different result.

Q. Take the two lines of New York, the Hudson River and the Harlem?

A. Where there was no competition which would so regulate the local prices as to put it out of the power of the railroads to make any more money out of them than they were at any particular period making, they would of course bo interested to add to the local rates as much as they lost on the through.

Mr. COBB—Will you explain that again?

A. I say that where there are no local rates which could not be controlled beyond the will of the company by some competing interest, then the local rates, if members of the directory had any regard for the stockholders, as trustees of their property, would have to raise the local rates to compensate for the loss of doing no through business. I cannot conceive that through business can be done without the same elasticity attaches to the New York roads that would attach to the roads in opposition to them, and that, if taken away, I do not see how long business can possibly be retained. If the long business is not retained either the company must lose a considerable portion of its revenues or it must derive them from some other source. I have no doubt, on the Michigan Central road, if we lost our through business, we should raise our local business at once. We could not afford to do local business so cheaply if the sources of revenue incident to the through business were cut off. Therefore it follows, that the profits made on long business does strengthen the company to a certain extent; enabling it to do its local business at better rates.

Q. Can a competing route with a longer line fix low prices for you, and yet not be able to carry as cheap?

A. I have said before that all of the lines freighting between common points must carry at the same prices. There is no question about that. Let any company, or any line of companies, charge a higher rate from Chicago to New York their rival lines will take the business. The question as to how much profit the rival lines will make on that is a question of their own. I will instance an extreme case. The Grand Trunk Railroad is taking cotton from Memphis, far south of the southern lines in competition for western business to the English factories. They say they make money on it, whether they do or not, the policy of the British government to work a large portion of the traffic of the Western States through the Provinces will probably be persevered in. I have no doubt it will. They have built, without any question, the best line of railroad on this continent. A line that can work the cheapest, setting capital aside, which costs them only three or four per cent a year, they have got relieved from their bonded indebtedness, having received large presents from the home government and releases from liens and taxes, and it is prepared to do this long business at a rate leaving but a moderate margin to the shortest line between the western markets and the seaboard. They will regulate the price, without any question, quite as efficiently as any other line trading between the seaboard and the west.

Q. If the through business was taken from the New York roads, would it, in your judgment, go to the canals or what other channels would it take?

A. I think that would depend to a very considerable extent upon how long the experiment of turning it away from the New York lines was carried on. I think that the first, second, third classes of freight would all take the other lines. The competition between the roads is for these three classes. The fourth class is divided between the roads and the canals. The property represented by the first three classes would scarcely any of it go to New York by the Grand Trunk road; I think it would go to Boston, all of it that went by the Grand Trunk road, and that the three classes going to New York would go by the southern roads, they being much the shortest. I should think that the wholesale business, the importing business for the western cities, would come from Baltimore and Philadelphia, because it would cost as little to put it there as in New York, and thence convey it to the west. It would cost less from London and Liverpool to Chicago and St. Louis, than it would cost to go through New York. The fourth class would be divided; a part of it would go on the canal and a part on these other lines; as wherever the second and third class goes to a certain extent, to a very large extent the fourth class goes. A good deal of the fourth class, that now goes upon the canal, would take these extreme southern lines. The importations would work their way to those cities. A portion of the fourth class, that now goes by canal, as well as a portion of the fourth class that goes on the rail, would go on these extreme southern routes, and the other portion of the fourth class that goes now by rail on the N. Y. roads, would take the canal.

Mr. CONKLING—How would it affect the transportation of passengers?

A. The passenger trade follows the freight. If the trade increased to the southern cities the passengers would follow more promptly the first, second, and third class freight than they would the fourth; because it requires more care to trade in each of these classes, more personal attention; but there is no doubt that the passenger trade would wear away with the freight, except in the case of passengers traveling for pleasure—passengers making short runs in the summer time to watering places, &c.

Mr. CONKLING—What would be the effect of that policy on the city of New York?

A. I do not see why it would not have the same effect upon the city of New York that it would have upon the roads—it would work the trade into the southern cities. We had some experience in that matter during the famous St. Nicholas compact, which has some fame as well as notoriety. The little experience we had at that time, showed the effect upon my own road as well as the roads here. It was very marked in the change which it made in the coffee trade, which was a large trade in the west, and the coffee trade was looked at carefully to see what effect it was having. We found that a considerable portion of the coffee, which had formerly been shipped to New York, and thence to the west, went to Baltimore. It went then over the Baltimore and Ohio road, to the Ohio river, down the river to Cario, up the Mississippi to Galena, and then turned eastward into the interior of Illinois; it went entirely around us. A few cents on a hundred pounds, amounting to about $3 a ton, of course turned that business. That was one of the articles of the fourth class, and I do not see why all the articles of that class would not follow in the same way, if treated in the same manner. I am sure the western importing man would feel it so at once, and others would follow.

Q. Did the New York roads have a fixed tariff prior to 1858?

A. They generally did, sir.

Q. You state that two or three dollars a ton turned that freight from you?

A. I do not recollect the rate. I recollect the effect of it was so strong against these New York and Northern lines, our own among the rest, that the compact was destroyed. It was found necessary; we could not live under that state of things. It astonished us by the promptness with which the goods began to change their routes.

Q. You stated that prior to 1858 they had a general fixed tariff?

A. Yes, sir, prior to then the elements of the competition which changed the entire character of the long business, had not begun to work. There was not then the competition between Baltimore, Philadelphia and New York that exists now. I will say, in regard to the Baltimore and Ohio, and the Pennsylvania Central, that they have the same objects to subserve to fulfill their destiny. They were built with city and state capital, to subserve a certain city and state policy, and unless they could secure a liberal portion of the trade of the West to these cities, they would not fulfill the destiny for which they were constructed. An investment of capital for revenue was not the moving cause for the construction of those lines. They are more severe competitors for the trade of the West, than they would be if they were built solely with the view to revenue, and of course they do not regard the procurement of revenue except as incident to their general arrangement.

Q. What lines of communication to the far West have been completed since 1857?

A. We regard all the elements introduced since then as incident to the three lines, the Pennsylvania Central, the Baltimore and Ohio, and the Grand Trunk railroads. There is another branch of business opened up to the West, which will probably grow to great importance pretty soon, I do not know how extensive it was last year, but the year before a large number of vessels loaded on the lakes for Liverpool, and returned with freights of merchandise for the West. That is the fourth element of the difficulty that has been introduced within the last three years, making, with the other three, four elements of competition. I suppose that will grow up to be one, for I have understood they were pretty successful. The trips that were made I believe amounted to something like thirty or forty vessels.

Mr. THACHER—In 1859?

A. Yes, Sir. I do not know the number; I followed them up until they reached twenty, when I lost track of them; I presume somebody here can give the number exactly.

Q. What induced the change in the policy of the New York roads, and the conflicts they had to retain that western business? How did it arise? State the facts.

A. The first conflict—guerrilla warfare—in the shape of competition. Such competition always arises when new elements are brought in, until some settlement is made; and the St. Nicholas compact was the first permanent settlement of the difficulties; or rather, it was understood to be permanent. In that, the Northern lines were out-generaled entirely; they conceded to the Southern lines because of their increased nearness of those States to the interior—a different rate to the Southern cities—so strong a difference as to have a serious effect on the trade of those cities. We know that trade began to move to and from those cities in a rapidly increasing ratio—that merchants trading with New York began to get their stocks through other cities, and that the change was increasing so rapidly that it had the effect to break up the St. Nicholas compact. It was decided that the New York and other Northern lines should fix their rates so as to be as near to the west as Philadelphia and Baltimore.

Mr. CONKLING—What were the general terms of that compact?

A. The general terms were, to carry freights at uniform rates—at stated rates, which we agreed upon with a difference.

Mr. CONKLING—A sort of pro-rata arrangement, was it?

A. The lines pro-rata—that is—let me explain. Though that question does not enter into the case, the Pennsylvania Central practically owns the Pittsburgh, Fort Wayne and Chicago Railroad. It is all one with them; and whether they pro-rated with that road is a fact that exists in their own counsels. But their connection with the west forced other lines to make combinations to work against them, as they had one line working straight through to the seaboard it would not do for other lines to have divided counsels. It resulted in the lines generally running to the Northern States, from the seaboard to the west, dividing the receipts of the business, pro rata per ton, per mile, with some small trifling allowances for ferriage, to the persons keeping those ferries; and with these exceptions it is a general pro rata.

Q. Is or is not one man President of both roads from Philadelphia to Chicago, by way of the Pennsylvania Central, Fort Wayne and Chicago roads?

A. One man is President of the line from Philadelphia to Chicago—one set of agents speak for the management of the whole, and one man manages the whole line, so far as the public is concerned.

Q. You say that was broken up in consequence of this large traffic moving to the west, leaving the lines which it formerly followed?

A. Yes, Sir.

Q. What was the result of the breaking up of that compact? How did it effect the trade and commerce that went there?

A. We all felt, when it was broken up, that we were to get thence onwards our legitimate share of the business again.

Q. Was that the effect, or not?

A. I have no doubt that it was the effect. I recollect that during the last two years there has been less business, and we have all felt that we didn't get quite our share.

Q. But you have got your relative share?

A. Yes, sir. But we got less in proportion than we did before these new carriers came into the market.

Q, You stated something about what it was that created this warfare; state whether or not it was the insisting by the southern lines on carrying out that compact, and sticking to it.

A. Yes, sir; and the refusal by the northern lines to do it.

Q. The southern lines understood that if that compact was carried out, they would get the trade to the West?

A. I think they didn't appreciate that more fully than we did who lost it.

Q. Will you state what course of action the southern roads adopted to get the trade again?

A. They are just in the same position in which we now are. All these long lines have agencies and offices established in the great centres of business in the West. By centres, I mean those cities and large places where business concentrates, by having a good many interior lines reaching to those points. Wherever there is a considerable quantity of business to be got at the West, all these competing avenues of trade have their agencies established, soliciting business with a good deal of industry and perseverance.

Q. State what means they have in the western States, and New York city, in the east, for the procurement of freight and passengers.

A. As far as New York is concerned, they have, on Broadway, a very large number of offices. I do not know how many. I should think there were ten or fifteen offices belonging to these lines, and in some other parts of the city less expensive ones; and there are some in Boston, in a less degree, however, because there is less business. And so in the cities at the West; at all the large places they have offices established and maintained, with solicitors who communicate directly with the owners of freight.

Q. Making personal application to the owners of freight?

A. Yes, sir; making contracts for it constantly. I should think that such a city as Chicago might have, perhaps, no less than twenty men, whose sole business it is to confer with the owners of freight, and endeavor to make contracts for it—for the different interests.

Mr. COBB—They are denominated drummers, are they not?

A. Perhaps that is what they would be called.

Mr. THOMPSON—Fifers, too!

A. They generally act as if they were the owners of the road, and controlling the State in which they reside.

Mr. CONKLING—How many are there in Chicago?

A. There may be four or five contending interests in Chicago: the north side of the lake line, the south side of the lake line, Pennsylvania Central, Baltimore and Ohio, and the Grand Trunk lines. But each one of these is made up of several interests. The New York Central road is connected with the Great Western, North Shore, South Shore, Michigan Central, and Boston and Worcester lines. All these interests are represented. Some of the larger interests employ separate agents, while some join together in maintaining an agency.

Q. Is it the habit of the freight agents on these southern lines to demand a uniform rate for the transportation of freight?

A. There is a sort of effort of the agents of the different lines to agree upon some rate; from day to day some one cuts down the price once or twice a day, and then the others come down. Then they have a conference. The interest of these lines have to be put into the hands of these persons who act with sufficient promptness to keep them strait.

Q. Suppose one line was unable to drop their prices?

A. I think it would be gratifying to the others. They would get along a great deal more harmoniously.

Q. They would lose the business, would they not?

A. They would do no more business until they got out of that fix.

Q. And the others would eat them up?

A. They would take the business.

Mr. CONKLING—In crossing high elevations by railroad, how far does the diminished cost of conducting trains down descending grades serve to compensate for the augmented cost of ascending grades?

A. I think it would be found that nearly all the saving rests in the simple economy in fuel. When you get to the top of a grade you cannot get any more cars to go down the grade to lessen the cost of the service and men connected with the train, brakemen, enginemen, &c.; there is no means of lessening this per car per ton. You do save fuel. The strength of the southern lines in overcoming their mountain grades consists in the cheap cost of their fuel. They use coal at a very insignificant cost. I think it is inside of a dollar per ton; Mr. Hubby says that, on the Baltimore and Ohio road, the cost is about seventy cents a ton. A ton of coal is more efficient than a cord of wood; and if it can be used in such a way as to secure the saving of all heat it is as valuable as two cords of wood; but it has not been so economized. We pay from $2 to $2.50 a cord. They get the same amount of fuel in a ton of coal at seventy cents. With that advantage the disadvantage of their grades is overcome, which places them in a condition to compete, to a certain extent, with the three Northern lines.

Mr. CONKLING—Is it your opinion that a locomotive engine can conduct a no more heavy train down a descending grade than it can haul up an ascending grade? that each engine has got to get up the grade with its load? do you know of no practice of using increased locomotive power?

A. Yes, sir. If the grades are isolated so that they can manage it, they, of course, economize very much. Some roads have grades of a greater length, incident to long districts; where they occur thus frequently it has not been found practicable to use this assisting power. I do not know how the Baltimore and Ohio road is managed, but I think it is used there very little, because they have long grades, and not many of these difficulties. I think that the great saving on those lines is in the cost of fuel, rather than in the advantage of the descending line.

Q. Has not the shortness of the route something to do with it?

A. The fact that it brings them down to a measure of miles in length, is a measure of its capacity for service.

Q. Can all roads that compete from common points, get the same pro rata per mile?

A. No, sir. A moment's thought will show you it could not be done. These roads most all carry freight, as I have said before, from common points to market, at the aggregate price, and not at the same price per ton per mile. It is the same aggregate price from source to market. The longer line will get less per ton per mile than the shorter. For example, from Chicago to New York, over the New York Central and Michigan Central, they will get more per ton per mile than they will get by the Baltimore and Ohio; and from Cincinnati to New York they will get more per ton per mile, on the Baltimore and Ohio road, than they would on the New York Central. In the one case, the Baltimore and Ohio forms a part of the long line, and the New York Central a part of the shorter, and, in the other case, the reverse, It follows that the same kind of freight must be carried at different rates by each road—at higher rates when they form part of the short line, at lower rates when they form part of the long line. The New York Central cannot say that they will take a barrel of flour over their line in the long traffic, in competition with the other railroads, at the same price per mile as the others. In some lines it forms a part of the long competing route, and in others, a part of the short competing route, and they have got to take their proper pro rata share.

Q. So that, in your judgment, it is impossible to apply that theory in practice for the transportation of freight on the longer lines of road?

A. It has been strongly for my interest, that that practice should be gone into at the North, in connection with the New York Central line from Chicago. We have felt as if we formed a part with this New York Central road, of the shortest line for that traffic. If we could have procured the New York Central road to take flour from us as cheaply as they could take it from Cincinnati, it would have been greatly to our advantage; but we have never felt justified in asking for that. So far as the Michigan Central line is concerned, we have always treated the question in that way. We have taken flour cheaper to Detroit when it came from St. Louis, than when it came from Kenosha, Galena or Milwaukee; because, when we go to St. Louis, they have a shorter line to take their freight to market, running east, northeast, than ours. We form part of the longer route, and we carry everything cheaper to the market than freight which came from the Northwest. We must do that, or else abandon our St. Louis business. So I may say with regard to all points that are on the shortest roads, we get the highest prices, and on the long lines a less price, for the same articles, in the same train, at the same time with the articles on the short line.

Q. Does the Grand Trunk Railway connect at Detroit? If so, how—what are its connections?

A. Temporarily, the Grand Trunk has got a narrow gauge from Port Huron; the wide gauge ends at Port Sarnia, on the east side of the river. Port Huron is on the west side, opposite—and the narrow gauge commencing there comes down to Detroit. It was in contemplation, when it was building, to have a broad gauge; but as they were very short of stock they laid a narrow gauge. They have leased locomotives for the line, and the cars of the Michigan Central, and the Michigan Southern roads go up to Port Huron The transhipment is there effected by ferry, as is the case here; they take the cars across so as to ship the freight from car to car; instead of a ferry boat they have a long boat upon which the cars are taken across. But it is in contemplation to have a broad gauge to Detroit; they have built transfer houses at Detroit, preparatory to the transfer business, when the broad gauge shall be brought there. They are now discussing the question as to the advisability of putting a broad gauge into Boston over one of the lines from Portland, and putting a third rail on the road to Chicago, so as to haul broad cars from Chicago to Boston.

Mr CONKLING—Is there machinery employed at any of these termini for the loading of cars?

A. It is all done by manual labor. Where grain is carried in bulk it is generally run into the car, afterwards shoveled out of the cars into pits below, and then elevated in the usual way. Beyond that I don't know of any machinery being used.

Q. If the rate on the New York roads was fixed at so much per ton per mile, what would be the effect on long freights?

A. It would depend upon how frequently that rate could be changed. If it could be changed every day it would be better.

Q. Suppose it could be changed once a month?

A. It would give twenty-nine days of that month to the other lines, unless the rate on that line was so low that it afforded no profit; then they would have their share of the business. I believe I have answered that question once before.

Mr. THOMPSON—Not exactly in that shape, and only incidentally.

Mr. BROOKS—You asked me that last question. I have not alluded to one point in relation to it, which has just come into my mind. If the New York roads charge for the long and local freight one rate of transportation, it would introduce to the western business, that comes by water, a new terminus. As a matter of course, it would put Oswego in the position of Buffalo. If you had to put the price by rail per ton, per mile to Oswego, at the same rate as to Buffalo, of course the water-bound business would come to Oswego. The New York Central road, as now regulated, has the power to make its long business, the principal business—has power to put business on the long end of its line instead of having it cut through in the middle. If the power to protect itself from inroad at the side is lost, water-bound business would come to Oswego, and the west half of their line would be of no use for the purposes of long freights.

Q. What is the effect of these low long freights on the country, on the price of land? State what your experience upon that subject has been, whether it has tended to diminish the price?

A. I once had that question raised upon me a good many years ago, very agreeably, and I look back upon it now with an inclination to smile. Somewhere about the year 1850 we opened our Michigan Central railroad to Lake Michigan, in 1852 we opened it to Chicago. We there met on the lake the waterborne carriers in boats. Not getting long business, we had to carry that long business at a lower rate than we carried our local business, owing te the competition of these boats. We carried our local business at a very great reduction upon the charges which the state had charged. The state had built the road to Kalamazoo, which was the entrepot. We took the road from the state and reduced the rates twenty-five per cent below the allowance in the charter, as we thought the rates called for in our charter too high. But when we got to Chicago we had to reduce them much lower; we had to commence at Niles, which is situated on a navigable river where we crossed it, about twenty or thirty miles from the lake. There were these little steamboats taking freight down the lake, which came thence around. When we got to Niles we took that business from the river at the rates charged by the boats, and as our route was the best we took the whole of it, and broke up the system completely. The Kalamazoo people met and prepared an address to us saying that we had ruined the price of land in Kalamazoo county by carrying freight at lower rates from Berrien county. I wrote them a letter which was printed in pamphlet form, of which I have not seen a copy for several years, but the purport of it was this, that unless it increased the price of grain, and influenced the price raised upon the Mediterranean and the wheat-growing countries of the world, it would not affect the price of their land unless we damaged them, or raised the price between Kalamazoo and the markets, their land would be as it was before, as we had reduced the price between Kalamazoo and the market more than 25 per cent, we had increased the value of their land, and as we had not carried wheat any cheaper from Berrien county any cheaper than other lines we had not increased the price of land there.

Q. State that principle in its application to the lands in the State of New York?

A. I say, in regard to the lands of New York, that if the New York Central Railroad has not raised the price of products from any particular district to the common markets, they have not reduced the value of land in that region, unless they have done something which should deteriorate the prices in this common market, which they have not the power to do, because from all the sources of the west they have done business at the rates of other lines; therefore, they did not open up any more lands by their own acts in competition. I take it, that if all the lands in the west were opened up, it would not affect the price of grain in the world. The grain-growing regions are very large, and as the New York roads carry grain at the same prices as their competitors, they exercise no influence upon that. As the canal has been the regulator of prices, so if the canal tolls are lowered so as to bring rail prices down with them, they will put western lands nearer market than they now are, to a certain extent; but they would have to introduce a vast amount of grain from regions now uncultivated in the west, to the markets of the world, before it would be affected by it.

Mr. COBB—Do you refer to the effect of individual lines of the railroad system?

A. I refer to the effect upon the State of New York. If the whole system of railways could be blotted out from the west at once, it would cut off certain districts of lands of the west from the eastern markets, except by the Mississippi and St. Lawrence. Whether it would compel them to grow more at a less price, I do not know.

Q. Do you know whether or not the local rates which the produce of the western states have to pay to reach the competing points at the west, are as high or higher than the local rates on the New York lines?

A. I think it will be found that they are generally not less than 25 per cent higher; I should say more than that. I know our own rates on the Michigan Central road are over 25 per cent higher, from a 100 to 150 miles from Detroit or Chicago, are very far in advance of the New York Central's local rates. I think that will be found to be so over the whole west. There may be isolated exceptions, but the general rule is such as I state.

Q. State to the Committee the relative cost of carrying wheat and carrying flour on the railway, the same distance?

A. I do not know as there is much difference, provided if the wheat is put in bags; but it is hardly considered practicable to do so when you come to the bulk, it is more difficult to carry than flour. West of the Mississippi the plan is, to put up the grain in bags for the St. Louis market; but where it is carried in bulk, as it is east of the Mississippi, there is a broad margin in favor of carrying flour.

Mr. COBB—Have you often attended railroad conventions, during your 25 years' experience on railroads?

A. I have attended quite a number of them.

Mr. COBB—How extensive are they attended by other lines?

A. I think we had one once at Cleveland where we figured 800 millions of dollars of capital.

Mr. COBB—But how many different lines?

A. I do not know as I could say; we had a vast number of roads.

Mr. COBB—Are these four roads, the Baltimore & Ohio, the Pennsylvania Central, the New York & Erie, and the New York Central, are they ordinarily conspicuous in those conventions?

A. I believe there was no one present from those roads at that convention, except Mr. Moran.

Mr. COBB—Is that the case with all the conventions?

A. I should think, as a general thing, one or two of them are present at about a half of the conventions, perhaps a little more. When they have had their compacts between themselves they have generally stood aloof from conventions held by the western lines. It depends a little upon what they are called for. If they are called for the fall or spring, to make running arrangements, they have to be present. Sometimes they are represented by their principal officers; sometimes by their train managers.

Mr. COBB—When the arrangements are being made for their summer's business they are ordinarily represented?

A. Yes, sir—and in the fall when the arrangement are being made for winter trains.

Mr. COBB—Represented by somebody?

A. Yes, sir.

Mr. COBB—While the St. Nicholas compact was in existence they were present in the conventions less than before?

A. Yes, sir.

Mr. COBB—In these conventions has any particular line a controlling influence?

A. I don't think there is. We have sometimes felt when we voted, (as we generally do, and have always done, by railroads,) that lines south of the south shore of Lake Erie, there was an undue representation. There are a good many roads in Ohio, and a good many short ones.

Mr. COBB—I refer to the four lines?

A. These short lines all carry the same vote as the long lines. We have frequently been embarrassed by the multitude of votes coming from roads of a short distance, and lines less interested in the east and western trains than the long lines were.

Mr. COBB—How are the roads represented—by miles?

A. Each road carries one vote—the long road the same as the short one.

Mr. COBB—As far as the Baltimore & Ohio, the Pennsylvania Central, the New York & Erie and the New York Central are concerned, has any one of them a controlling influence to any extent?

A. I do not think they have; I think the northern roads have always felt that the south has always exercised too much influence.

Mr. COBB—That is a mere matter of opinion?

A. Yes, sir. Each one cast his vote to carry his point, otherwise I don't think there has been any undue influence.

Mr. COBB—Which of the roads do you regard as your allies?

A. The New York Central and the Grand Trunk.

Mr. COBB—You ship over either as occasion offers?

A. We are unfortunate because our long lines cast but one vote.

Mr. COBB—But the Pennsylvania Central has only one vote?

A. Yes, sir. But the lines running into it always vote with the Pennsylvania Central and against the Michigan Central.

Mr. COBB—You have no feeders of that kind?

A. They are very small. Our feeders lie west of Chicago, and with them it is immaterial whether they vote with us or with the Pennsylvania Central. We have felt it to be very embarrassing to have the roads vote by routes and not by miles.

Mr. COBB—You have alluded to the St. Nicholas compact; did you state that the southern roads adhered to that rigidly?

A. I think they cut freights even on that. I think they were much in favor of keeping it up by us, but I think there was a little want of faith in keeping it up with them.

Mr. COBB—Did they not charge that on your northern routes?

A. They always charge it on each other, under such circumstances, and I dare say the charges are very true.

Mr. COBB—These railroad compacts are more on paper than anywhere else?

A. They are very apt to result so. It is almost impossible, by law or agreement, to make the thing work steady. The best way is to put in the hands of freight agents the right to drop rates when anybody else does. We have come to that as the only practicable method.

Mr. COBB—Then to the public, who do not know that there is no fault in railroad compacts, there is a liability of being largely deceived?

A. I think you might find some railroads as mean in their business operations as men in other lines of business. I do not know of any peculiar quality of mind or nature in railroad men, which should make them different from other men.

Mr. COBB—I was not calling for a pro rata distinction, but for your opinion upon the subject?

A. I have seen contracts that worked well for a long period, but it is very rare. If one party will live squarely up to the agreement, you will find some other party to it will cut under and take the business. When that is done the time for the dissolution of the compact is at hand, and while it exists it has a weakly life.

Mr. COBB—It is a paper contract without any seal?

A. Yes, sir. When business gets short, there is a struggle for it, and when somebody drops prices to secure it, then the compact dies out pretty quick?

Mr. COBB—In the spring these four lines hold a convention, and in the winter also?

A. The conventions are generally held in the spring and fall?

Mr. COBB—Can you tell me what are the relative prices between spring and summer; are they higher or lower or is there anything like a uniformity?

A. In the winter they are higher than in the summer.

Mr. COBB—What is the cause of this advance?

A. The cost of doing the work in the winter is a great deal higher than it is in the summer. I think if we were compelled to work in the winter at the rates we receive for summer business, it would be better for us to leave the business and shut up our offices.

Mr. COBB—Is that the only cause which produces an advance in prices?

A. I have no doubt that the closing of the canals and lakes has a very great influence. When the lakes are closed from Chicago to Buffalo we can get a higher rate. When the St. Lawrence, the Ohio river (though the Ohio river is more unsteady) and the canal is closed, and the Northern Mississippi, we can all get rates higher, and perhaps it gives us as much profit on our business as we get on our summer business at lower rates.

Mr. COBB—Are not your winter rates ordinarily remunerative?

A. I should think that, one year with another, they are.

Mr. COBB—How would it compare with your summer remuneration ?

A. I rather think we get quite as much net out of the summer.

Mr. COBB—Take the traffic together on one line of it ?

A. Of course we make more money out of passengers, because our rates are not much higher in winter than in summer—not near as much as the cost is. We make more in summer than in winter. I do not think we get more than 10 or 12 per cent for running our passenger business more.

Mr. COBB—You speak of a large number of freight agents in Chicago. Have the lines over which they engage, a tacit understanding to pro rate with each other on any contracts which they make ?

A. I think that is generally understood The Pennsylvania Central has its own counsels in its management. Our understanding is, that if we keep within reasonable limits the others will hold to it. If the rates are unreasonably low, the remedy is to call a convention.

Mr. COBB—Then they have a power of attorney to make contracts, and you carry them out ?

A. That has not been formally given, but there is a general understanding.

Mr. COBB—It amounts to an understanding. Do you ever repudiate contracts entered into ?

A. I do not say that. If we take a contract at below paying rates it is held to as a matter of courtesy. There is no compulsion. The Great Western road in Canada do have some bickerings.

Mr. COBB—But it ends in a settlement by which the property is carried ?

A. Sometimes the person making the contract has to pay the loss. We at the west think that the agents of the four lines at the east can judge whether they can get business from them better than we can. We at the west have better opportunities for judging of the prospects for business at the west. Sometimes ships carry to and from New Orleans very cheaply, and particularly when it comes to the cotton trade going to the north. We are quite willing at such times to drop our prices at the west to keep the trade in the northern channels, which, in the west, has a chance to go down the rivers. They feel that we can best judge at the west end of the route, and we feel that their judgment is better at the east. It is the same way as partners in a certain business living at different points, and where both are interested in the result of the operations at both places. Each would rely upon the other to look after their joint interests at his own end of the line, because each in his own position can better serve the other's interest than the other could himself.

Mr. COBB—Have the New York Central and the New York and Erie, in their agencies at Chicago, signs over their doors ?

A. They have agents there. I am not certain whether the New York Central has an office there or not. I dare say they have. The New York and Erie has.

Mr. COBB—They are as much represented as at the city of Albany ?

A. Not as much as the city of Albany, perhaps, Albany being one of the termini of the road.

Mr COBB—I mean for the purpose of engaging business ?

A. Yes, sir.

Mr. COBB—How much further west do they have agencies ?

A. I cannot tell you that.

Mr. COBB—They extend, at all events, from Chicago to New York city ?

A. It is generally understood that in the large sources of business there are men who look out for the interests of these great lines, extending from the centres of business.

Mr. COBB—You remarked, that previous to 1857, '58, your rates were made up by yourselves, and there was less cutting down ?

A. Yes, sir.

Mr. COBB—What was the position of the Michigan Central at that time, compared with the present ?

A. We got very much better rates.

Mr. COBB—What was its financial condition, compared with the present ?

A. Better—much better. There were fewer lines to divide the business among. It is partly owing to financial disaster, and the great depression of the trade of the country. How much is owing to that, and how much to the division of the business among the different lines, is a matter of judgment.

Mr. COBB—What proportion of your business is called through business ? That which comes from Chicago ?

A. I don't think I have seen the figures in regard to that subject for the last three or four years. I should think that one-third of the number of tons we move was through. The long tons moved would be less than half of the local.

Mr. COBB—That would be about one-third of the total ?

A. Less than half of the whole. I think it is more than one-third. As a mere matter of judgment, I should say that the through tons put into the car, were two-fifths of the total number of tons. But what proportion of the tonnage moving one mile it is, is another question. The long business goes the whole length of the road ; the short business, ten miles and upwards.

Mr. COBB—What are the present quotations of the Michigan Central stock ?

A. I think the last I saw was 38 ?

Mr. COBB—What was it in 1857 ?

A. In the spring of 1857 business was much better than in the fall. That was the year when everything broke down.

Mr. COBB—Previous to July, how was it ?

A. I cannot recollect; I should think it was more than 50 ; I may be mistaken.

Mr. COBB—Was there ever any time when its stocks were worth 100 ?

A. There was a time when it was over par.

Mr. COBB—How long since ?

A. A good many years. It was not within 5 or 6 years.

Mr. COBB—Was it within 6 or 7 ?

A. It may be ; I am very bad at remembering dates.

Mr. COBB—What were the relative rates of compensation for the traffic you performed then, compared with now ?

A. Our rates must have been a good deal higher than now; I cannot tell the relative rates; it would be a hard matter to go back 5 or 6 years.

Mr. COBB—But you must have a general recollection?

A. Our passenger rates were not any higher than now.

Mr. COBB—I refer to freight.

A. I cannot tell.

Mr. COBB—What was the relative amount of tonnage you moved at that time compared with now?

A. That I am unable to tell you.

Mr. COBB—What was about the relative value of Great Western stock in 1857, previous to July, as compared with its value now?

A. It was very high until they commenced to build their branches, about par; when they commenced them it began to drop.

Mr. COBB—What is its value now?

A. I cannot tell.

Mr. COBB—Very considerably lower?

A. I have never seen a quotation of that in my life. I do not know that there ever has been a share sold in the market so as to have a quotation.

Mr. COBB—What is the lowest rate at which you ever transported freight?

A. I should think we had carried for less than a cent a ton per mile. Once and a while we have worked for the purpose of putting the price down, when the cutting at Chicago has been so irregular that we could not work with satisfaction, we have then put down prices to bring the rates again to a paying point.

Mr. COBB—Your object was to punish your competitors?

A. The object was to secure a meeting at once. When we found they were charging 95, when we asked 100, we dropped to 95; then they fell to 90; we followed, and they dropped to 85. When that course is pursued, as it is occasionally, then we put rates down to such a figure as will call the attention of the officers of the road at once, and an arrangement is promptly made by which paying rates may be secured.

Mr. COBB—What is the cost of the movement of freight per ton per mile, as you estimate it?

A. I made one explanation of what I considered as new business.

Mr. COBB—I mean new business.

A. I dont think I have ever figured that on our road.

Mr. COBB—Do you suppose that your road is operated dearer or cheaper than the New York Central?

A. I do not think it should be much different. Our grades are not very much different from those of the New York Central.

Mr. COBB—Do you suppose the cost to be smaller?

A. I think we have mutual advantages. They have grades easier a little, but we have fuel cheaper. It is about the same.

Mr. COBB—Is there any difference between the cost of moving fourth class merchandise and other commodities? Are there any distinctions in the value of handling a barrel of flour and a barrel of beef or pork?

A. Not very appreciable. I would rather carry flour a little, than the others.

Mr. COBB—Do you regard it that a ton of flour or a ton of beef may be carried as cheap as a ton of anything else?

A. I should regard all those articles as being very favorable to cheap transportation.

Mr. COBB—Then do you regard it that a ton of either of these commodities costs no more than a ton of anything else to transport?

A. I do not think it does much. I would rather carry flour than some other articles.

Mr. COBB—Then there is very little difference in the cost of movement. No matter what the commodity is, whether first, second or third class; a ton of flour would represent a ton of anything else?

A. I cannot say that. I would rather carry flour than molasses. Some kinds of sugar we have trouble with.

Mr. COBB—Will a ton of flour fairly represent, as near as may be, a ton of anything else?

A. I would rather carry a ton of flour than a ton of anything else.

Mr. COBB—What is the difference?

A. I don't think I would make much difference.

Mr. COBB—How would it be with pork in barrels? Would a ton of that fairly represent a ton of anything else?

A. I think that rolling freight is better than other freights.

Mr. COBB—Would you regard a ton of molasses as about the worst?

A. I should think a ton of that or a ton of beef would be an average.

Mr. COBB—And the cost of transporting that would represent the cost of moving anything?

A. Almost anything. Gentlemen can judge as well as I. It is a mere question of the safety of the article and of its destructability.

Mr. COBB—I am not a railroad man, and we call upon railroad men for information about that which we have only a theoretical knowledge. You mentioned that the Pennsylvania Central is actually now running to Chicago; is not the western end of that road in the hands of a receiver?

A. Yes, sir. I believe it is the Pittsburgh, Fort Wayne and Chicago.

Mr. COBB—It is in the hands of the receiver?

A. Yes, sir.

Mr. COBB—I think you said the southern roads, the Baltimore and Ohio, and the Pennsylvania Central were less affected by the extremes of heat and cold than the northern?

A. Yes, sir, very much. I believe with regard to the receiver of the Pittsburgh, Fort Wayne and Chicago, that it was made satisfactory to Mr. Thompson, the president of both roads, it and the Pennsylvania Central, and that the arrangement is such as not to embarrass the business at all.

Mr. HOVEY—You have stated to the committee that, in your judgment, if the fourth class freights should be taken from the railroads in this state, instead of going by the canal, a large portion would go by roads outside of the state?

A. I said a considerable proportion. How large a proportion I did not state. A considerable proportion would go to the railroads of other states, along with the other three classes. I thought some, now going upon the canals, would follow. I stated that the trade of the southern cities would increase, drawing from all classes from the northern cities. Whether the aggregate result would be a reducing or increasing the canal or not is a question of judgment.

Mr. HOVEY—Do you know what proportion the fourth class freight, moved by the canals is, compared with that by railroads?

A. I have no doubt of it.

A. I have not the slightest idea.

Mr. HOVEY—Do you not know that it is much larger than that carried by all the freights carried by the railroads of this state?

A. I do not know anything about it. The fourth class carried by railway, covers certain specified articles. If you put all canal freights into the freight cars, it must be very immense.

Mr. HOVEY—Do you make your prices on heavy articles, beef, pork and flour, and freight of that character, with direct reference to the canal prices in the summer?

A. No, sir. So far as we are concerned we make them more with reference to lake transportation. If we are running back our cars to Chicago empty, we fill them at very low rates. If we are running them back full, and getting low rates, we would let the lake take the whole freight.

Mr. HOVEY—I asked with reference to your connection with the New York Central?

A. In summer it makes no difference to the New York Central whether it goes by lake or by rail, and we have to go squarely against lake. The New York Central cannot give us any freight to help us in the summer.

Mr. HOVEY—In your judgment is there any route from Lake Erie to New York cheaper than the New York Central or Hudson River?

A. I have no knowledge of the capacity of the canal.

Mr. HOVEY—I speak of the railroads.

A. I do not.

Mr. HOVEY—You think no route can do it better?

A. I think not. I think that long lines can put down rates so as to make it unprofitable. Long lines have the capacity to take away the profitable margin of the short lines. If the New York Central can make 25 per cent, these other longer lines have to be satisfied with 10 or 12 per cent.

Mr. HOVEY—You stated to the Committee, that if prices were fixed for freight from east to west, that unless they were fixed so low that the business would pay no profit, it would go to other roads?

A. It would.

Mr. HOVEY—Do you mean that this immense business would be done at a loss to get it?

A. I do not think it would do it at a loss. I think the Pennsylvania Central and Baltimore and Ohio would work at a loss for a time, under the impression that it would strengthen their road from the East in the trade with the West, so that they would, eventually, make considerable profit. We frequently open a business which is dependent for its future hopes of success in doing business at rates, for the present, that are not at all remunerative. If I was the controller of the affairs of the Pennsylvania Central and Baltimore and Ohio railroads, I would do a large amount of business at cost, to these cities, with the idea that it would result favorably to them in the future.

Mr. HOVEY—Having expressed the opinion that the New York Central can do business as low as any other route, do you think there would be danger of a final loss to that road if they were compelled to do business at a fixed published rate for a month?

Mr. HOVEY—They would lose the whole business?

A. Unless they fixed the rates so near cost that other roads would not accept the rate dictated, they would. I think the New York Central worked in this way for five years. It would severely try the patience of the Pennsylvania Central railroad, but I think she would work for such an advantage.

Mr. HOVEY—Does that bring yon to the conclusion that the long business now on these roads, is done at little or no profit, with such competition as now exists?

A. I think that the long business is done at a considerable profit. I think it can be kept up at the rate it is now done. None of the roads can reduce the rates of long business unless the others do it, and there is nothing to be gained by it. Suppose you fixed the rates on the New York Central where they now are, for a month. The agents of other lines at Chicago would drop their prices two cents, or five cents per hundred pounds, and get the business. They would continue to reduce the price from month to month, until the rates were very near cost.

Mr. HOVEY—What will be the effect of this competition on the stock of the road for the next five years?

A. It is hard to tell. I have generally been of the opinion that the longer this competition continued, the more it would make the roads pursue a conservative course, and stick to the rates, finding that, in cutting prices, they were met with promptness by a similar reduction by other roads.

Mr. HOVEY—Do you regard the action of these roads, during the past year, as having been conservative?

A. I cannot say I do.

Mr. HOVEY—Has not competition been going on without any regulation or order?

A. The competition has been very severe; it is almost always so when a new road enters into a traffic and attempts to get it away from old ones. It is generally very strong and very persevering. Such was the case with the Southern lines, and such is the case with the Grand Trunk now. They have got to make patrons for their new avenue, and introduce the public to it. People are attached to old avenues and inducements have to be made to secure their patronage for the new ones. The inducements are lower rates. When at last they had formed acquaintenances and secured patronage, they would consent to organize and fix prices at fair rates with the other lines. In another year another new line, without friends and without patrons, comes into competition, and again the arrangements are thrown into pi by their cutting rates to get patrons. This being secured, they of course would be conservative.

Mr. HOVEY—Then the establishment of business is no avail unless you do it as cheap as anybody else?

A. I don't think it is of much value in the freight business; in the passenger business it may have; but even there it has a wearing off tendency which would result injuriously.

Mr. HOVEY—Do you know the distances from Detroit to Boston, Portland and New York, by the Grand Trunk?

A. I do not; I think it is as near from Detroit to Boston as it is from Detroit to Portland, considerably nearer; if so, it is a hundred miles nearer from Detroit to Boston by the Grand Trunk than by the New York Central, and Albany and Western. The Grand Trunk, I might mention, has introduced a new element in the traffic, that of advancing money on freights.

Mr. COBB—Is not the New York Central represented in the Board of Directors of the Michigan Central?

A. Mr. Corning is a member of our board.

[During a subsequent stage of the proceedings, Mr. Brooks appeared before the Committee and made the following additional statement, in explanation of a part of his testimony. Reporter.]

Mr. BROOKS—I understand that I said in reply to the last gentleman, that all freights could be carried at about the same rates. I understood the gentleman to mean fourth-class freights, goods carried at about the same rates as molasses and beef. I did not understand the question to cover the first, second and third classes. It would be absurd to suppose that a ton of chairs or grain cradles, of which you cannot carry more than a ton or two in a car, would be as cheap as the others. I supposed I had so stated the facts as not to be mistaken. I supposed that the question referred to what was a fair average for fourth-class freight.

Mr. COBB—Can you load your cars fully with first and second class goods?

A. Some of the kinds we can. There is a wide difference. Of furniture you can get but very little.

Mr. COBB—Dry goods in boxes and bales?

A. You could, I should think; you would only suffer greater risk of loss or damage. High priced goods are more susceptible to damage. Some goods we can get only one or two tons in a car that carries ten tons, and with some we get in the full weight.

Mr. COBB—What do you suppose is the average tonnage per car, the season through, of first and second class goods?

A. I could not guess any better than yourself. Some may carry ten tons and others not more than two tons. They range between those two figures.

Mr. COBB—Taking goods in boxes and bales which are pretty heavy, would you estimate the cost of moving these as greater than moving the fourth class?

A. I do not think the simple difference in the cost of movement amounts to much, but the hazard and liability to damage makes the difference.

Mr. COBB—Then it depends upon the value of the commodity, whether heavy or light?

A. Yes, sir.

Mr. COBB—Take the third class goods; do not the cars ordinarily go fully loaded when you carry that class?

A. So far as the third class is concerned, I cannot now name any articles which belong in that class—I am ignorant of that detail as to what belongs to one class or the other. I could not divide the articles into their respective classes at all.

Mr. COBB—Is there not a wide dissimilarity in the price of movement of articles which you can't put eight or ten tons in a car, and does not the only difference consist in the value of the article?

A. Yes, sir, and the liability to damage?

STATEMENT

Of SOLOMON DRULLARD, General Freight Agent of the New York Central Railroad Company.

I have been General Freight Agent of the New York Central Railroad Company, since September, 1854; and previous to that time was General Freight Agent of the Buffalo and Hornellsville Railroad. I was formerly engaged in the canal transportation business, from 1827 up to the time of my appointment to the General Freight Agency of the Buffalo and Hornellsville Railroad.

I think the cost of moving way-freight, exceeds by one-third the cost of moving through-freight, and perhaps more, inasmuch as way-trains, do not, in the course of business, take or convey more than two-thirds the number of cars that through-trains do—perhaps less; that the way-cars are very frequently but partially loaded. It also requires a longer time to go a given distance, in consequence of the frequent stoppages—going on and off the switches to get to the freight houses, for loading and unloading freight, thus increasing the cost of motive power, and the men employed on freight trains; that from two to five and six men are required at the several way-stations, to load and unload, to make out way-bills, collect charges, deliver and receive freight, making the cost of conveying way-freight, as compared with through, from 40 to 50 per cent greater. The way-business is chiefly independent of the through, requiring separate men and management, and is necessarily governed by different rules, and should be conducted under different tariffs, and must be, if the difference in cost of transportation is taken into account.

I have examined the way-freight tariffs, of the eighteen different and principal freight roads, presented to the Committee in the testimony of Mr. Spaulding, as well as the local freight tariffs of many other roads, and find that no roads do their local freighting at rates as low as those charged by the New York Central on all their way-freights; nor do I believe, that greater accommodations, or more dispatch, are afforded to shippers of local freight on the line of any other road, than are given on the New York Central.

From my knowledge of the freighting business on the New York Central Road, I am confident, that it could not do a way and through-business under a pro rata law; nor could it do a through-business in competition with the rival lines, if compelled to make and publish a tariff, which could not be varied for thirty days; for, as soon as a tariff was published, competing lines would drop sufficiently under it to secure the business from all competing points. In a competing business, like the transportation of property, without the power of immediate change in prices, we become the prey of aggression, without the power of self-protection; our right to change, even if not used, is our only and strong safeguard.

A measure like the one asked for in the petitions, would, in my judgment, divert the trade from New York, and her roads, to a very serious extent, and injuring materially the large investments made by the business interests of the State.

While in Chicago, last week, I found that the

agents of the Grand Trunk Railroad, had actually contracted to convey a large quantity of provisions from Chicago to Liverpool, at eighty-seven and one-half cents per one hundred pounds. This freight was offered to the New York Central and Erie Roads at the same price, but it was declined at so low a rate. The Grand Trunk Road is to be a formidable competitor to the New York Roads, and is now taking business to the seaboard from them at Chicago, St. Louis, Cincinnati and other common western towns, at prices considerably below those at which property has heretofore been transported through New York.

The case alluded to in the New York Tribune, of December last, about which one of the Committee made inquiry, must be a mistake. I have no knowledge of cattle being driven from Bergen to Buffalo, to take the cars for Albany. Cases of this kind have occurred. Parties living at Bergen, and other places on the line of the Central Road, west of Rochester, have at times been allowed, when the rates of transportation were fair, to ship their cattle from Buffalo to points on the line of the road east, unload them with a view of a few weeks' pasturage, then take them up and transport them to Albany without extra charge. At one time, last summer, when the competition was sharp, and prices very low, one of the shippers, who had previously enjoyed the privilege just mentioned, desired to avail himself of its benefits again, but was refused at the then low rates ; the cattle were therefore sent through without charge at the competing prices.

Mr. Cobb is very much mistaken in his statement before the Committee, that no property was shipped for the citizens of Buffalo, between Oct. 20th and Nov. 20th, on the Central Railroad. They had, it is true, large quantities of freight to be forwarded at that time, but it did not prevent shipments of Buffalo freights, between the dates just mentioned. It frequently occurs in the fall, when the canal has more than it can do, that forwarders are desirous of making large shipments on the railroad on short notice, at a time when there is a large quantity of property in the railroad freight houses, which has been previously received. This delays property for the Buffolo forwarders for a few days, as property must be dispatched in the order it is received. But this state of things never lasts but a few days at a time.

I have examined the case charged against the Central Road, by Mr. Parsons of Rochester, who said that flour was taken from Rochester to New York for sixty cents per barrel, while eighty-seven and a half cents was charged from Fisher's Station, sixteen miles east of Rochester. The explanation given by Mr. Briggs, before the Committee, is correct. The flour was shipped by the Central Road to Albany, to the care of the Swiftsure Line of tow boats on the river, at fifty-two cents per barrel to Albany. It did not reach Albany in time to take the river before its close, was carted over the river by the Swiftsure Line to the Hudson River Road, at an expense of five and half cents per barrel, and was charged on the Hudson River Road, the usual winter tariff thirty cents per barrel to New York. There was no fault on the part of the Central Road in regard to it.

A complaint was made on the part of the petitioners, that the Central Road, last fall, in Buffalo, received flour to ship at the company's convenience, and that property belonging to Buffalo was detained until that received from the west had gone forward. It is the usual and proper course for the company to transport property in the order in which it is received, giving preference as far as they can, to perishable property, and late in the fall or early in December, at about which time the river closes, the company will not receive property to ship through except at their convenience after property previously received, has gone forward. There is generally for a few days at about the close of navigation a press of freight at Buffalo and other points to go east, which makes a few days' delay absolutely necessary before all property offered can be shipped, but it always goes forward in the order which it is received, and as fast as the large equipment of the road can transport it. November 1st, 1854, the tariff on flour from Buffalo to New York, was seventy cents per barrel, and to Albany sixty cents. This continued until the boats on the Hudson river put up their freight, which made a corresponding advance from Buffalo to New York necessary. The advance was five cents per barrel, so that on the 13th November, flour from Buffalo to New York was seventy-five cents. On the 21st November, freights were advanced on flour to seventy-eight cents to New York, and sixty-five cents to Albany. December 9th the tariff on flour from Buffalo to Albany, was seventy cents, from Rochester to Albany, fifty-five cents, and Canandaigua to Albany fifty cents per barrel. On the 2d January all the freight at Buffalo was cleared out, so that no complaint could be made on account of delay. January 4th, the rate on flour from Buffalo to New York was ninety-five cents, of which the Hudson River Road received thirty-seven and a half cents per barrel. January 10th, the rates on flour to New York were advanced to $1.10 cents per barrel, of which the Hudson River Road received forty-five cents per barrel, leaving to the New York Central Road sixty-five cents per barrel from Buffalo to Albany. In February, the Hudson River Road reduced their prices, and the tariff was again established at ninety-five cents per barrel from Buffalo to New York. No freights at this time was taken from western points, at a different tariff from the above. Arbitrary rates were maintained at Dunkirk, Buffalo and Suspension Bridge, on freights from the northwest, and generally so from the southwest, with the exception of cases where the roads of New York were brought into competition with the southern lines, until the lines of the southern roads were extended through to Chicago, which so much increased the competition for through business that arbitrary rates could no longer be maintained without a loss of the business to the New York lines. The cases mentioned by Mr. Cobb, where discriminations were made, have almost all of them occurred within the past two years, when the competition with rival lines has been unparalleled, and when it was necessary to take freights from common competing points at very low prices, in order to show the rival lines that it was better to return to fair and established prices, and that they would get as much business by so doing, as they did under extreme low rates. I find as much discrimination between long and short distances, and against the people of this state, in the transportation, on the canals as is made by railroads, and I give a few cases which have mostly come under my observation the past year, in the document marked A, appended to this statement. My experience is, that discriminations between long and short freights are general on all lines of transport.

January 31*st*, 1860. S. DRULLARD.

A.

CANAL DISCRIMINATIONS.

May, 1859. New York to Buffalo, 514 miles, 10 cents per 100 lbs. New York to Rochester, 415 miles, 12 cents per 100 lbs. At pro rata it should have been 8 4-100 cents per 100 lbs., or one-third less than was charged to Buffalo.

June, 1859. New York to Lockport, 483 miles, 16 cents per 100 lbs. New York to Cleveland, 700 miles, 12 cents per 100 lbs. A pro rata to Lockport would be 7 87-100 per 100 lbs., or less than half the amount charged.

June, 1859. New York to Lockport, 16 cents per 100 lbs., 483 miles. Brockport to Medina, 10 cents per 100 lbs. At pro rata, the rate between Brockport and Medina, would be 9 mills, or less than one-tenth that was charged.

July, 1859. New York to Syracuse, 8 cents per 100 lbs., 366 miles. Syracuse to Manlius, 10 miles, 8 cents per 100 lbs. At pro rata, the rate between Syracuse and Manlius, would have been 3 mills per 100 lbs., instead of 10 cents.

July, 1859. Albany to Syracuse, 166 miles, 12 cents per 100 lbs. New York to Syracuse, 316 miles, 8 cents per 100 lbs. A pro rata, between Albany and Syracuse, would be 4 1-5 cents, or about one-third the amount charged.

July, 1859. Albany to Rochester, 269 miles, 14 cents per 100 lbs. New York to Rochester, 419 miles, 10 cents per 100 lbs. At pro rata, from Albany, to Rochester, would be 6 42-100 per 100 lbs.

July, 1859, Albany to Rome, 125 miles, 10 cents per 100 lbs. New York to Syracuse, 316 miles, 8 cents per 100 lbs. At pro rata, from Albany to Rome, it should have been 3 27-100 cents per 100 lbs.

July, 1859. Albany to Utica, 100 miles, 10 cents per 100 lbs. New York to Detroit, 12 cents per 100 lbs. A pro rata would be, from Albany to Utica, 1 96-100 cents per 100 lbs., or less than one-quarter the price charged.

Aug., 1859. Albany to Amsterdam, 47 miles, 10 cents per 100 lbs. New York to Cleveland, 12 cents per 100 lbs. A pro rata, from Albany to Amsterdam, would have been 8 mills per 100 lbs.

Aug,, 1859. New York to Brockfort, 17 cents per 100 lbs. New York to Sandusky, more than double the distance, 12 cents per 100 lbs.

Aug., 1859. New York to Chicago, 1,400 miles, 18 cents per 100 lbs. New York to Rochester, 415 miles, 12 cents per 100 lbs. A pro rata would have been, from New York to Rochester, 5 14-100 cents per 100 lbs.

Aug., 1859. New York to Detroit, via Oswego, 14 cents per 100 lbs. Syracuse to Canastota, 20 miles, 10 cents per 100 lbs. A pro rata, from Syracuse to Canastota, would have been 4 2-3 mills, or less than half a cent per 100 lbs.

Sept. 1, 1859. On the day the Canal Convention was held in Rochester, the freight on flour was 35 cents per barrel, by canal, both from Buffalo and Rochester, to New York, one 514 miles, the other 415 miles. At pro rata rate, it should have been only 29 64-100 cents per barrel from Ro-Rochester. Difference against Rochester millers, nearly 6 cents per barrel.

Oct. 21, 1859. Buffalo to New York, 50 cents per barrel for flour. New York to Cleveland, 12 cents per 100 lbs. A pro rata on flour, from Buffalo to New York, would be 19 cents per barrel, or considerable less than one-half charged.

These cases have all occurred within the present year, and they might be multiplied to fill up as many books as have been published by the Clinton League. They are of every day occurrence, and show quite as glaring a difference as can be found on any of the railroads in the State. They show one prominent feature in the carrying trade—that short distances pay higher rates than long ones, by the same mode of transit.

S. DRULLARD,

Genl. Frt. Agt. N. Y. C. R. R.

January 30, 1860.

The testimony of Mr. Brooks and Mr. Drullard was fully corroborated in all its details, by the evidence of Messrs. Stone, Minot, Marsh, Hubby, Phillips, Boody, Briggs and Spaulding, all experienced and enlightened railroad men. And it was clearly shown that it cost at least one-half more per ton per mile, to transport way freight than through; that it was impossible to do both way and through on the pro rata principle; that the through business would have to be given up, and an increased charge by the railroads made for carrying way freight. That it costs, at least thirty per cent more, to do freighting in the winter than in the summer, on the northern roads. That a fixed tariff on the part of the New York roads, that could not be changed for thirty days, would enable competing lines to take all the through business from the New York roads, by dropping a little under the fixed tariff. That it would not increase business upon the canals, but would be likely to take it from them, from the state, and from the city of New York.

LEGISLATIVE RESTRICTIONS

ON THE

CARRYING TRADE

OF THE

RAILWAYS OF THE STATE OF NEW YORK:

VIEWED IN CONNECTION WITH OUTSIDE COMPETITION.

ADDRESSED TO THE CITIZENS OF THE CITY AND STATE OF NEW YORK.

NEW YORK:
PRINTED BY WM. L. S. HARRISON,
80 AND 82 DUANE STREET.
1860.

LEGISLATIVE RESTRICTIONS

ON THE

CARRYING TRADE OF THE RAILWAYS OF NEW YORK.

To the Citizens of the City and State of New York:

FROM the memorable struggle which, through the exertions of the indomitable Clinton, resulted in the construction of the Erie Canal, the people of the State of New York have in no instance been called upon to decide a graver question than that presented in the proposition to place legislative restrictions upon the carrying trade of our railways. Those who favor this policy argue that railway competition works a two-fold injury to the State: that it promotes the farming, manufacturing and industrial interests of other States to the detriment of our own, and that it materially lessens the revenues of our canals. To remedy these evils they propose that the Legislature shall enact the "*pro rata* freight bill" of 1858, and reimpose tolls on the railroads. On the other hand it is contended that the proposed measures would operate disastrously on the railroads, would increase the burthens of our agricultural and manufacturing interests by a still further increase of the cost of transportation within our own State, would drive a large portion of the through traffic upon rival thoroughfares outside of the State, and hence would fail to benefit the canals. To understand properly the comprehensiveness and momentousness of the issue, let us, at the outset, survey our present commercial position as a State.

For a time, and up to the period of the completion of the several great railway thoroughfares connecting the Atlantic coast with the region beyond the Alleghanies, the bulk of our inland commerce, between the East and the West, pursued interchangeably one undeviating course over the water lines traversed by the Hudson, the Erie Canal, the great lakes, and the Western canals and rivers. Within the last few years, however, a silent but mighty revolution has taken place. Iron rails, starting from our principal seaboard ports south of us, may now be seen winding their way through the valleys and along the lateral slopes of the Alleghanies, climbing over the back of the huge monster, tieing themselves as they pass to numerous intersecting roads, and to landing-places on the Ohio, the Mississippi and other rivers, and at Pittsburgh, Chicago, Wheeling, Cleveland, Columbus, Cincinnati, Indianapolis, St. Louis, Louisville, and places of lesser note, connecting with that vast railway net-work which collects and concentrates to those points the produce of the prairies, the great basin, and the trade of the interior towns. Thousands of untiring locomotives, harnessed to long trains of laden cars, regardless of the darkness of night, snow-drift or storm, are hastening to and fro; some to deliver the merchandise of the East to the West, and others to return the products of the West to the East. North of us the mountains of Vermont and New Hampshire yield their patient backs to similar iron bands, which stretch from the seaports of New England to the St. Lawrence, to Lake Ontario, and through the Canadas to the upper lakes, where they interchange commodities with the people of the Northwest. In addition to these, the improvements in steam navigation, in the construction of steamers and propellers—improvements which have kept equal pace with those of the railway—have brought into active and formidable competition a mammoth coasting line, which receives freight from all our Atlantic ports, delivers it at New Orleans, and returns with the products of the valley of the Mississippi and the Ohio. Its influence is sensibly felt even as far towards the Northwest as Indiana and Illinois. We may also remark here that the same improvements which enable this line to compete succcessfully for our carrying trade, are brought into use by the competing railways, where they connect with the waters of the interior, and also in drawing business to themselves from localities North and South of their termini on the coast of the Atlantic.

We will now consider more specifically the capacities of these rival routes. First in order, South of us, is the Pennsylvania Central Railroad. This road runs from Philadelphia to

Pittsburgh, and there, in connection with the Fort Wayne and Chicago Railroads, forms a continuous line to Chicago. It also connects with roads running direct to Cleveland, Columbus, Cincinnati, and all the important points of the West and Southwest. Pittsburgh, having its site at the confluence of the Alleghany and Monongahela rivers, which there form the Ohio, is the receiving and distributing point for the commerce of a vast area of country, and has a navigable water communication of many thousand miles. From the Alleghany, during a portion of the year, it receives business by means of small boats from the northward as high up as Olean in our own State. On the Ohio river, which bears southwesterly, passing by Wheeling, Cincinnati, Louisville, and numerous other enterprising towns on the borders of Ohio, Pennsylvania, Kentucky, Indiana, and Illinois, it commands 959 miles of navigation by large class steamers to the Mississippi, and thence to all the prominent places on that great "Father of Waters," from the highest accessible point to the Gulf of Mexico. Such are the connections of the Pennsylvania Central Road at the West. At its eastern terminus it connects with New York by means of the New Jersey roads and the Raritan Canal, also with New York, with Boston, and other New England cities, by regular lines of propellers, which it directly controls, and which pour into its depôt at Philadelphia immense quantities of freight taken from under our own eyes, and diverted from our own thoroughfares. Nor is this all. Few seem to know that the Pennsylvania Road places Philadelphia on an average more than 100 miles nearer the commercial cities of the West than is the city of New York. Philadelphia is nearer by the Pennsylvania Road than New York is by her roads:

To Cleveland, by	123 miles.
To Chicago, by	136 miles.
To St. Louis, by	161 miles.
To Columbus, by	190 miles.
To Cincinnati, by	190 miles.

More still, New York *itself* is brought nearer to the West *viâ* the Pennsylvania Road, than *viâ* the New York Central or the New York and Erie. New York merchants and Western shippers save in distance by the Pennsylvania Road, as against the New York Central or Erie as follows:

To Cleveland, ...	33 miles.
To Chicago, ...	46 miles.
To St. Louis, ...	71 miles.
To Columbus, ...	100 miles.
To Cincinnati, ...	100 miles.

As an evidence of the capacities of this road we instance the fact that its total tonnage in 1858 exceeded by 281,482 tons that of the New York Central. It increased its *through* freight in 1858, as compared with 1857, nearly 50,000 tons, while that of the New York Central fell off 19,531 tons. We take these facts from official reports. The cost of the road is over $30,000,000, contributed jointly by individuals, the city of Philadelphia, and the State of Pennsylvania—the latter having loaned its credit to the extent of $7,400,000. Combining so many natural and artificial advantages, with the fostering patronage of the State, favored by State pride, and by the strong ties which identify it with the life and prosperity of the second city in the Union, a city of only one-fifth less population than the city of New York, this road now boldly and confidently strives to wrest from our own roads their carrying trade, and from New York State and city their commercial supremacy. Already do its Directors assume, and act upon the assumption, of a certain triumph. In their report for 1858 they *officially* proclaimed it to be their settled policy to effect a transfer of our carrying trade to themselves, and the subversion of the commercial ascendency of New York city by a like transfer of its business to Philadelphia. We speak from the record.

On page 3 of their report for 1858, they say: "The city of Philadelphia has expended millions in the completion of internal improvements to draw to her the trade of the West, and her great work, *undertaken for that object*, is now finished and connected with all its principal avenues; yet it is without the proper means of transferring from cars to vessels the vastly increasing tonnage anticipated from these connections." On page 4 they continue: "In the opinion of your Board of Directors, a new impetus would be given to the growth of Philadelphia by the extension of the Pennsylvania Railroad to the Delaware River, tending more to revive our commerce than any other measure attainable at so small an outlay. The cost of transportation to the Delaware River, with the exemption from city tolls, city teaming, or cartage, would thus be reduced so much below that to other eastern cities, that vessels would be drawn to *our harbor* for their freights; the difference in favor of Philadelphia over New York or Boston, in the cost of transportation between the West and shipboard, or *vice versa*, would be so apparent *that shipowners or foreign merchants would take advantage of circumstances so greatly to their interests.*

A merchant receiving flour at both New York and Philadelphia from the same western consignor, and selling it at precisely the same rate in each city, returns to the consignor a *larger per centage* on his Philadelphia than on his New York sales—arising solely from the cost of transportation *in favor* of Philadelphia: consequently, cheap transportation to the river front secures to her a large trade which otherwise she cannot obtain, and no doubt *vessels will be brought here for the trade thus created.* This advantage will not be left unimproved by those controlling the commercial interests of our city." Again, on page 5, they say: "In conclusion, your Board of Directors are of the opinion that the Pennsylvania Railroad has not *accomplished the object* of its construction until a connection is effected with tide-water on the Delaware, thus opening an avenue by which every variety of mineral and agricultural production can be conveyed to a proper point for shipment, and furnishing facilities for the trade of this city at least equal to those of any location on the Atlantic coast."

In regard to the advantages enjoyed by New York, furnished by the Erie Canal and Hudson River, they further say, on page 16: "The removal or equalization of these advantages must return to it (Philadelphia) a large share of this *export trade*, bringing with it a *corresponding increase in the imports.*" The italics in the foregoing extracts are our own.

After these explicit avowals had been thus officially announced, and it was discovered that they had aroused a feeling of marked uneasiness among the citizens and merchants of New York, G. W. Cass, Esq., one of the most active and energetic of the directors of the road, published in the *New York Times* a communication, dated April 25, 1859, designed to allay apprehension, and to cajole them into the belief that the Pennsylvania Road was as essential to the prosperity of New York as to that of Philadelphia. We call the particular attention of the reader to the following language quoted from that communication:

"That the Pennsylvania Road will contribute to the rapid growth and commercial development of Philadelphia we claim; but such a claim is not inconsistent with the fact that the Pennsylvania Road carries a very large amount of the business done by both New York and Boston with the West. We cannot state to-day the amount of this tonnage, but of the 263,204,721 pounds of twelve classes carried to Philadelphia, in 1858, paraded so triumphantly by 'New York,' in proof of his position, a large quantity was merely *in transitu*, when it arrived at Philadelphia, for New York and New England. And herein is the explanation of the great prosperity of the Philadelphia (?) Road; it not only enjoys most of the interior carrying trade of the city of Philadelphia, but being the shortest and best route from New York City to the greater part of the West, the Western merchants (who in fact control the route by which four-fifths of the freights between the East and the West shall be shipped,) prefer to make their shipments to and from New York over this route. During a good portion of every year, goods may be carried from New York to Cincinnati and points in that direction, with but 353 miles of rail (portage) transportation, whereas it is double that over the New York Central route. In lineal distance, the Pennsylvania Road has more than 100 miles the advantage in all-rail route to the same portion of the West; and in *directness*, few seem to be aware of the favorable location of the Pennsylvania Road as to the City of New York. The New York Central Road runs on a parallel of latitude *about two and a half degrees north of the City of New York; whereas the Pennsylvania Road preserves a parallel about one-half degree south of that City.* The Pennsylvania Road, then, being in a geographical position to avail itself, or rather to command, the carrying trade of Philadelphia, Baltimore, New York, and Boston, to and from the West, by river, and by the new Western rail connections lately completed, fully accounts for her increased trade in 1858, and is, moreover, a sure promise of still greater increase in the future, without in any way damaging the merchants in New York. Such a state of things is not only consistent with, but would be promoted by, the most flattering increase of the business of the City of New York its truest friend could wish. As we have before intimated, it is because the Pennsylvania Road carries trade to and from New York in legitimate and successful competition with the Central, and thereby increases her (Pennsylvania Road) receipts, that so much exercises the New York Central Managers, and *not* the lesser rate from Philadelphia to the West." In a letter dated only two days later, and addressed to "the Merchants of Chicago," this same Director reiterated these views as applicable to that city. "The trade of Chicago and the business of the Northwestern roads have the advantage of this *less* rate from Philadelphia, to the same extent that other cities and other roads have it. And we do not believe that there is a single merchant in Chicago or the Northwest, who buys goods in Philadelphia, that will insist, when his freight bill is presented to him, that the Freight Agent has made it out *too low*, and that he must add to it, to make the rate equal to what he paid on his New York or Boston purchases. Nor do we believe that a packer of provisions in Chicago, who has shipped 1000 barrels of pork to New York at the current rates, will insist, when he goes to ship 1000 kegs of lard to Philadelphia, that the Freight Agent shall charge him the New York rates. When the Freight Agent informs the shipper that the distance to Philadelphia is about 150 miles less than to New York, and that he can carry his lard at $2 per ton less to Philadelphia than his meat was carried to New York for, who supposes he will indignantly refuse the offer on the ground that it will injure the packing business at Chicago?'"

Now, with these premises before us, and the statistical facts we have given, who does not see that we have in the Pennsylvania Road alone a competitor which threatens the ascendency of our New York roads?

Next in order as a competing route, is the Baltimore and Ohio Railroad. What the Pennsylvania Road is to Philadelphia, the Baltimore and Ohio Road is to Baltimore. It has its principal terminus on the Ohio river at Wheeling, 379 miles from Baltimore, and another at Parkersburgh, about 200 miles below Pittsburgh, 96 miles below Wheeling, and 383 miles from Baltimore. Its water connections are the same as those of the Pennsylvania Road, which we have described. In conjunction with the Central Ohio Road at Wheeling, the Marietta and

Cincinnati at Parkersburgh, and their affiliated lines, it places Baltimore in direct rail communication with the valleys of the Ohio and Mississippi. Baltimore has an advantage over the City of New York, the latter taking her own roads, of a less rail distance

To Columbus by	250 miles.
To Cincinnati by	298 miles.

Even New York merchants can ship goods by rail to Baltimore, and thence to Cincinnati, *viâ* the Baltimore and Ohio Road, and save 100 miles in distance, as between that and the New York Central Road. Alluding to the recent completion of the Louisville and Nashville Road, the Directors of the Baltimore and Ohio Company, in their annual report just published, say: "The operation of this and other Southern and Western lines, combined with the superior advantages of Parkersburgh as a port for the great river traffic, and the excellent location of Baltimore, will enable this company to outflank their Northern competitors in the contest for the Southwestern trade." Coasting steamers are also used by this Company, to draw trade from New York and New Englond. Our New York roads, in consequence of these new facilities afforded to Eastern and Western shippers for transporting merchandise and produce over the Baltimore and Ohio road, at reduced rates, have lost largely of the Southwestern trade already, and are, therefore, forced to conform to the same low rates in order to retain the business they now have. To show the powerful agency of these coasting steamers as a means of diverting our freight over that route, we again quote from the report of the Directors of that Company. On this point they say: "Since the opening of the Baltimore and Ohio road to the Ohio River, and the completion of its Western rail connections, the large supplies of agricultural products over the route have furnished bases for the profitable employment of numerous steamers which regularly ply between Baltimore and the principal Northern and Southern cities on the seaboard.

During the contest for the freighting business last Spring, the New York Central Company demanded from the Southern lines an equality of rates to common points at the West. To this, John W. Garrett, Esq., President of the Baltimore and

Ohio Road, responded as follows: "The New York Central Company demands that the rates from New York, Boston, Philadelphia, and Baltimore to the common centres of the West and Southwest shall be the same. The illustration of the case, in connection with the city of Baltimore, will exhibit the error and absurdity of the principle announced. Cincinnati, as the leading city of the Ohio valley, has commanded the most attention in the discussions of the conventions of the four lines. What are the relative positions of New York and the New York Central Company, and Baltimore and the Baltimore and Ohio Company, to that city? The distance from New York *via* the New York Central Road and the shortest railway line to Cincinnati, is 880 miles. The distance from Baltimore and the shortest railway line to Cincinnati, is 582 miles; leaving the difference in favor of Baltimore, 298 miles. It therefore clearly follows that, unless the New York Central Road concludes to render the service for its entire length without any remuneration whatever, if the connecting roads of the Baltimore and Ohio Company in Ohio can work at the same rates as the connections of the New York Central, it must abandon this demand.

"It has claimed great relative advantages during the season of river and lake navigation, and economy of working, arising from low grades, &c. What are the facts? Assume the use of the Hudson River to Albany, and of the lake from Buffalo to Cleveland, yet the actual transportation is, viz:

	Miles.
On New York Central Railroad, ...	298
And from Cleveland to Cincinnati, ...	255
Total, ...	553
Whilst from Baltimore to Parkersburg, on the Ohio River, 200 miles below Pittsburg, the distance is but	383
Exhibiting the transportation by rail from the City of New York to be (miles)	170

in favor of the Baltimore route, using canal or sea from New York to Baltimore, making the Baltimore and Ohio line the cheapest from the City of New York, and proving conclusively the absolute advantages of the location of Baltimore." Mr.

Garrett then goes on to show that the use of bituminous coal for fuel, which is supplied in inexhaustible quantities on the line of the road at a cost of about $1 per ton, enables that Company to work their motive machinery at an expense materially less per annum than the cost of fuel on the New York Central. If his statement (which he supports by comparative figures) be true, then this difference may be annually appropriated to the purposes of competition. While candor requires us to regard the amount stated by Mr. Garrett as somewhat exaggerated, there can be no doubt that the advantage derived from this source constitutes a most formidable element in the competing capacities of that road. It is, moreover, a permanent and increasing advantage. For as wood becomes more and more scarce every year, and advances in price, in the same proportion will the contrast be more marked, and the margin in favor of the Baltimore and Ohio Company be enlarged. Now, without lessening their own relative expenditure, they can use the entire amount they save in this respect to the injury of the business of their rivals. On the supposition that their cheap fuel lessens the cost of transportation one or two dollars per ton, they can then offer a premium to that extent to Eastern and Western shippers. The Directors, as the previously quoted extract indicates, fully appreciate this element in the competing capacities of their road, and will, beyond question, make the most of it.

In 1858, this road *increased* its through tonnage to within a fraction of 50,000 tons, which, added to a similar increase on the Pennsylvania road, equals about one-third of the *total* through tonnage on the New York Central for the same year. No road in the country has a better system of agencies, or a more active, vigilant, and persevering corps of agents. They are established in New York, Boston, and other New England cities, circulate handbills, mingle with our merchants, and bid temptingly for every pound of freight. An equally efficient, but more extensive organization, co-operates with them in the Western States.

It is proper also to remark that the State of Maryland and the City of Baltimore have contributed nearly ten of the $30,000,000 which the road has cost.

With all these circumstances, alliances, and appliances in its favor, it must take a prominent and energetic part for the future, as it has taken for the past, in the great struggle for the carrying trade between the East and the West.

A *third* railway route runs from Norfolk and Richmond to Louisville, on the Ohio river, to various places on the Tennessee, and to Memphis on the Mississippi.

A *fourth* route runs from Charleston to all the points last named.

A *fifth* route runs from Savannah to the same points.

All these lines have steamers plying regularly to and from our Northern ports, and they connect with other steamers on the Ohio and Mississippi at their western termini. Many local advantages contribute to their capacities of competition. Their original cost does not exceed an average of over $30,000 per mile; and a propitious climate materially lessens their operating expenses, repairs of roadway, &c., compared with our Northern roads. They are likewise fostered and strengthened in every possible manner by the legislation of the States through which they pass. Georgia has even conferred banking privileges on the Central Georgia Road, which forms a part of one of these lines. It is authorized to create and issue three dollars of paper-money to one of its capital.

A *sixth* line is nearly completed across the Peninsula of Florida, designed to open a shorter and cheaper communication between the Gulf ports and our Atlantic cities. This route, by means of the Alabama and Tombigbee rivers, will draw freight from as high a point as Columbus in the State of Mississippi. Gulf steamers plying in connection with it will tap the immense commerce of the Mississippi and Ohio rivers at New Orleans. Rail communication from New Orleans is also open to the mouth of the Ohio, 540 miles, where, by means of the Illinois Central, it forms a connection with the whole system of Western and North-western Railways—reaching into Michigan, Wisconsin, and Iowa. The Mobile and Ohio Railway will soon be finished to the mouth of the Ohio, which will place Mobile in a relation similar to that of New Orleans. Here then is another combination which is exerting, and must continue to exert, a powerful influence on the traffic between the Atlantic and the South-western interior.

A *seventh* great competitor is the steamship line between

New York and New Orleans. At New York it gathers freight, by means of confederated lines, from all the New England States, and at New Orleans from steamers on the Mississippi. As we have already stated, the improvements in steam-navigation tend every year to cheapen this mode of transportation That it is effective in the diversion of trade is evident, from the bare fact that it thrives and remunerates its proprietors.

An *eighth* competing element is seen in the numerous sail-vessels which interchange commodities between our Northern and Southern cities. In order to complete their cargoes, they frequently take freight at prices scarcely above the cost of handling. Yet to that extent they feed the Southern competing roads.

It is not generally known, but it is nevertheless true, that the item of *insurance* determines the course of freight to a large extent, and this item operates to the injury of our New York routes, when shipments are made by rail and water. Lake insurance is much higher at all seasons than on the Atlantic coast. Mr. Moran, late President of the New York and Erie Railroad Company, who has carefully studied the subject in its bearings on our railway traffic, in a correspondence with Mr. Garrett, President of the Baltimore and Ohio Company, an extract from which we take the liberty to copy, states the case as follows: "Insurance on the Lakes is never less than ½ of 1 per cent. in summer, and rises to 1 in September; 1½ in October, 1¾ on 1st November, and 2½ after 15th of November; whereas, on the Atlantic Ocean the insurance is only ¼ of 1 per cent. in summer, and ⅜ to ½ in winter." According to this, a ton of goods delivered at Buffalo after 15th of November, and worth $1,000, if it be sent from there by water to Chicago, would pay $25 insurance in addition to cost of portage; whereas the Pennsylvania Road would transport it from New York to Chicago at less than the simple Lake insurance. When the shipper determines to send by rail and water, he first ascertains the relative cost of insurance, and, if our Northern roads get the freight, they must make the margin on their rates of transportation equal to the difference in insurance —which is equivalent to paying that difference. They are compelled to meet this difficulty every hour of their daily transactions during the season of navigation.

This brings us to another important advantage possessed by the Southern routes. After navigation closes with us it is the best with them, and so continues till spring. They have both their short-rail distance, and their rail and water with a light rate of insurance on the Atlantic. They can, therefore, use either, as may suit their purpose, while our roads are limited to an all-rail price. We observe this feature of the subject, because a change of the current of traffic during the winter months induces a permanent tendency in the same direction, and, if you impose legislative restrictions on our carrying trade, that tendency will be confirmed and strengthened.

Would that we could stop here! But, unfortunately, we are assailed with equal vigor by rival thoroughfares on the north. Boston, the metropolis of New England, in order to carry on a successful competition against New York, by a more direct trade with the West, has formed a railroad connection with Lake Ontario, at Ogdensburgh, and with Montreal on the St. Lawrence. Over this route are transported the manufactures and merchandise of the Eastern States, and in return they receive flour and other produce, to feed the operatives employed in their factories, and to afford supplies for their shipping. Not long since, the Boston *Railroad Journal* stated that this route makes the rates as low from Boston to the West as from the city of New York; and then adds, that "goods shipped by this line arrive at Ogdensburgh in forty-five hours, are immediately put on the Lake propellers, and in three hours more are on their way to ports on the great Western Lakes. Property is transhipped only at Ogdensburgh, and there under great advantages for careful handling and protection."

Further north is that immense thoroughfare known as the Grand Trunk Railway. With $60,000,000 invested in it by English capitalists, including the $16,000,000 loaned by the Canadian Government—virtually without interest; with the patronage and wealth of Great Britain and her provinces in its favor; with a continuous track of nearly 1,000 miles from Portland through the Canadas to the Upper Lakes; with a solidity and durability of structure unsurpassed; with an extensive range of docks at Portland, on which its cars are brought alongside of ocean steamers; with an equipage corresponding to its length and magnitude; with *exemption from taxation the entire distance, from its Eastern to its Western terminus;* with abundance of cheap fuel at all its stations; and with a system of rail and water connections at the West leading to all points of the interior, it presents a capacity for competition unequalled by any other road on the American continent.

As an illustration of its actual operations, we have the fact that it has carried heavy merchandise the past season from Boston to Chicago at 22 cents per 100 pounds, and flour from Chicago to Portland at 60 cents per barrel. The Boston *Transcript* of Nov. 8 informs us that, for several weeks previous, the boats of the Grand Trunk Company had delivered at wharf in that city alone, 1,400 barrels of flour daily, and that its business was rapidly increasing. How many barrels in addition it may have distributed by railway to other parts of New England, or sent in vessels to Old England, is not stated. It has even sought the cotton trade, and has transported that staple from the Mississippi to Boston for $4 per bale. We learn from the Montreal *Herald* that it passed over the Victoria Bridge, eastward, for five days, at the rate of 2,334 barrels of flour daily. At the same rate for the year, it would move 855,560 barrels, or 20,014 barrels more than the total number transported by the Erie Canal to tidewater in 1857.

As a part of the same great Canadian system is the water communication with the interior Western States, *viâ* the river St. Lawrence and the St. Lawrence and Welland Canals. Vessels of 500 tons burthen pass through the St. Lawrence Canal, and will soon pass through the Welland Canal. The capacity of the latter is already sufficient to permit vessels loaded at Chicago to sail to Liverpool without breaking bulk. But it is found more profitable to reship at Montreal or Quebec, by means of iron sail vessels and propellers, which now make regular trips to and from England. These have been adopted because grain transported in them is less liable to damage from heat. They are supplied with cargoes by sail vessels from the Great Lakes, by the Collingwood rail route, which runs from Georgian Bay, on Lake Huron, to Toronto, and the Grand Trunk Railway, from the latter place, to Montreal. The navigable water line, extending from the Atlantic through Canada to the very heart of our Continent, is not less than 2,500 miles. Montreal receives at her docks vessels of 2,000 tons burthen laden with goods for the interior. Toronto, 333 miles west of Montreal, and on a longitude west of Buffalo, is *nearer to Liverpool than is the City of New York!* Possessing these enormous water and rail facilities, and measuring distance by the cost of transportation, the merchants of Great Britain are practically as near to the great West as our New York merchants. We have good authority for the statement that flour has been taken from Chicago through the Canadas to Liverpool at a *less* price per barrel than is exacted by our own thoroughfares from Chicago to New York.

At the present writing the tariff of the Grand Trunk Railway affords *lower* rates on shipments from Liverpool to our Western cities than the New York Central tariff does from the City of New York to the same points!

The following is a *verbatim* copy of one of the public handbills issued by the Grand Trunk Company, and will tell its own story:

"Grand Trunk Railway of Canada and Montreal Ocean Steamship Company.—New carrying route from England to the United States! Only two transhipments between Liverpool and Chicago, Cincinnati, or St. Louis. One contract throughout. The Grand Trunk Railway will be open from Portland, in Maine, to Detroit, in Michigan, in November next; which, in connection with the Montreal Ocean Line of steamships to Quebec, in Summer, and Portland, in Winter, will form the cheapest, most direct, and expeditious route from Liverpool to the Western States of America. The Agents in Liverpool are prepared to grant through contracts upon the terms, and to the places named below; which include wharfage, customs, bonding, and all charges except marine insurance.

Goods to the above places will go through in Bond.

To prevent delay, merchants are particularly requested to forward bills of lading and invoices of value by mail, prepaid, direct to the Agent of the Grand Trunk Railway, Portland, Maine; in order that the Customs' regulations may be complied with immediately on arrival of the goods.

Early notice of Summer rates of freight will be given.

During Winter the steamships will sail from Liverpool and Portland not less than once a fortnight.

Rates of freight for consignments of not less than twenty cubic feet, or 1000 *pounds, viâ Portland, from November,* 1859, *to April,* 1860:

From Liverpool to	Dry Goods, per 40 cubic feet.			Hardware in casks and cases, per 2,000 lbs.			Tin, Zinc, Steel and Chain, per 2,000 lbs.			Crockery, Iron, in bars, sheets, and plates, per 2,000 lbs.		
	Stg.	$	c.	Stg.	$	c.	Stg.	$	c.	Stg.	$	c.
Detroit, Mich.	90s	21	90	110s.	26	76	75s.	18	25	65s.	15	82
Chicago, Ill.	100s.	24	33	120s	29	20	85s	20	69	89s.	19	47
Quincy, Ill.	115s	27	98	140s	34	07	100s.	24	33	95s.	23	12
Galena, Ill.	120s	29	20	145s.	35	29	110s.	26	76	105s.	25	55
Milwaukie, Wis.	105s.	25	55	125s.	30	42	90s.	21	90	85s.	20	69
Burlington, Iowa	115s.	27	98	140s	34	07	100s.	24	33	95s	23	12
Dubuque, Iowa	120s.	29	20	145s.	35	29	110s.	26	76	105s.	25	55
Cincinnati, Ohio	100s.	24	33	120s	29	20	85s.	20	69	80s.	19	47
St. Louis, Mo.	110s.	26	76	135s.	32	85	95s.	23	12	90s.	21	90

Produce conveyed to Liverpool on very reasonable terms. For rates and other information, apply to

GRAND TRUNK RAILWAY COMPANY,
Office, No. 21 *Old Broad street, London.*

MONTGOMERIE & GREENHORNE,
Montreal Ocean Steamship Company's Office, London.

ALLAN BROTHERS & CO.,
Weaver Buildings, Brunswick street, Liverpool.

JAMES & ALEXANDER ALLAN,
No. 54 *St. Enoch square, Glasgow.*

J. S. MILLAR,
Agent Grand Trunk Railway, Portland, Maine.

T. D. HALL,
Agent Grand Trunk Railway, Detroit, Michigan.

JAS. WARRACK, Western Agent,
No. 74 *Dearborn street, Chicago, Illinois.*

C. R. CHRISTIE,
Superintendent of Western Division, Toronto, C. W.

EDMONDSTONE, ALLAN & CO., Agents,
Montreal Ocean Steamship Company,
Portland, Maine, and Montreal, C. E.

M. PENNINGTON, Freight Manager,
Grand Trunk Railway Company, Montreal, C. E.

Oct. 7, 1859.

By comparing the above tariff of the Grand Trunk Company with the tariff of the New York Central, it will be seen that the rates from Liverpool are LESS per ton of 2,000 lbs. than from

New York City to Detroit by	$2 10	per ton
To Chicago by	7 67	"
To Quincey by	7 02	"
To Galena by	10 00	"
To Milwaukee by	6 45	"
To Dubuque by	11 00	"
To Cincinnati by	5 67	"
To St. Louis by	9 24	"

Though these low rates may appear unremunerative, our roads are, nevertheless, compelled to contend against them, and, in the judgment of the writer, the contest must continue. Those who have carefully studied the commercial policy of England well know her far-reaching grasp. She procured the construction of this road not simply nor primarily for the profit which it was expected to yield to its stockholders, but with a view to open a direct trade with our Western interior cities, and thus to turn into the pockets of her own manufacturers, merchants, and bankers the profits and commissions now received by the factors of our Atlantic cities. Our people will ere long awake to a realization of the fact that, in one vastly important sense, the Grand Trunk Line does not terminate, nor was it intended to terminate, at Portland, but reaches across the ocean, to Liverpool, Glasgow, Sheffield, Manchester, Birmingham, and London. Contracts for the transportation of British manufactures and merchandise will include the Ocean and the Grand Trunk Railway, with its Western connections, and a return of the products of the West by the same line. This is the English idea of that mammoth undertaking. When that idea shall be more extensively developed in practice, orders for goods from Western wholesale merchants will go directly to England instead of New York, and consignments will be made by English merchants to their Western agents. If by this means Great Britain can make a wider margin of profit in favor of her own manufacturers as against those of ours, in favor of the merchandise she buys of other nations to sell to us, and in favor of her own purchasers of our produce, of which she is the chief foreign consumer, then the prize will amply compensate for the expenditure.

We are therefore destined to grapple with this giant competitor in a struggle from which there is no escape. Possibly the interposition of Congress might aid us, but in the absence of such interposition, and with our own Legislature against us, it requires no prophet to predict the result. Our internal traffic, too, is seriously menaced. Southwestern and Western New York have been tapped by the Williamsport and Elmira Road, which places Elmira only *two* miles further from Philadelphia than it is to New York, over the New York and Erie, and *twenty-one miles nearer* to Baltimore. Binghamton, *viâ* the Delaware, Lackawanna and Western and the New Jersey Central Roads, is seven miles nearer to New York than *viâ* the New York and Erie, and commands by railway a favorable position with respect to Philadelphia and Baltimore. On the north, all that portion of the State bordering on Lake Ontario, on the St. Lawrence, Lake Champlain, and east of the Hudson River, is likewise contested by the routes leading to Boston and Portland.

Already a number of our railroads, after struggling against the influences of adverse competition, have been driven to bankruptcy. When the New York and Erie was built the then position of affairs more than justified the wisdom of its projectors. It was no fault of theirs that they were not gifted with foreknowledge. If the same state of things had continued which then existed, and no other antagonistic thoroughfares had sprung up outside of our State, who does not believe that the New York and Erie would have been to-day a prosperous and paying road? It shows how the rapidity of progress baffles the calculations and forecast of our wisest men. Rip Van Winkle, after awaking from his twenty years' sleep, and noting the changes which had occurred, exclaimed, "Everything is changed, and I am changed; I can't tell what's my name or who I am!" We are equally bewildered by the events of a single year. A map of our country made to-day becomes obsolete to-morrow. No less remarkable are the tendencies of commerce. Enterprise waves her magic wand over other States besides the State of New York, and every touch of that wand, like the rod which smote the rock, opens a new current of trade.

What have been the effects upon us? In what position commercially are we placed? South of us, as we have shown, no less than eight great rivals have tapped and are diverting the flow of our commerce. All the Atlantic States from New Jersey to Florida bring to bear their legislation, the sympathies and patronage of their people, the energies of their cities, the wealth of their capitalists and every other possible influence to attain the same end, and the States of the southwest co-operate. The Lake States, and even those of the northwest, have become neutral. Maine, New Hampshire, and Vermont join with the great Northern lines, while Massachusetts, Rhode Island, and Connecticut are neutral. The Canadas, aided by the mother country, are hostile. From the moment we step across our own boundaries every inch of ground east, west, north, and south is contested. We have *no allies* outside of our boundaries, and are obliged to contend for even our internal traffic.

Yet, in these circumstances, our own Legislature are called upon to turn against us. In the face of the plain, palpable, stubborn facts presented, it is demanded that our assembled representatives shall erect an immense toll-gate across the breadth of the Empire State, or what is worse, enact the "*Pro Rata* Freight bill," either of which measures would effectually exclude from us and throw into the hands of our rivals, the benefits of our railway traffic. Should they do an act so suicidal, let no more be said of the great imperial wall which encircles China, or the policy which dictated its erection.

Here let us contemplate the bearings of this outside competition on the City of New York. Hitherto that City has been the chief factor both of our foreign and internal trade. For a long time she monopolized the only avenue of cheap transportation to and from the West. Before the completion of the Erie Canal, Philadelphia took the precedence. After the opening of the Canal a new impetus was given to the growth of New York, and she became what she is. But now Philadelphia possesses facilities of communication with the interior in some respects superior to New York. By the Pennsylvania road, as previously shown, she is nearer than New York is *viâ* the Central.

To Cleveland, by	123 miles.
To Chicago, by	136 "
To St. Louis, by	161 "
To Columbus, by	189 "
To Cincinnati, by	189 "

By rail and water her relations with the interior commercial centres are no less favorable. Within thirty hours from the sounding of the signal whistle in her depôt, steamers on the Ohio River receive and bear away the goods of her merchants. It will be seen that the Pennsylvania Road can carry freight by rail from Philadelphia to Cincinnati at a rate *below* that from New York by the New York roads, which will equal the *cost* of transportation on 189 miles. So to Cleveland, Columbus, Chicago, St. Louis, and other points, according to their relative proximity. Who reap the benefits? Chiefly the Philadelphia merchants. To prevent this, and to maintain an equality for New York City, the only course left for the New York lines is to lose the transportation on the excess of distance. Now if, in *addition* to the loss of 189 miles of transportation to Cincinnati, the same to Columbus, 123 to Cleveland, 136 to Chicago, and 161 to St. Louis, you force our roads to adopt a still higher scale of rates, how is it possible for them to retain the business or preserve the ascendency of New York? Unless, therefore, they be left untrammelled and free, New York must submit to a serious diversion of her trade. Can that great heart of commerce continue its vigorous pulsations while the veins and arteries which lead to it are tapped and drained? Will not the entire Empire State participate in the loss? Her supremacy is essential even to the canals, but it cannot be secured so long as her merchants have to contend against lesser rates to Philadelphia. It may be said that she is not in danger because the Southern routes place her also much nearer to the West than she is by her own routes. Very well; in that case her commerce will pass over those routes instead of ours. They gain it; we lose it. But, should New York transact her business with the Western centres *through* Philadelphia, then, too, she must lose on every shipment to or received from them, the cost of transportation over the 90 miles between the two cities. Besides, will it add to the prosperity of New York to subject her to the necessity and humiliation of paying tribute to her great rival as the carrier of her commerce? Would she be likely to receive justice from a State whose legislation is adverse, and from a city whose interests are really and avowedly antagonistic to hers? to a city which aspires to supplant her as the commercial metropolis? a city whose continual policy is to wrest from her her importing and exporting, as well as her inland trade? Baltimore, the next great Southern rival of New York, is 298 miles nearer to Cincinnati by rail, and possesses numerous advantages in competing to that point. We have shown that the policy of England in building her canals from Lake Erie to the St. Lawrence, and the Grand Trunk Railway from Detroit to Portland, aims a fatal blow at the commerce of New York. Is it of no account that these thoroughfares transport freight from Liverpool to the Western cities at an average of $7 per ton *less* than the *cost from New York to the same points!* Is it of no consequence to the citizens of New York that Great Britain has opened the contest for a direct trade with the West by the active employment of seven monster steamers to run in connection with the Grand Trunk Railway at Portland and her inland water routes at Quebec? When she offers to the farmers and merchants of the West a cheaper transportation to and from Liverpool than they have to and from the City of New York, is it possible for the latter to retain her trade unless her own railways come to her rescue? New York, therefore, the moment her own roads are compelled by legislative restrictions to relinquish their through traffic, has tremendous odds against her. Will our Legislature subject her to the unequal contest? Commerce is the life of cities, the soul of their prosperity. God forbid that ill-advised legislation should stifle that life in the Empire City of the Empire State.

We should not overlook the fact that railroads everywhere are developing an astonishing ability to move freight. Senator Prosser, of Buffalo, one of the staunchest advocates of the "*Pro Rata* bill," and an old canal forwarder, expressed the opinion before the Utica Convention, that the railroads have the ability to transport freight at *lower rates than the Canal.* We quote from his speech on that occasion the following remarkable words:—

"It is the ability of the railroads to work cheap which I fear.

Not but that they have often taken property at less than cost; that is undoubtedly so; but they have the ability to do the work extremely low in warm weather. The calculation that so great a loss accrues to railroads on the transportation of flour, &c., is a mistake. Those who are conversant with this business, who come to different conclusions, do so because they take the whole number of tons carried, and estimate the cost of all through freight the same. This is wrong. The stock trade being only one way, is more expensive than that in which the cars are loaded both ways. Freight of the latter class in Summer can be carried very cheaply on a well-balanced rail. If we make the estimate correctly, we shall find that the cost comes down to prices startlingly low. Deduct from these prices the cost of the Winter amount, and we arrive, in my judgment, at an ability to move enormous quantities at a cost of not over $3, from Buffalo to New York. Now, sir, I come to inquire if we have this ability in our public works? Have we got the ability to move property from Buffalo to New York at the low rate of $3 per ton? *No, sir, we have not got it.*"

Assuming that gentleman's opinion to be correct, we desire to ask him a few simple questions. Have not the railroads out of the State—some of them having much shorter distances and cheaper fuel in their favor—the same ability to carry freight at low rates as those within the State? And if, by your legislation, you force high rates upon our railroads, pray tell us is there any earthly reason to doubt that our carrying trade will be transferred to these thoroughfares?

Those who advocate these legislative restrictions are not agreed, as to the plan to be adopted. A large party insist on the enactment of the "Pro-Rata" freight bill of 1858. They allege, in support of this measure, that our railroads make exorbitant discriminations against the citizens of our own State; that the rates on *local* being much higher than they are on through freights, have the effect to depreciate the value of our farming lands, and to enhance the value of Western lands. Suppose they do charge higher on local than on through freights? What then? Will the remedy proposed relieve our farmers from Western competition? Were the Legislature to enact a prohibitory law—a law absolutely restraining our roads from carrying through freights, it would not change the relative positions of the farmers of the State of New York with respect to those of the West, except to the still greater injury of the former. Western produce would still find the same cheap and rapid transit to the seaboard by other outlets. No law whatever, unless it were to bring within its scope the railways of the South and North, the Canadian canals, the Ohio and Mississippi rivers, and the Atlantic, could by any possibility benefit our farmers or relieve them from competition with the cheap lands of the West. Our relative conditions in this respect are fixed and governed by a "higher law" than any the Legislature can enact.

But what are the facts in regard to the alleged discriminations? The record will show that our people pay to our railroads less per ton, per mile, on rail transportation within their own State than the people of Ohio, Indiana, Michigan or Illinois pay their railroads for the same service. Our local tariffs will exhibit a favorable comparison with those of any State in the Union. Whenever this statement shall be contradicted by the leading advocates of restrictive measures, it will be time to furnish the data for a just comparison. For the present we shall move one step further, and affirm and prove that the railroads of the West have established as wide, if not wider, discriminations between their local and through tariffs.

Take the following examples:

OHIO AND MISSISSIPPI RAILROAD.

From Cincinnati to St. Louis, 342 miles, the local tariff is higher than the through—

By $4 80 per ton on first class.

By $5 40 per ton on second class.

By $6 00 per ton on third class.

By $4 80 per ton on fourth class.

This gives an average of $5 25 per ton more on local for the same number of miles.

From Cincinnati to Trenton, though the distance is 31 miles less, the average *local* is $5 75 per ton more than the *through* rate.

CLEVELAND, COLUMBUS AND CINCINNATI RAILROAD.

From Cleveland to Columbus, 135 miles, the average *local* is $2 32 above the through rate.

From Cleveland to Delaware, 113 miles, the average *local* is $1 60 above the through rate.

SANDUSKY, DAYTON AND CINCINNATI RAILROAD.

From Sandusky to Dayton, 154 miles, the *local* is $2 25 above the through rate.

MICHIGAN SOUTHERN AND NORTHERN INDIANA RAILROAD.

From Toledo to Chicago, 243 miles, the average *local* is $2 90 per ton above the through rate.

From Toledo to White Pigeon the average *local*, though the distance is 119 miles *shorter*, is $2 50 per ton above the through rate.

MICHIGAN CENTRAL RAILROAD.

From Detroit to Kalamazoo, 143 miles, the average *local* is $2 65 per ton above the through price on 283 miles.

ILLINOIS CENTRAL RAILROAD.

From Chicago to Mattoon, 172 miles, the *local* average is 55 cents per ton greater than the through rate to Cairo, 365 miles.

The Pennsylvania road, the Baltimore and Ohio, the Grand Trunk Railway, and other competitors, discriminate far more against their *local* than our New York roads do. We might multiply illustrations to any extent, showing similar results. Now, while like discriminations exist in the Western States, and while the farmers on the lines of those roads are subject to them in sending their produce to the central points where it is collected for shipment to the sea-board, how can it be shown that they possess in this respect any relative advantage? Do the Western farmers all live in Cincinnati, or Chicago, or Detroit? Then do not the discriminations to which they are subject fairly offset similar discriminations in the State of New York. Carry out the principle of the *pro rata* scheme, and relieve the Western farmers also by applying it to their roads as well? Will that improve the condition of the farmers of New York? Have they contemplated the retroactive consequences they will bring upon themselves by a practical application of this doctrine to the Railroads of the Great West?

Nor is it a sufficient answer to our reasoning to say that the rates from the central points to the seaboard are disproportionately low. It proves too much. For the Erie Canal holds the same relation that our railroads do to those central points. Canal forwarders enjoy precisely the same advantages on the Lakes, and form the same alliances with the canals and railroads leading westward from the Lakes. In 1858 they had better contracts with the two Michigan roads than the New York Central had. Hence, if the low through rates on our railroads damage our farmers, much more are they injured by the canals. Besides, the canal forwarders have always adopted large discriminations against local and in favor of through freights. They carry from Buffalo to New York cheaper than from Brockport or Medina, and from New York to Buffalo cheaper than from New York to Utica. Every locality on the line pays as large differences to the canal forwarders as are paid to the railroads. If, therefore, the argument be sound that the low through rates depreciate the value of our farming property, all of *three-fourths* of the depreciation must be attributed to the canals; for, according to a statement of Canal Commissioner Ruggles, they carry more than three-fourths of the total tonnage! Will the advocates of the *pro rata* measure apply its provisions likewise to the transportation companies on the canals? Why not? Unless they do so, how are our farmers to be relieved from the alleged oppressive inequality? What do they gain? We need go no further for the causes which operate to the disadvantage of our farmers than the cheapness, easiness of culture, and superior fertility of the Western lands.

The process of equalization is at work, and no legislation under Heaven can arrest it, least of all the *pro rata* scheme. At the several *so-called* "Canal Conventions" held within the past year, a mass of statistics was presented to show that the New York and Erie and Central Roads had made ruinous discriminations against our own people, and in favor of the farmers of the West. To those who are familiar with the railroad freighting business the absurdity of these statistics will be at once apparent. To those who are not familiar with the details of such matters we would say that the pretended facts are not correctly given, and also that two radical *fallacies* underlie them all. First—Instead of comparing the *actual proportions* on through freights *received* by our roads with their local tariffs, these skilful reasoners take the *entire through rates* to the West, and compare them with the local. Whereas most of the alleged discriminations were caused, not by *our roads*, but by other connecting lines. Its second fallacy is seen in the fact that the through rates by rail *and water* are compared with our local *all-rail* rates, as if both rates were *all-rail*. The two fallacies here exposed are fatal to the correctness of their assumed premises, and equally so to their conclusions. No comparison can be just or trustworthy which rests on bases so glaringly fallacious.

It is simply idle to suppose that our railways would voluntarily adopt the present rates were it possible to obtain higher. Self-interest precludes the idea. They are forced to submit or abandon the business. The obvious design of the "*pro rata*" scheme is to place the roads in a position where, in order to preserve their local prices, they will be forced to adopt a proportionate scale on through freights. Its projectors hope by this course to transfer the through business to the canals. They know perfectly well that with the new scale of high rates the roads cannot possibly retain it.

We agree with them that the effect would inevitably be to deprive our roads of the business. But then comes the question, and a question, too, of momentous significance to the people of the State of New York, where and to what channels of transport will it be transferred? To the New York canals? or to rival thoroughfares outside of the State? To the latter beyond the possibility of doubt. Has it ever occurred to the advocates of the proposed law that all perishable articles, all the lighter and more costly goods, which require rapidity of transit, and which constitute what are denominated first and second class, and also the entire live-stock trade, never seek the canals? The live-stock trade and the trade in dressed hogs pay to the New York roads over $2,000,000 per annum. Competing roads desire all these classes of freight, and it is simply a question whether they shall have them or we. While the canals will not gain them our roads will lose them. Other roads will transfer this traffic to themselves, other cities will reap the profits, and the people of other States will receive the contingent disbursements pertaining to the process of transportation.

His Excellency Gov. Morgan, with a significant silence, ignores the *pro rata* scheme in his recent Message, but endorses and recommends the policy of imposing tolls.

We have watched the Governor's course too closely to question his patriotism, or to doubt for an instant the purity of his intentions; but, with all due respect, we express the belief that, should this hazardous experiment be tried, it will bring upon our noble State a series of calamities from which neither he nor we will ever live to witness a recovery. Commerce, like persons, will bear burdens which it cannot shirk; but at no period of the world's history has it ever voluntarily submitted itself to any burden whatever. It is the only thing in America which really knows no North, no South, no East, and no West. It goes where it finds the cheapest pathways, without regard to latitudes and longitudes or the boundaries of States. Toll-gates are institutions from which it instinctively recoils, and it will never patronize where it is possible to elude them. Does the existing situation of our carrying trade warrant the erection of these gates across the railways of the State of New York? Will they invite outside commerce? Will they preserve our internal commerce?

Our respected Auditor of the Canal Department, in his Annual Report for 1858, argues that "the imposition of canal rates of toll on the New York lines would not cause any diversion of trade from our own lines of railroads, or from our own commercial metropolis." To support his position he gives the following as the comparative rates of transportation from three of the seaboard cities to the West in 1858:

COST PER TON FROM	
Baltimore to Chicago	$23 07
Philadelphia to Chicago	20 16
New York to Chicago, by New York and Erie Railroad	13 38
New York to Chicago, by New York Central Railroad	10 82
New York to Chicago, by Canals, &c. . . .	7 12

Because the costs per ton, as he alleges, were higher in 1858 from Baltimore and Philadelphia to Chicago, than he says they were from New York, he argues that the imposition of tolls will not divert our trade.

Mr. Benton is extremely unfortunate in his statement of facts. Take the first item above as an example. We have in our possession, and can show to Mr. Benton, one of the original handbills of the Baltimore and Ohio Railroad Company, which were generally posted about New York in August, 1858, wherein they solicited freight from *New York* to Chicago by steamer and railroad, and offered to carry, first class, $10 per ton; second class, $8 per ton. Here, then, the fact turns out to be that the Baltimore and Ohio Railroad Company actually took freight from New York to Chicago at an average of more than $1 per ton *less* than the price Mr. Benton gives as the rate on the New York Central, and at $14 per ton *less* than the rate given by him from Baltimore to Chicago? Had Mr. Benton taken the trouble, he could easily have ascertained that it has been and still is the settled policy of the Baltimore and Ohio Company to make much *lower* rates from Baltimore to common points of the West than from New York. By the terms of the notorious St. Nicholas Compact, the comparative rates were, by all rail:

FROM BALTIMORE TO

Cincinnati	30	25	17	15	15	Less than from New York.
Columbus	30	25	20	15	15	
Cleveland	5	0	5	5	5	
Indianapolis	30	25	20	15	15	
Chicago	20	15	10	10	10	
St. Louis	30	25	20	15	15	

A similar scale existed in favor of Baltimore by rail and water. So with the Pennsylvania road. The New York merchants were alarmed by these low rates from Baltimore and Philadelphia, and appealed by earnest memorials to the Presisidents of the New York Central and New York and Erie Companies, to afford them relief. What relief could they afford? There was but one remedy, and that was to meet their antagonists by a corresponding reduction. It became with our roads a matter of necessity. They had to abandon the merchants of our great City to the mercy of their opponents, to a continued drain upon their trade, and suffer an equal loss to their own traffic and that of the State, or else equalize the cost of transportation by placing New York on a par with her rivals. This state of affairs still exists, and must exist. The operations of the Grand Trunk Railway, which the Auditor does *not* notice in his report, add immensely to the antagonism brought to bear against our New York roads, and against our commercial metropolis. Mr. Benton has been led into similar errors respecting the rates from Philadelphia. Yet it is from such fallacious statistics the advocates of restrictive measures deduce the conclusion that, if enacted, they would not operate injuriously upon our general trade.

But why did not Mr. Benton allude to the practical workings of this measure on our internal traffic? He does not explain to us how he expects property will go from Elmira to New York, over the New York and Erie, and pay tolls on 273 miles of railway, while it can reach Philadelphia, which is only two miles further, and Baltimore, which is twenty-one miles nearer, and pay *no tolls* at all. He does not allude to the fact that produce from Suspension Bridge to Philadelphia, *via* the Williamsport and Elmira road, would pay tolls on 171 miles in the State of New York; whereas, if it took our own roads from Buffalo, it would pay on 300 miles; nor does he tell us whether it would naturally choose the more costly or less costly route. He does not inform the people that from Buffalo to Philadelphia, *viâ* the Williamsport and Elmira road, it would save over 150 miles of tolls, which it would be compelled to pay if it were to take our own roads. Indeed, every town in the southern tier of counties, most of the towns in the central counties, and all of the northern towns and counties, will find it to their interests, in order to save tolls, to ship to rival seaboard cities rather than to New York, whenever the markets are equal, and even when they ship to New York, they will take the outside routes that intersect the southern part of the State.

For similar reasons a large portion of Western produce would avoid Buffalo and Rochester, and strike the State at Oswego or Cape Vincent, and shipments from New York to the West would turn off at the same points. We believe that practical experience will demonstrate that the effect of tolling our roads will be to materially *diminish* the traffic of the State both in local and through freights. Were it not for the *permanent loss* which must result to the City and State, we would not say a word against a trial of this experiment. We know that the clamor for repeal, within twelve months, would be a thousandfold more loud and potent than that which now calls for restriction. But we also know that when trade once passes under the control of rival interests, rival localities, and rival associations, all act upon it like so many magnets, and it cannot again be recovered except at a vast sacrifice and at a vast expense.

One of the last acts of that quiet, unassuming, noble man,

the late Isaac Newton—a man who was thoroughly conversant with these matters, was to appear before a Committee of the Senate, and utter his solemn protest against this ruinous policy.

More than eighteen hundred years ago, He who comprehended the blindness of mankind proclaimed that though one were to rise from the dead and bear witness to the truth, yet it would not be believed. It may be so in the case before us; but, nevertheless, that voice from the dead shall be heard, and its eloquent warnings be repeated, though they may not be heeded. Said Mr. Newton: "I affirm that instead of the New York and Erie and New York Central Railroad taking business from, they give business to the canals, by keeping the traffic of the West in this channel, by opening and cheapening the modes of transportation between the Lakes and the City of New York. * * * * * * But, Mr. Chairman, I feel an interest in this subject beyond dollars and cents. If you impose these tolls one of two things must take place. The railroads must either, in order to retain the trade, carry freight at prices that will ruin them, or charging a price that will enable them to live, the property will seek other routes. Every hoof, horn, and bushel must go by other routes if tolls are imposed upon the goods of this State. By so doing you may get a few dollars out of commerce, but the effects—the throwing of trade out of the State—will not be arrested in years. Your people will be impoverished and your treasury without funds. The world is not asleep. The railroads we have now are but a moiety of the railroads we will have in a few years. The object is to keep the control of the commerce until the great work, in which we all have so just a pride—the canals—are finished."

If the people of the City and State of New York could appreciate *all* the facts and considerations which bear upon this great issue, we would not fear the result. They would see, what must be evident to every reflecting mind, that this is not a question between our canals and railroads, but between all the thoroughfares of our State and those of other States. With the watchwords, "*Freedom to our railroads and an enlarged canal*," and the adoption of a corresponding policy, we may still retain our position as the *Empire State*, and our City will continue to be the Empire City. Herein is our only hope and our only safety.

NEW YORK.

Read and Circulate.

STATE OF NEW YORK,

IN ASSEMBLY, JANUARY, 1860.

PRO RATA SELECT COMMITTEE.

Proceedings before the Committee, and proofs and arguments offered against the Pro Rata measure, fraught with so much injury to the People, to the commerce and business of the State, and to the Railroads themselves.

WEDNESDAY, Jan. 25th, 1860.

The Special Committee met at 9 o'clock.

PRESENT—Mr. FLAGLER, Chairman, and Messrs. Varian, Conkling, Emerick, Smith, Fulton and Moulton.

The chairman announced that the committee was ready to hear additional statements.

Mr. SETH C. HAWLEY said: I wish to make an explanation of one item of the proof that was put in yesterday, lest it should be misunderstood, and mislead somebody as to our design in reference to it. I refer to the figures that were given to show the amount of the through freight and way freight, and the revenue of each, and the amount per ton per mile on each. The problem I stated, was what it would cost per ton on way freight, provided the railroad company made up the amount of receipts on both, by increasing the rate of way freight. The figures which you have are correct, except the rate per ton on the way freight, which should be $2.66, instead of $2.27; and before increasing the way rate, we should deduct from the gross amount received on the through freight the amount that it cost to carry it, leaving the profit on the through freight to be added to the way freight, to make up from the way freight an equal revenue. The receipts on the through freight were $8,325,055. The problem of exactly how much of the receipts are profits, is one that has not been proven to the satisfaction of everybody on any road. The best that can be done is to make approximate estimates sufficient for the purposes of business. Nobody will ask that we show positively the amount of profit for carrying a specific quantity a specific distance. I will suppose a case: we show that our through freights produce an average of one and three-quarters of a cent per ton per mile. I will assume that the naked cost for carrying was one cent per ton per mile. In that case, our profits would be three-quarters of a cent per ton per mile. The gross amount of this three-quarters of a cent per ton per mile, would make this problem complete by adding on way freights a price that would bring us an equal sum. That is to say, so much money as was profit on the through freight we would be entitled to on the way freight, to get the same amount of earnings if we carried through freight.

Mr. A. STONE, Jr., of Cleveland, Ohio, was then introduced as a witness, Mr. M. F. Seymour conducting the examination.

Q. State your place of residence and your business?

A. I reside at Cleveland, Ohio, and am President of the Cleveland & Erie Railroad Company; the Cleveland, Painsville and Ashtabula Road is the corporate name; it runs from Cleveland to Erie.

Q. How long have you resided in Cleveland?

A. Ten years.

Q. What has been your business for the last ten years in the State of Ohio?

A. Building and operating railroads.

Q. On what particular line?

A. From Cleveland to Columbus; I went there as contractor for that line, and have been a director since its completion; I was a contractor on the Cleveland & Erie road.

Q. You are now the president of the road you name?

A. Yes sir.

Q. Before going to Cleveland, were you connected with the construction of railways?

A. I was.

Q. In what way?

A. In the construction of different parts mechanically, and other parts, in the construction and operating; I was engaged in operating the road in 1845, between Springfield and New Haven.

Q. The people of the State of New York, or a portion of the people, are petitioning the legislature to pass a law to contain the following general provisions: [Mr. Seymour then read the provisions]. Will you please state in your own way the effect which you think the passage of that law would have upon the railroad interests of this state and the carrying trade from the west to the East?

A. There was a law introduced, or rather proposed, in Ohio, in 1852 and 1853, with similar provisions; it was then regarded as impracticable; it did not pass the legislature; after it was fully discussed, I thought it would be impracticable to put such a law in force, particularly upon through freights, as there are at least five thoroughfares from our place, Cleveland and the Atlantic, and the least embarrassment in trade over any one would tend to throw the trade on the other lines.

Q. What are the principal competing lines from Cleveland to the eastern markets?

A. The Baltimore and Ohio.

Q. Can you give the distance by it from Cleveland to New York?

A. Over the Baltimore & Ohio Railroad, from Cleveland, I think, by rail, is about 500 miles.

Q. From Cleveland to Baltimore?

A. Yes sir; to Philadelphia is about the same; there are two routes from Cleveland, and there is but little difference between them; the Pennsylvania Central and Baltimore & Ohio; the Pennsylvania Central to Philadelphia and Baltimore; then there is the New York & Erie and the New York Central; the Ogdensburgh route to Boston and the Grand Trunk route to Boston and Portland, making six routes by rail, beside the Erie canal.

Q. What is the distance from Cleveland to New York and Philadelphia by the Pennsylvania Central road?

A. From Cleveland to New York by the Central is about 625 miles; by the New York and Erie it is about 600; by the Pennsylvania Central a little less than 600,—595 miles.

Q. To New York City?

A. Yes sir: to New York City, by the Baltimore and Ohio road, all rail to New York, it is a little further—I do not recollect exactly the distance.

Q. How do you regard the relative capacities of these different lines for the carrying trade?

A. The Pennsylvania Central claim that they have the cheapest route. They have always been in the market for business at the lowest prices, and they have often been below the lowest rates. Whether the Grand Trunk is cheaper or not, I do not know, but they have still lower prices than any other lines.

Q. Has there been much competition at Cleveland for the eastern freight, between these different lines?

A. There has been very great competition, amounting to the transportation of property at about net cost to the Atlantic cities.

Q. The Grand Trunk road does not compete so directly with these for through freight at Cleveland, as it does for the west?

A. It does not when navigation is open. It only competes by striking some tributaries at places west of us.

Q. What are these tributaries further west?—Cincinnati, Cleveland, Chicago?

A. At Columbus is the furtherest point where they have been felt. They strike Columbus and they compete with all the other thoroughfares north and west of Columbus.

Q. State any other fact you think pertinent in connection with that branch of the subject?

A. I can only say that the present policy of advancing on freights at the present rates, if it can be carried out in the manner which the Grand Trunk has taken, is such that no other line, embarrassed or unembarrassed, can carry property at a profit from the points they reach. They have made prices so low that no other line can take freight if it is to be continued. They have commenced advancing money on freights transported by them through to the Atlantic cities and England. They have made rates at less than one cent per ton per mile, and have taken large quantities of freights at these rates.

Q. Do you know of their having contracted for freight to Liverpool?

A. I saw their tariff distributed over the west, giving the rates from all the prominent points to Liverpool and London; and I have heard that contracts have been made according to those tariffs. It is undoubtedly the case that contracts have been made, and are being made daily, at those rates, from those points to Liverpool and London.

Q. Suppose the railroads of this state, competing for the western trade, should be compelled to fix permanent rates for a month, on their different lines, and post them up in conspicuous places, how would it affect the chances of their obtaining much of this through business, in competing with other roads?

A. If such a tariff were published and fixed without change—if it were at or below net cost, the line might do a proportion of the business; but if it afforded a profit, to any extent, the competing lines would take it at enough below to entirely control the trade; ten cents per ton would change it from one route to another.

Q. You mean to say that they could not do any through business except at a loss?

A. That would be the practical result.

Q. That would be the effect at Cleveland, and other points west, Cincinnati and Chicago. Would the same principle apply at those points?

A. It would.

Q. We would like to have you give your views in regard to the comparative cost of transporting through freight and way freight, with reference to the pro rata principle, as suggested in that petition?

A. It is difficult to estimate the accurate comparative cost between through and way freight. There are very many elements that change that. A large amount of local traffic is done at a loss, as there are many stations on different routes that do not receive as much income as it costs to maintain them. As a whole, local tariffs have been regarded as not more profitable than through, heretofore. The increase cost per mile is varied according to circumstances, and varied from 25 per cent to two or three hundred per cent or more. I think that the amount of dead weight carried in proportion to the productive freight in local business, as a whole, compared with the through, is two to one, as the cars are not fully loaded. Besides, the local trains, from necessity, average very much less than the through trains. On one part of the road the train may not have more than five cars, and on another part may have twenty-five. They average at least from 20 to 40 per cent less cars in the transportation of local than in through trains.

Mr. HAWLEY—You mean less cars in the train?

A. Yes, sir; less cars in the train. Another element is, more weight per ton carried, in proportion, on way trains than on through.

Q. I would like to call your attention to one of the elements of extra cost to which you have alluded. Your remark has been more particularly in reference to the running of the trains. What do you regard as the per centage chargeable to the supply of stations, switches, furniture and outfit of the road for transacting way business, such as would not be required if no way business were done? I would like to have that explained a little, in detail, to show to the committee the extra cost chargeable to that element of business?

A. The outlay varies very much upon different roads, to accommodate the local and through business. My judgment would be that it would vary from 15 to 30 per cent.

Q. On the entire cost of the road?

A. Yes, sir.

Q. I suppose you mean to include the permanent fixtures, or do you intend to include the switching and extra men employed at these stations?

A. I understood your question to refer to the permanent outlay, and had no regard to the running.

Q. That was it. Are there other charges connected with it?

A. Yes, sir; charges for delay, transportation, men employed at the way stations. A man may be employed at a way station at a cost of $40 per month, and not ship more than a ton of freight per week.

Q. Do you think of any other items of expense?

A. I do not now.

Q. How much longer does it require to run way trains than through trains, and what are the causes of the extra length of time in running the same distance?

A. It depends very much upon the amount of way business. But generally the way train is given about 20 per cent more time. The record shows that the engine consumes about 20 per cent more fuel for the same number of cars, or about 25 per cent, and that it takes about 20 per cent more time to do the way than the through business.

Q. Do you think there is any difference in the cost of transportation of freights between the winter and the summer seasons?—and if so what are the causes of it.

A. It costs more in the winter. It has been as high as 40 per cent more, and again it might not exceed more than 15 or 20 per cent in a mild winter.

Q. Will you state why it costs more?

A. The average number of cars hauled in a train through a series of years, I think is about 25 per cent less in the winter than in the summer, with the same engine.

Q. Are there breakages of rails, &c.?

A. The breakages are perhaps four to one in winter as compared with the summer. Some winters it has been so great as to almost stop the traffic, caused by the breaking of wheels, axles and rails; metal of any kind is more weak when it is frosted than at other times.

Q. Do you generally run trains in the winter at as high a rate of speed as in summer?

A. It is generally reduced about 10 to 15 per cent.

Q. Which of the through routes from Cleveland are the less liable to obstructions from snow?

A. It has been the least upon the Pennsylvania Central, I think, and on the Baltimore and Ohio.

Q. From that and other circumstances, do you regard those roads you have mentioned, as in any way formidable competitors for the carrying of these freights to the more northern routes—freights from the south and southwest?

A. The practical result has been that they have always made as low rates since the roads opened for business, as either the northern routes, and with the same rates have had their full proportion of the traffic. They show their ability to do it by their net results at the end of the year.

Q. What is the relative cost of fuel on those roads, and the New York Roads?

A. Not to exceed one-third, on the Baltimore and Ohio, as compared with the New York Roads.

Q. They use coal there?

A. Yes sir.

Q. And on the Pennsylvania Central, is it cheaper generally?

A. It may be about one-half.

Q. That I suppose is an important element in the running of the road?

A. A very important item.

Q. What is the effect of reducing the tolls on the Erie Canal, on the carrying rates from the West by railroads?

A. My impression is that there has been about the same carried by rail and canal.

Q. I mean its effects upon prices?

A. It effects prices in the proportion as the lowering of the tolls. Prices have been more than as much lower than the difference in the toll, for the last two years. I think the Erie Canal rates control the rates in the South West as far as Cincinnati, control the rates from all points on the Ohio River, from Portsmouth to Cairo, and up the Mississippi. Whatever are the rates on the Erie Canal, they determine the rates and the other competing lines all compete with those rates. It has been more evident, since the reduction of the tolls, that the New York routes could maintain their position, in the summer as against the other routes, than ever before, their ability to do the carrying trade, to control it at a rate above the present rates. It would seem to me a very small per cent above the present rates by the Erie Canal, would throw the traffic on to other roads.

Q. Are you familiar with the New York and Erie Railroad?

A. I am somewhat.

Q. Have you ever been over it?

A. I have traveled over it several times, and have done business in connection with it for the last ten years.

Q. Before going into the details in reference to the Erie road, I will ask you: Suppose this policy of the pro rata be adopted, and it amounts, as you think it would, to a prohibition of the carrying of through freights over railroads of this state, what course do you think freight would take?—would it go over the canals of this state, or other competing railroads, as near as you can judge?

A. It would diminish from the canal and increase upon the other roads.

Q. Why would it diminish by the canals do you think?

A. The proposition was, if they increased the tolls.

Q. If this policy was adopted requiring pro rata rates, I think you said it would prevent any carrying over the roads of this state of through freights; what route—what channel would it take?

A. The tendency of all freights of value now is, to go by rail; it would seek the rail lines as it can go so much quicker; the loss of interest, too, is so much less, and various influences tend to throw freight on the railroads, as the difference is so small between the cost on rail lines and the canal.

Q. Is the absolute cost of transportation the controlling influence in fixing the rate, or is it the demand for the article in the market and the rate of exchanges?—I would like to have you state the influences?

A. There are two—time and cost; to certain parties time is of no account—to other parties it is everything.

Q. A sudden demand for instance?

A. Yes sir.

Q. In your railroad experience, have you ever known railroads to do a through and way-freight business at the same rate—at a pro rata rate?

A. No sir.

Q. Do you think it can be done successfully on any road with which you are acquainted, in doing both classes of business under the same rate of charges per ton per mile?

A. It might be done if other thoroughfares, both by water and rail, adopted the same plan; but while every point has two or more modes of transportation—thoroughfares—it would be impracticable.

Q. Will you state the reasons to the Committee why it would be impracticable?

A. The through rate, controlled by the net cost pro rata, would be so high, that it would enable the competitor, who is not restricted, to make profits on the through business, and to extend and control it. A pro rata making a through rate which would be based upon net cost for local, would be so high as to afford a profit to competing lines, and lines restricted by the pro rata would be deprived of its entire business, and would have to do either a through or local business entirely; that is so far as profits are concerned.

Q. Which do you think the New York roads would have to do under this regulation, a through or a way business? What would be the result in that respect?

A. I am not prepared to answer that question.

Q. If they had to do a freight business at pro-rata charges, I would like to know which in your judgment they would sacrifice, the way or the through freight?

A. One line might do one and another the other. They could not do both on the same tariff on that basis.

Q. Will you give me your opinion as respects the New York and Erie road, which it would be likely to do under such a restriction, whether it could do any through business under that arrangement at a paying rate?

A. I think it could not do any in the summer season. In the winter it might. You could not make a summer tariff and do any business on a basis of that kind.

Q. What would be the effect of such a restriction upon any one railroad, as to increasing the amount of business done by it, or increasing the value of its stock, or enabling it to pay the interest upon its indebtedness, or anything of that kind? Whether it would be considered beneficial as a measure, or one quite the reverse generally?

A. I think, if any one line was restricted from the Mississippi valley to the Atlantic cities and all the rest were left free, it would annihilate its value practically.

Mr. CONKLIN—Take these five or six several routes which you have described, is it your opinion that the adoption of this policy would tend to the destruction of the value of both the New York Central and the New York and Erie railroads?

A. It would destroy the entire value of the Erie, and would injure the Central very much, although its local business might pay something over its running expenses.

Mr. CONKLIN—Is it your opinion that the adoption of this policy would tend to the augmentation of the rates on through freights, and not to the diminution of the rates on the way business?

A. I think it would leave the through rates about the same. There are so many other thoroughfares that the entire freight can be carried by other routes to the Atlantic cities.

Mr. CONKLIN—I don't know as I made myself fully understood. We will suppose the case of the New York and Erie Road. The Legislature enacts a law that the rates of transportation on way and through business shall be the same per ton per mile. Now, in your opinion, would that policy tend to increase the present through rates, or to diminish the present way rates?

A. I think the tendency would be to increase the way rates, and not to affect the through rates much. If there was but one thoroughfare, the result would be to increase the way and through rates the same.

Mr. FLAGLER—Does your road (the Cleveland, Painesville and Ashtabula) ever pro rate with either of the New York and Erie, or New York Central, in rates of freight passing over one or the other of these New York roads?

A. Yes, sir.

Mr. FLAGLER—Divide in proportion to the distance carried?

A. Not on everything, at all times; but in a large proportion we do.

MR. FLAGLER—You stated that the competition you meet with on through freights, is so great, that at times, freights are transported at cost. Have you any opinion as to what proportion of this business you speak of is carried at cost, and without profit?

A. During the last eight months a very large proportion has come to very near cost.

Mr. FLAGLER—And on the balance, will you give us your opinion, whether there is much of any profit on that, even?

A. There is a very fair profit on certain portions of the through traffic.

Mr. FLAGLER—Can you give us an opinion with regard to this through business you speak of, as a whole? Is it, or is not profitable, or very profitable to the railroads dividing it?

A. I think it has not been very profitable for the last year. I think the time will soon come when it will be.

Cross-Examination.—Mr. COBB—What is the distance from Cleveland by the Grand Trunk road to New York?

A. I cannot give you the distance accurately. I think the rail used on the Grand Trunk is about 750 miles. We do not regard it as a competitor at Cleveland, but at points beyond.

Mr. COBB—Then from Columbus, via the Grand Trunk to New York, you regard the Grand Trunk as in direct competition?

A. Perhaps you misunderstood me in the remark I made in relation to the Grand Trunk.

Mr. COBB—I understood you to say that at Columbus the Grand Trunk came in competition from the west by cutting off supplies for Cleveland?

A. Yes, sir. Allow me to explain how it is. Portland is a point where a great deal of traffic has gone, but heretofore from Cincinnati and Columbus to Baltimore, and thence by propeller to Portland. By the Grand Trunk the business can go from Cincinnati and Columbus direct to Portland. I do not regard the Grand Trunk as a competitor for New York business, except as it may affect the Liverpool and London trade.

Mr. COBB—You mentioned that there was 25 per cent less to run the engine in summer than in winter. Does that grow out of the inability of the engine to haul, or because you wish to run a given number of trains, or that the number of cars ——— ?

A. The friction of the cars is much greater.

Mr. COBB—Then it is the inabilty to haul?

A. Yes sir.

Mr. COBB—You mentioned the appreciation or depreciation of the rates of freight as compared with the rates of the canal. What periods of the year are these manifested?

A. From June to August are the lowest rates generally, on account of the small amount of freight to be carried, going west or coming east.

Mr. COBB—Is there any period of the year, for a series of years, about which time the rates have either appreciated or depreciated?

A. I have no general impression upon that. I think the opening of the Erie canal has generally been the time at which the rates have usually changed on both classes to the west. There has been a reduction at that time.

Mr. COBB—At any period of the year has there been an advance?

A. On the closing of the canal the rates have changed again.

Mr. COBB—Is that confined only to third or fourth class merchandise, or is it confined to provisions, flour, &c.?

A. Provisions and flour are rated as fourth class?

Mr. COBB—When rated at all?

A. Yes sir.

Mr. COBB—But are they not carried at special rates without reference to classification or the prices of that class?

A. It is done so to quite an exent from the west. But since there has been an agreement between the different lines for common rates they have often put them in the fourth class. But a large proportion has been carried under special contracts from important points at the west.

Q. I think of one question which I would like to ask you. Being president of a road, I suppose you have attended these railroad conventions, which has been held at different points, to agree upon freights and passenger rates, &c.?

A. I have generally attended them for the last ten years.

Q. Will you explain to the Committee the effect of these meetings on prices of freight, whether at these conventions rates have been agreed upon and advanced generally, and which are considered to be binding by those carrying interests?

A. General conventions have been held which have had a very favorable effect in that direction, but they have not been a cure of low rates. It is by the ability of one line to change its rates at three hours notice which has kept rates up. Conventional rules have not been very much regarded.

Q. Explain that a little more fully—the keeping of rates up or below a losing rate?

A. Conventional rates are agreed upon and are publicly known to the world. If any one line holds strictly to these rules, there is some other of the great lines that would be quite apt through their agents to make lower rates; but if it is known that others are prepared to change on the same day they do, there is but little inducement to change. The rate is being adhered to more than formerly—more generally than it was a few years ago. It is only the ability to change rates at once that keeps them up; there is no other process that seems to answer the purpose—no other policy.

Q. Do you think the railroads of our State would have the ability, if the provisions in this proposed bill were carried out, of appearing in these conventions by their agents to fix these rates?

A. If your State has the ability to support a line below cost, and sustain it, you would probably do all the business; but if you published rates through the west, that afford a profit, to be binding for thirty days, other lines would put their rates just enough below to get the traffic until you published another tariff.

Mr. HAWLEY—Is there certain classes of freight that are deemed railroad freight, under certain circumstances, and others which go on railroads always? if so, what classes have that tendency?—I mean, supposing that there are rail lines to transport it.

A. Where there are rail lines, at least 95 per cent of the third and fourth classes go by rail, at all times, as against the canals.

Mr. CONKLIN—Which classes ?

A. The third and fourth classes—no, the first and second—not the third and fourth.

Mr. CONKLIN—You have several times alluded to first class merchandize where railroads and canals do not come into competition. What are they ?

A. The first class embraces all valuable goods—dry goods, &c. The first and second—

Mr. CONKLIN—You mean goods valuable in proportion to their bulk ?

A. Hats and caps—dry goods. New England domestics are generally classed in second class.

Mr CONKLIN—You mean cotton sheetings, &c. ?

A. Yes, Sir. They generally go on rail, except where there are propeller lines. Those goods go on propeller lines to a large extent. It is in fourth class generally that the canal competes with the railroads.

Mr. CONKLIN—What articles are in the fourth class ?

A. Sumber, provisions, flour, grain.

Q. Ores, iron and coal ?

A. Yes, Sir. Iron, coal and lumber nearly all go by canal when navigation is open.

Mr. ALLEN—In what are groceries classified ? the third and fourth classes ?

A. Sugar in large quantities, and molasses and coffee are generally in the fourth class. Coffee is about the only article that the rail competes with the canal in the fourth class in the summer time. It is an article that they carry a larger per cent of than any other of that class; it is more valuable.

Mr. ALLEN—In speaking of railroad conventions, would the prices established during the season of canal navigation by these conventions, be somewhat regulated by the prices of transportation on the canals, and, to a degree be governed by them in making the prices ?

A. Yes, Sir, they are generally governed by them in the fourth class—the higher classes.

Mr. ALLEN—Of heavy goods ?

A. Yes, Sir.

Mr. ALLEN—In connection with this subject what is the difference generally—the extreme difference between the prices of first and fourth class articles—charged usually by rail ?

A. The first class is generally not less than one hundred per cent more than the fourth class and is often one hundred and twenty-five per cent more. Once and a quarter, and once and a half more in some tariffs.

Mr. CONKLIN—Do these rates vary according to the value of the goods—for instance—does the consumer pay any more on $100 worth of goods in the first class than he does on the same value of the fourth class ?

Mr. HAWLEY—The same quantity you mean ?

Mr. CONKLIN—Take $100 worth owing to the value of the goods ?

A. On some articles it would be the same—the same price for the same value—on others it would not.

Q. Do you transport any milk on your western roads ?

A. No, Sir, not to any extent worth noticing.

Mr. CONKLIN—You have found in the prosecution of your business as president of the Cleveland, Painesville and Ashtabula road that the competition between the Erie canal and the railroads of this state is exclusive or chiefly in the transportation of merchandise of the fourth class ?

A. Yes, Sir, but not entirely.

Mr. HAWLEY—I want to ask you if the low rates of last year have had any effect in extending the region through which we compete to the southwest, and what effect it has had in drawing trade from that quarter ?

A. Last year—the last two years—a greater area has been controlled and covered by the northern lines than previous years.

Mr. HAWLEY—Is that due to the low prices, do you think ?

A. It is. The present tolls on the Erie Canal will control a large portion of the freights from the Ohio Valley.

Mr. HAWLEY—Has the increase or diminution of the tolls on the Erie Canal extended the area of trade in that direction ?

A. It has always had a very decided effect at Cairo.

Mr. HAWLEY—Have you been able to observe when the tolls were reduced, that there was an effect produced of extending the reach of the canal in the southwest ?

A. Yes, Sir. Prior to the opening of the Baltimore and Ohio and Pennsylvania Railroads, to the southwest, the Mississippi river was the competing route.

Mr. HAWLEY—What effect did the late reduction of tolls on the canal have on the prices of freights on railroads ? Did the reduction enable canals and railroads to receive so much per ton for freight or did they have to go down also ?

A. They did go down in proportion to the reduction of tolls upon the canal.

Mr. ALLEN—Are you governed by the valuation of goods or their bulk and weight ?

A. Both have an influence in determining the rates, as we are insurers on the rail and charge higher for valuable goods in consequence of their liability to destruction in our hands.

Mr. ALLEN—What proportion do you charge upon the valuation—I mean approximatively ?

A. There can be no fixed rule. Pig iron, for instance, cannot be damaged.

Mr. ALLEN—I speak in reference to the bulk of articles, such as dry goods, hats and caps, furniture, what you generally class as second class goods ?

A. We cannot adopt any rigid definite rule with regard to that. It is a matter of general judgment. There are a good many very valuable silks which necessarily have to go in a stock of goods in the same class with certain other kinds of cheaper goods. They go in, and though they have the same bulk, they are of much greater value. It is impracticable to control that entirely without making too many classes.

Mr. ALLEN—Then you are governed generally by bulk ?

A. Yes Sir.

The committee took a recess to three o'clock.

The committee re-assembled at three o'clock, all the members being present.

CHARLES MINOTT made the following statement, the examination being conducted by Mr. Hawley.

Q. What is your present occupation?

A. I am superintendent of the New York and Erie Railroad.

Q. State what length of time you have been in that relation to the New York & Erie Railroad, and when you were appointed?

A. For nearly five months back, and from May 1st, 1850, to May 1st, 1854.

Q. Something over four years?

A. Four years and five months nearly.

Q. Had you been familiar with railroad business prior to that?

A. I had been on the Boston and Maine Railroad, in Massachusetts, and on the Michigan Southern road in the west.

Q. For what length of time, about, on all these roads?

A. Nearly 19 years in all, on different roads.

Q. During that time has it been in your line of business and duty, to investigate and understand the carrying traffic between the East and the West, over the regions which you have mentioned?

A. It has.

Q. Will you state to the Committee the length of the New York and Erie road, and the divisions in which it is operated?

A. The distance from Jersey City to Dunkirk is 460 miles; the eastern division is 88 miles.

Q. Reaching to what point?

A. To Port Jervis; the Delaware division from Port Jervis to Susquehanna is 104 miles; the Susquehanna division from Susquehanna to Hornellsville is 140 miles, and the Western division, from Hornellsville to Dunkirk, is 128 miles.

Q. What are the grades and curvatures as respects the Eastern and Western divisions?

A. On the Eastern division there are quite a number of grades of 60 feet to the mile; on the Western division there is no grade over 50 feet; on the Susquehanna there is none over 10 feet to the mile; and on the Delaware division none over 15 feet, except at Deposit—between there and Susquehanna, where the grade is 60 feet, for 15 miles, going over the summit.

Q. Will you state the railroad connections of the New York & Erie road, commencing at Dunkirk and going east?

A. At Dunkirk, with the Buffalo and Erie and Lake Shore roads; at Hornellsville, with the Attica aud Buffalo roads.

Q. Leading to Buffalo?

A. Yes, sir, leading to Buffalo; at Corning with the Buffalo and New York road, which goes to Rochester and Buffalo; at Elmira with the Williamsport road, which connects with roads leading to Philadelphia.

Q. Is there a route to New York through that connection?

A. There is.

Q. How does that route to New York compare with your own?

A. It is considerable further.

Q. What is the next connection East?

A. At Owego, it connects with the road to Ithaca; at Binghampton, with the road to Syracuse; at Great Bend it connects with the Delaware, Lockawanna and Western road to New York.

Q. Can you tell the distance by the Delaware and Lockawanna road to New York, as compared with your own?

A. It is a little longer, I cannot give the number of miles.

Q. Is there any further connection East of that?

A. None except our own branch to Newburgh, and the branch to Piermont; at Corning we connect with the Blossburgh road which leads to the coal regions.

Q. I wish you to state to the Committee what you consider the competing lines of transportation, competing with your road for the great traffic between the East and the West and South-West, and the North and East?

A. The Baltimore and Ohio, the Pennsylvania Central, through Philadelphia, and with its Allentown connection, not going through Philadelphia, but making a short cut to New York.

Mr. CONKLIN—Connecting with the New Jersey Central?

A. Yes, sir. The New York Central, the Erie Canal and the Grand Trunk.

Q. The Grand Trunk terminates at Portland, does it not?

A. At Portland.

Q. What is the character of Portland as to its harbor, compared with New York, Philadelphia and Boston?

A. It is the best harbor in the United States. They have the deepest water there, and it is never frozen.

Q. How much nearer is that to Liverpool than New York, about?

A. It is a little over three hundred miles.

Q. What is the present Railroad connection of the Grand Trunk, with the roads of the United States?

A. They own the line to Detroit.

Q. Is there any connection between them and Toronto, with the Canada and Great Western road?

A. Certainly.

Q. Then, at Detroit, they connect with all the roads connecting with the Michigan Central west, and the Michigan Southern west?

A. Yes, Sir; and the Dayton and Michigan road to Cincinnati, and the northwest with the Detroit and Milwaukie?

Q. By that route they cross Lake Michigan?

A. Yes, Sir, on boats.

Q. Considering the traffic that is now the subject of investigation, to be between that wide western, northwestern, southwestern, and the east and northeast to Europe, state, in your opinion, how small an amount of ascertained and certain advantage would turn the freights of the country.

A. A very small price per ton, with the same time.

Q. I mean all things considered as an advantage?

A. A very small difference in freight—say 20 cents per ton. I could hardly say it would be so small.

Q. Do you not consider that the lines of competition you have named, are really in the field of competition against the New York and Erie and the New York Central roads?

A. They all are, except the Allentown connection of the Pennsylvania, which will be the coming season. They are all in active competition.

Q. Can you tell me how much the Allentown route reduces the distance—about how much?

A. I forget; but I think, from Chicago, 60 miles over the Erie; I am not sure; I may be wrong.

Q. That is the last and newest route?

A. Yes, Sir; it and the Grand Trunk, which completed its western connection this year.

Q. Can you, from recollection, name the route of all these from the West to the East which, in the summer, presents the shortest line of rail to New York.

A. From Chicago, do you mean?

Q. From the west; from Chicago?

A. The Pittsburgh, Fort Wayne and Chicago.

Q. I want to call your attention to the distance by rail from Buffalo to Albany, and from Oswego to Albany, supposing the freight to go by Lake to Oswego, and by river from here to New York; how much rail line is there?

A. I don't know the distance to Oswego.

Mr. HAWLEY—It is 183 miles.

A. I know it is so much less that the freight would go to Oswego instead of Buffalo or Dunkirk.

Q. Under pro rata?

A. Under pro rata, certainly. It would be 183 miles by rail against 300 by the Central.

Q. From here to Buffalo?

A. Yes, sir; and while on the Lakes the transportation would be very small.

Q. In reaching out for this traffic what motives govern your road in fixing its rates of tariff?

A. We try to fix them at such a rate as will give us the most money for the least work.

Q. Then I understand you that there is no tendency to carry freights lower than is necessary to get them?

A. Certainly not.

Q. In making out a tariff of this kind, when you are in full competition with these routes, are there times when, in a business point of view, you would be justified in carrying freight below what it would cost to carry it?

A. It might, to bring other roads to terms, and make them agree upon some fair tariff, for a short time to carry lower than cost.

Q. Then in competition it is deemed good business policy at times to carry at less than cost for the purpose of forcing competitors on compensating ground?

A. Most certainly, it is occasionally done.

Q. Which do you consider the greater, the cost of transporting through or way freights on your road?

A. There can be no question, the way freight costs more than the through.

Q. Give in detail the elements of the increased cost on way over through freights, as you view it in your railroad offices?

A. One element is that we take, on our road, twice the time to get a way train over, than a through freight train. We have to start with one or two cars at the commencement and by the time it gets through we calculate to have a full train. Frequently we do not get it; we have to run that risk. Therefore the average load of a way train is less than that of the through train, with which we start at the end of the road with as many cars as we can haul. Then at every station, with the way trains, we have to stop and back into the switches.

Mr. FLAGLER—Don't you have a regular time for starting through trains?

A. We start the train on time. We start the way train with few cars and empty.

Mr. FLAGLER—When your time comes you start a through train?

A. I did not understand you. When we have no business for a through train we do not start them.

Q. But your way business demands that you run them regularly?

A. Yes, sir, we must get some freight.

Q. You depend upon the accident of getting freight?

A. We do.

Q. Does it ever occur that you do not get as much way freight as you can draw?

A. We rarely do. It is an accident if we do. In loading as we do at way stations, we have to do it hastily, and they cannot get it so closely packed as it is in through trains. We carry twice the number of men, brakemen, that we do on through freight trains, because they have to do this loading.

Q. Is there any element of increased expense in the wear and tear of train and track, by reason of these frequent stoppages?

A. Of course there is; in stopping and starting, applying the brakes to the trains.

Q. Is there a larger consumption of fuel per ton?

A. Yes, sir, every stop is a large element of cost.

Q. Does it cost a larger amount of wages per ton for your employees?

A. That is so, because we only run way trains about half as fast, and it takes nearly twice the men.

Q. State, if you please, the increased cost of the original investment in a road on account of way stations, switches, turn-outs, side track, and increased expense of stations, that are called for by way business as compared with through business. State if you can, what per cent of cost it is more than through freight?

A. If the Erie Railroad was only arranged for doing through business, more than seven-eighths of the expenses would be saved.

Q. In stations?

A. Of stations, turn-outs and those accommodations for freight houses, certainly seven-eighths would be saved.

Q. Can you make an approximate estimate of the cost of these stations?

A. I cannot, and the same would apply to the help, the help at the stations would be diminished in the same way.

Q. What proportion is there between the number of cars on a through train and on a way train on your road?

A. I never looked to see; we start with one or two, and we pick up all the way; we do not carry so many; I have never looked to see, but the number is much less, of course.

Q. This petition asks that each railroad in this state publish their tariff once each month, the same to remain fixed for the month, and that each company be compelled to charge pro rata an equal sum per ton per mile, or quantity per mile, on the whole length of the road, what effect would that restriction have upon your road when you were in the western market competing for through freights—how would it operate?

A. It would be very injurious, for we could not meet the competitions of other roads by coming down as low as they, and we should lose a great deal of business; they would have it in their power to fix their tariff so that we could not get any through business, or very little, if any; the other roads, knowing our tariff, would arrange theirs so as to get the whole of it.

Q. The other roads chose to make special rates, do they not?

A. They do very often.

Q. If they knew your rate on the first day of May, and you were bound to charge those rates during the month, would you stand any chance of getting any freight as against them?

A. I think they would be very apt to get the freight at rates a little less than ours.

Q. Are there any points on your route where other roads can compete for your way business to New York?

A. The Delaware & Lackawanna can compete for our way business west of Great Bend.

Q. How is it as to Elmira?

A. The Elmira and Williamsport could compete, but the competition would not be very great, because the road is not a good one; in transporting freights, a little additional distance does not make much difference.

Q. Is it not in the power of longer routes to fix the rates of shorter routes to bid against them?

A. The Grand Trunk is giving all our roads our through rates.

Q. They are able to fix the minimum to you by bidding down?

A. Yes, sir; they are doing it.

Q. Will that principle apply to the Elmira and Williamsport road?

A. Yes sir.

Q. Under all the circumstances, suppose you were subject to that restriction, what, in your judgment, would be the necessary course of the New York & Erie road in deciding which branch of that traffic they would retain, and which they would give up?

A. I think they would give up the through business, beyond all doubt.

Q. Could you get the through business at way rates?

A. Not by any means; we should get none at all.

Q. Suppose you fixed your pro rata way rates so that they would pay you a small compensation, could you get through freights at any such figure?

A. At any reasonable compensation, I do not think we could get any through business at all.

Q. Could you do way business at the rate you would be required to do through business in competition?

A. Not profitably at all. We might save ourselves. There would be no profit in the investment, or profit over and above the actual cost of doing the work.

Q. You mean over and above the current expenses of the work, and not the interest on the debt?

A. Not at all.

Q. Then if they had no other business than that, at that rate you would be running in debt?

A. Yes, sir; every year.

Q. What would be the effect on prices of way freight, by your road attempting to live by getting a compensating revenue out of the way freight, upon the prices of way freight?

A. We should have to increase the price to get a reasonable interest on our investment, to pay the interest on our bonds. We should have to increase the way freight beyond all question.

Q. And if you were cut down to such a business is there any economies you could introduce in the way of dispensing with stations or other things that would economize your work; I mean those establishments which you have set np for the accommodation of way freight?

A. There are stations at which the profits of the business done do not pay the expenses.

Q. Then true economy would require you to abolish these?

A. Looking only to the interests of the road and not to the accommodation of the people, it would require it.

Q. In your opinion what proportion of the expenditure for way stations, to accommodate way freight, would be saved if you confined yourself to through business?

A. Seven-eighths of it would be saved, I am convinced.

Q. Assuming that you were compelled to pro rata, to charge equal prices per quantity and distance on all articles, what would be the effect of the traffic in small articles, as, for instance, those usually taken by express?

A. There could be no express over the road. It would ruin the Express Companies beyond question.

Q. Will you explain what would be the difficulty of Express Companies doing business under such an arrangement, where quantities were pro rated?

A. Their profits are on small packages, on whtch they get from 25 to 50 cents upon two or three pounds. Under a pro rata bill that would have to be carried at a regular price per ton, and the Railroad Companies would have to do it, and all the Express Companies would have remaining to do, would be carrying money, packages and valuable papers, &c.

Q. What would be the effect on the express business by the increased time that would result from running way trains alone?

A. If it was ruined before, I suppose it would be to ruin it again. [Laughter.]

Q. Would it not compel the Express Companies to do business on other routes?

A. It would throw the Express on roads out of the State, that is certain.

Q. What is your opinion as to the necessity of competing railroads having the power to fix rates from day to day for long freights?

A. It is a very great element of power to enable us to keep up prices, by our being able to meet our competitors, if they are taking a course that we think injurious.

Q. The railroad companies have conventions at times, the object of which is to fix prices so that they should not go too low?

A. They do.

Q. They never meet for the purpose of lowering prices, do they?

A. They generally meet when they have got them down so low that they can't live any longer.

Q. Suppose you were doing business under a pro rata bill, how much respect, do you think, you would command in such a convention as that—your road?

A. We should be powerless under those circumstances.

Q. What is the general practice of railroads in regard to having their agencies, roads outside of the state having them in this state, and the roads of New York having agencies in Western cities?

A. Most of the important lines have agents west, and most of the Western lines in New York to look after their freight business.

Q. Is fuel considered a large element of expense?

A. It is a very large element.

Q. Are you able to state about the cost per mile for fuel on your road?

A. On some roads it is from 23 to 24 cents; on the Baltimore and Ohio road it is only two or three cents.

Q. What is the reason of this difference?

A. They run through a coal mining country, where fuel costs almost nothing.

Q. What are the figures?

A. I saw in the paper that the cost was from two to three cents a mile.

Q. Has the Pennsylvania Central also an advantage over you?

A. In a large degree, but not so much as the Baltimore and Ohio.

Q. Do these roads have any advantage over your road in respect to climate in winter?

A. We are obstructed more or less every year by snow.

Q. More than they?

A. Always; and we have, from the frost, more broken rails, axles and wheels, beyond question.

Q. Will you state whether your cost of transportation and carrying is actually greater in winter than in summer, and if so, the reasons.

A. Beyond all question much greater in the winter.

Q. State the elements of the increased cost?

A. I have no doubt it costs 50 per cent more to do the business in the winter than in the summer.

Q. What are the elements of the increase?

A. The engines cannot draw so heavy loads; the rails break, often causing accidents to the wheels and cars; when there is snow on the track the power is diminished in a much greater degree than from the common causes, and we cannot haul as much.

Q. Are there occasions when the expense of the removal of the snow is very great?

A. Many times more than all the receipts and passengers for the day.

Mr. COBB—You mentioned that the Grand Trunk had its connections at Detroit, do you mean to say that the Grand Trunk runs to Detroit?

A. By crossing the river. They commonly run on the East side of the river to Detroit.

Q. Do they not run to Sarnia?

A. There is a road to Detroit from opposite Sarnia. The Grand Trunk are building a road at the crossing of the Michigan Southern roads I inferred that they run from it. They have control of that road, I am sure of that. The cars of course do not cross the river.

Mr. COBB—You remarked that you would be compelled to increase the rates on your way freight, if you wished to secure enough to pay interest on your bonds. How is the interest paid at the present time?

A. The interest on the first mortgage bonds is paid from the receipts of the road. The interest on the other bonds is not being paid at present.

Mr. COBB—In the answer, do you contemplate raising more money?

A. I suppose we are under obligation to.

Mr. COBB—Did you intend, if you make your revenue on way freight, to pay interest on mortgage?

A. By the profits on way freight and the passenger business altogether of our business, we should try to get it from the way freight and passenger business, but we should have to increase our rates for way freight to get enough money to pay interest.

Mr. COBB—On the first mortgage bonds?

A. All the mortgage interest.

Mr. COBB—Then you contemplate paying more than you are now paying?

A. Yes, sir.

Mr. COBB—If you abandoned way freight you would save seven-eighths of the expense?

A. Yes, sir, those that are built for way freight. If we only carried through freight from Dunkirk we would save seven-eighths of our investment for these things.

Mr. COBB—How do your prices now compare with those of the Baltimore and Ohio Road and the Pennsylvania Central to Western Points?

A. We try to keep them alike.

Mr. COBB—They are essentially alike?

A. They are.

Mr. COBB—How do your rates in Summer compare with those rates?

A. They have the ocean in the Summer and the river.

Q. How do your rates to common points in the West compare during the summer and winter?

A. It is since the summer that I resumed my connection with the road. I do not know what our rates were last summer.

Mr. COBB—Are the present rates of steam carrying compensating?

A. They pay some profit.

Mr. COBB—How do you account for it that while you are obstructed in the winter that you can carry freight as cheap as they?

A. We agree upon the rates, but they make more money than we do.

Mr COBB—You agree upon winter rates and you go by the agreement?

A. Yes, sir.

Mr. COBB—What is the difficulty in making an agreement for the summer, as to this rate, and thus keep up prices?

A. Because they have more water than we; they have the ocean at one end of their rail route and the river at the other.

Mr. COBB—If the pro rata policy were adopted, where would the through freight of Ohio and Indiana go?

A. It would go over the Pennsylvania Central, the Baltimore and Ohio or the Grand Trunk railroads.

Mr. COBB—Suppose you were compelled to adopt the pro rata, where would the freight of Ohio and Indiana go. What avenue would it probably seek?

A. It would seek the Pennsylvania Central or the Baltimore and Ohio.

Mr. COBB—Why would it seek them in preference to the canal?

A. The more costly goods, the rail good, would take the southern lines.

Mr. COBB—How about the rest?

A. They would take the canal as they do now.

Mr. COBB—Take Chicago as a starting point, during the summer, suppose you were compelled to adopt the pro rata principle, where would that trade go?

A. I think the Grand Trunk would get a large portion of it?

Mr. COBB—You spoke of the express business. What did you refer to?

A. The United States Express Company which runs over our road, and the American Express Company on the Central.

Mr. COBB—Have you examined the provisions of the bill before the committee?

A. I have read it over.

Mr. COBB—Do you suppose that its provisions reach express goods?

A. I so understood it.

Mr. COBB—It is not generally so understood. It is to prevent them from receiving a commission for attendance; but I do not suppose it prevents them from receiving a commission for delivery?

A. I suppose the price would be so low on the railroads that it would go to the railroad instead of the company

Mr. COBB—How do you explain the idea that prices would be advanced?

A. The business of the express is carrying small packages; the price per ton has very little to do with it, and $5 or $10 per ton would make but very little difference, the prices are so small on each package.

Mr. COBB—But the aggregate is very large?

A. Certainly it is.

Mr. COBB—How many cars over your road each train?

A. We average a car load each day, each way. That is about the average, I should think.

Mr. COBB—In your opinion would the Grand Trunk take the New York city business from Chicago during summer?

A. I have not been here for three or four years in the summer season.

Mr. COBB—What is your opinion based, upon 19 years experience on railroads?

A. I think the canal would get no more than it now does.

Mr. COBB—I am asking about the Grand Trunk. Would it get the New York city trade from Chicago during the summer season. I ask you as an expert familiar with these things.

Mr. HAWLEY—You mean under a pro rata law?

Mr. COBB—Yes, Sir, under a pro rata, if you please.

A. I think they would get a good deal of it. They charge only ⅘ of a cent per ton per mile.

Mr. COBB—Do you estimate ⅘ of a cent per ton per mile cheaper transportation than the ocean, lake or canal?

A. Taking into consideration time, insurance, &c., it would be a preferable price.

Mr. COBB—In point of dollars and cents?

A. For a great many goods.

Mr. COBB—What goods?

A. I think that provisions and flour would go round that way.

Mr. COBB—You think they would take provisions and flour to New York by that route as a matter of economy?

A. They seem determined to get it, by making their prices to get it.

Mr. COBB—How would they take it from Chicago?

A. One way would be to take it by propellers from Portland to New York.

Mr. COBB—How would they bring it from Chicago? Describe.

A. They would take the Michigan Southern to Toledo, and the Toledo and Monroe to Detroit, then the road to opposite Sarnia, which they have control of, and then their own road to Portland.

Mr. COBB—And that route you estimate would be the cheapest in dollars and cents, considering insurance, for flour and provisions for New York during the summer season?

A. I do not know as it would be the cheapest. I have not been in the summer's business for several summers. I came on the road in September, and their road was not then completed. I do not know what the tolls on the canal were last summer.

Mr. COBB—Then I understand that you do not pretend to answer the question. What changes in the through tariffs have occurred since September? If any, when were they made?

A. The changes are made by the receiver, and not by me; I know they have been increased, but what the increase is I do not know; the general freight agent is here and can answer the question.

Mr. COBB—What time did that take place?

A. It generally takes place at the close of canal navigation.

Q. Does the Grand Trunk Railway present superior facilities for transporting, from the west to Portland and to Europe, freight of the class that have been accustomed to go to New York and thence to Europe, provisions, flour, &c.?

A. I do not know; their distance is greater.

Q. I mean their price—whether they made better offers for transportation?

A. They are far better than ever before known for rail rates.

Q. Suppose they continue their offers, would it not have the effect to divert from New York City and from the lines through this state, some portion of the freight that goes to Europe, of that class?

A. Certainly; that is the object of the Grand Trunk Railway.

Q. Would you not understand that to be a diversion of freights from the State and City of New York?

A. Most certainly.

Q. If there is any considerable amount of freight in that direction, what is the probability of importations coming back by the same line?

A. They have an arrangement by which goods coming to Portland go over that road immediately without any detention in the custom-house.

Q. Are their rates for return freights from there equally low?

A. I have understood they are; but I do not know any thing about return freights.

Mr. COBB—In your opinion, would not heavy freights take the canals to a large extent—fourth class goods, on the supposition that the railroads should raise local freights?

A. That would be the effect more than it is

now, from the places where there is canal competition.

Mr. COBB—You mentioned the rates from Chicago by the Grand Trunk Railroad to Europe, can you name any article that they propose to take?

A. Not from my own knowledge; I saw an article to-day, in the New York Times, on that subject.

Mr. COBB—Has not your road an arrangement with Europe for importation in the same way?

A. We have made an arrangement; I have understood the Central has also on roads next parallel with them.

Mr. COBB—Can you compete with the Grand Trunk in doing business?

A. I am afraid not.

NATHANIEL MARSH was next introduced, he gave the following testimony, the examination being conducted by Mr. Hawley.

Q. State your present relation to the New York and Erie Railroad?

A. I am the Receiver appointed by the authority of the Supreme Court to take charge of the property, and manage and run the road.

Q. How long has it been in your charge as Receiver?

A. Since the 16th of August last.

Q. How long have you been connected with the management of the New York and Erie Railroad altogether?

A. About 15 years.

Q. Have you been in some relation to enable you to intimately understand the traffic and operation of the road?

A. I have occupied the office of Secretary until I was appointed Receiver.

Q. Has that road during later years had a severe competition with other lines competeing for the traffic to the next?

A. Yes, sir.

Q. Can you tell from recollection about how many years since the Pennsylvania Central Railroad came into the field as a competitor?

A. I think it is two or three years since they made their connections complete with the West.

Q. So as to reach all Western Points?

A. Yes, sir.

Q. Do you know whether that road is owned in part by the city of Philadelphia and what its relations are to that city?

A. I believe that the city of Philadelphia owns one third of its stock.

Q. Do you know whether that road has the management of and control of the canals of Pennsylvania?

A. Yes, sir. The main line of canals through the State of Pennsylvania is owned by the Pennsylvania Railroad Company.

Q. Do you know whether the road is operated largely, with reference to getting trade to Philadelphia?

A. That is the avowed object of the construction and management of the road.

Q. Can you state whether the reduction in the rates, by competition, have had the effect to extend the field from which you draw freights in the west and south?

A. Yes, Sir, very largely.

Q. How far in the southwest do you reach in bringing and carrying freights?

A. The extreme point is New Orleans in the southwest.

Q. In reference to the capacity to carry cheap, how will the Pennsylvania Central compare with the New York and Erie, take it altogether?

A. Do you mean the Pennsylvania Central road only, or through its connections to reach distant points?

Q. I mean in what respects has it an advantage over the New York and Erie, for engaging in this traffic successfully—say in the matter of fuel?

A. I should think that the cost of fuel on the Pennsylvania Central was about one-half that on the New York and Erie.

Q. Do you know whether the curvatures and grades of the Pennsylvania Central is greater than on the New York and Erie?

A. I believe that they have some grades higher, but on the whole their grades are quite as favorable as those of the Erie.

Q. In what respect is that an advantage in the price of fuel, and how far will it compensate for the advantage possessed by the New York Central in the matter of grade and curvature?

A. It would give the Pennsylvania Central a decided advantage.

Q. What do you understand to be their advantage over yourselves in the price of fuel—what per cent?

A. I should think their fuel cost them about one-half.

Q. Take their line to Philadelphia from the common points west, are they nearer than your road to New York?

A. Yes, Sir.

Q. Do you know any motive in fixing the tariff on freights other than to get the largest remuneration for the business?

A. I know of none other.

Q. With the liberty to do the best on this subject, has your road been able to pay so as to get out of the hands of the receiver?

A. Yes, Sir.

Q. Will you explain what has been the difficulty in placing it in its present position?

A. It has been the diversion of its earnings to other purposes.

Q. Then it has not been lossses in business but financial mismanagement?

A. Yes, Sir.

Q. Do you understand it to be a sound business rule for a road, or individual in charge, to do business at times below cost?

A. I believe it is an admitted rule.

Q. What is the object of doing business below cost under certain circumstances?

A. One great object would be to retain business which in future might be profitable, as merchants sometimes sell goods below cost to secure and retain a good customer. In the same way a railroad would carry freight two months in the year at a loss, with the fair chance of making a profit in the same traffic during the other ten months. Then there is the other reason stated by Mr. Minot to maintain the position of the road with reference to travel.

Q. To drive those who control other roads into a frame of mind which will induce it to come to compensating rates?

A Yes, sir.

Q. I come now to the subject of the comparative cost of through and way freights, what, in your judgment, after all your opportunities for observation, as to the difference in the cost of transporting through freight and way freight?

A. It would be different on different parts of the road; on some parts of the road the cost would not be 25 per cent more; on others, it would be 50 per cent, and on some portions of the road, say the Delaware division, it would be double.

Q. With reference to the whole of the business you have done, what is the difference between the through business and way business—what per cent?

A. That is susceptible of an accurate answer, which I am not able to give without an examination of the figures.

Q. I mean an approximate amount, not the actual?

A. I should think that the cost of the way freight was 50 per cent greater than the through; but there are a great many elements that enter into the calculation, and it might vary somewhat; I do not propose that the Committee should understand me as saying that it would cost exactly so much more or so much less, but that the tendency is larger because of these elements, which they can see as well as we.

Q. State those elements of increased cost on way freight, chargeable to it, and not chargeable to through freight?

A. The elements are the diminished work done by the motive power, the additional cost of labor, the additional cost of fuel, the additional cost of station expenses, additional track expenses, track repairs, station-houses, side-tracks and their maintenance, and the interest on the additional capital required to do it; these are some of the main items.

Q. Can you give an approximate estimate or statement of what way stations and fixtures have cost on that road, which would not be needed if you did a through business only; I speak of an investment, not of current expenses?

A. I understand your question to be, this: How much more has been expended on the road to enable it to give facilities for doing a way business than would have been expended if the object had been to do a through business only?

Q. Yes, sir, as an investment?

A. I should think from six to eight millions of dollars.

Q. Then the interest on the capital would be chargeable as current expenses on that account, in addition to other items you have mentioned, wages, &c.?

A. Yes, sir.

Q. Assuming that the prayers of this petition are granted, which requires you by statute to arrange and publish a tariff of prices for freight per ton per mile, or a pro rata tariff on quantity and distance, what would its effect be upon your ability to compete in the Western marts for through traffic with other lines?

A. We should have no power to compete.

Q. Suppose on the first day of May, you fixed a tariff according to your best judgment, and sent it to your agents in Chicago, how would they be met when they were canvassing for freight?

A. If they offered to transport freight from Chicago to New York for 80 cents a hundred, the agents of the Pennsylvania would offer to do it for 79 cents and would take the freight.

Q. Suppose you were to come down a little the next month, and published another tariff, what would be the result?

A. The same small reduction would take away the freight.

Q. How far would you come down before you would get rid of the pertinacious competition?

A. I would not undertake to say, but we would get down below cost.

Q. They would probably leave you then?

A. If they were compelled to carry it below cost, they would give it to us.

Q. What is your judgment as to the possibility of retaining that branch of business under such a statute in the present condition of competing lines?

A. It could not be retained and would not be attempted.

Q. I desire to call your attention to your power to control the whole of your way freight under such a pro rata tariff. What is your judgment as to your being able to carry way freight within reach of your competing rival at Great Bend?

A. I don't believe we could carry them at all.

Q. Would they be able to fix a low price for you at Elmira at that route?

A. They are already carrying freights to Philadelphia at very low prices.

Q. Could your road do a way business at figures so low as to enable you to compete for the Western business, suppose that you pro rated?

A. No, sir, on a road as long as the Erie, a pro rato near the terminus would amount next to nothing.

Q. Then your conclusion is that you would have to abandon through traffic?

A. Yes, sir.

Q. Then upon way traffic, what would be the necessary course that you would have to pursue in endeavoring to get an amount of revenue sufficient to carry on your enterprise?

A. The most profitable part of the way business is done on the eastern division nearest New York of course, where the population is greater and the products sent to market, and the consumption of goods and merchandise from the city the greatest. That is on all roads the most profitable and desirable to preserve. In order to maintain those rates at anything like a remunerative price, it would be necessary to fix such prices at the western terminus of the road, Dunkirk, so high as to be absolutely more than double the rates ever charged by any road.

Q. If you fixed them lower at the west end, what would be the effect on the eastern route?

A. It would run to nothing. If the road terminated at Port Jervis it would alter things very much. If there were four roads instead of four divisions of one road, it would alter things very materially.

Q. Each one could then pro rata for itself?

A. Yes, sir.

Q. Are you able to give a tariff on the milk trade on the eastern division. Explain how it would operate on the actual business you have now?

A. The milk is produced and shipped from a verys mall portion of territory extending along the line of the road about 35 miles from near the eastern boundary of Orange county to the neighborhood of Otisville. Perhaps the extreme distance is 35 to 40 miles. The great bulk is shipped from the neighborhood of Goshen and Chester. The charge upon milk is seven-eighths of a cent per quart any distance, no distinction being made with regard to the length of the haul. The milk is carried on a very rapid train, run for the especial accommodation of that trade. It is carried at a rate of speed as fast as any passenger train is run on the road. It requires the most prompt and regular delivery. A delay of two or three hours in the arrival of the milk train costs the whole freight, the milkmen declining to take the milk. The milk is carried under the pressure of speed and dispatch all the time. The milk cans are returned to the owners free of charge by the same train returning, it being run for no other purpose. The charge upon milk, as I said, is seven-eighths of a cent per quart which produces 35 cents for a can of 40 quarts, and a can of 40 quarts weighs about 100 pounds, milk and can.

Q. The cost of 100 pounds is about 35 cents?

A. That charge pro rated to Dunkirk, putting milk into first class, would make the rate from Dunkirk about $60 per ton, or about three times as high a rate as was ever charged, at any charge which would be fixed for bringing in way freight west of Deposit, or perhaps I should say east of that point, a milk business at the prices now paid would be a losing business and would not pay the cost of transportation, and on ordinary freight trains it would not be carried at all.

Q. By reason of the time?

A. Yes, sir. In the summer season, and indeed in all seasons, trains run in the night, and are run at a greatly increased expense. There is a large amount of labor required in handling the milk, loading and unloading cars; and carried on ordinary freight trains, milk would all spoil in the summer season, and necessarily irregularity would cause great inconvenience.

Q. Have you at hand any document showing the extent of that trade. Do you remember it per year or month?

A. During the year ending December 31, 1859, we transported on the road over 25 millions of quarts.

Q. At seven-eighths of a cent a quart, produced how much?

A. About $205,000.

Q. Can you state the condition of the milk trade over the Harlem road, whether it is carried largely there?

A. I believe it is about the same, and is done about the same way and at the same price.

Q. Do you know how much territory it spreads over?

A. About as large a territory. I think the extreme points are about 40 miles distant.

Q. Subject to the same regulations?

A. To the same regulations exactly.

Q. Would it be practicable to continue the express business on your road under a pro rata?

A. I think not, sir. That is in the assumption that express matters are freight. I judge from a remark on the other side [Mr. Cobb] that it is not so contemplated. I supposed it was.

Q. Will you state the reason for that, why it could not be carried?

A. It is a pro rata in quantities as well as distances.

Q. Could they carry small quantities at any price that large quantities would bear?

A. The road could not carry it.

Q. Because they would not allow others to carry on your road what they would not allow you?

A. I suppose not.

Q. You are familiar with the general features of the Grand Trunk line of railway. Do you know what they are proposing to do and are doing in the way of carrying western freight to Europe?

A. They are proposing and are actually making contracts to carry freight from Cincinnati, Chicago, and any other points in that region, making a through price from from any western point to Liverpool, including all charges, all commissions, free deliveries, and in all respects making a good or a better mode of transportation than is now offered on any other route.

Q. How does the rate compare with the rates to Liverpool by New York?

A. The rates are lower than were ever known before.

Q. Are you aware of any attempts or offers to bring freights from the West, by that route, to Boston and New York?

A. Boston freight has been carried over the Grand Trunk, and within a very few days freight has been taken from New York to Portland, to go thence by the Grand Trunk road to Chicago.

Q. By what means is it carried from New York to Portland?

A. By propellers—a line of propellers recently established.

Q. Did they get that freight by accident or did they compete for it?

A. They competed and took it away from other lines by lower prices.

Q. Do you know the amount of capital invested in the Grand Trunk railway in round numbers?

A. I think it is sixty millions of dollars.

Q. Do you know the distance by that road from Chicago to Portland?

A. I think the distance is about 1120 or 1130 miles—it is 1133 miles.

Q. Do you know the object of building the Grand Trunk road?

A. The avowed object, as set forth in their own reports and statements, to the Parliaments of Great Britain and Canada, is to transport the products of the west to England on freight lines of steamers, by way of Quebec and Montreal, and to use Portland as a harbor in the winter, when those ports are closed by the ice.

Mr. CONKLIN—Who furnished the capital?

A. Different parties.

Mr. CONKLIN—Is it British capital?

A. A portion is, sir; a portion is furnished by the bonds of the Company, guaranteed by the Provincial Government, and some of these bonds have been guaranteed anew by the British Home Government, and the Provinces released from the payment of interest for a long time to come, and it may be regarded as a free gift to the Canadas, of that immense railroad.

Q. It has made financial and other arrangements, such as indicate that they don't expect to get interest or dividends on their capital?

A. I think so; I have seen nothing in their reports, which I have read with care, which looks to the payment of dividends, while the

Governments have assumed the payment of a portion of their debts. They get their capital at from three to four per cent per annum, which is another advantage they have.

Q. Can you state the time since, when New York has out-grown Philadelphia in size?

A. I think it was about the time of the completion of the Erie Canal, in 1825 or '26.

Mr. COBB—About the time of the completion of the Canal?

A. Yes, sir. I am not posted up in that matter; it is not purely a railroad question.

Q. Is it practicable as a business question to carry on a large interior traffic without a corresponding foreign traffic to balance it?

A. No sir, it is not.

Q. If by any circumstances or means the great commodities of this nation could be collected at other points than at New York, would it be possible for New York, under any circumstances, to retain the import foreign trade?

A. Of course it could not.

Q. These elements must balance according to the law of trade?

A. What has given New York its importance, is its power to control the export trade.

Q. What is your opinion of the facilities, by the Erie canal in early years and the recent superior facilities, having caused the growth of New York, as compared with Philadelphia and Baltimore?

A. New York, of course, owes its growth to those facilities; the great shipping interest has been built up by its export and import trade; the import trade following the export.

Q. What would be the effect, in your opinion, of another point, say Philadelphia or Portland, securing decidedly superior facilities of internal traffic, to New York City?

A. The effect on New York would be to take away the export trade from her, and a large corresponding amount of the import trade; a case in point is the traffic that has grown up within the last three months at Portland.

Mr. COBB—That is upon the hypothesis of the Grand Trunk Railroad running to Portland?

A. The effect would be still greater when they took the property to Montreal.

Q. What is the effect upon the city of New York in taking the emigrant business?

A. The effect has been felt during the past season; we know that it has diverted a large portion of the emigrant business to the Canadian and Nova Scotian ports.

Mr. SEYMOUR—Since you have been receiver, have you had any correspondence or negotiation with any line of Liverpool or European steamers with the view to compete with this Portland route, with reference to carrying freight over the New York and Erie Railroad?

A. I have.

Mr. SEYMOUR—Will you state the object of it?

A. I made these inquiries with the view to ascertain if freights destined for English ports could not be carried over the New York and Erie road and be shipped from New York as cheaply as from Canada; I commenced that investigation some three months since; at that time prices could be given, and lines were ready to make prices at which property could be carried; the Grand Trunk Railroad had not been givlng any Eastern prices, but shortly after they published prices which carried the rates so much below what steamships of New York had ever thought of carrying freights, that the agent of these lines said it was useless to contend. I subsequently renewed the inquiries, for then the prices of the Grand Trunk road had been given for these freights, and I ascertained that propellers running from New York took a small amount of freight at rates which left the Grand Trunk about a cent a ton per mile from a few of the ports of the west, not all; I have learned within a few days that the Grand Trunk are making prices—taking off about 25 to 30 per cent when the St. Lawrence river opens, making about two-thirds of the rates of freight now existing between New York and Liverpool; of course they would abandon the carrying business to the Grand Trunk Railway from Chicago, and terminate at Liverpool. There is another thing to which I would like to call your attention, with regard to the greater facilities which are offered by the Grand Trunk road than ever given by any American line. They are given in this way: arrangements have been made by the Grand Trunk road, through their agents in Liverpool and London, to advance upon property shipped by their route from Cincinnati to Liverpool or London; thus, making a market in these places for this property, instead of having it marketed in New York, as has been the case heretofore. These bills of lading and bills of exchange drawn against these shipments are beginning to form, in New York, an important feature in the exchange market. I have seen these bills of lading and exchange, and am familiar with the manner in which the business is done, and it would be exceedingly difficult to make an arrangement as satisfactory from the port of New York.

Mr. SEYMOUR—You spoke of knowing something of the milk trade on the Harlem road—what is it worth?

A. The President of the road told me that it was worth $260,000 a year.

Q. Will you tell the Committee how many miles it is from New York on the Erie road to the first milk station?

A. About forty-five miles; Turner's is the first place where any quantity is shipped, which is forty-six miles from New York.

Q. The furtherest point is how far?

A. Otisville, about seventy-six miles.

Q. Do you charge any difference in price, per quart, for a greater or less distance?

A. No, sir.

Q. What, in your opinion, would be the effect upon the milk trade of charging a pro rata price upon that milk, as is asked for in this petition?

A. It would destroy the business.

Q. Suppose you should fix the price at seven-eighths of a cent per quart, for the shortest distance, and greater pro rata for the long distance?

A. It would cut it all off—an increase of a quarter of a cent would cut it all off.

Q. If called upon to determine the question of long and way freights, and settling the policy of that road, what course would you take to get at it?

A. I should collect the best information in my power on the subject, and then present a petition to the Supreme Court, asking them to direct me, giving my own views in the matter, precisely as I go to the Court for any directions, not specifically laid down in the authority given me.

Q. The Court would have to determine that question for you on the facts before it?

A. Yes, sir. I should be compelled to represent my inability with any orders I possessed to run the road, and to ask for instructions.

Mr. COBB—Can you inform me what were the net receipts on your road from freight for the current past year?

A. I believe that testimony has been furnished the Committee; I cannot give it from recollection.

Mr. COBB—Can you give them, about?

A. I would not venture to say; our accounts are made up to the 30th of September for the year; that is, in the report to the Legislature, which is on file. They are in a sworn statement in the hands of the State Engineer, and are accessible to the Committee.

Mr. COBB—What part of these net receipts were derived from the through summer receipts last year?

A. I could not separate them so as to answer that question.

Mr. COBB—Have you any means of knowing?

A. I could if an analysis of the whole, for the whole year were made; but our accounts are not kept in a way to show that, unless it is an object of interest to ascertain it.

Mr. COBB—Have you any general knowledge upon the subject without coming to exact figures?

A. I would not guess the figures when the matter is susceptible of exact information. If the committee desire the information I will furnish it.

Mr. COBB—Can you tell what proportion of your net receipts?

A. Yes, sir. That can be given; any information of that kind, which is in our power, we will give?

Mr. COBB—I believe you did not separate your way freights from your through freights last year.

A. Yes, sir, we did. I can only say if the committee desire that information, the receiver has no sort of objection to furnish it.

Mr. COBB—Your report does not separate the way tonnage and the mileage?

A. I believe they do. The report is made out in exact conformity with the requirements.

Mr. COBB—Do you esteem your road, 460 miles in length, competent in the summer to compete with the Central with only 300 miles of rail, and 150 miles by water?

A. Yes, sir.

Mr. COBB—Would you esteem yourself better able to transport freight than the New York Central with that advantage?

A. I think we have advantages over the Central route. I have seen nothing in my administration of the road to shake the opinion I had previously formed.

Mr. COBB—What would be the advantage of your road; how much per ton?

A. That would be coming down pretty close. I certainly do not want to say anything derogatory to the Central road.

Mr. COBB—What is your custom from points like Binghamton, Elmira and Corning, compared with points east of that, as respects the prices?

A. I do not know. They are lower pro rata.

Mr. COBB—What is the reason for that, if there is any?

A. At these points there is a sharp competition.

Mr. COBB—What with?

A. At Binghamton with the Delaware, Lackawanna, and Western, and the New Jersey Central road to New York. And at Elmira with the Williamsport and Elmira road.

Mr. COBB—Is there a canal at either of these places?

A. There is at both of them.

Mr. COBB—Do the canals enter into competition?

A. At Binghamton I do not think it does. the distance is so much greater by canal. I doubt if there was no other competition if we should pay much attention to it.

Mr. COBB—You have spoken of the Grand Trunk, and a prospect of a diversion of business from the city of New York, and the extent of the business which the Grand Trunk should do; do you mean to be understood that any business goes over the Grand Trunk and centers at Portland?

A. I do not think Portland is the competing point. I think the competing point is Montreal and Quebec, to which the railroad distance is so much less. Portland is the port which the Grand Trunk will use during the winter; and it has been demonstrated that they can compete with all our lines running over our longest railroad distances; but with the opening of navigation the steamers which run from Liverpool to Portland will run to Liverpool and Montreal, so that Montreal and Quebec become the competing points, with 350 miles less railroad transportation.

Mr. COBB—What is the ordinary transportation to the continent, from Montreal, compared with New York?

A. I am unable to say what it has been in the past; I can tell what it is to be in the future; the prices have been given for the coming season at 30 shillings per ton from Quebec.

Mr. COBB—On what articles?

A. Fourth class articles, heavy goods, beef, pork, salt, &c.

Mr. CONKLING—Is that ton a forty feet measurement?

A. Yes, sir.

Mr. COBB—Is that 30 shillings sterling?

A. Yes, sir; or it is about 32 cents per hundred pounds.

Mr. COBB—What is the ordinary price for ocean transportation, from New York, by the same method?

A. I am giving it by steamer, by sailing vessels it is cheaper; the rates are much higher from New York than from Quebec.

Mr. COBB—Has that long been the case?

A. No, sir.

Mr. COBB—When did the change take place?

A. Very recently.

Mr. COBB—Then it is prospective rather than present?

A. I think you do not quite comprehend; the prices from New York have hitherto been much higher than that. No prices were so low, by steam to Liverpool, as those announced by the Grand Trunk Line. The agents in New York say they will not carry at those prices; I mean the agents of the principal lines in New York—that they will go out of business at those prices.

Mr. COBB—Is not the route from New York

to Liverpool a preferable one than that by Quebec? Is it not better for safety?

A. There are different opinions about that; the rates of insurance are no higher.

Mr. COBB—What is the financial credit of the Grand Trunk Railway in the city of New York?

A. I do not know as they have ever appeared as money borrowers in the city of New York; but the bills of exchange, drawn against produce shipped by that route, find ready purchasers.

Mr. COBB—That is not the credit of the Grand Trunk Railway, but the credit of the drawers.

A. The credit of the Grand Trunk is involved so far as carrying out the contract is concerned; these bills drawn upon property sent by an irresponsible road would not sell.

Mr. COBB—Is it not within your knowledge that bills are sold every day in New York, predicated upon property from the west passing over the New York and Erie Railroad?

A. Yes, sir.

Mr. COBB—Then it does not hold good with reference to the one as to the other?

A. Why not?

Mr. COBB—Because the one is supposed to be an irresponsible concern.

A. That supposition is not correct.

Mr. COBB—Are not all the other canal routes through the state, and also the Southern routes destined to be eclipsed by the Grand Trunk Railway?

A. To a certain extent it would necessarily; under a pro rata it would carry all; under existing circumstances, as long as their policy is not to do business for a profit, but with a view solely of securing the business, they will get it.

Mr. COBB—How long will that kind of business last?

A. As long as the financial condition of the Company will permit.

Mr. COBB—As a business man, do you think it profitable for the New York or Southern roads to attempt a competition with that route during the time they are carrying on that thing?

A. That depends entirely upon the rates fixed; if the rates prevail that they now propose to charge during the coming season, I can say for one that the New York and Erie road don't want any of the business at those prices. Other roads may speak for themselves.

Mr. CONKLING—You have spoken of the extraordinary grants and immunities of the British Government to the Grand Trunk Railway Company—have you any reason to believe that there was a political design on the part of the British Government?

A. It is avowed in the reports to the British Parliament, and to the Provincial Parliament—the reports of the Grand Trunk road itself. The object stated there is to improve the condition of the Canadas, to stimulate emigration for the occupation of their vacant lands, and the building up of their towns and cities. That has been publicly avowed ever since the road was begun.

Mr. CONKLING—To build up a great independant power on this continent—a kind of Vice-Royalty?

A. That has evidently been hinted at.

Mr. CONKLING—And interposing insuperable barriers to any connection between this country and the Canadas?

A. It would certainly have that tendency; there has doubtless been a great change in the policy in the Home Government towards the Colonies within the past two years—a more liberal policy; and gentlemen will also observe that the tone and feeling within the past few years, on the part of Canada towards the Home Government, is much better. You hear of no disloyalty, no dissatisfaction, and so long as money is furnished as it has been for the last two or three years, you will probably not hear of any.

Mr. CONKLING—The whole policy looks to the building up of a great independent power on the north of the United States, which would be able to operate as a sort of check upon this country?

A. Yes, sir; it looks like that. I asked a very intelligent English gentleman, who is largely interested in railroad management, and who has large means of getting information and knowing public sentiment, what his opinion was in regard to the Grand Trunk road. His answer was, "that the Grand Trunk must not be looked upon as a railroad; it was a political affair." Then I said, I suppose you don't hold any of the securities. He said that the securities guaranteed by the Government were very good, but those that depended upon the business profits of the road he thought were very dubious. Then in a conversation he explained, giving views similar to those I have mentioned.

The Committee took a recess until seven o'clock.

SPEECH OF MR. THOMPSON,

Before the Select Committee of the Assembly.

Mr. THOMPSON said he had endeavored to demonstrate, by way of protest to these petitions, as follows:

It is plausibly urged that by the low rates charged from Chicago or other Western points to New York, the millers of Rochester or Oswego are *injured*, and that as they are compelled to buy grain in Michigan or Wisconsin, they cannot freight it to Rochester, flour it, barrel it and get it to New York as cheaply as the Millers at Chicago or Detroit. Might admit all that to be true, and would it therefore follow that the Rochester miller is the *final cause* of all railroads, that the natural course of trade, the products of agricultural, the prosperity and enterprise of all the Empires of the New World are to bend to the thrift of Rochester millers, and go through the hoppers of Rochester mills? It is a strange assumption that any business become unprofitable in our own state by the *nature of things*, should be protected and kept up by unjust discrimination against all that may come into competition, might be applied equally to our *mills* here, our *wool* growing. It ought never to be thought of in reference to the great staple of life, *bread*, and especially when for seven months the Rochester mills has canal at its door and for balance the markets of Portland and Boston, but thus *demonstrated* by way of protection to these petitions.

1. The fallacy of the assumption, that railroad companies have any *privileges* or exemptions from the burdens borne by other trading or mercantile interests of the state, but on the contrary they are subjected to all the burdens of taxation, on their real estate, rolling stock and capital, working our highways, their own rivals, building our school houses and thus aiding our educational interests, and bring the wealth of the states to be invested in their stocks and bonds to one hundred and fifty millions of dollars, penetrating remote districts, and enhancing fourfold the price of lands where they go, building up villages, equalizing the value of property, affording large districts a valuable market for wood, and contributing by these means as well as by the employment of labor to the wealth and prosperity of the whole state. Grand Trunk exempt from a long entire line. I endeavored to establish that it was the purpose of the state in former times to foster and encourage these public enterprises, by putting them on a *footing of equality* with other forms of *associated* wealth and private enterprise, giving only such *general* regulation to their modes of operation, as experience had demonstrated would work no injury to them, and at the same time give assurance that no abuses should be tolerated where the remedy laid within the purview of legislative correction.

That within these general principles Railroads were on the *same footing as individuals*, in the transaction of their business, being governed by the laws of trade, the law of demand and supply and by the *usages* of business, as it develops, and that these laws of *trade* like the principles of the common law are progressive and changeable; changing with the growth and development of the country which they intersect, with the character of the business and merchandise which employs them, and that no rule can or should be imposed by the Legislature to cripple their usefulness or destroy their income.

I endeavored further to show that *political and moral right* ought to back and fortify *naked powers* before it is exercised to interfere with the natural commerce of corporations, and that in this respect all they should and did stand upon the footing of individuals, being entitled to the same legal protection and the same legislative regard. That *commerce* made her *own laws*, and that any interference with these, within the limits and between the states of this confederacy, was contrary to the spirit of the constitution of the United States, in direct violation and usurpation of the powers of Congress over *commerce*. Operating as effectually and disastrously as the erection of a custom house at Dunkirk or Buffalo or Oswego or Albany, to *levy a duty on all western tonnage before it should be permitted* to pass their own borders.

That such a policy would inevitably destroy what it professed to *protect*. That such hasty ill-advised legislation to protect *class interest*, always recoiled upon the very interest it was designed to foster, and instead of giving each a fair chance in the race of honorable competition ruined both.

2. That the allegation, that our railroads unjustly discriminated between *citizens of our own state* and citizens of western states was *unfounded* and unjust, the same rates being demanded of *every one shipping from the same point*, and that any discrimination in prices of transportation have *relation simply to distances and not to persons*, and that in this respect the *way* business and the *through* business of our railroads were kept on separate footings, and carried on by the companies at different rates of expense.

That no person could complain living on the line of the road, while the business was done promptly, cheaply and more to his advantage than in any other mode. That the Company might be able to carry from more distant points, for the same or a less price per ton per mile.

That the idea of the same price per ton per mile, is as absurd as if applied to a New York city omnibus or railroad car, permitting 6d for the longest ride, and demanding a pro rata diminution for any shorter distance, or lighter weight.

That the way business of the road, resting on its own footing, and conducted on a separate basis, is to be considered and regulated, if at all, solely in reference to itself

That it is neither increased nor diminished by the passage of western merchandise over the road. That its expense is regulated by what it costs, with a small ordinary profit, depending upon grade of the road, time employed in delivering and receiving freight, cost and consumption of fuel, freight houses to be built at the stations, labor to be employed along the line, most of these being items of cost, not necessarily entering into the cost of through transportation, in respect of which, most of it passes on the road, simply without reloading or handling—being loaded at Cleveland, or Toledo, or Chicago, or other western points, from whence it comes passing direct to New York, by the Erie, or to Albany on Central.

That way transportation could not, in the nature of things, be carried on as cheaply as that between distant points—and that to this rule there is no exemption.

That way freight on the ocean, in the coasting trade, on all our rivers, canals, and railroads, pays and must pay a higher rate for short distances than for longer ones.

That a locomotive carried usually 30 cars filled with through freight, with few stoppages, and no loss of time. While the same power on a way train, carried not to exceed 20 cars, and these only partly filled, with greater loss of time, and consumption of fuel, and expenses of handling.

And the only legitimate question before the committee is: Are the rates of freight too expensive, from any station, on the line of the road to New York?

That any other view of the case, is a prostitution of the road and its uses, to operate as a limitation and check to the free enterprise of the whole country and any part of it.

That there is no power in the Legislature, to *directly prohibit* the roads from carrying cars, coming on from other States; and that it is equally unjust to compel them to charge such prices, as to effectually exclude them from the roads—thus, doing that *indirectly*, which they have no power to do directly.

That it should be the wish and effort of enlightened statesmanship, to force through our State, and into its metropolis, these streams of western merchandise, and to aid our channels of communication, in diverting it from rival lines by a fostering Legislature, instead of so crippling our own roads, as to drive this trade away from us; for it is as absurd to suppose, that the human heart can carry on its pulsations, sending blood through all its channels to the extremities, as that New York, the mart of the State, can remain wealthy, or retain her influence and prestige, when these channels of trade are strangulated or dried up.

That cheap transportation on through lines, is benefit to producer and consumer, and merchant alike.

It costs a less price when delivered in the market, which is divided between production and consumption; each receiving a portion of that by the *regularity* of railroad transportation, merchants are enabled to do business with less capital, supporting their families, and employing labor, and increasing the growth and resources of the metropolis.

I had further endeavored to demonstrate the fallacy of the allegation, that the canals were thus deprived of their "legitimate traffic," as false *in principle* and unfounded in *fact*.

That the State is no more entitled to the carrying trade, as her legitimate and peculiar field of profit, than an individual or a corporation; and that she has the same right to embark in the manufacture of iron, or quarrying of stone, or raising of agricultural products, and they lay a tax on all these branches of business for her own protection, as to compel the railroad to charge rates so high, as to throw the business they now do into the hands of *forwarders* on the canals.

If the canals cannot be supported without the destruction of all private business that may interfere with them, they had better be *abandoned, and the sooner the better*.

That it is unfounded in fact, inasmuch as the bulk of freight now carried on the railroads would not pass the canals, if the railroads were unable to carry it. That all that part of it which consists of live stock, and dead hogs, which is made up of light, valuable or perishable materials, and which must get *rapidly* to market, would seek other rail lines in getting to seaboard; and that this trade once diverted, would never return to its former channels.

That if the through freight was abandoned, as it would be through the imposition of higher prices, the way freights would require to be *largely advanced* all along the line, to enable the roads to continue their business; and upon the Erie Road this would be a calamity without any relief, as there is no other means of communication, which would therefore depreciate the price of property all along the line, from the increased expenditure required to send it to market, and along the Central. While it might aid canal transportation a little in the summer, it could not affect freights in the *winter season*, when the canal is frozen. And that unless the State desires to attempt a confiscation of the railroads, and running them on its own account (a worse boon to her than the canals), she cannot justly interfere in the matter.

That a new and cheaper mode of transportation is never, in a wise government, burdened with the expenses of the old and inferior.

There could be no progress in civilization, no advances in political or social or commercial life, under such a barbarian rule. We, on the contrary, reward the inventor with a right to the exclusive use of his invention; but of what avail is his patent, if he must buy out all the old churns, scows and machinery his invenion is designed to supersede? And that on this principle, the river craft on the Hudson, and all the dock owners along its borders, might apply to the Legislature, to compel the Hudson River Railroad to pay the price of all property which this new mode of transportation has rendered unprofitable.

3. I also attempted to expose the fallacy of the allegation that the railroad was carrying *through* freight for less than they can afford.

1. Because the petitioners have and can have no knowledge on the subject.

2. Because it is safe usually to leave com-

panies to be governed by their own instincts and experience, they being better judges of this matter than any one else can be, and that the benevolence of these petitioners towards the stockholders and bondholders of these roads is altogether quixotic and misplaced.

That the allegation that this loss is made up by excessive way freights is not true, and if true would, in summer aid, and not injure the canal; and that it is equally unjust to the company to charge it as the reason of advanced rates on *winter* transportation, as

1. The canals do not thus conflict with them; and,

2. The actual cost of winter transportation is increased in about the same ratio. And that no person along the line was compelled to delay his shipments for winter transportation, and if so, he ought, in justice, to pay the necessarily increased cost.

4. I endeavored, moreover, to expose the folly that "parties all along the line had yielded equal "rights for the erection of railroads, and were "entitled as a consideration to be placed on the "footing of through freight." That as these lines had conferred benefits and benefits only on the country at large, no one had *yielded anything*, his land was increased in value; his products found a market, cities and villages and towns were increased and built up, and other certain places and taverns on the canal might suffer, it was only the same thing that happened to the old turnpike and some of its villages by the construction of the canal. They yielded nothing, the course of trade *retreated* and left them high and dry.

I endeavored, moreover, to demonstrate the absurdity of pro rata freight charges, having reference to long *lines and freights out of the State.*

That with efficient agencies, now employed in all western cities and the inducements at present offered, to bring it through our state it is only by continued struggle that our railroads retain it at all, and that the imposition of any new burden or charge upon it would send it off on rival lines, all equally anxious to divert it; and that once gone from us, as the course of trade is to carve its own channels deeper and deeper, we could offer under legislative resolutions no means for its recovery.

That there was no less than eight different lines of communication from the southwest, to the sea coast south of us, and two rival lines north of us, all in eager competition for this trade, which will bear no burdens it can avoid, but will seek such market as it can get at the cheapest.

That the products of Ohio, Indiana, Illinois, have natural and feasible outlets, through the Pennsylvania Central and the Baltimore and Ohio Rail Road, which are fostered and encouraged by the States; and run lines of vessels from those cities to New York, carrying up coal, and wood and lumber, and take freight back as ballast, or at nominal prices in return.

That produce, and pork and beef on the Ohio and at Chicago, goes either to the river for preparation, slaughter and packing, and so round by water to the seaboard, or down the lakes, and through the Grand Trunk Rail Road to Boston and Portland.

That Chicago has, in fact, opened a direct trade with Liverpool, sending one vessel, the Dean Richmond, *in* 1856; *in* 1857, 13 *vessels*, and in 1858, 40 *vessels.*

That Boston is on the wing, through all the northwest, soliciting and paying a premium on this freight. We sit here deliberating whether we shall not notify them we shall tax. I am half suspicious, the finger of Boston is on these petitions on your table. If they had paid ten thousand dollars for them, they are worth it all if they accomplish what they desire.

TESTIMONY OF J. W. BROOKS.

Mr. J. W. Brooks, President of the Michigan Central Railroad, then gave testimony as follows—Mr. Thompson conducting the examination:

Q. Where do you reside?

A. At Newton, near Boston.

Q. What is your business?

A. I am President of the Michigan Central Railroad Company.

Q. How long have you been in the railroad busness?

A. Something over 20 years—between 20 and 25 years.

Q. Will you state where your stations have been during that period—the points at which you have been located?

A. For the last 16 or 17 years I have been connected with the Michigan Central Railroad, and the roads running from it to Missouri; but my attention during that time has been confined to that line.

Q. You were President of that line during the time you spoke of?

A. I constructed the Michigan Central road, commencing in 1846, and was not President of the Company until some time after 1850—I do not recollect the year—perhaps it was 1853 or '54. Previous to that I was local manager at the west, and constructor.

Q. Are you acquainted with railroad transportation and the movement of freight and passengers on those western roads, through to the east, and the general course of business?

A. I am, as far as a person who had control of one of the long lines would be likely to have, sir.

Q. As a manager of a road I ask you this question: what is the difference in the cost of railroad transportation of through freight as compared with way freight?

A. Almost every road would present a somewhat new case. But there is no doubt that upon all roads it costs a good deal more to transport the local than the through freight. On some roads the difference in the two classes would be very much greater than on the others. There are so many causes that affect it more in some cases and less than in others, one can hardly fix a stated per cent difference. The cars in the one case do not run as full as in the other, nor do the trains take as many cars. The maximum number of cars of a full train is about thirty. The local train takes one or two on and picks others up on the route, as it picks up and drops cars on the route, the average will differ from station to station. I have generally supposed that more money could be made at two cents per mile per ton on long business, than at three cents on local. That must make a difference of 50 per cent. Some roads will make that figure smaller. There are cases where it might be larger. There is entering into that question a phase that is not always thought of. New business is generally long business. New business can be done somewhat cheaper than old business. If you will allow me to go into an explanation I will try to make myself understood in that regard. The fixed business, for which the road is built, has fairly charged upon it the whole expense of the operation of the road. The fixed business, which may be regarded as legitimately belonging to the line, is that which the public depends upon it to perform, and for which it was built. There are certain classes of expenses connected with the management, not incidental to the increase of business; as, if you please, the decay of the perishable materials connected with its structure. The roadway, the ties, the care of its bridges, its culverts, its drainage, ditches, the sliding of its banks, the wooden material connected with its rolling stock. The decay of that goes on as much in a smaller as in a larger business. There is a certain class of agencies connected with it, not influenced by the greater or less quantity of business. All the principal agents at the extremities of the line, these are not influenced in any appreciable degree by new business brought upon the line. I have generally supposed that perhaps nearly one-third of the expenses of railway management, was not increased by the increase of business. Therefore, I would say, that if the total cost of working the road or business was a cent a ton per mile (I state that not as representing the cost, but as a mere example), then new business could be done for two-thirds of a cent, and the other trade would not be affected by increased tonnage. It will follow from that that if new business is taken at the exact cost of the current business of the line, there is a profit incident to that business, which if you take the whole business at that cost, your line is worthless. In my own judgment I have always regarded that theory and have sought new business as the exigency of trade seemed to make it expedient. If we had current trade one way and empty cars the other, we would take freight at a very low rate, to fill up the empty cars. There are seasons of the year when our rolling stock is unemployed, that we would enter it upon any business at these low rates to make something out of it. The new business thus sought, not being legitimate business belonging to the road, and for which the road was not constructed, has been almost always taken at rates which are near the cost of movement. It is that element which I have endeavored to describe, which generally rendered it desirable for long lines to seek distant business.

Q. You have stated the occasion of this difference; will you now state the cost of winter transportation on these Northern routes, the principal lines, the New York Central and the New York and Erie, as compared with the cost in summer.

A. We all know and feel that there is a good deal of difference between the winter and summer expense of working lines of railroads. There is generally very much more difference than appears in the monthly figures that make up the cost; the rigidity of the railway, caused by freezing, of course would wear out rails much more rapidly. They may be fresh in fall, and partially fresh in the spring, but they are not taken out until the wear of years completes their destruction, when they have to be taken out in the regular course of repairs; winters vary very much. Then in regard to the rails, I will cite an example in the Lowell Railroad. When the rails were first laid they were laid on stone, which made the track as rigid as if frozen; it was found that the rails and machinery wore out the iron, which was bolted on the stone sleepers; the rails wore out quickly by reason of the rigidity with which the track was laid; they took them up and inserted a wooden block between the rail and the tie, to give them an amount of elasticity which would relieve the rail from the rigidity. I suppose that state of things is incident to rails frozen up; but winters are different. Within a few years, I do not recollect the time, we had two successive winters during which I do not believe many roads in this climate made any money at all. We, almost all of us, did not find ourselves clear of the damage until the succeeding July or August; that is, our machinery went into the winter business in better repair than they were subsequently, until the following July or August; so that the expense of it remained until the fall business following. We were pretty busy on the Michigan Central in getting ready and repairing machinery, injured by the hard winter service. Then there are other winters which are far different. We never have a winter but what the track freezes, but there are winters when we are not troubled so much with snow, so that the operation of the road during the winter season varies in the difficulties that are attendant upon it with the severity of the season. I speak now of the latitude in which we are. North of New York it is very different. South of New York, where the climate is considerably changed, it might be still worse than it is here; though I do not know when we get down to the freezing point, how much additional influence it has upon it. Of course, in the south, this does not amount to anything as their winters are not severe.

Q. As the result of this action upon the rails, the wear and tear of machinery and the repair of track, what, in your judgment as a railroad expert, is the average difference in the cost of winter and summer transportation?

A. I think I could only give it as a matter of judgment; I have never given the subject an accurate investigation.

Q. That is all we expect.

A. We, of course, are compelled to run smaller trains in the winter; we are liable to the difficulties of frosty stock, and we do less service with the same stock. I think few people would place it as low as one-third; I think I should place it at that figure; I think I could make more money at two cents in the summer than three in the winter. You can calculate, very nearly, what can be done in the summer; the winter has surrounding the business so many risks that trains have to be lighter, everything has to be handled more delicately, and necessarily greater destruction and damage ensues. The difficulty of estimating the damage is, that a great deal of the repairing is done during the ensuing season; but we know that the rails are hammered in the ends, and early in the spring we have to take out a multitude of rails; it is difficult to measure the damage in dollars and cents.

Q. I ask you, as a distinct question, what an advantage has the Southern over the Northern routes in the winter?

A. I do not see if you get south but what the Southern routes have an advantage exactly equal to the inconvenience and extra expenditure of the Northern lines, caused by their cold climate. Whatever measures the one, will measure the other; if we had not winters here we would be free from all this inconvenience and expense; they have a sort of advantage beyond that, which generally would not be estimated very high, but I think it is worth something; I should regard it, in long lines of competition, as an advantage; the current of their business is not disturbed by the exigencies of our line of service; therefore it is easy for them to take and retain business at certain prices the long traffic, that would be regarded as valuable in the carrying business against competing lines.

Q. In case of a stated published tariff by any of the roads, not variable for a month, and published throughout the east and west, what would be its effect on the through business?

A. I think that question almost every one can judge of; it is a sort of mixed commercial and carrier question; it may be said to be not very different from the case of certain merchants on one side of a street having their prices fixed and unchangeable, while on the other side they were not so restricted; I should think that the people on the other side would do the business for that month certainly; in the long traffic we all meet in the centres of trade—the western sources of business (I speak of centres as being those points where, from the number of railroads centering from the interior, make them common points), what we call common points, points from which we reach the seaboard markets. If any one of these several lines puts out its rates as fixed and unchangeable for a month, the others would certainly do the business, unless the rate was fixed at a point where no profit could be made; then I think the line having the fixed rate would do the business. I have had a little experience on that question in relation to the passenger business; I cannot recollect the year, but it was very soon after we opened our line to Chicago. The Michigan Southern line were entering into competition for the long traffic for passengers; we all had our offices in the sources for business along the west and northwest of Chicago; we thought we did wisely in playing a very conservative part in regard to cutting rates; we placed fixed rates, which we had agreed upon, in the hands of our agents, leaving them no discretionary power to go below them; we found, immediately after this arrangement was made and the price settled upon, the traffic began to lessen and divert; it grew out of small changes, sometimes cutting fifty cents under price for a passenger to New York, or if that did'nt answer the purpose, a dollar. We had a great deal of difficulty growing out of this changing of rates, and I finally gave orders to ask the price which was asked by the other route. From that time rates were steady; no advantage could be taken by reducing rates, because the other was changed at the same hour. That settled the question definitely.

Mr. CONKLING—This practice to which you refer, not only enables you to retain your share of the business, but it operates as a regulator of the rates?

A. It keeps the rates steady; there was not gain to be made; for if one man lowers, he knows his neighbor is ordered to lower at the same hour; so that it is a question only whether he will carry a passenger at a dollar loss, for of course he gets no more passengers than if he had adhered to the rates.

Q. You say, in regard to freight, that the road having the fixed tariff would lose the freight; why would it lose it?

A. What I said in regard to passengers, will apply to freight. I look upon these two as being affected by the same causes; but one in a greater degree than the other. I instanced the passenger question because it is one in which I had had experience. Passengers will not leave at once the line on which they have been accustomed to travel, because of a slight reduction of price on a competing line; but if the reduction is adhered to for a long time, they will gradually leave it for the line which has the less price. But with regard to freight, it makes very little difference with the owner of property, whether it is carried in a red car or a brown one, so that it gets to market in a stated reasonable time. There is not much difference in the time in which freight reaches the market on any of these lines. There is less than a day's travel in the distance of carriage, between the longest and the shortest one. The time on freight has little or nothing to do with it. While I know that the passengers would leave a line gradually, I have no doubt that freight would leave it *en masse* at once. I know when we had an arrangement which we could not change, and the other parties could change, we could not get any of the other parties' traffic, and they did get some of ours. You cannot get freight from a given point unless you transport it as cheap as any one else. There is another reason which affects passengers to a certain extent, so long as the passenger has business to do along the line, a half dollar nor even a dollar would change the passenger from one line to another; but freight has no such stopping necessity.

Q. In your judgment, as a railroad man, can the way and through business be done at the same rates practicably?

A. I have no doubt about its being impractic able. There may be a good many definitions of the word impracticable, but as it is generally understood the business could not be conducted with any profitable result; the two are widely different in their character. One of them, to be done at all, situated as these lines are, has got to be done under the same elasticity on one line which the other has, it would very much derange business to have that changed every day or every hour. I do not think there is any profit of the long business that amounts to much if you have got to connect it in any way with the local business. You have got to use the long business to make it profitable, to fill up the gaps as it were. You must rely upon the local business to a great extent as a steady business, running all the year pretty nearly equal as the business of the country runs.

Q. What effect would result, in your judgment, to the way freights if the through freights were abandoned?

A. On different roads it would bring about a different result.

Q. Take the two lines of New York, the Hudson River and the Harlem?

A. Where there was no competition which would so regulate the local prices as to put it out of the power of the railroads to make any more money out of them than they were at any particular period making, they would of course be interested to add to the local rates as much as they lost on the through.

Mr. COBB—Will you explain that again?

A. I say that where there are no local rates which could not be controlled beyond the will of the company by some competing interest, then the local rates, if members of the directory had any regard for the stockholders, as trustees of their property, would have to raise the local rates to compensate for the loss of doing no through business. I cannot conceive that through business can be done without the same elasticity attaches to the New York roads that would attach to the roads in opposition to them, and that, if taken away, I do not see how long business can possibly be retained. If the long business is not retained either the company must lose a considerable portion of its revenues or it must derive them from some other source. I have no doubt, on the Michigan Central road, if we lost our through business, we should raise our local business at once. We could not afford to do local business so cheaply if the sources of revenue incident to the through business were cut off. Therefore it follows, that the profits made on long business does strengthen the company to a certain extent; enabling it to do its local business at better rates.

Q. Can a competing route with a longer line fix low prices for you, and yet not be able to carry as cheap?

A. I have said before that all of the lines freighting between common points must carry at the same prices. There is no question about that. Let any company, or any line of companies, charge a higher rate from Chicago to New York their rival lines will take the business. The question as to how much profit the rival lines will make on that is a question of their own. I will instance an extreme case. The Grand Trunk Railroad is taking cotton from Memphis, far south of the southern lines in competition for western business to the English factories. They say they make money on it, whether they do or not, the policy of the British government to work a large portion of the traffic of the Western States through the Provinces will probably be persevered in. I have no doubt it will. They have built, without any question, the best line of railroad on this continent. A line that can work the cheapest, setting capital aside, which costs them only three or four per cent a year, they have got relieved from their bonded indebtedness, having received large presents from the home government and releases from liens and taxes, and it is prepared to do this long business at a rate leaving but a moderate margin to the shortest line between the western markets and the seaboard. They will regulate the price, without any question, quite as efficiently as any other line trading between the seaboard and the west.

Q. If the through business was taken from the New York roads, would it, in your judgment, go to the canals or what other channels would it take?

A. I think that would depend to a very considerable extent upon how long the experiment of turning it away from the New York lines was carried on. I think that the first, second, third classes of freight would all take the other lines. The competition between the roads is for these three classes. The fourth class is divided between the roads and the canals. The property represented by the first three classes would scarcely any of it go to New York by the Grand Trunk road; I think it would go to Boston, all of it that went by the Grand Trunk road, and that the three classes going to New York would go by the southern roads, they being much the shortest. I should think that the wholesale business, the importing business for the western cities, would come from Baltimore and Philadelphia, because it would cost as little to put it there as in New York, and thence convey it to the west. It would cost less from London and Liverpool to Chicago and St. Louis, than it would cost to go through New York. The fourth class would be divided; a part of it would go on the canal and a part on these other lines; as whereever the second and third class goes to a certain extent, to a very large extent the fourth class goes. A good deal of the fourth class, that now goes upon the canal, would take these extreme southern lines. The importations would work their way to those cities. A portion of the fourth class, that now goes by canal, as well as a portion of the fourth class that goes on the rail, would go on these extreme southern routes, and the other portion of the fourth class that goes now by rail on the N. Y. roads, would take the canal.

Mr. CONKLING—How would it affect the transportation of passengers?

A. The passenger trade follows the freight. If the trade increased to the southern cities the passengers would follow more promptly the first, second, and third class freight than they would the fourth; because it requires more care to trade in each of these classes, more personal attention; but there is no doubt that the passenger trade would wear away with the freight, except in the case of passengers traveling for pleasure—passengers making short runs in the summer time to watering places, &c.

Mr. CONKLING—What would be the effect of that policy on the city of New York?

A. I do not see why it would not have the same effect upon the city of New York that it would have upon the roads—it would work the trade into the southern cities. We had some experience in that matter during the famous St. Nicholas compact, which has some fame as well as notoriety. The little experience we had at that time, showed the effect upon my own road as well as the roads here. It was very marked in the change which it made in the coffee trade, which was a large trade in the west, and the coffee trade was looked at carefully to see what effect it was having. We found that a considerable portion of the coffee, which had formerly been shipped to New York, and thence to the west, went to B ltimore. It went then over the Baltimore and Ohio road, to the Ohio river, down the river to Cario, up the Mississippi to Galena, and then turned eastward into the interior of Illinois; it went entirely around us. A few cents on a hundred pounds, amounting to about $3 a ton, of course turned that business. That was one of the articles of the fourth class, and I do not see why all the articles of that class would not follow in the same way, if treated in the same manner. I am sure the western importing man would feel it so at once, and others would follow.

Q. Did the New York roads have a fixed tariff prior to 1858?

A. They generally did, sir.

Q. You state that two or three dollars a ton turned that freight from you?

A. I do not recollect the rate. I recollect the effect of it was so strong against these New York and Northern lines, our own among the rest, that the compact was destroyed. It was found necessary; we could not live under that state of things. It astonished us by the promptness with which the goods began to change their routes.

Q. You stated that prior to 1858 they had a general fixed tariff?

A. Yes, sir, prior to then the elements of the competition which changed the entire character of the long business, had not begun to work. There was not then the competition between Baltimore, Philadelphia and New York that exists now. I will say, in regard to the Baltimore and Ohio, and the Pennsylvania Central, that they have the same objects to subserve to fulfill their destiny. They were built with city and state capital, to subserve a certain city and state policy, and unless they could secure a liberal portion of the trade of the West to these cities, they would not fulfill the destiny for which they were constructed. An investment of capital for revenue was not the moving cause for the construction of those lines. They are more severe competitors for the trade of the West, than they would be if they were built solely with the view to revenue, and of course they do not regard the procurement of revenue except as incident to their general arrangement.

Q. What lines of communication to the far West have been completed since 1857?

A. We regard all the elements introduced since then as incident to the three lines, the Pennsylvania Central, the Baltimore and Ohio, and the Grand Trunk railroads. There is another branch of business opened up to the West, which will probably grow to great importance pretty soon, I do not know how extensive it was last year, but the year before a large number of vessels loaded on the lakes for Liverpool, and returned with freights of merchandise for the West. That is the fourth element of the difficulty that has been introduced within the last three years, making, with the other three, four elements of competition. I suppose that will grow up to be one, for I have understood they were pretty successful. The trips that were made I believe amounted to something like thirty or forty vessels.

Mr. THACHER—In 1859?

A. Yes, Sir. I do not know the number; I followed them up until they reached twenty, when I lost track of them; I presume somebody here can give the number exactly.

Q. What induced the change in the policy of the New York roads, and the conflicts they had to retain that western business? How did it arise? State the facts.

A. The first conflict—guerrilla warfare—in the shape of competition. Such competi ion always arises when new elements are brought in, until some settlement is made; and the St. Nicholas compact was the first permanent settlement of the difficulties; or rather, it was understood to be permanent. In that, the Northern lines were out-generaled entirely; they conceded to the Southern lines because of their increased nearness of those States to the interior—a different rate to the Southern cities—so strong a difference as to have a serious effect on the trade of those cities. We know that trade began to move to and from those cities in a rapidly increasing ratio—that merchants trading with New York began to get their stocks through other cities, and that the change was increasing so rapidly that it had the effect to break up the St. Nicholas compact. It was decided that the New York and other Northern lines should fix their rates so as to be as near to the west as Philadelphia and Baltimore.

Mr. CONKLING—What were the general terms of that compact?

A. The general terms were, to carry freights at uniform rates—at stated rates, which we agreed upon with a difference.

Mr. CONKLING—A sort of pro-rata arrangement, was it?

A. The lines pro-rata—that is—let me explain. Though that question does not enter into the case, the Pennsylvania Central practically owns the Pittsburgh, Fort Wayne and Chicago Railroad. It is all one with them; and whether they pro-rated with that road is a fact that exists in their own counsels. But their connection with the west forced other lines to make combinations to work against them, as they had one line working straight through to the seaboard it would not do for other lines to have divided counsels. It resulted in the lines generally running to the Northern States, from the seaboard to the west, dividing the receipts of the business, pro rata per ton, per mile, with some small trifling allowances for ferriage, to the persons keeping those ferries; and with these exceptions it is a general pro rata.

Q. Is or is not one man President of both roads from Philadelphia to Chicago, by way of the Pennsylvania Central, Fort Wayne and Chicago roads?

A. One man is President of the line from Philadelphia to Chicago—one set of agents speak for the management of the whole, and one man manages the whole line, so far as the public is concerned.

Q. You say that was broken up in consequence of this large traffic moving to the west, leaving the lines which it formerly followed?

A. Yes, Sir.

Q. What was the result of the breaking up of that compact? How did it effect the trade and commerce that went there?

A. We all felt, when it was broken up, that we were to get thence onwards our legitimate share of the business again.

Q. Was that the effect, or not?

A. I have no doubt that it was the effect. I recollect that during the last two years there has been less business, and we have all felt that we didn't get quite our share.

Q. But you have got your relative share?

A. Yes, sir. But we got less in proportion than we did before these new carriers came into the market.

Q, You stated something about what it was that created this warfare; state whether or not it was the insisting by the southern lines on carrying out that compact, and sticking to it.

A. Yes, sir; and the refusal by the northern lines to do it.

Q. The southern lines understood that if that compact was carried out, they would get the trade to the West?

A. I think they didn't appreciate that more fully than we did who lost it.

Q. Will you state what course of action the southern roads adopted to get the trade again?

A. They are just in the same position in which we now are. All these long lines have agencies and offices established in the great centres of business in the West. By centres, I mean those cities and large places where business concentrates, by having a good many interior lines reaching to those points. Wherever there is a considerable quantity of business to be got at the West, all these competing avenues of trade have their agencies established, soliciting business with a good deal of industry and perseverance.

Q. State what means they have in the western States, and New York city, in the east, for the procurement of freight and passengers.

A. As far as New York is concerned, they have, on Broadway, a very large number of offices. I do not know how many. I should think there were ten or fifteen offices belonging to these lines, and in some other parts of the city less expensive ones; and there are some in Boston, in a less degree, however, because there is less business. And so in the cities at the West; at all the large places they have offices established and maintained, with solicitors who communicate directly with the owners of freight.

Q. Making personal application to the owners of freight?

A. Yes, sir; making contracts for it constantly. I should think that such a city as Chicago might have, perhaps, no less than twenty men, whose sole business it is to confer with the owners of freight, and endeavor to make contracts for it—for the different interests.

Mr. COBB—They are denominated drummers, are they not?

A. Perhaps that is what they would be called.

Mr. THOMPSON—Fifers, too!

A. They generally act as if they were the owners of the road, and controlling the State in which they reside.

Mr. CONKLING—How many are there in Chicago?

A. There may be four or five contending interests in Chicago: the north side of the lake line, the south side of the lake line, Pennsylvania Central, Baltimore and Ohio, and the Grand Trunk lines. But each one of these is made up of several interests. The New York Central road is connected with the Great Western, North Shore, South Shore, Michigan Central, and Boston and Worcester lines. All these interests are represented. Some of the larger interests employ separate agents, while some join together in maintaining an agency.

Q. Is it the habit of the freight agents on these southern lines to demand a uniform rate for the transportation of freight?

A. There is a sort of effort of the agents of the different lines to agree upon some rate; from day to day some one cuts down the price once or twice a day, and then the others come down. Then they have a conference. The interest of these lines have to be put into the hands of these persons who act with sufficient promptness to keep them strait.

Q. Suppose one line was unable to drop their prices?

A. I think it would be gratifying to the others. They would get along a great deal more harmoniously.

Q. They would lose the business, would they not?

A. They would do no more business until they got out of that fix.

Q. And the others would eat them up?

A. They would take the business.

Mr. CONKLING—In crossing high elevations by railroad, how far does the diminished cost of conducting trains down descending grades serve to compensate for the augmented cost of ascending grades?

A. I think it would be found that nearly all the saving rests in the simple economy in fuel. When you get to the top of a grade you cannot get any more cars to go down the grade to lessen the cost of the service and men connected with the train, brakemen, enginemen, &c.; there is no means of lessening this per car per ton. You do save fuel. The strength of the southern lines in overcoming their mountain grades consists in the cheap cost of their fuel. They use coal at a very insignificant cost. I think it is inside of a dollar per ton; Mr. Hubby says that, on the Baltimore and Ohio road, the cost is about seventy cents a ton. A ton of coal is more efficient than a cord of wood; and if it can be used in such a way as to secure the saving of all heat it is as valuable as two cords of wood; but it has not been so economized. We pay from $2 to $2.50 a cord. They get the same amount of fuel in a ton of coal at seventy cents. With that advantage the disadvantage of their grades is overcome, which places them in a condition to compete, to a certain extent, with the three Northern lines.

Mr. CONKLING—Is it your opinion that a locomotive engine can conduct a no more heavy train down a descending grade than it can haul up an ascending grade? that each engine has got to get up the grade with its load? do you know of no practice of using increased locomotive power?

A. Yes, sir. If the grades are isolated so that they can manage it, they, of course, economize very much. Some roads have grades of a greater length, incident to long districts; where they occur thus frequently it has not been found practicable to use this assisting power. I do not know how the Baltimore and Ohio road is managed, but I think it is used there very little, because they have long grades, and not many of these difficulties. I think that the great saving on those lines is in the cost of fuel, rather than in the advantage of the descending line.

Q. Has not the shortness of the route something to do with it?

A. The fact that it brings them down to a measure of miles in length, is a measure of its capacity for service.

Q. Can all roads that compete from common points, get the same pro rata per mile?

A. No, sir. A moment's thought will show you it could not be done. These roads most all carry freight, as I have said before, from common points to market, at the aggregate price, and not at the same price per ton per mile. It is the same aggregate price from source to market. The longer line will get less per ton per mile than the shorter. For example, from Chicago to New York, over the New York Central and Michigan Central, they will get more per ton per mile than they will get by the Baltimore and Ohio; and from Cincinnati to New York they will get more per ton per mile, on the Baltimore and Ohio road, than they would on the New York Central. In the one case, the Baltimore and Ohio forms a part of the long line, and the New York Central a part of the shorter, and, in the other case, the reverse, It follows that the same kind of freight must be carried at different rates by each road—at higher rates when they form part of the short line, at lower rates when they form part of the long line. The New York Central cannot say that they will take a barrel of flour over their line in the long traffic, in competition with the other railroads, at the same price per mile as the others. In some lines it forms a part of the long competing route, and in others, a part of the short competing route, and they have got to take their proper pro rata share.

Q. So that, in your judgment, it is impossible to apply that theory in practice for the transportation of freight on the longer lines of road?

A. It has been strongly for my interest, that that practice should be gone into at the North, in connection with the New York Central line from Chicago. We have felt as if we formed a part with this New York Central road, of the shortest line for that traffic. If we could have procured the New York Central road to take flour from us as cheaply as they could take it from Cincinnati, it would have been greatly to our advantage; but we have never felt justified in asking for that. So far as the Michigan Central line is concerned, we have always treated the question in that way. We have taken flour cheaper to Detroit when it came from St. Louis, than when it came from Kenosha, Galena or Milwaukee; because, when we go to St. Louis, they have a shorter line to take their freight to market, running east, northeast, than ours. We form part of the longer route, and we carry everything cheaper to the market than freight which came from the Northwest. We must do that, or else abandon our St. Louis business. So I may say with regard to all points that are on the shortest roads, we get the highest prices, and on the long lines a less price, for the same articles, in the same train, at the same time with the articles on the short line.

Q. Does the Grand Trunk Railway connect at Detroit? If so, how—what are its connections?

A. Temporarily, the Grand Trunk has got a narrow gauge from Port Huron; the wide gauge ends at Port Sarnia, on the east side of the river. Port Huron is on the west side, opposite—and the narrow gauge commencing there comes down to Detroit. It was in contemplation, when it was building, to have a broad gauge; but as they were very short of stock they laid a narrow gauge. They have leased locomotives for the line, and the cars of the Michigan Central, and the Michigan Southern roads go up to Port Huron The transhipment is there effected by ferry, as is the case here; they take the cars across so as to ship the freight from car to car; instead of a ferry boat they have a long boat upon which the cars are taken across. But it is in contemplation to have a broad gauge to Detroit; they have built transfer houses at Detroit, preparatory to the transfer business, when the broad gauge shall be brought there. They are now discussing the question as to the advisability of putting a broad gauge into Boston over one of the lines from Portland, and putting a third rail on the road to Chicago, so as to haul broad cars from Chicago to Boston.

Mr CONKLING—Is there machinery employed at any of these termini for the loading of cars?

A. It is all done by manual labor. Where grain is carried in bulk it is generally run into the car, afterwards shoveled out of the cars into pits below, and then elevated in the usual way. Beyond that I don't know of any machinery being used.

Q. If the rate on the New York roads was fixed at so much per ton per mile, what would be the effect on long freights?

A. It would depend upon how frequently that rate could be changed. If it could be changed every day it would be better.

Q. Suppose it could be changed once a month?

A. It would give twenty-nine days of that month to the other lines, unless the rate on that line was so low that it afforded no profit; then they would have their share of the business. I believe I have answered that question once before.

Mr. THOMPSON—Not exactly in that shape, and only incidentally.

Mr. BROOKS—You asked me that last question. I have not alluded to one point in relation to it, which has just come into my mind. If the New York roads charge for the long and local freight one rate of transportation, it would introduce to the western business, that comes by water, a new terminus. As a matter of course, it would put Oswego in the position of Buffalo. If you had to put the price by rail per ton, per mile to Oswego, at the same rate as to Buffalo, of course the water-bound business would come to Oswego. The New York Central road, as now regulated, has the power to make its long business, the principal business—has power to put business on the long end of its line instead of having it cut through in the middle. If the power to protect itself from inroad at the side is lost, water-bound business would come to Oswego, and the west half of their line would be of no use for the purposes of long freights.

Q. What is the effect of these low long freights on the country, on the price of land? State what your experience upon that subject has been, whether it has tended to diminish the price?

A. I once had that question raised upon me a good many years ago, very agreeably, and I look back upon it now with an inclination to smile. Somewhere about the year 1850 we opened our Michigan Central railroad to Lake Michigan, in 1852 we opened it to Chicago. We there met on the lake the waterborne carriers in boats. Not getting long business, we had to carry that long business at a lower rate than we carried our local business, owing te the competition of these boats. We carried our local business at a very great reduction upon the charges which the state had charged. The state had built the road to Kalamazoo, which was the entrepot. We took the road from the state and reduced the rates twenty-five per cent below the allowance in the charter, as we thought the rates called for in our charter too high. But when we got to Chicago we had to reduce them much lower; we had to commence at Niles, which is situated on a navigable river where we crossed it, about twenty or thirty miles from the lake. There were these little steamboats taking freight down the lake, which came thence around. When we got to Niles we took that business from the river at the rates charged by the boats, and as our route was the best we took the whole of it, and broke up the system completely. The Kalamazoo people met and prepared an address to us saying that we had ruined the price of land in Kalamazoo county by carrying freight at lower rates from Berrien county. I wrote them a letter which was printed in pamphlet form, of which I have not seen a copy for several years, but the purport of it was this, that unless it increased the price of grain, and influenced the price raised upon the Mediterranean and the wheat-growing countries of the world, it would not affect the price of their land unless we damaged them, or raised the price between Kalamazoo and the markets, their land would be as it was before, as we had reduced the price between Kalamazoo and the market more than 25 per cent, we had increased the value of their land, and as we had not carried wheat any cheaper from Berrien county any cheaper than other lines we had not increased the price of land there.

Q. State that principle in its application to the lands in the State of New York?

A. I say, in regard to the lands of New York, that if the New York Central Railroad has not raised the price of products from any particular district to the common markets, they have not reduced the value of land in that region, unless they have done something which should deteriorate the prices in this common market, which they have not the power to do, because from all the sources of the west they have done business at the rates of other lines; therefore, they did not open up any more lands by their own acts in competition. I take it, that if all the lands in the west were opened up, it would not affect the price of grain in the world. The grain-growing regions are very large, and as the New York roads carry grain at the same prices as their competitors, they exercise no influence upon that. As the canal has been the regulator of prices, so if the canal tolls are lowered so as to bring rail prices down with them, they will put western lands nearer market than they now are, to a certain extent; but they would have to introduce a vast amount of grain from regions now uncultivated in the west, to the markets of the world, before it would be affected by it.

Mr. COBB—Do you refer to the effect of individual lines of the railroad system?

A. I refer to the effect upon the State of New York. If the whole system of railways could be blotted out from the west at once, it would cut off certain districts of lands of the west from the eastern markets, except by the Mississippi and St. Lawrence. Whether it would compel them to grow more at a less price, I do not know.

Q. Do you know whether or not the local rates which the produce of the western states have to pay to reach the competing points at the west, are as high or higher than the local rates on the New York lines?

A. I think it will be found that they are generally not less than 25 per cent higher; I should say more than that. I know our own rates on the Michigan Central road are over 25 per cent higher, from a 100 to 150 miles from Detroit or Chicago, are very far in advance of the New York Central's local rates. I think that will be found to be so over the whole west. There may be isolated exceptions, but the general rule is such as I state.

Q. State to the Committee the relative cost of carrying wheat and carrying flour on the railway, the same distance?

A. I do not know as there is much difference, provided if the wheat is put in b gs; but it is hardly considered practicable to do so when you come to the bulk, it is more difficult to carry than flour. West of the Mississippi the plan is, to put up the grain in bags for the St. Louis market; but where it is carried in bulk, as it is east of the Mississippi, there is a broad margin in favor of carrying flour.

Mr. COBB—Have you often attended railroad conventions, during your 25 years' experience on railroads?

A. I have attended quite a number of them.

Mr. COBB—How extensive are they attended by other lines?

A. I think we had one once at Cleveland where we figured 800 millions of dollars of capital.

Mr. COBB—But how many different lines?

A. I do not know as I could say; we had a vast number of roads.

Mr. COBB—Are these four roads, the Baltimore & Ohio, the Pennsylvania Central, the New York & Erie, and the New York Central, are they ordinarily conspicuous in those conventions?

A. I believe there was no one present from those roads at that convention, except Mr. Moran.

Mr. COBB—Is that the case with all the conventions?

A. I should think, as a general thing, one or two of them are present at about a half of the conventions, perhaps a little more. When they have had their compacts between themselves they have generally stood aloof from conventions held by the western lines. It depends a little upon what they are called for. If they are called for the fall or spring, to make running arrangements, they have to be present. Sometimes they are represented by their principal officers, sometimes by their train managers.

Mr. COBB—When the arrangements are being made for their summer's business they are ordinarily represented?

A. Yes, sir—and in the fall when the arrangement are being made for winter trains.

Mr. COBB—Represented by somebody?

A. Yes, sir.

Mr. COBB—While the St. Nicholas compact was in existence they were present in the conventions less than before?

A. Yes, sir.

Mr. COBB—In these conventions has any particular line a controlling influence?

A. I don't think there is. We have sometimes felt when we voted, (as we generally do, and have always done, by railroads,) that lines south of the south shore of Lake Erie, there was an undue representation. There are a good many roads in Ohio, and a good many short ones.

Mr. COBB—I refer to the four lines?

A. These short lines all carry the same vote as the long lines. We have frequently been embarrassed by the multitude of votes coming from roads of a short distance, and lines less interested in the east and western trains than the long lines were.

Mr. COBB—How are the roads represented—by miles?

A. Each road carries one vote—the long road the same as the short one.

Mr. COBB—As far as the Baltimore & Ohio, the Pennsylvania Central, the New York & Erie and the New York Central are concerned, has any one of them a controlling influence to any extent?

A. I do not think they have; I think the northern roads have always felt that the south has always exercised too much influence.

Mr. COBB—That is a mere matter of opinion?

A. Yes, sir. Each one cast his vote to carry his point, otherwise I don't think there has been any undue influence.

Mr. COBB—Which of the roads do you regard as your allies?

A. The New York Central and the Grand Trunk.

Mr. COBB—You ship over either as occasion offers?

A. We are unfortunate because our long lines cast but one vote.

Mr. COBB—But the Pennsylvania Central has only one vote?

A. Yes, sir. But the lines running into it always vote with the Pennsylvania Central and against the Michigan Central.

Mr. COBB—You have no feeders of that kind?

A. They are very small. Our feeders lie west of Chicago, and with them it is immaterial whether they vote with us or with the Pennsylvania Central. We have felt it to be very embarrassing to have the roads vote by routes and not by miles.

Mr. COBB—You have alluded to the St. Nicholas compact; did you state that the southern roads adhered to that rigidly?

A. I think they cut freights even on that. I think they were much in favor of keeping it up by us, but I think there was a little want of faith in keeping it up with them.

Mr. COBB—Did they not charge that on your northern routes?

A. They always charge it on each other, under such circumstances, and I dare say the charges are very true.

Mr. COBB—These railroad compacts are more on paper than anywhere else?

A. They are very apt to result so. It is almost impossible, by law or agreement, to make the thing work steady. The best way is to put in the hands of freight agents the right to drop rates when anybody else does. We have come to that as the only practicable method.

Mr. COBB—Then to the public, who do not know that there is no fault in railroad compacts, there is a liability of being largely deceived?

A. I think you might find some railroads as mean in their business operations as men in other lines of business. I do not know of any peculiar quality of mind or nature in railroad men, which should make them different from other men.

Mr. COBB—I was not calling for a pro rata distinction, but for your opinion upon the subject?

A. I have seen contracts that worked well for a long period, but it is very rare. If one party will live squarely up to the agreement, you will find some other party to it will cut under and take the business. When that is done the time for the dissolution of the compact is at hand, and while it exists it has a weakly life.

Mr. COBB—It is a paper contract without any seal?

A. Yes, sir. When business gets short, there is a struggle for it, and when somebody drops prices to secure it, then the compact dies out pretty quick?

Mr. COBB—In the spring these four lines hold a convention, and in the winter also?

A. The conventions are generally held in the spring and fall?

Mr. COBB—Can you tell me what are the relative prices between spring and summer; are they higher or lower or is there anything like a uniformity?

A. In the winter they are higher than in the summer.

Mr. COBB—What is the cause of this advance?

A. The cost of doing the work in the winter is a great deal higher than it is in the summer. I think if we were compelled to work in the winter at the rates we receive for summer business, it would be better for us to leave the business and shut up our offices.

Mr. COBB—Is that the only cause which produces an advance in prices?

A. I have no doubt that the closing of the canals and lakes has a very great influence. When the lakes are closed from Chicago to Buffalo we can get a higher rate. When the St. Lawrence, the Ohio river (though the Ohio river is more unsteady) and the canal is closed, and the Northern Mississippi, we can all get rates higher, and perhaps it gives us as much profit on our business as we get on our summer business at lower rates.

Mr. COBB—Are not your winter rates ordinarily remunerative?

A. I should think that, one year with another, they are.

Mr. COBB—How would it compare with your summer remuneration ?

A. I rather think we get quite as much net out of the summer.

Mr. COBB—Take the traffic together on one line of it ?

A. Of course we make more money out of passengers, because our rates are not much higher in winter than in summer—not near as much as the cost is. We make more in summer than in winter. I do not think we get more than 10 or 12 per cent for running our passenger business more.

Mr. COBB—You speak of a large number of freight agents in Chicago. Have the lines over which they engage, a tacit understanding to pro rate with each other on any contracts which they make ?

A. I think that is generally understood The Pennsylvania Central has its own counsels in its management. Our understanding is, that if we keep within reasonable limits the others will hold to it. If the rates are unreasonably low, the remedy is to call a convention.

Mr. COBB—Then they have a power of attorney to make contracts, and you carry them out ?

A. That has not been formally given, but there is a general understanding.

Mr. COBB—It amounts to an understanding. Do you ever repudiate contracts entered into ?

A. I do not say that. If we take a contract at below paying rates it is held to as a matter of courtesy. There is no compulsion. The Great Western road in Canada do have some bickerings.

Mr. COBB—But it ends in a settlement by which the property is carried ?

A. Sometimes the person making the contract has to pay the loss. We at the west think that the agents of the four lines at the east can judge whether they can get business from them better than we can. We at the west have better opportunities for judging of the prospects for business at the west. Sometimes ships carry to and from New Orleans very cheaply, and particularly when it comes to the cotton trade going to the north. We are quite willing at such times to drop our prices at the west to keep the trade in the northern channels, which, in the west, has a chance to go down the rivers. They feel that we can best judge at the west end of the route, and we feel that their judgment is better at the east. It is the same way as partners in a certain business living at different points, and where both are interested in the result of the operations at both places. Each would rely upon the other to look after their joint interests at his own end of the line, because each in his own position can better serve the other's interest than the other could himself.

Mr. COBB—Have the New York Central and the New York and Erie, in their agencies at Chicago, signs over their doors ?

A. They have agents there. I am not certain whether the New York Central has an office there or not. I dare say they have. The New York and Erie has.

Mr. COBB—They are as much represented as at the city of Albany ?

A. Not as much as the city of Albany, perhaps, Albany being one of the termini of the road.

Mr COBB—I mean for the purpose of engaging business ?

A. Yes, sir.

Mr. COBB—How much further west do they have agencies ?

A. I cannot tell you that.

Mr. COBB—They extend, at all events, from Chicago to New York city ?

A. It is generally understood that in the large sources of business there are men who look out for the interests of these great lines, extending from the centres of business.

Mr. COBB—You remarked, that previous to 1857, '58, your rates were made up by yourselves, and there was less cutting down ?

A. Yes, sir.

Mr. COBB—What was the position of the Michigan Central at that time, compared with the present ?

A. We got very much better rates.

Mr. COBB—What was its financial condition, compared with the present ?

A. Better—much better. There were fewer lines to divide the business among. It is partly owing to financial disaster, and the great depression of the trade of the country. How much is owing to that, and how much to the division of the business among the different lines, is a matter of judgment.

Mr. COBB—What proportion of your business is called through business? That which comes from Chicago ?

A. I don't think I have seen the figures in regard to that subject for the last three or four years. I should think that one-third of the number of tons we move was through. The long tons moved would be less than half of the local.

Mr. COBB—That would be about one-third of the total ?

A. Less than half of the whole. I think it is more than one-third. As a mere matter of judgment, I should say that the through tons put into the car, were two-fifths of the total number of tons. But what proportion of the tonnage moving one mile it is, is another question. The long business goes the whole length of the road ; the short business, ten miles and upwards.

Mr. COBB—What are the present quotations of the Michigan Central stock ?

A. I think the last I saw was 38 ?

Mr. COBB—What was it in 1857 ?

A. In the spring of 1857 business was much better than in the fall. That was the year when everything broke down.

Mr. COBB—Previous to July, how was it ?

A. I cannot recollect; I should think it was more than 50 ; I may be mistaken.

Mr. COBB—Was there ever any time when its stocks were worth 100 ?

A. There was a time when it was over par.

Mr. COBB—How long since ?

A. A good many years. It was not within 5 or 6 years.

Mr. COBB—Was it within 6 or 7 ?

A. It may be ; I am very bad at remembering dates.

Mr. COBB—What were the relative rates of compensation for the traffic you performed then, compared with now ?

A. Our rates must have been a good deal higher than now; I cannot tell the relative rates; it would be a hard matter to go back 5 or 6 years.

Mr. COBB—But you must have a general recollection?

A. Our passenger rates were not any higher than now.

Mr. COBB—I refer to freight.

A. I cannot tell.

Mr. COBB—What was the relative amount of tonnage you moved at that time compared with now?

A. That I am unable to tell you.

Mr. COBB—What was about the relative value of Great Western stock in 1857, previous to July, as compared with its value now?

A. It was very high until they commenced to build their branches, about par; when they commenced them it began to drop.

Mr. COBB—What is its value now?

A. I cannot tell.

Mr. COBB—Very considerably lower?

A. I have never seen a quotation of that in my life. I do not know that there ever has been a share sold in the market so as to have a quotation.

Mr. COBB—What is the lowest rate at which you ever transported freight?

A. I should think we had carried for less than a cent a ton per mile. Once and a while we have worked for the purpose of putting the price down, when the cutting at Chicago has been so irregular that we could not work with satisfaction, we have then put down prices to bring the rates again to a paying point

Mr. COBB—Your object was to punish your competitors?

A. The object was to secure a meeting at once. When we found they were charging 95, when we asked 100, we dropped to 95; then they fell to 90; we followed, and they dropped to 85. When that course is pursued, as it is occasionally, then we put rates down to such a figure as will call the attention of the officers of the road at once, and an arrangement is promptly made by which paying rates may be secured.

Mr. COBB—What is the cost of the movement of freight per ton per mile, as you estimate it?

A. I made one explanation of what I considered as new business.

Mr. COBB—I mean new business.

A. I dont think I have ever figured that on our road.

Mr. COBB—Do you suppose that your road is operated dearer or cheaper than the New York Central?

A. I do not think it should be much different. Our grades are not very much different from those of the New York Cent al.

Mr. COBB—Do you suppose the cost to be smaller?

A. I think we have mutual advantages. They have grades easier a little, but we have fuel cheaper. It is about the same.

Mr. COBB—Is there any difference between the cost of moving fourth class merchandise and other commodities? Are there any distinctions in the value of handling a barrel of flour and a barrel of beef or pork?

A. Not very appreciable. I would rather carry flour a little, than the others.

Mr. COBB—Do you regard it that a ton of flour or a ton of beef may be carried as cheap as a ton of anything else?

A. I should regard all those articles as being very favorable to cheap transportation.

Mr. COBB—Then do you regard it that a ton of either of these commodities costs no more than a ton of anything else to transport?

A. I do not think it does much. I would rather carry flour than some other articles.

Mr. COBB—Then there is very little difference in the cost of movement. No matter what the commodity is, whether first, second or third class; a ton of flour would represent a ton of anything else?

A. I cannot say that. I would rather carry flour than molasses. Some kinds of sugar we have trouble with.

Mr. COBB—Will a ton of flour fairly represent, as near as may be, a ton of anything else?

A. I would rather carry a ton of flour than a ton of anything else.

Mr. COBB—What is the difference?

A. I don't think I would make much difference.

Mr. COBB—How would it be with pork in barrels? Would a ton of that fairly represent a ton of anything else?

A. I think that rolling freight is better than other freights.

Mr. COBB—Would you regard a ton of molasses as about the worst?

A. I should think a ton of that or a ton of beef would be an average.

Mr. COBB—And the cost of transporting that would represent the cost of moving anything?

A. Almost anything. Gentlemen can judge as well as I. It is a mere question of the safety of the article and of its destructability.

Mr. COBB—I am not a railroad man, and we call upon railroad men for information about that which we have only a theoretical knowledge. You mentioned that the Pennsylvania Central is actually now running to Chicago; is not the western end of that road in the hands of a receiver?

A. Yes, sir. I believe it is the Pittsburgh, Fort Wayne and Chicago.

Mr. COBB—It is in the hands of the receiver?

A. Yes, sir.

Mr. COBB—I think you said the southern roads, the Baltimore and Ohio, and the Pennsylvania Central were less affected by the extremes of heat and cold than the northern?

A. Yes, sir, very much. I believe with regard to the receiver of the Pittsburgh, Fort Wayne and Chicago, that it was made satisfactory to Mr. Thompson, the president of both roads, it and the Pennsylvania Central, and that the arrangement is such as not to embarrass the business at all.

Mr. HOVEY—You have stated to the committee that, in your judgment, if the fourth class freights should be taken from the railroads in this state, instead of going by the canal, a large portion would go by roads outside of the state?

A. I said a considerable proportion. How large a proportion I did not state. A considerable proportion would go to the railroads of other states, along with the other three classes. I thought some, now going upon the canals, would follow. I stated that the trade of the southern cities would increase, drawing from all classes from the northern cities. Whether the aggregate result would be a reducing or increasing the canal or not is a question of judgment.

Mr. HOVEY—Do you know what proportion the fourth class freight, moved by the canals is, compared with that by railroads?

A. I have no doubt of it.

A. I have not the slightest idea.

Mr. HOVEY—Do you not know that it is much larger than that carried by all the freights carried by the railroads of this state?

A. I do not know anything about it. The fourth class carried by railway, covers certain specified articles. If you put all canal freights into the freight cars, it must be very immense.

Mr. HOVEY—Do you make your prices on heavy articles, beef, pork and flour, and freight of that character, with direct reference to the canal prices in the summer?

A. No, sir. So far as we are concerned we make them more with reference to lake transportation. If we are running back our cars to Chicago empty, we fill them at very low rates. If we are running them back full, and getting low rates, we would let the lake take the whole freight.

Mr. HOVEY—I asked with reference to your connection with the New York Central?

A. In summer it makes no difference to the New York Central whether it goes by lake or by rail, and we have to go squarely against lake. The New York Central cannot give us any freight to help us in the summer.

Mr. HOVEY—In your judgment is there any route from Lake Erie to New York cheaper than the New York Central or Hudson River?

A. I have no knowledge of the capacity of the canal.

Mr. HOVEY—I speak of the railroads.

A. I do not

Mr. HOVEY—You think no route can do it better?

A. I think not. I think that long lines can put down rates so as to make it unprofitable. Long lines have the capacity to take away the profitable margin of the short lines. If the New York Central can make 25 per cent, these other longer lines have to be satisfied with 10 or 12 per cent.

Mr. HOVEY—You stated to the Committee, that if prices were fixed for freight from east to west, that unless they were fixed so low that the business would pay no profit, it would go to other roads?

A. It would.

Mr. HOVEY—Do you mean that this immense business would be done at a loss to get it?

A. I do not think it would do it at a loss. I think the Pennsylvania Central and Baltimore and Ohio would work at a loss for a time, under the impression that it would strengthen their road from the East in the trade with the West, so that they would, eventually, make considerable profit. We frequently open a business which is dependent for its future hopes of success in doing business at rates, for the present, that are not at all remunerative. If I was the controller of the affairs of the Pennsylvania Central and Baltimore and Ohio railroads, I would do a large amount of business at cost, to these cities, with the idea that it would result favorably to them in the future.

Mr. HOVEY—Having expressed the opinion that the New York Central can do business as low as any other route, do you think there would be danger of a final loss to that road if they were compelled to do business at a fixed published rate for a month?

Mr. HOVEY—They would lose the whole business?

A. Unless they fixed the rates so near cost that other roads would not accept the rate dictated, they would. I think the New York Central worked in this way for five years. It would severely try the patience of the Pennsylvania Central railroad, but I think she would work for such an advantage.

Mr. HOVEY—Does that bring yon to the conclusion that the long business now on these roads, is done at little or no profit, with such competition as now exists?

A. I think that the long business is done at a considerable profit. I think it can be kept up at the rate it is now done. None of the roads can reduce the rates of long business unless the others do it, and there is nothing to be gained by it. Suppose you fixed the rates on the New York Central where they now are, for a month. The agents of other lines at Chicago would drop their prices two cents, or five cents per hundred pounds, and get the business. They would continue to reduce the price from month to month, until the rates were very near cost.

Mr. HOVEY—What will be the effect of this competition on the stock of the road for the next five years?

A. It is hard to tell. I have generally been of the opinion that the longer this competition continued, the more it would make the roads pursue a conservative course, and stick to the rates, finding that, in cutting prices, they were met with promptness by a similar reduction by other roads.

Mr. HOVEY—Do you regard the action of these roads, during the past year, as having been conservative?

A. I cannot say I do.

Mr. HOVEY—Has not competition been going on without any regulation or order?

A. The competition has been very severe; it is almost always so when a new road enters into a traffic and attempts to get it away from old ones. It is generally very strong and very persevering. Such was the case with the Southern lines, and such is the case with the Grand Trunk now. They have got to make patrons for their new avenue, and introduce the public to it. People are attached to old avenues and inducements have to be made to secure their patronage for the new ones. The inducements are lower rates. When at last they had formed acquaintenances and secured patronage, they would consent to organize and fix prices at fair rates with the other lines. In another year another new line, without friends and without patrons, comes into competition, and again the arrangements are thrown into pi by their cutting rates to get patrons. This being secured, they of course would be conservative.

Mr. HOVEY—Then the establishment of business is no avail unless you do it as cheap as anybody else?

A. I don't think it is of much value in the freight business; in the passenger business it may have; but even there it has a wearing off tendency which would result injuriously.

Mr. HOVEY—Do you know the distances from Detroit to Boston, Portland and New York, by the Grand Trunk?

A. I do not; I think it is as near from Detroit to Boston as it is from Detroit to Portland, considerably nearer; if so, it is a hundred miles nearer from Detroit to Boston by the Grand Trunk than by the New York Central, and Albany and Western. The Grand Trunk, I might mention, has introduced a new element in the traffic, that of advancing money on freights.

Mr. COBB—Is not the New York Central represented in the Board of Directors of the Michigan Central?

A. Mr. Corning is a member of our board.

[During a subsequent stage of the proceedings, Mr. Brooks appeared before the Committee and made the following additional statement, in explanation of a part of his testimony. Reporter.]

Mr. BROOKS—I understand that I said in reply to the last gentleman, that all freights could be carried at about the same rates. I understood the gentleman to mean fourth-class freights, goods carried at about the same rates as molasses and beef. I did not understand the question to cover the first, second and third classes. It would be absurd to suppose that a ton of chairs or grain cradles, of which you cannot carry more than a ton or two in a car, would be as cheap as the others. I supposed I had so stated the facts as not to be mistaken. I supposed that the question referred to what was a fair average for fourth-class freight.

Mr. COBB—Can you load your cars fully with first and second class goods?

A. Some of the kinds we can. There is a wide difference. Of furniture you can get but very little.

Mr. COBB—Dry goods in boxes and bales?

A. You could, I should think; you would only suffer greater risk of loss or damage. High priced goods are more susceptible to damage. Some goods we can get only one or two tons in a car that carries ten tons, and with some we get in the full weight.

Mr. COBB—What do you suppose is the average tonnage per car, the season through, of first and second class goods?

A. I could not guess any better than yourself Some may carry ten tons and others not more than two tons. They range between those two figures.

Mr. COBB—Taking goods in boxes and bales which are pretty heavy, would you estimate the cost of moving these as greater than moving the fourth class?

A. I do not think the simple difference in the cost of movement amounts to much, but the hazard and liability to damage makes the difference.

Mr. COBB—Then it depends upon the value of the commodity, whether heavy or light?

A. Yes, sir.

Mr. COBB—Take the third class goods; do not the cars ordinarily go fully loaded when you carry that class?

A. So far as the third class is concerned. I cannot now name any articles which belong in that class—I am ignorant of that detail as to what belongs to one class or the other. I could not divide the articles into their respective classes at all.

Mr. COBB—Is there not a wide dissimilarity in the price of movement of articles which you can't put eight or ten tons in a car, and does not the only difference consist in the value of the article?

A. Yes, sir, and the liabflity to damage?

STATEMENT

Of SOLOMON DRULLARD, General Freight Agent of the New York Central Railroad Company.

I have been General Freight Agent of the New York Central Railroad Company, since September, 1854; and previous to that time was General Freight Agent of the Buffalo and Hornellsville Railroad. I was formerly engaged in the canal transportation business, from 1827 up to the time of my appointment to the General Freight Agency of the Buffalo and Hornellsville Railroad.

I think the cost of moving way-freight, exceeds by one-third the cost of moving through-freight, and perhaps more, inasmuch as way-trains, do not, in the course of business, take or convey more than two-thirds the number of cars that through-trains do—perhaps less; that the way-cars are very frequently but partially loaded. It also requires a longer time to go a given distance, in consequence of the frequent stoppages—going on and off the switches to get to the freight houses, for loading and unloading freight, thus increasing the cost of motive power, and the men employed on freight trains; that from two to five and six men are required at the several way-stations, to load and unload, to make out way-bills, collect charges, deliver and receive freight, making the cost of conveying way-freight, as compared with through, from 40 to 50 per cent greater. The way-business is chiefly independent of the through, requiring separate men and management, and is necessarily governed by different rules, and should be conducted under different tariffs, and must be, if the difference in cost of transportation is taken into account.

I have examined the way-freight tariffs, of the eighteen different and principal freight roads, presented to the Committee in the testimony of Mr. Spaulding, as well as the local freight tariffs of many other roads, and find that no roads do their local freighting at rates as low as those charged by the New York Central on all their way-freights; nor do I believe, that greater accommodations, or more dispatch, are afforded to shippers of local freight on the line of any other road, than are given on the New York Central.

From my knowledge of the freighting business on the New York Central Road, I am confident, that it could not do a way and through-business under a pro rata law; nor could it do a through-business in competition with the rival lines, if compelled to make and publish a tariff, which could not be varied for thirty days; for, as soon as a tariff was published, competing lines would drop sufficiently under it to secure the business from all competing points. In a competing business, like the transportation of property, without the power of immediate change in prices, we become the prey of aggression, without the power of self-protection; our right to change, even if not used, is our only and strong safeguard.

A measure like the one asked for in the petitions, would, in my judgment, divert the trade from New York, and her roads, to a very serious extent, and injuring materially the large investments made by the business interests of the State.

While in Chicago, last week, I found that the

agents of the Grand Trunk Railroad, had actually contracted to convey a large quantity of provisions from Chicago to Liverpool, at eighty-seven and one-half cents per one hundred pounds. This freight was offered to the New York Central and Erie Roads at the same price, but it was declined at so low a rate. The Grand Trunk Road is to be a formidable competitor to the New York Roads, and is now taking business to the seaboard from them at Chicago, St. Louis, Cincinnati and other common western towns, at prices considerably below those at which property has heretofore been transported through New York.

The case alluded to in the New York Tribune, of December last, about which one of the Committee made inquiry, must be a mistake. I have no knowledge of cattle being driven from Bergen to Buffalo, to take the cars for Albany. Cases of this kind have occurred. Parties living at Bergen, and other places on the line of the Central Road, west of Rochester, have at times been allowed, when the rates of transportation were fair, to ship their cattle from Buffalo to points on the line of the road east, unload them with a view of a few weeks' pasturage, then take them up and transport them to Albany without extra charge. At one time, last summer, when the competition was sharp, and prices very low, one of the shippers, who had previously enjoyed the privilege just mentioned, desired to avail himself of its benefits again, but was refused at the then low rates ; the cattle were therefore sent through without charge at the competing prices.

Mr. Cobb is very much mistaken in his statement before the Committee, that no property was shipped for the citizens of Buffalo, between Oct. 20th and Nov. 20th, on the Central Railroad. They had, it is true, large quantities of freight to be forwarded at that time, but it did not prevent shipments of Buffalo freights, between the dates just mentioned. It frequently occurs in the fall, when the canal has more than it can do, that forwarders are desirous of making large shipments on the railroad on short notice, at a time when there is a large quantity of property in the railroad freight houses, which has been previously received. This delays property for the Buffolo forwarders for a few days, as property must be dispatched in the order it is received. But this state of things never lasts but a few days at a time.

I have examined the case charged against the Central Road, by Mr. Parsons of Rochester, who said that flour was taken from Rochester to New York for sixty cents per barrel, while eighty-seven and a half cents was charged from Fisher's Station, sixteen miles east of Rochester. The explanation given by Mr. Briggs, before the Committee, is correct. The flour was shipped by the Central Road to Albany, to the care of the Swiftsure Line of tow boats on the river, at fifty-two cents per barrel to Albany. It did not reach Albany in time to take the river before its close, was carted over the river by the Swiftsure Line to the Hudson River Road, at an expense of five and half cents per barrel, and was charged on the Hudson River Road, the usual winter tariff thirty cents per barrel to New York. There was no fault on the part of the Central Road in regard to it.

A complaint was made on the part of the petitioners, that the Central Road, last fall, in Buffalo, received flour to ship at the company's convenience, and that property belonging to Buffalo was detained until that received from the west had gone forward. It is the usual and proper course for the company to transport property in the order in which it is received, giving preference as far as they can, to perishable property, and late in the fall or early in December, at about which time the river closes, the company will not receive property to ship through except at their convenience after property previously received, has gone forward. There is generally for a few days at about the close of navigation a press of freight at Buffalo and other points to go east, which makes a few days' delay absolutely necessary before all property offered can be shipped, but it always goes forward in the order which it is received, and as fast as the large equipment of the road can transport it. November 1st, 1854, the tariff on flour from Buffalo to New York, was seventy cents per barrel, and to Albany sixty cents. This continued until the boats on the Hudson river put up their freight, which made a corresponding advance from Buffalo to New York necessary. The advance was five cents per barrel, so that on the 13th November, flour from Buffalo to New York was seventy-five cents. On the 21st November, freights were advanced on flour to seventy-eight cents to New York, and sixty-five cents to Albany. December 9th the tariff on flour from Buffalo to Albany, was seventy cents, from Rochester to Albany, fifty-five cents, and Canandaigua to Albany fifty cents per barrel. On the 2d January all the freight at Buffalo was cleared out, so that no complaint could be made on account of delay. January 4th, the rate on flour from Buffalo to New York was ninety-five cents, of which the Hudson River Road received thirty-seven and a half cents per barrel. January 10th, the rates on flour to New York were advanced to $1.10 cents per barrel, of which the Hudson River Road received forty-five cents per barrel, leaving to the New York Central Road sixty-five cents per barrel from Buffalo to Albany. In February, the Hudson River Road reduced their prices, and the tariff was again established at ninety-five cents per barrel from Buffalo to New York. No freights at this time was taken from western points, at a different tariff from the above. Arbitrary rates were maintained at Dunkirk, Buffalo and Suspension Bridge, on freights from the northwest, and generally so from the southwest, with the exception of cases where the roads of New York were brought into competition with the southern lines, until the lines of the southern roads were extended through to Chicago, which so much increased the competition for through business that arbitrary rates could no longer be maintained without a loss of the business to the New York lines. The cases mentioned by Mr. Cobb, where discriminations were made, have almost all of them occurred within the past two years, when the competition with rival lines has been unparalleled, and when it was necessary to take freights from common competing points at very low prices, in order to show the rival lines that it was better to return to fair and established prices, and that they would get as much business by so doing, as they did under extreme low rates. I find as much discrimination between long and short distances, and against the people of this state, in the transportation, on the canals as is made by railroads, and I give a few cases which have mostly come under my observation the past year, in the document marked A, appended to this statement. My experience is, that discriminations between long and short freights are general on all lines of transport.

January 31*st*, 1860. S. DRULLARD.

A.

CANAL DISCRIMINATIONS.

May, 1859. New York to Buffalo, 514 miles, 10 cents per 100 lbs. New York to Rochester, 415 miles, 12 cents per 100 lbs. At pro rata it should have been 8 4-100 cents per 100 lbs., or one-third less than was charged to Buffalo.

June, 1859. New York to Lockport, 483 miles, 16 cents per 100 lbs. New York to Cleveland, 700 miles, 12 cents per 100 lbs. A pro rata to Lockport would be 7 87-100 per 100 lbs., or less than half the amount charged.

June, 1859. New York to Lockport, 16 cents per 100 lbs., 483 miles. Brockport to Medina, 10 cents per 100 lbs. At pro rata, the rate between Brockport and Medina, would be 9 mills, or less than one-tenth that was charged.

July, 1859. New York to Syracuse, 8 cents per 100 lbs., 366 miles. Syracuse to Manlius, 10 miles, 8 cents per 100 lbs. At pro rata, the rate between Syracuse and Manlius, would have been 3 mills per 100 lbs., instead of 10 cents.

July, 1859. Albany to Syracuse, 166 miles, 12 cents per 100 lbs. New York to Syracuse, 316 miles, 8 cents per 100 lbs. A pro rata, between Albany and Syracuse, would be 4 1-5 cents, or about one-third the amount charged.

July, 1859. Albany to Rochester, 269 miles, 14 cents per 100 lbs. New York to Rochester, 419 miles, 10 cents per 100 lbs. At pro rata, from Albany, to Rochester, would be 6 42-100 per 100 lbs.

July, 1859, Albany to Rome, 125 miles, 10 cents per 100 lbs. New York to Syracuse, 316 miles, 8 cents per 100 lbs. At pro rata, from Albany to Rome, it should have been 3 27-100 cents per 100 lbs.

July, 1859. Albany to Utica, 100 miles, 10 cents per 100 lbs. New York to Detroit, 12 cents per 100 lbs. A pro rata would be, from Albany to Utica, 1 96-100 cents per 100 lbs., or less than one-quarter the price charged.

Aug., 1859. Albany to Amsterdam, 47 miles, 10 cents per 100 lbs. New York to Cleveland, 12 cents per 100 lbs. A pro rata, from Albany to Amsterdam, would have been 8 mills per 100 lbs.

Aug,, 1859. New York to Brockfort, 17 cents per 100 lbs. New York to Sandusky, more than double the distance, 12 cents per 100 lbs.

Aug., 1859. New York to Chicago, 1,400 miles, 18 cents per 100 lbs. New York to Rochester, 415 miles, 12 cents per 100 lbs. A pro rata would have been, from New York to Rochester, 5 14-100 cents per 100 lbs.

Aug., 1859. New York to Detroit, via Oswego, 14 cents per 100 lbs. Syracuse to Canastota, 20 miles, 10 cents per 100 lbs. A pro rata, from Syracuse to Canastota, would have been 4 2-3 mills, or less than half a cent per 100 lbs.

Sept. 1, 1859. On the day the Canal Convention was held in Rochester, the freight on flour was 35 cents per barrel, by canal, both from Buffalo and Rochester, to New York, one 514 miles, the other 415 miles. At pro rata rate, it should have been only 29 64-100 cents per barrel from Ro-Rochester. Difference against Rochester millers, nearly 6 cents per barrel.

Oct. 21, 1859. Buffalo to New York, 50 cents per barrel for flour. New York to Cleveland, 12 cents per 100 lbs. A pro rata on flour, from Buffalo to New York, would be 19 cents per barrel, or considerable less than one-half charged.

These cases have all occurred within the present year, and they might be multiplied to fill up as many books as have been published by the Clinton League. They are of every day occurrence, and show quite as glaring a difference as can be found on any of the railroads in the State. They show one prominent feature in the carrying trade—that short distances pay higher rates than long ones, by the same mode of transit.

S. DRULLARD,

Genl. Frt. Agt. N. Y. C. R. R.

January 30, 1860.

TESTIMONY RESUMED.

Mr. ——— Phillips, superintendent of the Boston and Worcester road, was then called as a witness. He gave the following testimony, Mr. Thompson conducting the examination:

Q. Where do you reside?

A. At Boston.

Q. What is your occupation?

A. I am superintendent of the Boston and Worcester railroad.

Q. How long have you acted in that capacity?

A. On that road about a year and a half.

Q. How long have you been in the railroad business?

A. Since 1850. From 1840 to 1843 I was on the Worcester road; from 1843 to 1852 I was freight agent on that road, and from 1852 to 1858 I was superintendent of the Cleveland and Toledo road.

Q. Then you have had experience on both ends of the line; the Boston end and the Cleveland and Toledo end?

A. Yes, sir.

Q. Will you state what in your judgment is the difference in the transportation of way freight compared with through freight?

A. Way freight must be considerably greater in the cost than through freight.

Q. Why so?

A. The engines draw less. A local train will start with one or two cars, and picks up others on the route. It has the largest load at the lsat end; and the largest will not average more than two-thirds the number of through trains. Then there are station expenses. More men are employed and more fuel consumed on way trains.

Q. What per cent difference do you make in the cost?

A. There must be from 25 to 50 per cent on most roads.

Q. Do you think of anything else in connection with the proposal to establish a pro rata?

A. There are other considerations.

Q What is the cost of winter transportation in comparison to summer transportation?

A. It is very much greater. During some months in the winter I have known it to be more than 100 per cent more than in summer. It varies in accordance with the intensity of the winter.

Q. State the elements which go to make up that increase in expenditures?

A. The engine draws less load in the winter, and there is a larger expense in clearing the track of snow and ice, and there is the expense of increased breakage of wheels, axles and rails. The rigidity of the track causes a greater wear and tear of iron.

Q. Any other elements that you recollect?

A. That makes the main features of it.

Q. What, in your judgment, is the per cent difference, as near as you can get at it, in the cost of winter and summer transportation?

A. It must be in this climate from 30 to 40 per cent more.

Q. In case of a stated published tariff, unalterable for a month by these northern roads, what would be the effect upon the through business?

A. The effect on the Boston road would be that unless we put our prices of freight very low per mile, so as to leave no profit, the business would go through on other routes, which is competing for it, would put their rates a little lower. The only safety that roads have in competition is to be able to follow the reductions of others at once.

Mr. EMERICK—It seems to me that we have had evidence enough upon these subjects.

Mr. FLAGLER—It is a settled matter that these gentlemen were to run this train to-day in their own way.

Mr. THOMPSON—Without being obliged to pro rate, can the way and through business be done at the same rates in a practicable manner?

A. No, sir; it cannot.

Q. Will you tell why?

A. The through business must be taken at a lower rate per mile than it can be made profitable to carry local freights for.

Q. Can a competing route, with a longer line, fix lower prices for you and yet not be able to carry at as cheap a cost to itself?

A. Yes, sir; we have a case now right in point. The Grand Trunk line to Boston has a longer line than we to the west, but at their reduction of rates, which they have announced, they will take our business away from us.

Q. Do you know what the local tariffs on southern roads are, compared with the local rates on the New York roads?

A. My impression is that they are higher.

Q. What is your judgment as to the direction which through business would take, if thrown off the New York roads by a fixed monthly tariff?

A. I think it would take the southern lines, a part of it at least, and a portion would go by the Grand Trunk, and probably the canal would take a portion of it.

Q. What class of freight, if any, would go by canal?

A. The fourth class. I do not mean to say the whole of it, but a portion of it would go.

Q. What effect would the losing of this trade have upon the passenger trade?

A. To a certain extent, the passengers would follow the freight.

Q. Do you know what was the habit of the New York roads prior to 1858 in regard to a fixed tariff for through freight?

A. They had a fixed rate and did not, until about that time, pro rate with the western roads.

Q. What was the occasion of the change of policy?

A. The competition with the southern lines.

Q. How did it happen that the southern lines competed at that time and not before?

A. They had just finished their roads to Chicago, Cincinnati, and other western points.

Q. What would have been the effect on the commerce passing through this state if these competing lines had adopted the rates which they did, and our roads not been able to reduce their rates at the same time with their competitors?

A. They would have taken the business.

Q. Do you know what means or agencies these roads have at the west for soliciting freights?

A. The southern lines have agencies both at the east and west.

Q. Where at the east?

A. At Boston and New York.

Q. And where at the west?

A. At Chicago, Cincinnati, Cleveland, Toledo, St. Louis and other places.

Q. In your judgment, can all roads competing for freight from common points, receive the same rate per mile pro rata?

A. They cannot; the shortest line gets the larger prices per ton, per mile, than the longer one.

Q. Where do freights from Maine, New Hampshire and Massachusetts bound for the west go?

A. Through New York.

Q. Where does it go?

A. Some by the Grand Trunk, some by the Ogdensburgh road, a part by the New York Central, a part by the canal, and some goes by the southern lines.

Q. How does it go by the southern lines?

A. By steam propellers or sailing vessels around to New York or Philadelphia, or Baltimore, and thence by rail.

Q. Do you know upon which, if any of these lines, this business is increasing?

A. I should think upon the Grand Trunk.

Q. Which do you regard as the greatest rival of the New York lines—the Northern or Southern competitors?

A. If you speak of the extreme eastern business, the Grand Trunk is. If you refer to Boston, the competition is perhaps as strong by the

Southern lines as by the Grand Trunk. They are both competing actively for the trade.

Q. What is the only protection which the railroads in the State of New York have to retain business?

A. To be able to make the rates equal with the Southern lines.

Q. If those rates were fixed at any point, what would be the result?

A. If they were fixed and the other lines had the power of reducing rates, the line reducing would get the business.

Q. Have other lines that power?

A. Yes, sir.

Mr. COBB—What are the relative rates charged on freight on your road from Boston to Farmingham, as compared with rates charged to western cities?

A. Very much larger.

Mr. COBB—About how much larger?

A. I could hardly say; it varies very much at the different points.

Mr. COBB—Take Chicago, if you please? Are the rates one, two or three hundred per cent dearer?

A. Two hundred per cent dearer.

Mr. COBB—The Ogdensburgh road runs in connection with your road, does it not?

A. No, Sir.

Mr. COBB—Does not the Vermont Central come into your road?

A. It does not.

Mr. COBB—Is it one of the competing routes to your road?

A. Yes, sir.

Mr. COBB—What is the present condition of the Ogdensburgh road?

A. I am not posted.

Mr. COBB—Have not you seen it quoted?

A. I do not remember to have seen it. I know generally that the road is very much embarrassed.

Mr. COBB—The inference in your mind would be that it is not worth quoting?

A. I know the stock is low.

Mr. COBB—Are any of the gentlemen holding seats in the Board of the New York Central or New York and Erie represented in your Board?

A. No, sir.

Mr. COBB—Are either of your Board of Directors represented in the New York Central?

A. No, sir.

Mr. COBB—What is the proportion of local to through business on your road?

A. The local is largely in excess.

Mr. COBB—What proportion should you think?

A. Did you mean the comparative tonnage?

Mr. COBB—I referred to business in tons.

A. Our foreign tonnage is greater than our local.

Mr. COBB—Your entire through tonnage is greater than your local?

A. Yes, sir.

Mr. COBB—Do you remember the tonnage?

A. I have not it in my mind.

Mr. COBB—Do you remember the comparative income of the local compared with the through business?

A. Our through business is greater.

Mr. COBB—Can you give the relative profits of the local as compared with the through business?

A. I am not prepared to give that.

Mr. COBB—Do the merchants of Maine do business over your road to any extent?

A. More or less.

Mr. COBB—Where do the goods passing to the merchants of Maine ordinarily come from—New York or Boston?

A. They come from both places.

Mr. COBB—Which do you think has the preponderance of the business?

A. I am not prepared to say.

Mr. L. M. Hubbie, president of the Cleveland, Columbus and Cincinnati Railroad Company, was introduced as a witness. His examination was conducted by Mr. Thompson, as follows:

Q. Where do you reside?

A. Cleveland, Ohio.

Q. What is your business?

A. I am president of the Cleveland, Columbus and Cincinnati Railroad Company.

Q. How long have you been thus engaged?

A. Some five years.

Q. How long had you been engaged in railroad transportation prior to that time?

A. Two years.

Q. Will you tell us what, in your judgment, is the difference in the cost of transportation between way and through freight?

A. It would be different on different roads. I think on our roads it is 75 per cent more than the through.

Q. Why?

A. The reason is, because the local business is picked up in smaller lots. Our trains start from Columbus to Cleveland with an engine and tender, and a necessary amount of men to manage it. They commence picking up cars at the first station, which continues until they reach the last. The cars are picked up at small stations where they are not half loaded, and the expense of running them equally as great as fully loaded cars from Columbus. Then the stopping at these stations, switching out the cars and switching them in again, consume more time and fuel than the through train does. The expense of men would be the same. The wear and tear of rails would be a little less on one end of the road, but it is equally as great on the other end.

Q. What amount of the station and other equipment is properly chargeable to way freight, and not to through freight? I mean what is the difference of equipment that you have to have on the road to do way business which would not be required if you did through business only?

A. We should require no local stations if we did a through business alone, and we could dispense with the men employed, the switching side tracks, &c., employed in consequence of our local business.

Q. What proportions are the cost of these or intermediate stations, compared with the termini of the road?

A. I could not exactly answer that question; I do not know.

Q. How long is your road?

A. One hundred and thirty-five miles.

Q. Do you know how many stations there are on your road?

A. I do not know exactly; I should say from 18 to 20.

Q. What, in your judgment, is the difference between the cost of winter and summer transportation?

A. With us the difference is very little. We never change our rates in consequence of the season of the year.

Q. State why?

A. The cost of transportation is about the same. It may be 10 or 15 per cent more than in the summer, but the climate is such that we are troubled scarcely any at all with snow, and very little with hard frozen ground and consequent rigidity of our road-bed. We can do nearly as much business at the same expense in winter as in summer.

Q. So that the Southern routes have that advantage, among others, over Northern routes?

A. Yes, sir.

Q. Suppose a stated tariff was published by the New York Central and the New York and Erie, from which they could not vary for a month, what would be the effect?

A. If their tariff was so low that no profit could be made, they might retain their share of the business; but if it left any margin for profit the other routes would bid enough lower to get the business. We have had that tried. During the St. Nicholas Compact, under the rule of Mr. Moran, they gave us fixed rates for freight. At Cincinnati and Columbus we met the Southern roads, and we having fixed rates, they would vary the price just enough to take the business from us.

Q. With what lines do you run in connection?

A. The New York Central, the New York and Erie, and to a small extent the Pennsylvania Central. Its main connecting road, the Pennsylvania Central, crosses us nearly in the middle of our route.

Q. Where it crosses your road, what is the distance to New York by the Pennsylvania Central road, as compared with the distance by the Northern routes and Hudson River?

A. I do not recollect the exact distance but it is a hundred miles nearer by Philadelphia.

Q. Much nearer by the Southern route?

A. Yes, sir.

Q. In your judgment, as a railroad man, can way business and through business be done, practicably done, at the same rates?

A. Taking the business as it now is, with all these competing lines, it is impracticable—entirely so. Either one must be done at a loss or the other abandoned.

Q. In case of the abandonment of one, which, in your judgment, would have to be abandoned?

A. Each road must judge for itself. The one that was worth the least would be abandoned first.

Q. Suppose the law provided that the road must carry the way business as it was presented?

A. They would have to abandon the through business.

Q. That would be the only alternative?

A. Yes, sir.

Q. If the through business was abandoned, what would be the effect on the way business as to rates of tariff on prices?

A. It would be the same as in any other commercial transaction. If a man is confined to a smaller business, he has to charge a higher profit on what he does.

Q. In this case a higher rate on local freight?

A. Yes, sir.

Q. Can a competing line, with a longer route, fix low prices for you, though they would not be able to carry at as low a cost to themselves as you?

A. Yes, sir. A long route can fix rates low and the short route must carry at the same rates, or else they cannot get business. The route that carries for the lowest rates gets the business.

Q. How are the rates on the western and southern roads—the local tariffs—in comparison with the local tariffs on the New York lines?

A. I think they are higher generally. I examined some eighteen of these tariffs, and fourteen of them were higher than the New York Central, and four not far from the same.

Q. Suppose your through business was taken from the New York roads, where, in your judgment, according to the present facilities for diversion by rival lines, would it go?

A. It would go by those routes which would do it to the best satisfaction of the owners of the property. If the rail routes did not offer any greater inducements than the canal, it would go by the canal. The railroads now reach every point in the west, southwest and northwest, and the business would take just the same channels it now does, provided the southern roads could do it; if not, and there was a profit in the business, they would increase their facilities. I do not think it would change the course of trade as between rail and water.

Q. You think water could not take the trade as against the rail?

A. Not if the rail was the best. If the water routes were improved, so as to compete with the rail they would undoubtedly get more.

Q. What is the rule on railroads as to freight being followed by the passenger traffic?

A. I do not know as there is any such rule. The supposition would be that if a person sent property by a particular route, he would travel that route. There might be inducements to travel that route connected with the sale of his property. If he was sending his property by Baltimore or Philadelphia, he would naturally inquire the state of the markets on those routes.

Q. Do you know what was the action of the New York roads, prior to 1858, as regards a fixed tariff?

A. They generally gave us a fixed tariff.

Q. When was that system altered?

A. The first deviation as a rule from that was in 1858.

Q. What was the occasion of that?

A. The competition of the southern lines. The business was something in this wise. The southern lines, the Pennsylvania Central for instance, by its own aid, completed or helped to complete the connecting roads, and by so doing retained a certain control over the roads, by which they were able to make contracts pro rata. The Baltimore did the same thing in helping the Central Ohio, and retained the same control. When that system came to be adopted we immediately felt the effects at Columbus, and at various other points, in the competion of these lines. As the New York lines had given us fixed rates, we had in the competition to bear the whole burden of the reduction ourselves. We then appealed to the New York roads to pro rate with us, as being the only way we could successfully meet that competition. When they became satisfied that by so doing they could only be able to compete, they came into the arrangement.

Q. It was the result of experience?

A. Yes, sir. It was a matter of actual necessity, or else abandon the business.

Q. What is your location—Cleveland?

A. Yes, sir.

Q. Do you know what facilities the rival lines, north and south, have all through the west for the solicitation of business?

A. They have agencies at all the important points; all the sources of business pretty much. Cincinnati, Columbus, St. Louis, almost every little town throughout the west that furnishes them business.

Q. What is the reason that uniformity of rates is now somewhat preserved between the different lines?

A. The reason is that each line is satisfied that they can make nothing by reduction; that the relative position of competing lines would be the same, for if one line reduces the other reduces also.

Q. Then the safety of lines in this respect consists in their ability to change their rates?

A. Yes, sir.

Q. Can all roads competing from common points get the same price pro rata per mile?

A. They cannot. The short roads get more per mile than the long roads. The prices must necessarily be the same from one point to another, or there would be no competition.

Q. What is the cost of fuel on those southern roads, as compared with the cost on the northern roads? State what they burn, and what relation coal bears to wood.

A. The managers of the Baltimore and Ohio road told me that their fuel cost them 70 cents per ton—merely, the expense of mining and moving. The cost of fuel on the northern roads I don't know exactly, but I suppose it is from $3 to $5, or $6 per cord. A ton of coal, with us, is considered equal to about one cord of wood, but whether it bears the same proportion in a locomotive, I do not know. On the Pennsylvania Central road, the same fuel is something about the same. They have the same kind of coal, and I suppose they get it just as cheap.

Q. Do you know what the consumption of a locomotive ordinarily is, for fifty or one hundred miles, either in coal or wood?

A. It varies with different locomotives, and with the amount of load they haul.

Q. Say a 20 or 25 ton locomotive?

A. Our freight locomotives would burn, between Cleveland and Columbus, from three to five cords of wood; while a locomotive on a passenger train would burn from two to four cords.

Q. You would burn the most in the freight train?

A. Yes, sir.

Q. How much longer does it take a freight train to run through than a passenger train?

A. About twice as long, perhaps a little more.

Q. Do you burn coal or wood entirely?

A. Wood entirely.

Q. What does wood cost you on your line?

A. About $1.75 a cord—150 cubic feet to the cord.

Q. What does it come to per mile?

A. I could not now recollect.

Q. Do you know the local rates on the western roads, your own and others?

A. I have seen them.

Q. How are they in comparison with the local rates on the New York Central and New York and Erie?

A. Generally higher.

Q. Does that apply to all roads west of the New York Central and New York and Erie, and running in connection with them?

A. They are generally higher, so far as I know.

Mr. COBB—Explain what you mean by local and through business. Is the tonnage delivered to the New York Central road at Buffalo for Albany through business?

A. Through business.

Mr. COBB—Then freight from Dunkirk to New York would be through business?

A. Yes, sir. I would consider through business that which goes over the whole length of the road.

Mr. COBB—Say from Louisville to Boston and New York?

A. I put that among through business, and all that passes over the whole length of the road.

Mr. COBB—Why is it that that portion of the business would have to be abandoned if the pro rata principle was adopted?

A. For the reason that to pro rate local rates, to receive property and transport the same 20 miles, at the same rate per mile as in through business, if they charged anything like cost for transportation, would make the through rates so high that it could get no business.

Mr. COBB—Suppose you had the power to fix the compensation yourself, would there be any necessity of abandoning it?

A. I do not know as there would.

Mr. COBB—You could so fix the price for freight delivered by the Central at Albany that you would not have to abandon it?

A. Unless the business could be diverted from the Central at its source.

Mr. COBB—Then your meaning of through business would put it back to its source?

A. Where there are competing lines.

Mr. COBB—Then your remark would apply to the far west; the business between competing lines, and not immediately at the terminus of the road?

A. Yes, sir, unless there was competition at that terminus.

Mr. COBB—Then if one rule of pro rata applied to both competitoss it still would save it?

A. Yes, sir.

Mr. COBB—The stocks of your road, I believe, are at par or near it?

A. A trifle less.

Mr. COBB—In your Board of Directors is there any member of the Erie or Central boards?

A. No, sir.

Mr. COBB—About what relative rate of compensation, compared with other Ohio roads, does your road get for through business—say the Mad River; do you get higher prices than they?

A. Not any higher; probably a little lower per ton per mile, because they receive the same price from Sandusky to Cincinnati that we do from

Cleveland to Cincinnati, and they have a shorter route.

Mr. COBB—So that you have to run to Columbus, Zania and over the Little Miami?

A. We pro rate; but as our road is of greater length, we get less per ton per mile.

Mr. COBB—But taking an equal number of miles, do you get a higher or a lower scale of compensation than the Mad River?

A. That would depend upon the local tariff.

Mr. COBB—Take your through tariff from Columbus to Cleveland?

A. I think our rates and the Mad River's would be about the same.

Mr. COBB—Your local business is very small compared with your through?

A. About one-half.

Mr. COBB—I believe that your passenger trains run at a pretty high rate of speed?

A. Yes, sir.

Mr. COBB—Have you ever made a computation of the cost of moving a passenger train, compared with cost of transporting a ton of freight?

A. The wear and tear of rail is impossible to come at; but the wear and tear of machinery we know.

Mr. COBB—Have you ever made an approximate estimate?

A. I do not know that I have; it costs more, the greater the speed.

Mr. COBB—Then the mathematical rule holds good on railroads as elsewhere—that the higher the speed the greater the resistance, and the more wear and tear?

A. Yes, sir.

Mr. COBB—And the lower speed the less resistance and the less wear and tear?

A. Yes, sir.

Mr. COBB—If not deemed impertinent, and you choose to answer it, will you state how low is your lowest through rate, at which you have pro rated this summer, between your place and Louisville or Cincinnati, on a ton or a hundred pounds?

A. I was informed that one lot of freight went through from Cleveland to Cincinnati at 8 cents per hundred pounds.

Mr. COBB—Has the bulk of your through freight gone this summer to New York or Boston, at anything near that figue?

A. The whole season through averaged from 15 to 17 cents per hundred pounds.

Mr. COBB—How was it upon cattle?

A. Our rates this season have been less than a year ago.

Mr. COBB—What is the lowest that you have received per car this summer?

A. I should think the lowest price would pay us $20 from Columbus to Cleveland?

Mr. COBB—Have not some roads carried to Cleveland cheaper than that?

A. The competition from Chicago and west has been greater than on our road. Our competition is not very great on cattle.

Mr. COBB—How low have you known cattle to come from Chicago to Cleveland by rail?

A. I could not state in figures; I know that they were carried below cost.

Mr. COBB—Do you consider 8 cents per hundred from Columbus to Cleveland cost?

A. No, sir.

Mr. COBB—Do you consider 15 cents cost?

A. Yes, sir.

Mr. COBB—Would 12 be?

A. You must take the question with all its surroundings. If all our business should be done at that price it would not pay us any profit. But an increase of business—a certain amount of through business could be done without any material increase of expense.

Mr. COBB—Then if all your business was done at that rate, it would not pay?

A. It would not?

Mr. COBB—Has your road ever been importuned to discriminate against the canal in freight passing over it?

A. I do not recollect anything particular about that.

Mr. COBB—Was not a proposition made to your road to discriminate in the prices you should charge between property consigned to a Buffalo forwarder and property consigned to the Central Railroad?

A. I made a proposition to the other roads something to that effect. The prices were very low and our pro rata on the road was not a remuneration. We proposed to the New York roads to advance these rates and that the canals should advance at the same time. I saw some of the canal forwarders and they consented to advance; but the New York roads had no confidence that the canals would sustain the rates. I then said we will protect you in this wise: we will give the canals the same rates, and if they cut these rates we will advance the rates on them, as they reduce them on you.

Mr. COBB—Who objected to going into this arrangement?

A. It was generally objected to by railroad transporters, on the ground that they had not any confidence in the canals.

Mr. COBB—Where did that occur?—at the Niagara Falls convention?

A. I think not.

Mr. COBB—Where did it, then?

A. I made the proposition last fall, or perhaps it may have been in August.

Mr. COBB—The canal people assented but the railroad people refused to concur?

A. I did not say they assented. They were anxious to have an advance, but the railroads had no confidence in the "wild boatmen."

Mr. COBB—Did the Baltimore and Ohio urge the same arrangement?

A. They wanted an advance.

Mr. COBB—Were they any more willing to trust the canal forwarders?

A. I do not know.

Mr. COBB—Did they express faith in the canal forwarders?

A. I do not recollect that anything was said about the forwarders. They said that while a few of the lines would keep to the rates, there were a good many wild boatmen who could not be controlled, and who would not adhere to any prices under the agreement.

Mr. COBB—Did the New York roads propose to your road that a different price should be made by your road for freights that came by railroads than on those which came by canal, and that you should discriminate against the canal?

A. I do not know of any proposition of that kind being made to me.

Mr. COBB—Did you make any to them?

A. No, sir.

Mr. HOVEY—You have had some knowledge of canal business in this State?

A. Yes, sir.

Mr. HOVEY—About what was the tonnage of canal boats when you left?

A. Line boats, I believe, were something like 30 tons.

Mr. HOVEY—Take Crestline, the crossing-point of yours and the Pittsburgh, Fort Wayne and Chicago road; could property be transported by that route as cheap as it could be thence to Cleveland, by lake to Buffalo, by canal to Albany and steamboat to New York, in a canal boat of 250 tons?

A. My impression is it could not. It certainly would be transported cheaper from Cleveland.

Mr. HOVEY—Do you think there would be any danger of the diversion of trade from the canals by the railroad lines from Crestline to New York in competition with the canal?

A. I think there would.

Mr. HOVEY—You think it might?

A. You might carry it cheaper, but they would carry it quicker.

Mr. HOVEY—I am speaking of fourth-class freight?

A. We can only judge from what they have done. They do carry cheap, and do get business.

Mr. HOVEY—How do you manage to get freight from Cincinnati to Cleveland, thence to go by the New York Central or the canal, if they compete with you at Crestline?

A. We do it at the same price as they, and upon as good terms, and in as good time.

Mr. HOVEY—You think there is no danger of diversion?

A. No, sir. At the same prices.

Mr. HOVEY—How would it be at Fort Wayne and Toledo, on the Wabash and Western Railroad—a hundred miles from Cleveland?

A. I do not think there is any particular danger of diversion, so long as the New York roads can do it as cheap and as well as the Pennsylvania Central.

Mr. HOVEY—I understood you that they can do it as cheap?

A. They have done it.

Mr. ALLEN—Of the different modes of transportation from these points, mentioned by Mr. Hovey, Cleveland, Toledo, Crestline, &c., including the receiving and forwarding, which do you think the cheapest method of transportation?

A. I think the canal would be the cheapest. I think it is cheaper by water than by rail, but it depends very much on the condition of the Erie canal.

Mr. ALLEN—Then, in your opinion, during the season of navigation, the canal is the regulator of these prices?

A. I think so.

Q. On what class of merchandise?

A. On heavy goods.

Q. So that the canals keep our rates down?

A. Yes, sir.

Q. Supposing the canal tolls were raised, what would be the effect on railroad freights?

A. I think the freights in the lower class would be advanced.

Mr. HOVEY—Suppose tolls were put on the railroad freights also?

A. The same rule would apply.

A. I think that the rates are reduced lower this year on fourth class goods by competition between the canals and railroads than by competition between the railroads.

Mr. ALLEN—Are you acquainted with the value of Pennsylvania capital stock?

A. I have seen quotations of its stock, but I cannot tell what they were.

Mr. ALLEN—Can you approximate?

A. A little below par—from 40 to 45, on shares of $50. The Baltimore and Ohio I don't recollect what the value is.

Q. How about Mad river?

A. I cannot tell.

Q. Has there been any dividends on Pennsylvania Central?

A. I think there has.

Q. They keep up the dividinds?

A. I think so.

Mr. M. B. SPAULDING, a forwarder, of New York, was next examined as a witness by Mr. Thompson, as follows:

Q. What is your occupation?

A. I am in the forwarding business.

Q. Where do you reside?

A. In the city of New York.

Q. How long have you been engaged in the forwarding business?

A. Twenty-five years.

Q. On what routes?

A. Over the routes of the State of New York.

Q. To what points?

A. To the west and southwest.

Q. With the principal lines in the course of transit?

A. Yes, sir.

Q. You have freighted by railroads as well as by canals?

A. Yes, sir.

Q. Will you state in your judgment what is the cost of through as compared with way freight?

A. My knowledge would be only general on that subject. But the way freight would cost very much larger than the through.

Q. Does that apply to all modes of transportation—ocean, river and canal?

A. Yes, sir.

Q. Short routes pay larger than smaller ones to be remunerative?

A. Yes, sir.

Q. Do you know what the practice of the canal has been in the mode of discrimination; how it has been between longer and shorter routes?

A. Higher rates have been charged on canals for shorter distances than for longer.

Q. Is that the universal practice?

A. Yes, sir.

Q. On the Hudson river, canal and rail you say that is so?

A. To the best of my knowledge it is.

Mr. CONKLING—Does that discrination appear to be inseparable in all modes of communication, whether by land or water—has it been the case in all you have known anything about?

A. I do not recollect of any exceptions to that.

Q. What is your judgment in reference to a published tariff, at the west, of the prices of freight on the New York roads which cannot be departed from for 30 days. What would be the effect on through freights to the west and east?

A. The lines confined to these fixed rates would be likely to get little or no business.

Q. Have you made an examination in reference to the local rates on the New York Central railroad, for produce and all freights carried as compared with the local rates on other roads in different parts of the country?

A. I have on a few.

Q. I would like the result of that examination on the important freight routes?

A. I have taken 12 or 14 of the large freight roads and I have compared the rates from one of the termini, a distance of 100 miles, which is one-third of the length of the New York Central road. The rates are contained in this table:

TABULAR STATEMENT OF COMPAARTIVE RATES FOR LOCAL FREIGHTS.

ROADS.		1st Class.	2d Class.	3d Class.	4th Class.	Miles.
New York Central,	Albany to Oriskany,	27	22	20	17	99
New York and Erie,	New York to Port Jervis,	33	25	19	15	88
Michigan Southern and Northern Indiana,	Toledo to Bronson,	44	34	30	14	98
Sandusky, Dayton and Cincinnati,	Sandusky to Bellefontaine,	32	27	21	21	97
Ohio and Mississippi,	Cincinnati to Bownstown,	28	24	20	16	98
Terre Haute, Alton and St. Louis,	Terre Haute to Pana,	41	28	21	21	94
Michigan Central,	Detroit to Albion,	42	32	26	23	95
Detroit and Milwaukee,	Detroit to St Johns,	46	37	27	22	98
Chicago, Burlington and Quincey,	Chicago to Arlington,	30	25	19	19	97
Galena and Chicago,	Chicago to Dixon,	28	23	19	19	98
Milwaukee and Mississippi,	Milwaukee to Madison,	35	30	25	25	96
Pittsburgh and Chicago,	Pittsburgh to Lilly's,	40	35	30	25	99
Baltimore and Ohio,	Baltimore to Flagg's Mills,	37	30	26	23	98
Cleveland, Columbus and Cincinnati,	Cleveland to Cardington,	27	20	16	16	97

Q. How many of these are higher than the New York Central?

A. I think they are all higher, except the Cleveland and Columbus.

Q. Have you made any computation in regard to the effect of a pro rata law in this state upon any particular locality, and if so state how it would operate upon the two lines of this state?

A. The computations I have are very brief owing to the limited time I have had.

Q. Will you read your statement?

A. I have made a computation of the cost of the transportation of flour at three, four and five cents per ton per mile, which is as follows:

COST OF TRANSPORTATION UNDER A PRO RATA REGULATION.

	Rates per ton per mile at 3 cents.	4 cents.	5 cents.
5 miles,	15	20	25
10 "	30	40	50
20 "	60	81	1 00
40 "	1 20	1 60	2 00
80 "	2 40	3 20	4 00
100 "	3 00	4 00	5 00
200 "	6 00	8 00	10 00
300 "	9 00	12 00	15 00
400 "	12 00	16 00	20 00
450 "	13 00	18 00	22 50

I have made a computation exhibiting the effects of a pro rata law in giving advantages to those places which, by means of water communication, afford western produce a means of getting to New York with less rail transportation.

The distance from Albany to Buffalo is 300 miles, from Rochester 229 and from Oswego 183 miles. The cost of transporting grain from Cleveland to Buffalo by lake is three cents per bushel; elevating at Buffalo, one cent; canal transportation to Rochester, four cents; making eight cents from Cleveland to Rochester. Cost of lake transportation to Oswego from Cleveland is six cents per bushel; elevating at Oswego one cent; making seven cents, or one cent in favor of Oswego over Rochester, where the wheat is to be ground. Under a pro rata, the cost of flour on rail from Rochester to Albany, 229 miles, at three cents per ton per mile, is seventy-four cents per barrel; same from Oswego to Albany, 183 miles, at same rate, forty-five cents, a margin in favor of Oswego of twenty-nine cents. The cost of flour from Buffalo to Albany, 300 miles, at three cents per ton per mile, is ninety-seven cents. From Oswego to Albany, 183 miles, at same rate, fifty-nine cents—a margin of thirty-eight cents in favor of Oswego. The distance from New York to Smith's mills, on the New York and Erie road, is 449 miles; distance from Smith's mills to Dunkirk, 12 miles. The cost of transporting 100 pounds of fourth class freight from New York to Smith's mills, at three cents per ton per mile, would be sixty-seven cents. Cost of the same from Smith's mills to Dunkirk, 12 miles, at same rates, would be one cent and eight mills. Butter and cheese are now carried from Little Falls to Albany 74 miles, at seventeen cents per 100 pounds, or about 5 cents per ton per mile. At this rate the cost from Smith's mills to New York, on the New York and Erie, would be $1.12 per hundred pounds.

Mr. CONKLING—Do you say that the present rate on the New York Central is 5 cents per ton, per mile?

A. That is the present local rate.

Mr. CONKLING—Is it not an unusually high rate?

A. That is $3.40 per ton, from Little Falls to Albany.

Mr. COBB—You have paid pretty close attention to this subject of transportation, and the political economy which pertains to the movement of these things?

A. I have been engaged in the business

Mr. COBB—You have written some articles which have been published?

A. I have written some and talked some.

Mr. COBB—Are you the author of a publication which appeared over the signature of "New York," with these views?

A. That is a private matter.

Mr. COBB—Is it your opinion that a pro rata measure would work prejudicially to Buffalo?

A. I only show the figures.

Mr. COBB—It would appear so from them?

A. Yes, sir.

Mr. COBB—Is there any inference that wheat would take the rail at Rochester after being made into flour?

A. The owner would consult his own interest in regard to that.

Q. At what rate do you think railroad transportation could be made profitable from Buffalo to Albany, per ton, per mile?

A. There are various circumstances which might be called into question, which materially increase or decrease the cost of transportation between those points.

Mr. COBB—Are you the New York freight agent of the New York Central?

A. No, sir.

Mr. COBB—What road are you connected with, if any?

A. I ship goods over the Central, and I am connected with the Sandusky, Dayton and Cincinnati road.

Mr. COBB—You ship over the New York Central?

A. Yes, sir.

Mr. COBB—Is that road an ally of the Central?

A. She is an ally with other roads in connection. We use the Pennsylvania Central, the New York and Erie and the New York Central.

Mr. COBB—You have a pretty intimate acquaintance with the rates which have been received for transportation from New York to the upper lake ports?

A. Yes, sir.

Mr. COBB—What have been the lowest and highest rates on fourth class freight taken the past season by rail and lake to Chicago?

A. I could hardly go behind the tariff. There have undoubtedly been special contracts, of which I have no knowledge.

Mr. COBB—I ask within your range of knowledge?

A. Probably 28 to 60 cents.

Mr. COBB—That is the lowest you have known?

A. From 27 to 28 and 30 cents a hundred pounds.

Mr. COBB—What would that give to the New York Central in a pro rata division as they have pro rated this summer?

A. It would depend altogether what they got for the lake transportation.

Mr. COBB—Have you any knowledge as to what the division has been?

A. I think they would get 20 cents?

Mr. COBB—From Albany to Buffalo?

A. From New York to Buffalo.

Mr. COBB—What would the Hudson river get by barge?

A. I suppose about five cents.

Mr. COBB—What would the Hudson river railroad get?

A. I am not familiar with that division, having had nothing to do with it?

Mr. COBB—Have you not known, during June and July, considerable quantities of goods taken from New York to Chicago at 22 and 24 cents?

A. I have not. I have no recollection of any going as low as 24 cents.

Mr. COBB—Has common rumor brought any thing of that kind to your knowledge?

A. We hear a great many things upon which we place no dependence.

Mr. COBB—Have you never contracted, during the past season, from New York to Chicago, at 24 cents?

A. No, sir. I do not do much Chicago business.

Mr. COBB—Have you to Milwaukee?

A. No, sir. My business lies more on the south side of Lake Erie.

Mr. COBB—What have been your lowest rates to Cleveland, Sandusky and Toledo?

A. The lowest rate to Cleveland was 22 cents.

Mr. COBB—The same to Toledo?

A. All the lake ports are the same—Detroit, Cleveland, &c.

Mr. COBB—Do you know what proportion the lake received of that?

A. Probably a dollar a ton.

Mr. COBB—That would leave the New York Central railroad 12 cents a hundred.

A. These are exceptions to the general rule, made in cases of extreme competition.

Mr. COBB—How long was that exceptional style of business prevalent?

A. A month or two.

Mr. COBB—Did it extend to July and August?

A. Not one day after the 15th of June.

Mr. COBB—But from the opening of the canal to that day the exception and not the general rule prevailed?

A. Yes, sir.

Mr. COBB—Did you contract any goods over Central road to Buffalo?

A. I did if I had the opportunity.

Mr. COBB—Have you had the opportunity?

A. I do not recollect of making a contract to Buffalo this year.

Mr. COBB—Did you to Rochester or Syracuse?

A. If I had the opportunity.

Mr. COBB—Did you have the opportunity?

A. I do not recollect of any.

Mr. COBB—What were the lowest rates for which you contracted goods to Cincinnati, during the months of April, May or June?

A. Thirty-four cents I think.

Mr. COBB—What route would that take?

A. Hudson river to Albany, rail to Buffalo, lake to Sandusky, and rail to Cincinnati.

Mr. COBB—What proportion of that would the road from Sandusky to Cincinnati receive?

A. They would receive a pro rata proportion according to the distance.

Mr. COBB—Would the lake share in that pro rata?

A. No, sir.

Mr. COBB—Then the compensation on the lake remains the same?

A. It is so usually, though sometimes it varies.

Mr. COBB—Then the difference between 34 cents and the cost of river and lake transportation would be pro rated between the Ohio road and the New York Central?

A. Yes, sir.

Mr. COBB—Can you remember the sum paid over the Ohio road?

A. No, sir, I cannot.

Mr. COBB—Can you remember the sum received by the Central?

A. If I knew that I could tell the other.

Mr. COBB—At what rates have you contracted goods from New York to Dayton?

A. To Dayton and Cincinnati the rates are about the same.

Mr. COBB—How are they to Columbus?

A. Two or three cents less than to Cincinnati. There is a very strong competition between Dayton and Columbus.

Mr. COBB—How are they to West Liberty on the line of the Mad river?

A. They pay local rates.

Mr. COBB—How as to Miamisburgh or Franklin?

A. That is on the Dayton and Hamilton road. We only make a price to Dayton when we have goods to those places.

Mr. COBB—Then where there is no competing route local rates prevail?

A. We take them to the nearest point.

Mr. COBB—What proportion would the New York Central get on goods shipped to West Liberty?

A. The same as they would on goods shipped to Dayton.

Mr. ALLEN—I wish to make an inquiry. You have given a statement of the values of transportation to and from different points, Rochester and Oswego, stating that at three mills per mile per ton, the cost of flour to Oswego would be 45 cents, and the cost to Rochester would be 74 cents. You give also the transportation from Cleveland to Buffalo and Oswego. Now comparing one at eight and the other at seven cents, I want to know what we are to deduce from that idea. What was the idea to be conveyed to the minds of the committee?

A. I merely stated the fact that under a pro rata the fixed rate per ton per mile would produce that result.

SMITH BRIGGS, freight agent of the Hudson River railroad, was the next witness. He testified as follows, the examination being conducted by Mr. Thompson:

Q. What is your place of residence and occupation?

A. I reside in Albany, and am freight agent of the Hudson River Railroad Company.

Q. How long have you been engaged in that business?

A. Six years.

Q. Have you investigated the facts in reference to the rates charged on the flour from Pittsford, referred to in the letter of Jesse Hoyt & Co., about which Mr. Parsons made charges, and if so what are the facts?

A. On the 20th of December I received from the Swiftsure Line, of which Van Sanford & Co. are proprietors, 270 barrels of flour, consigned to Jesse Hoyt & Co., from Fisher's station on the New York Central road. On that flour the charges were 52 cents per barrel. Van Sanford's charges for commissions, cartage, &c., were $5\frac{1}{2}$ cents per barrel, and our local rates, from East Albany to New York, were 30 cents per barrel, making $87\frac{1}{2}$ cents; the whole bill being $236.25. On the 26th of December we received from the Swiftsure Line 180 barrels at the same rates, the charges being $157.30. by

[This testimony refers to a charge made by Mr. Parsons, based upon a letter of Jesse Hoyt & Co., of New York, that the New York Central Railroad had received $87\frac{1}{2}$ cents for the transportation of flour from Pittsford to New York, while the charges from Rochester to New York were but 60 cents per barrel. REPORTER.]

Q. That was the flour referred to by Mr. Parsons?

A. Yes, sir.

Q. Have you any estimate in your mind of the difference in the cost of transportation of way and through freight on your own road especially?

A. I have.

Q. What is your judgment upon that subject?

A. I think the difference in cost of transporting the way freight, as compared to the through, is equal to 50 per cent.

Q. How is it in reference to the summer and winter business—which is the most expensive?

A. It is much more expensive on our road in the winter.

Q. Why so?

A. On account of the snow, cold weather, wear and tear of machinery, switching, &c.

Q. What, to the best of your judgment, is the additional cost of way freight or a through?

A. I think it is at least 50 per cent, for this reason: We have to start our way trains with comparatively no freight and pick it up in the manner that has been explained to you by other witnesses.

Q. You have to have a larger complement of cars for your winter than for your summer business?

A. Yes, sir.

Q. Explain the cause of that?

A. Our business is much larger in winter than in summer. The result of it is, we have to have a larger portion of it for winter service and a smaller portion for the summer service.

Q. State what your habit and practice is, and must be, running for freight in the summer season in competition with the Hudson River boats?

A. We have no fixed rates at all, but change 20 times a day, if need be.

Q. Why?

A. Because of competing with the boats. We go into the market for the business.

Q. Is it not necessary in the summer to keep up your organization for freight business the same as in winter when you have a larger quantity?

A. It is.

Q. That is the experience on your road?

A. That is the rule adopted.

Q. Do you recollect how many landings there were, years ago, which were accustomed to send rival lines of boats down?

A. I was not at that time fully acquainted with the localities, but there were a great number to my knowledge.

Q. Did those local boats send both freight and passengers?

A. Yes, sir, and they are still doing so.

Q. In the carrying of your freight, have you any reference to the procurement and transportation of passengers and getting them off the rival lines of boats?

A. We have.

Q. State how it operates with these boats in carrying passengers?

A. At all these localities where these boats run, to and from Albany, they do a great deal of trading and marketing; if we get that trade, we get the passengers—the parties doing that trade. In so doing, we take their freight at the same rates that the boat offers, whatever they may be; we consider it for our interest to do so.

Q. What would be the effect of compelling the Hudson River road to fix a tariff of prices, unalterable for a month, between New York and Albany?

A. We could do nothing at all.

Q. How would it affect your cattle trade?

A. We could not touch it.

Q. Would it, in your judgment, destroy the trade of all the four classes of freight transported on your road?

A. It would, in my judgment.

Q. Will you state the custom of the Harlem and Hudson River roads, with reference to the carriage of milk to the city of New York?

A. We commence at Castleton, 20 miles below Albany, and pick the milk up at differe nt stations until within 20 miles of New York; we charge the same rate per gallon from Castleton to New York as we do at all the stations below—three cents per gallon; I think it is the same on the Harlem.

Q. The same train that starts from here stops at all of these milk stations and takes on the cans?

A. Yes, sir.

Q. So that the station 20 miles this side of New York, takes the train from here, and pays as much as is paid on the milk from Castleton?

A. Yes, sir. A gallon of milk weighs about 12 pounds.

Q. What would be the effect of a pro rata regulation on the milk trade?

A. You can judge. It could not be carried.

Q. It would sour the whole train?

A. It would be apt to. It would bring the price of transportation to $20 to $30 per ton from the upper end. The milk trade is a pretty important trade with us.

Q. If present rates were continued, as the rates from Castleton, would the milk be worth handling as freight under a pro rata?

A. No, sir; the larger portion of our milk business is done from the lower end.

Q. What is the practice on all roads, north and south, and on the river, as to these through and way rates—are the latter larger than the former?

A. That is our practice. We get larger rates for way than for through freights, per ton, per mile.

Q. Is that so on the river?

A. It is so.

Q. Do they not charge as much per barrel for flour from New York to Sing Sing, as from New York to Albany?

A. They charge more. That is the case with us, and it is so with the boats too, sir.

Q. Was it so on the canal in your experience there?

A. When I was on the canal it was so. I left the canal six years ago.

Q. What was the difference according to your best recollection, on the canal, between short and long freights, say from here to Schenectady, as compared from here to Buffalo?

A. I cannot give the exact figures, it was very large, from 45 to 50 per cent. We always made our rates on short distances much higher than on long distances.

Q. On the better classes of freight is not the risk on the transportation of property greater on the short routes than on the long ones—the danger of misdelivery, &c.—the amount of damage to be paid in case of loss?

A. Yes, sir, the danger of misdelivery is greater by the frequent opening of the cars.

Mr. COBB—Why do you esteem it neccssary to compete with Hudson River transportation?

A. To maintain our identity and keep up our business connection.

Mr. COBB—Do you esteem yourselves able to cope with the Hudson River successfully?

A. We have done so very well.

Mr. COBB—What is the value of your stock?

A. I think it is 41. I have not looked lately.

Mr. COBB—What price did you get for cattle during the summer, per car?

A. We have taken them as low as $5 per car.

Mr. COBB—Do you esteem that compensating?

A. No, sir. We did not.

Mr. COBB—Then cattle at that price you do not consider compensating?

A. We consider it compensating rather than lose the business.

Mr.COBB—How so?

A. We don't want business to go from us.

Mr. COBB—You would rather do it at $5 per car, than lose it?

A. Yes, sir. We have done that business ever since I have been on the road, but probably not as low as the present year. The present year has been an exception.

Mr. COBB—To all previous years?

A. Yes, sir.

Mr. COBB—Do you esteem it costs more to deliver a car load of property at Sing Sing than it does at Albany?

A. I think it does.

Mr. COBB—How as to Hudson?

A. A full car load?

Mr. COBB—Yes, sir.

A. I judge it would not.

Mr. COBB—But you think to Sing Sing it would?

A. A through train would go through. We would have to put this on the way.

Mr. COBB—How many cars could you add to a locomotive without increasing the expense?

A. I suppose that every car added to a train increases the expense.

Mr. COBB—Then it would cost more to take it from New York to Albany, than from New York to Sing Sing?

A. Those cars all go on the way freight trains and not in the through trains at all. We start our local trains about one o'clock with a passenger car attached. We pick up some passengers, but we seldom have a full car load.

Mr. COBB—How low have you carried beef from Buffalo to New York by the hundred or barrel?

A I think it has been as low as a dollar a ton —5 cents a hundred.

Mr. COBB—Do you esteem that remunerative?

A. In a certain degree, I do.

Mr. COBB—But on its merits?

A. Our business from New York is much larger than our down business, and consequently we do not have loads for our cars and we have to send them empty to bring goods up, or else take freight at a low figure. If we can get ten tons in a car and charge $10 per car it is better than to run our cars empty.

Mr. COBB—Do you compete in down freight such as flour, with the Hudson River?

A. We have never done that by rail.

Mr. COBB—How low would you put the point of compensation before you would esteem it better to give it up than to carry it?

A. Ten cents a barrel.

Mr. COBB—You would rather give it up than carry it below ten cents a barrel?

A. Yes, sir.

Mr. COBB—Do you run in connection with the New York Central?

A. Yes sir.

Mr. COBB—I believe the Harlem road is totally within the state?

A. Yes, sir.

Mr. COBB—You stated that if a pro rata bill was passed it would injure you;—suppose it applied to both?

A. If it applied to through freight, we could not touch it. Our freight from New York to Albany, with the central in the winter time, we consider compensates.

Mr. COBB—Taking the season through?

A. We consider that it compensates.

Mr. COBB—Do you pro rate with the Central on its Western contracts?

A. In the winter we do.

Mr. COBB—Do not you in the summer?

A. No, sir; we would like to, though.

Mr. COBB—That freight takes the river during the summer?

A. Yes, sir.

Mr. COBB—Do the Hudson river and Harlem roads charge the same prices?

A. They have in a measure this winter. Last winter we were rival routes, and we went in and got the best we could.

Mr. COBB—You went in on your nerve? [Laughter.]

A. Yes, sir, on our nerve.

Mr. COBB—Which do you think the best able to do that on the nerve?

A. We consider ourselves.

Mr. COBB—But your present winter rates you consider are compensating?

A. We do.

Mr. COBB—Can you tell what it is per ton per mile; take the average of it?

A. I have not computed it and I cannot tell you at present; I can give you our through rates.

Mr. COBB—What is your relative tonnage, way and through?

A. From way stations to way stations?

Mr. COBB—What is strictly way tonnage?

A. Our way business would be largest.

Mr. COBB—What proportion?

A. About one-half larger.

Mr. COBB—Then your through business would be one-third.

A. I am not giving you any thing accurate; I am only estimating.

Mr. COBB—This milk business must be limited? You could not bring milk from Ohio, or the western part of the state?

A. We could not.

Mr. COBB—It is a purely local business?

A. Yes, sir.

Mr. COBB—And must be done at rates peculiar to itself?

A. Yes, sir.

Mr. COBB—You could not bring it a long distance and have it valuable when it arrived in market?

A. I should judge not.

Mr. COBB—Is there any other article of similar character?

A. We carry dressed meat. We have transported 80,000 dressed sheep for one man last year.

Mr. COBB—In refrigerator cars?

A. No, sir. But in cars built for the purpose, in which they can be hung.

Mr. SMITH—Do you estimate the cost of way business to be 50 per cent over through?

A. Yes, sir. That includes all classes of way business.

Mr. SMITH—How much more would it cost to do way business than through, provided the way business was done by the car load?

A. If it was done by the car load it would reduce the expense very much.

Mr. SMITH—It would?

A. Yes. If we knew just exactly how much we were going to get at every station when we started, and what we were going to deliver.

Mr. SMITH—There is a good deal of this business done on other roads?

A. On our road it is picked up in all kinds of little parcels.

Mr. CONKLING—In how small parcels?

A. Quite small. Bundles and baskets and all sorts. People living in the country and doing business in New York send them up by the local trains.

Q. What would be the effect of a pro rata freight law upon the express business?

A. In my judgment it would be to discontinue it entirely.

ALBANY, *January* 30, 1860.

N. RANDALL, Esq.:

Dear Sir—With less promptness than I could wish, but as soon as my business permitted, I obeyed your message of the 23d, addressed to me at Chicago, and hastened to this city to state, as you requested, my views to the House of Representatives of your State, having charge of the petitions and proposed legislation, in accordance with the prayer of the petitioners, to establish and inaugurate "A pro rata freight policy on your Railroad." On my arrival in this city, I found the hearing of the case before the committee on behalf of the Railroads had closed, and the committee listening to counsel, representing the petitioners.

I gave attention to the arguments adduced by said counsel, and have since read, in part, the report of evidence introduced on behalf of roads. I regret, on my own account, that circumstances prevented my responding to your call in time to have listened to the testimony given by men of such wide experience and well-known capacity, on this most interesting and important subject. With the conclusions and most of the reasons given in support of those conclusions, as stated by the gentlemen called before the committee, I most fully concur.

My experience in the handling of freights by

rail, commencing in 1838, has been altogether in the West, from which the long freights of the N. Y. Roads are gathered. During the last eight years in Chicago, and during the last five years I have had charge of the Chicago, Burlington and Quincy railway, having a terminus at Burlington, Iowa, on the Mississippi, and another terminus at Quincy; also, on the Mississippi nearly opposite the Hannibal and St. Joseph railroad, leading to the Missouri at St. Joseph. All the long or through business coming to our line, is taken from the strong competition of the Mississippi river fleets, who have long held undisputed sway on that noble stream, since the inauguration of steam has driven off the flat boats.

Until a very recent period, this competition has not feared the influence of railroads on the commerce that enriched and strengthened it. Of course, this has been a stronger competition than can be presented by any artificial communication, no tolls to be exacted, no right of way to be secured.

From the Falls of St. Anthony to the Gulf, except in extreme cases of drought, the navigation for eight months, and for most of the distance the whole twelve months, was uninterrupted. Not only so, but by means of the Ohio, a shorter rail connection was made with the Atlantic, via Wheeling and Pittsburgh, than can be made by the northern routes which has compelled the managers of the Mississippi river lines, centering in Chicago, especially the Chicago, Burlington and Quincy line, to meet this question of through and way rates, and decide what line of policy would best subserve the interests of the community through which it was built, and the stockholders owning it.

The result to which we have come, and the practice we maintain, and the reasons for our course, perhaps will as well express my views of the proposed pro rata measure, now agitated at Albany, as direct answers to any set of interrogations that may be put.

Looking upon the line in a twofold aspect, as a convenience and necessity to the community of the State of Illinois, through which it passes, and as an investment for its stockholders, who are entitled to a fair return upon their investment, the question how it can be made best to subserve both their interests must be met. If it is so managed as to disregard either the one or the other of these aspects, its directory is faithless to its trust. For, if it does not subserve in a proper manner the interests and convenience of the public, it cannot long be profitable to its stockholders; and if for a series of years it shall be so managed as to ignore reasonable returns to its stockholders, it will cease to exist to be run as corporate property. In that event, the State having all the advantage of it, may well be called upon to assume its ownership, and the people who are benefited respond by payment of taxes to support it. It is evident that the first and chief reliance of the line must be upon way business. For the sake of brevity, I will not speak of passenger business. Way freight must, except in exceptional cases like the Panama Railroad, be the chief dependence for freight revenue; and, first, the tariff of charges must be such as to stimulate production in a healthy manner, enabling it to enter into a fair competition with the market of the world; else there be no other outlets for the products of industry, the road will soon have nothing to carry; products will cease. Second, the tariff of rates must not exceed, with the element of time considered, the rates by which these products can be otherwise transported. This would defeat revenue entirely. Third, when the tariff on way freight is made with an intelligent appreciation of, and a due regard to these simple principles, the question to be settled is, what amount have you got? Does the revenue thus arising meet all the demands for repairing and maintenance of road, rolling stock, and payment of interest, with a fair return to your stockholders? In our case, the answer is in the negative.

Then comes the question, can you add to this income by long freights? In our case we could by competing with the great inland highway of our nation, the Mississippi river. But we could not reach a pound of that freight at the rate per ton per mile of way freight. Would it do to carry it less as a medium of revenue? Would it do to transport it less as a matter of justice to shippers of way freight? And here lies the whole question: If these two questions are answered in the affirmative, and, more, if it is shown to have been our duty to our way freight shippers to reach out after long freight, even at a less rate per mile than we carry way freight, the question is solved. We decided that it would do to carry it less as a matter of revenue, for the reason that the cost of carrying it was greatly less.

The depreciation of all wooden structures of railroad bridges, ties, station buildings, sliding of banks, filling up of ditches, and the expense of a large number of men, are not materially increased by additional business.

The difference in expense in the transportation of through and way freight, is *real, substantial*, and not imaginary, and although it may not be demonstrated with mathematical accuracy, it is believed to be at least 33 per cent less. It follows, then, of course, that if I transport a given number of tons of way freight a given number of miles, and receive therefor $100, and the operating expenses were $50, and transport the same number of tons of long freight the same number of miles, and receive therefor only $50, the operating expenses for which were only $33.33, that I have made $16.67 to go to income account. This is put as an extreme case. It is seldom, perhaps, that the line is compelled to carry long freight at half the price of way freight per mile. As a medium of revenue, then, it is clear that a road may carry long freight at a less rate than way freight. As a matter of justice to the shipper of way freight, it seemed our imperative duty, in operating the Burlington and Quincy line, to reach after this long freight, because by so much profit as we could thus make, we were enabled to bring the way freight from competing points cheaper. Neither does it change the relative value of the farms of the producers of long and way freight.

We carry the produce of the way freight at a reasonable price—lower than by any other mode of conveyance, taking into account the element of time, and lower, as is seen above, from the fact that we carry the long freight, while we do not add to his competition in the market of the world, because the long freight producer had another route of transit.

Neither have we carried his freight any cheaper than the rival route would have carried it. Upon these principles, and for these reasons, briefly stated, we have always made a difference in favor of long freights, or freights for which other lines were competing. We cannot run our road on any other principles without practically abandoning all hope of a fair return to our stockholders. If compelled to charge equal rates per ton, per mile, on all freights of the same class, our most remote way freight shippers would have to pay a price absolutely prohibitory, if those prices were made with reference to dividends in any degree.

Now what is true of our road, leading from the Mississippi to Chicago, is eminently true of the New York roads. The price at which they must take freight at Chicago for the sea-board, is fixed by lines north and south of them having the capacity and disposition to carry these freights. The New York roads cannot therefore take these freights except they conform to the prices fixed for them by these roads, and these prices change from day to day.

They do not increase the quantity carried to the sea-board by a single barrel by reaching to Chicago for this freight; they do not thus injure the citizens of New York by increasing the competition in the market; they do not confer any favor upon the western producer except to add two other lines by which he can be served at the same price.

Under the proposed pro rata bill, the New York lines cannot take a pound of this freight from Chicago—neither will very much go by the New York canals, as I believe.

The first, second and third classes will go round New York routes, and the fourth class will be divided. The element of time will, through all the future, be a governing element in transportation. This fact, to which dealers are accustoming themselves with great rapidity, and which so greatly augments the value of a moderate capital, enabling property to be converted many times in a year, compels the New York and other roads to keep their lines open for freight at all seasons of the year.

This greatly enhances the value of railway transportation in this latitude. It should be borne in mind that the frosts of winter, as they are more or less severe, add also more or less to the cost of transporting freight. In the severe winters of 1855 and 1856, it is not pretended that any road west of Lake Michigan, made anything in their freight departments.

In the more moderate winters that have succeeded, less difficulty and expense has been met from this cause. But as a rule it may be said that the difference of expense, in the transportation of freight by rail in summer and winter, in the latitude of central Illinois, is from 20 to 30 per cent. In New York the more severe winters would undoubtedly justify a large estimate.

The New York roads would be justified therefore in raising their winter tariff to meet this increased cost. It should be borne in mind, also, that the New York lines and their connections do not reach the home of the producer, and bring his products from that home to market, at the reduced or way freight rates. They reach only the centres of trade, to which the freight has first paid a local tariff, off-setting the local freight paid by the New York producer in getting his freight to New York city.

This should be borne in mind, whenever the objection is raised against the present practice of distributing rates upon freight, that the value of the far off lands is enhanced to equal your own. I need not say that if there is anything at all in this objection, it should have prevented the building of the New York and Erie canal—that the Mohawk farmer had a right to complain of the advantages given thereby to the farmer of Genesee valley; nay, more—that the Hudson River farmer had a just cause of complaint, against this State, for aiding the Mohawk farmer.

I am, dear sir, most respectfully,
Your obedient servant,
C. H. HAMMOND.

The Watertown and Rome Rail Road Company, in answer to the application pending before the Select Committee of the Assembly for a *Pro Rata Law*, respectfully submit the following statement:

This Company is not advised of the particular features of the law asked of the Legislature and therefore is unable to anticipate how and to what extent any particular bill which may be framed, will affect its business and its interests, or those of the state and her citizens as connected therewith. We can only speak of the general proposition of a *Pro Rata Law* and of its injustice and impolicy so far as applicable to our road.

The Watertown and Rome Rail Road is not a rival of the canals of this state, but on the contrary is tributary to them. It may be alleged that it attracts some freights that would otherwise enter the canals at Oswego. To a limited extent this is true. But we affirm that, taking into consideration the freight which it brings to the canal at Rome, which would otherwise go down the St. Lawrence River, or over the Northern Rail Road to Boston or other places in New England, or over the Canadian Grand Trunk Road to Montreal, or via Portland to an Atlantic or foreign market, the Watertown and Rome Road is, in the aggregate, a feeder of the Erie Canal, and if the Committee would aid the canal business and revenues, should be encouraged, rather than embarrassed in its freighting business, by legislation.

During the season of canal navigation, for 1859, this company delivered to the canal at Rome

Way freight,	17,480 tons
Through freight,	23,462 do.
Total	40,942 do.

as per statement annexed.

On all of which the state collected canal tolls from Rome to the place of destination, which was for nearly all of it, tide water.

Of the 23,462 tons of through freight, considerably over one-half was lumber, from points in Canada, below Kingston, and which would have gone to Montreal had it not come over our road. A large portion of the residue of the through freight, consisted of Canadian freights which, except for our road, would have sought transportation over the Grand Trunk or down the St. Lawrence.

The Watertown and Rome Road extends from the Erie Canal at Rome, to Cape Vincent—opposite Kingston—on the St. Lawrence River. Instead of diverting freights from the canal, its natural effect is to bring Canadian freights in the vicinity of Kingston, or which are brought to that point by the Grand Trunk Rail Road, to the Erie Canal and through it to our great commercial city, instead of their going to a market beyond the state and over other thoroughfares.

The Watertown and Rome Rail Road cannot reduce its way freight tariff. It cannot afford to do so without rendering its stock wholly unremunerative to its owners. This road, by economy in its management has maintained its pecuniary credit and afforded small dividends to its stockholders. Its main reliance is way business, which it cannot afford to reduce the prices and consequently the profits on, by adopting any pro rata tariff adapted to securing through business.

By a pro rata tariff, founded on its present rates for way business, its through freights would be almost entirely cut off at once. Nor would the canal be the gainer. These freights would go to the Grand Trunk railroad, or to the St. Lawrence river. They have only been secured to our road by low rates of freight, and we had to carry them at these rates, or not at all. If we were able to make a very small profit in the operation, and at the same time give this business to our own Erie canal, and our own markets, we supposed ourselves not unpatriotic citizens, or deserving to be arrested in our course by hostile legislation. It only requires an examination of the subject, to satisfy the committee that the effect of a *pro rata law* upon our road would be to divert business from the canals. We should be unable under such a law to continue to deliver to the canal, at Rome, our past amount of tonnage.

It may be said, that the discrimination on our road in favor of through freights, has been a matter of necessity. As to these, it was a choice between something, or nothing. We have got what we could, and as we have only diverted freights from our Canadian neighbors, and towards our own canals, surely, our State has no reason to complain.

But in point of fact, the discrimination in price in favor of through freights, is not unjust on any basis, especially on our road, looking at its peculiar circumstances. Our through freights are carried in full laden cars, and in the most economical form. But the way freights on our road are collected from numerous small stations, which seldom supply a car load at one time. From no way station on the road, except Watertown, do we, except in some instances, get a car load of freight at one time. We have to pick up small quantities of freight as a train passes over the road. Thus we are are compelled to draw trains of empty or partly laden cars of way freight, at equal or greater expense than our through trains of full laden cars; the latter frequently at lower rates, paying more than the former at higher rates. As a matter of equity, therefore, and on the basis of actual expense, we do not deem a somewhat higher tariff for way freights, unjust or unfair.

With these suggestions to the committee, we submit that a Pro Rata Freight Bill, would be unjust towards the Watertown and Rome railroad, and at the same time would not benefit the canal revenues, or any class of the citizens of this State. We, therefore, respectfully protest against such a law.

ADDISON DAY,
Superintendent of Watertown & Rome R. R.

Dated *January* 27, 1860.

Statement showing the number of tons of freight delivered to the Erie Canal by the Watertown and Rome Railroad, for the year ending December 31st, 1859.

	THROUGH.	WAY.	TOTAL.
April,	623 tons.	1,906 tons.	
May,	1,558 "	3,001 "	
June,	2,664 "	2,342 "	
July,	3,790 "	1,641 "	
August,	2,832 "	1,686 "	
September,	2,813 "	2,243 "	
October,	3,760 "	2,710 "	
November,	5,422 "	1,951 "	
	23,462	17,480	40,942 tons.

Testimony Resumed.

GEORGE POWERS, Superintendent of the Hudson and Boston Railroad, was the next witness. He testified as follows, Mr. Thompson conducting the examination:

Q. State your occupation and residence?

A. My residence is at Hudson, and I have charge of the Hudson and Boston Railroad.

Q. How long have you been connected with that road?

A. Eight years, not all the time under that title. It was formerly called the Hudson and Berkshire Railroad.

Q. It has been purchased by the Boston line since?

A. Yes, sir.

Q. What was your occupation prior to that?

A. I was in the forwarding business on the river?

Q. State what is the invariable habit of forwarders in the Hudson river, on reference to increasing the compensation for way freight over through freight?

A. It has been as now, that the charge on way business is fully up to the through rates, to all points.

Q. To all points between where?

A. Between Albany and New York.

Q. Have you been practically acquainted with locomotives and the cost of running them?

A. I have, sir.

Q. Will you state what it costs per mile, on your road, to run your locomotives?

A. Nineteen cents per mile it cost last year.

Q. Was that reckoning one way or both ways?

A. All ways, the entire running of the year?

Q. What are your grades?

A. We start with a very heavy grade—probably the heaviest grade operated by a locomotive anywhere; at least anywhere within my knowledge.

Q. What would be the effect of a rigid tariff—the same amount per ton per mile for all distances—the same to remain for a month?

A. It would have a very serious effect.

Q. State what it would be?

A. We would have to lose on our way freight to enable us to hold the through freight.

Q. Which part of your business is carried at the greatest cost, the through or way business?

A. The way business.

Q. Have you any competing routes? if so, what are they?

A. In connection with the Western Railroad we have several competing routes.

Q. Name them ?

A. The Hartford and New Haven, the Providence and Worcester, the Canal road, the Troy and Boston, the Housatonic and the Harlem.

Q. And the Hudson river ?

A. Not so much.

Q. Do you know a road in Massachusetts built on the side of a canal—the canal being discontinued ?

A. Yes, sir; that is what we call the Canal road.

Q Are they both in use ?

A. No, sir.

Q. The canal given up and the railroad substituted ?

A. Yes, sir.

Q. It passes through Westfield ?

A. Yes, sir.

Q. Do you know its length ?

A. I do not.

Q. What was the freights from Albany to Hudson, as compared with those from Albany to New York, when you were engaged in the carrying trade ?

A. I have been connected with a concern which has been carrying from Albany to Catskill for about 15 years, and am still connected with it. The rates have been invariably twelve and a half cents, from Albany to Catskill, for a barrel of flour, or to any point between.

Q. What is it from Albany to New York ?

A. I have known it to be as low as five or six cents per barrel.

Q. Is it ordinarily beyond a shilling ?

A. No, sir.

Q. And not as much as you charge for way freights ?

A. Not generally. We could not afford to carry it in the quantities we carry as low, if we had larger quantities. We carry smaller lots in steamboats which make all the landings, and cannot carry so economically as they do where there are several thousand barrels on a barge.

Q. Do you carry milk ?

A. No, sir.

Q. Don't you bring milk from the eastward to the Hudson river ?

A. No, sir.

Q. Will you state any other circumstances in connection with your road ?

A. I was present this morning when some questions were asked in reference to the cost of operating railroads by coal as a fuel. My experience has shown that the cost of coal, as compared to the cost of wood, is as 12 cents to 19 cents per mile.

Mr. ALVORD.—On the same road ?

A. On the same road.

Q. What coal do you use ?

A. Bituminous.

Mr. SMITH.—I do not understand your statement, perfectly.

A. The cost of fuel using wood for a whole year, was nineteen cents per mile. About the first of January, I think it was, we commenced running a coal engine over the same road. The cost of coal per mile was twelve cents.

Mr. CONKLING.—How much did you pay for the wood ?

A. Our wood varied from three to five dollars per cord.

Q. How much for coal ?

A. We allowed six dollars per ton, thirty cents per hundred, which was a very liberal allowance.

Q. At these relative prices, the cost of fuel was as twelve to nineteen cents per mile ?

A. Yes, sir. There was a time last summer, when the coal would not have probably cost so much by a half dollar a ton.

Mr. COBB.—Your road starts from Hudson; what does it connect with to Boston ?

A. The western road at Chatham Four Corners.

Q. What does your through traffic consist of?

A. We have grain, and flour, and meal, produced and milled in the county; considerable of that. We have, also, a very heavy coal trade on our road.

Q. Any iron ore ?

A. We have a good deal of iron ore mined at Berkshire.

Mr. HOVEY.—You stated that there was a road called the Canal road, built on the line of a canal which has been discontinued. What was the length of that canal ?

A. I cannot tell. It was a canal extending from New Haven up to the neighborhood of Westfield river. I think that was the terminus.

Q. What was its capacity ?

A. It has not been in operation since I became acquainted with it.

Q. What means and sources had it for getting business ?

A. The same sources that would apply to the railroad.

Q. If there is any significance to the introduction of this subject, it is intended to convey the idea that canals cannot live by the side of railroads. Did it run from Northampton to New Haven ?

A. Yes, sir.

Q. And had seventy miles of that country to drain ?

A. Yes, sir.

Q. It was in operation until the Hartford and New Haven railroad was built ?

A. Yes, sir.

Q. It had no capacity of getting other than local business ?

A. Yes, sir.

Azariah Boodie, President of the Toledo and Wabash Valley Railroad, was next examined as a witness, by Mr. Thompson. He testified as follows :

Q. Where do you reside ?

A. In New York.

Q. What is your occupation ?

A. I am in the railroad business.

Q. In what part of the country does your field of operations lie ?

A. In the west.

Q. Between what points ?

A. The road I represent at present, runs from Toledo to the Illinois line, following the Wabash valley.

Q. You are President of the road ?

A. Yes, sir.

Q. How long have you been engaged in the railroad business ?

A. Twenty-four years.

Q. During that time have you paid particular attention to the transit of freight and passengers ?

A. I have for the last six years given more attention to the transit of passengers than before. I was a builder of railroads until within five or six years, since when I have been operating

Q. Will you give us your judgment as to the difference in the cost of transportation on railroads between through and way freights?

A. It depends upon localities to a very great extent; but my opinion is, that there is a greater difference than has been mentioned here. Through freight is carried on our road exceedingly cheap, compared with local; for the simple reason that it is brought to the road in bulk. It may be compared to a wholesale business, while to local is a retail business. It costs the roads nothing to gather the business. You hitch to the train, and take it through. It costs nothing to the agencies on the line during its transportation. There is none of the difficulties attending at the depots, &c., that you have with local freight. You receive a car full, and it goes directly through and you receive full pay from the car; while in the other case perhaps you cannot have more than five tons in a car. Taking all these things into consideration, I should think there was from fifty to sixty per cent. difference.

Q. Will you now state what in your judgment is the difference between the cost of winter and summer transportations in the north, where the roads are affected by snow and frost?

A. If we in the winter season should have the same account of business to do as in the summer, the difference would not be so great. But there is every difficulty in operating in winter. We not only have frost and snow, but we do not as much business. We run the same trains, but do not have half of the amount in the trains.

Q. Which roads are those of which you speak?

A. I mean the northern roads, at the south there is no frost; they can operate quite as cheap as in the summer.

Q. What in your judgment would be the effect of a stated tariff, unalterable for thirty days on the road which establishes it, as regards its ability to get through freight?

A. I can speak only for the roads I represent, which cover three states, from Toledo to Burlington on the Mississippi river, and Quincy on the Mississippi, a hundred miles below Burlington; a fixed tariff for three days would divert that business from the State of New York. At the end of our lines there are four or five different routes that will take our freights as cheap as the New York lines. If you fix an arbitrary or unalterable rate on the roads of New York, as soon as it becomes known that that fixed rate is made, that moment the rival routes, those outside of New York, would drop their rates, just enough to take the business, and they would continue to do so as long as the business would pay.

Q. Has that already been the effect of a fixed tariff by the New York roads, prior to 1858?

A. Prior to 1858, they did not have the rival lines that they have at the present day. The Baltimore and Ohio has been finished since 1858; the Pennsylvania Central has been in operation about two and a-half years, and the Grand Trunk has just been put into operation. The consequence is, that, prior to 1858, the New York roads had almost a monopoly of the western carrying trade.

Q. The advantage of a monopoly is now almost entirely cut off?

A. There is a different state of things. It is now utterly impossible for one to have the carrying trade of the west as a monopoly, owing to the opening of other roads.

Q. Does the rivalry and competition between the northern and southern roads affect the commerce of the canals as well as the railroads?

A. Precisely the same, so far as my observation goes. I cannot state exactly the proportions. We classify freight into first, second, third and fourth classes. The first, second and third will stick to the railroads; at any rate, that has been our experience. The fourth, and perhaps some portion of the third, will go to the canals. I am speaking now of through freights, not of local. If there is an arbitrary rate in New York on the railroads, it will not affect the first, second and third classes of freights, because they can get to the seaboard as cheaply by other roads as by those of New York. I had offers last season, repeatedly, while west, to take freights from our country, seeking the seaboard, to Portland, and even to Boston, by the Grand Trunk railway, and from the Pennsylvania Central, to take them over the Pittsburgh, Chicago and Fort Wayne. We might have done our business by them just as cheaply as by the New York roads.

Q. Is it, in your judgment, practicable to operate a road at the same tariff for through and way freights? Can it be done profitably?

A I answer your first question, yes. But profitably, impossible, because way freights cost largely more than through.

Q. In your judgment, what would be the consequence, on the New York roads, by the abandoning of the through freights, on the way freights?

A. I can only answer by stating how I should manage the New York roads if I owned them. If I were obliged to abandon the through freight, I should get the largest price I could for the local. If both through and local tariffs at present barely pay, it is very evident, if the through freight was abandoned, you would have to put the whole expense on the local tariff, and which, of course, would be increased in this degree.

Q. Do you know whether a competing route could have an influence in fixing your tariff, though not able to carry as cheaply as you?

A. I know they do.

Q. What is the cause of it?

A. A competing route to the same point may be 500 miles longer, and if they offer to take the goods a fraction under us to that point, we are obliged to come down to their price to be able to carry the goods. They may be losing money, and the only effect upon us would be that it would lessen our profits.

Q. Do you know what the tariffs for local freights on western roads are, in comparison with New York roads—say the Central?

A. I can tell you the tariff of the road I represent.

Q. How do they compare with the Central?

A. They are higher, both for passengers and freight.

Q. How does through freight affect the passenger carriage? what connection, if any, is there between them?

A. Passengers are very apt to follow freight. It would not be an immediate effect. Freights would be diverted from New York and go to other roads. As there would be new avenues of trade open, new relations would spring up with other cities, and eventually the passenger traffic would be to a great extent diverted.

Q. Do you know whether there are rival competing routes from the centers of trade at the west?

A. I know there are.

Q. What are those rival lines?

A. The principal and most powerful is the Pennsylvania Central; the next, perhaps, is the Baltimore and Ohio; but the most formidable at present is the Grand Trunk—a new line which they do not expect to bring in revenue, but is rather a national or political affair—and it is now striving to get the trade of the west.

Q. What advantages, within your knowledge, has the Grand Trunk over other roads?

A. I cannot say that it has any advantages over other roads, for they are all equally able to do the business, except thus: that the Grand Trunk is one of the best constructed and best equipped roads in this country.

Q. Does it pay any taxation?

A. I think it does not.

Q. Is it fostered by the government?

A. Yes, sir.

Q. To what extent?

A. There was from 13 to 14 millions of dollars of government assistance to begin; whether it has been fostered by the Home Government I do not know, but it has been helped by individuals on the other side.

Q. Is it not a road constructed differently from other northern roads?

A. Yes, sir.

Q. How?

A. The bridging of the road is very superior—a great many of them being of iron. The road bed is probably the best on the continent. It is all raised some three or four feet above the natural soil, is thoroughly drained, and is a finished road; and probably the wear and tear on the road for the next ten years will be less than on any road in this country.

Q. Has this road agencies in the western country?

A. Yes, sir, everywhere.

Q. What is your judgment as to whether all roads competing from a common center, can have the same rate per mile for carrying freight?

A. If they get the same rate per mile for doing the freighting, the shortest road will do the business.

Q. Is it practicable in your judgment?

A. No, sir, simply because the long routes will not agree to it.

Q. Do you know the practice on all rivers, lakes, canals and roads, of charging more per ton per mile for local freight than for through freight, and if so, in what did the practice originate, and what justifies it?

A. As far as my observation goes, it is invariable the case. Local prices have always been higher. I suppose the reason is that it costs more to do it, that is the origin of it.

Q. Did you ever know the canal from New Haven, where a railroad is now located?

A. The canal run from New Haven to Northampton. I think it was about seventy miles long, it may have been seventy-two or seventy-three. It was abandoned twelve years ago.

Q. How long was it in operation?

A. Some twenty-five years, or twenty years, parts of it.

Q. Do you not know that the Farmington canal has also been used to construct a railroad on its banks?

A. The canal from Providence to Worcester?

Q. Yes, sir.

A. Certainly. The railroad I represent, has a canal running along by it for two hundred miles.

Q. What is that?

A. The Wabash Valley canal.

Mr. COBB — You built the Rochester and Lockport railroad?

A. Yes, sir.

Mr. COBB—Did you also build the Toledo and Wabash road?

A. Yes, sir.

Mr. COBB—What do you call the terminus of your road?

A. It commences at Toledo, in the northern part of Ohio. It strikes Indiana seventy-three miles from Toledo, and reaches Fort Wayne; thence it runs to Lafayette, and eighteen miles beyond the Wabash it connects with the Great Western railroad, which leads across the state of Illinois to Quincy.

Mr. COBB—What do you call its western terminus?

A. The state line.

Mr. COBB—And it runs then in connection with the Great Western?

A. Yes, sir.

Mr. COBB—And the whole runs from Toledo to the Mississippi?

A. Yes, sir.

Mr. COBB—What route in this state do you consider your ally?

A. I do not consider that either of the routes in this state are our allies, one more than another. We, as western railroad men, who represent western interests, have all the facilities outside of New York to get our freight east, that we could ask for.

Mr. COBB—Does the New York Central pro rate with you in the contracts which you make for freight?

A. They do, to a very great extent. We have a discretionary power to a certain extent.

Mr. COBB—You consider yourself fully entitled to make any rate you please?

A. No, sir.

Mr. COBB—Does the Great Western also pro rate to the Mississippi?

A. It pro rates with us except with respect to local business. There is a very large proportion of the Great Western's freight gathered up at Decatur, and we pay the Great Western an extra rate as a local rate, making a discrimination in their favor.

Mr. COBB—Over that section of the road?

A. Yes, sir; business comes over the Great Western road, we pro rate there.

Mr. COBB—At what rates have you been taking freight from your western terminus?

A. I do not recollect.

Mr. COBB—Have you not received freight at your western terminus as low as 20 cents a hundred?

A. I do not recollect.

Mr. COBB—During the summer season did you ship from Toledo by the lake or by rail?

A. A very great item in the west is the transportation of cattle. Last year it was about equally divided between the rail and lake.

Mr. COBB—To whom did you deliver them when you shipped by the lake?

A. To the propellers of the New York Central and the New York and Erie.

Mr. COBB—At what rates have cattle been taken through by your road from its western terminus?

A. That I cannot tell, for the reason that we delivered the cattle at the lake at our price.

Mr. COBB—What was this price?

A. Forty dollars a car load on our road.

Mr. COBB—What is its total length?

A. Two hundred and forty-three miles.

Mr. COBB—Was that the way you carried all your cattle during the past summer?

A. I think there may have been an occasional exception.

Mr. COBB—Are any cattle sent over the Great Western?

A. A great many.

Mr. COBB—What rates do you get when they are sent over both roads?

A. When we did get a through rate, it gave us about $33 a car load; I do not pretend to be exact; I think that was it.

Mr. COBB—At what rate per ton per mile was your business during the summer season performed?

A. I can tell pretty near, but I cannot give the figures exactly. It was probably in the neighborhood—a fraction less than 2 cents per ton per mile.

Mr. COBB—At what rate was the way business done?

A. About three cents.

Mr. COBB—Which do you esteem gives the most profit?

A. The through business, I think.

Mr. COBB—What is the proportion of your way business to your through?

A. I cannot tell; I have not the figures here.

Mr. COBB—Is your road at present in first hands or second hands?

A. My hands were the first, and it is still there.

Mr. COBB—Has it not been latterly sold?

A. Yes, sir; I was the purchaser.

Mr. COBB—Then it has changed hands?

A. It has gone into a new organization.

Mr. COBB—What was its original stock?

A. I think about three millions.

Mr. COBB—Had it any bonds?

A. Yes, sir.

Mr. COBB—How much in bonds?

A. I could get you all of these details, but I do not see that it has anything to do with the question here. Still I have no earthly objection to give it.

Mr. COBB—What amount of stock and bonds were wiped out of existence at the sale?

A. If the committee wish an answer, I will endeavor to make myself understood. The sale of the road was not owing to the operation of any way or local tariffs.

Mr. FLAGLER—It is supposed Mr. Cobb may trace the relation between the cause and the effect.

WITNESS.—Three years ago last December, we got the road finished right to the state line. The road at that time was $900,000 in debt on its construction account, not on its operation account, and it was neither fenced, equipped, nor gravelled. Of course we were very poor. We took the question of our difficulties into consideration, and we thought the better way to get out of our difficulties, was to make an amicable arrangement and sell the road under a foreclosure, protecting every person's interest to the best of our ability. We did not get into debt nor any difficulty, by any operation of the road; but instead of that, we have from the operation of the road paid the interest on the first mortgage bonds, and on the second mortgage bonds, and have within six months, have fenced in, over two hundred and forty-three miles of the road, built nineteen houses, and done a great deal of gravelling; all that has been done from the income from the operation of the road. I hardly think you can infer that the road has broken down from a want of success in its operations.

Mr. COBB—Has your present, or had your former organization any member in its Board of Directors, who is a member of the New York Central, or New York and Erie's Board?

A. There has never to my knowledge been a Director of the New York Central, or New York and Erie, who had anything to do with our road as a Director,

Mr. HOVEY—The inference drawn from the statement you gave, is that the canal had been superseded by the operation of your road. What was the condition of the canal at the time your road was completed? What was its capacity, its length and its means of getting business?

A. I have not the statistics to give a definite answer to that question. I can say, generally, that the Wabash Valley canal was considered a failure prior to the finishing of our road.

Mr. HOVEY—That is all I wish to know.

WITNESS—I wish to give you a reason.

Mr. HOVEY—I am satisfied.

Q. You say you run parallel with the canal for what distance.

A. We run substantially parallel to the canal for two hundred and twenty-nine miles.

Q. Has your railroad been pro rated by the state for the purpose of protecting the canal?

A. No sir.

Q. What would be the effect on your road, as regards through freight, if the pro rata measure were to be passed on the New York roads?

A. I do not think it would be near so injurious to us as to the New York roads.

Q. Would it be injurious or otherwise?

A. It would be injurious, because you would have to throw off either one class of freight or the other. You put such a restriction on your roads and you throw the through business out of the state.

Mr HOVEY—Are you not aware that the New Haven and Northampton Canal had only from 2½ to 3 feet of water in it before the completion of the railroad?

A. The canal was made originally the ordinary depth.

Mr. HOVEY—What do you mean by the ordinary depth?

A. I suppose from three and a half feet to four feet four or five; I do not know; I never gave a great deal of attention.

Mr. HOVEY—It was never more than three and a half feet.

A. The Erie canal, if it did not take means to be cleared out and repaired, would not have more than three and a half or four feet of water in time.

Mr. HOVEY—Has the Grand Trunk road any advantage in grade, build or distance, or anything else that would enable it to carry freight from Toledo to Portland, 853 miles, cheaper than it could be carried by the New York road, or all the way by rail from Detroit to New York, 845 miles?

A. If the Grand Trunk road had no other object in view than revenue, and to get the most money out of the road practicable, I think they would not be able to compete successfully, either with the New York roads or the Pennsylvania Central, or Baltimore and Ohio.

Mr. HOVEY—That is to Portland?

A. Yes, sir.

Mr. HOVEY—Now, as regards Boston—the distance by the Grand Trunk, from Toledo to Boston is 964 miles; by the routes this way it is 734 miles, a distance of 224 miles in favor of this route. Can the Grand Trunk compete with this route under these circumstances?

A. I don't think they could for a series of years. I think that for the next two years their road can be kept in repair and operated cheaper than any road in this country.

Mr. HOVEY—You stated that the Grand Trunk road had received from 13 to 14 millions from the Provincial government of Canada.

A. Yes, sir.

Mr. HOVEY—None from the home government?

A. Yes, sir.

Mr. HOVEY—Is 14 millions of capital aid on a capital of 50 millions, which is that of the Grand Trunk, as much as three millions would be to the Erie?

A. That is a matter of figures which I am not capable of answering to.

Mr. HOVEY—How low do you contract flour from Lafayette, Indiana, to New York?

A. I do not recollect the lowest figure. The way we did our business last summer, on our line, was, to contract to Toledo. The competition was so destructive to all interests that we chose to contract only to the end of our own route and then let it take its own course.

Q. What is the length of the water communication on that line—on the Grand Trunk?

A. It is rail to Portland and water to New York.

Q. What would be the effect of this pro rata upon roads west that have been built to run in connection, in reference to bringing business to them?

A. The effect of a pro rata on the New York roads, on our roads would be for us to give up the business, so far as the New York roads are concerned, entirely, and take it to the other roads.

Mr. COBB—Would not that depend upon whether the roads would be willing to do it for nothing?

A. We know they have been ready at all times to take it, and continue to do so, so long as they can make a profit, however small; of course you could get it down to a figure where nothing could be made and then they would stop.

Mr. COBB—You said you did a very good business on your road without making any contracts beyond Toledo?

A. I say to a very great extent we brought only to Toledo.

Mr. COBB—Why could not other roads do as you have done, and succeed as well by limiting their operation to their own termini? Do you know of any impediment in their way?

A. If there were but one line of railroad there would be no impediment. We have done that way to as great an extent as we could.

Mr. CONKLING—Is there any road in the west except the Cleveland, Painsville and Ashtabula, which can properly be said to be dependent on the roads of this state?

A. No, sir. The Toledo and Cleveland freight can be diverted at Cleveland to the Pennsylvania Central; all the other routes southwest, west and northwest can reach the southern roads.

Mr. CONKLING—With reference to the Wabash Valley canal, connecting Toledo with Evansville on the Ohio river, it is 456 miles in length?

A. Yes, sir.

Mr. CONKLING—Did I understand you to say that the traffic on the northern part of that canal had been abandoned?

A. No, sir.

Mr. CONKLING—How is it between Toledo and Defiance?

A. It is not abandoned.

Mr. CONKLING—What is the size of the channel?

A. It is about the size of the old Erie canal.

Mr. CONKLING—About 45 feet wide and 4½ deep?

A. It is not to exceed 45 feet I should think.

Mr. CONKLING—At Defiance what are the connections of the canal?

A. It has a connection with a Cincinnati canal, at what is called the junction.

Mr. CONKLING—They used to join at Defiance and used the channel in conjunction for a distance. Do you recollect when there was an extensive passenger business done on it?

A. Yes, sir.

Mr. CONKLING—Is there any done now?

A. No. sir.

Mr. CONKLING—I refer to the business on that portion of the canal; is there any done now?

A. Very little is done now there, except the carrying of grain; there is scarcely any merchandise. There is some salt, some lumber, and some grain.

Mr. CONKLING—Prior to the construction of the railroad, the entire business of the region was done on that canal?

A. No, sir. Prior to the construction of the railroads of Indiana, pretty much all the business done on the canal was diverted from it to a very great extent by cross roads at the principal business points, such as Lafayette, Fort Wayne, the business within thirty or forty miles from the canal.

Mr. HOVEY—Do you not know that sixty ton boats were the largest that ever run on that canal?

A. I think that was the size.

Mr. CONKLING—That would be about the size of one of the original Erie canal boats—rather larger?

Mr. HOVEY—Not quite equal to it.

Mr. CONKLING—I make these inquiries because my personal knowledge extends back to 1844, when I passed over the canal from Toledo to Dayton.

Mr. HOVEY—I suppose it was abandoned by the English bond-holders a year ago?

A. No, sir. The English bond-holders, or trustees of the bond-holders, kept it in repair until last winter.

Mr. HOVEY—They did not maintain its depth?

A. They kept it in repair, but it pined and has been dying gradually for years.

Mr. CONKLING—During how long a portion of the year is it available for navigation?

A. It is generally open before the Erie canal, and closes about the first of December. They generally get it open in March—from the middle to the last part.

Mr. CONKLING—Has it an ample supply of water at all times?

A. There has not been any want of water since I had any acquaintance with it, but once, and that was only between Attica and Lafayette.

Mr. CONKLING—Then the canal is available for eight months in the year for navigation?

A. Fully eight months.

Mr. HAWLEY, said:

Mr. Chairman, Gentlemen of the Committee: I feel impressed that you must be weary of the subject, and of the parties, and that will impel me to hasten a conclusion, and to pass by everything which I deem to be not worthy of consideration, and a great many thimgs that shall be worthy of consideration. The testimony adduced befo e you has been of that clear character, and given under such circumstances as will save to the counsel who have the duty of summing up a very considerable labor. A general view of the subject. it seems to me, is the only one not pretty much exhausted. Nevertheless the subject is one that has more aspects, more details, more points, more facts, more interests and more serious consequences connected with it than any that has been debated in these halls, in a great many years; and I doubt whether there has been before the people of this state a subject of such momentous consequences, which reach so far, and cut so deep, since the day of the debate in this House which determined that the Erie canal should be built.

Trade marks the era of these years. This is the commercial century, and an improvement upon all the ages that have passed. What is commerce? What is the carrying trade in its relations to commerce? It is a very small part of it, but it is a link in the trade chain of the whole. On the soundness of your policy in reference to the carrying trade depends the soundness of the whole. The carrying of a commodity is labor and cost bestowed upon it. But that labor and that cost adds nothing to its intrinsic value. A barrel of flour, after having been carried across the ocean, will feed no more people. A piece of cloth, when carried a thousand miles, will cover no more nakedness. So it is—carrying adds nothing to the intrinsic value of the thing carried; therefore it is labor lost, so far as it is more expensive than is necessary. It is a waste of ingenuity, a waste of time, of human industry and capital, to spend anything more for carrying a commodity than is necessary to be spent upon it. I say it is as inevitable as the conclusions of logic, and as fixed as the laws of gravitation, that low rates of transportation are the healthy doctrine for commerce—the lower the better. I challenge criticism upon that position. That I state as a general proposition covering the whole kingdom of traffic. No man can deny it. He is an unwise statesman and a simple merchant who trades on any other basis. The State of New York was penetrated with that great doctrine when it bent its energies and achieved the greatest undertaking of the age by connecting the waters of our great lakes, presenting two thousand miles of inland navigation, surrounded by four thousand miles of lake coast, dotted with growing towns and cities with the Atlantic Ocean. Then it was understood to be a part of the system to so direct the energies of this state and its canal to enable the people to gather the commodities from the rich gardens of the west, to be distributed among the Atlantic cities and in Europe, at the lowest possible rate. It was never discovered that that was an error until my intelligent friends opposite found out that the interest of the people, and parties, and institutions were being ruined by too low rates of transportation!

Now, I admit, that under particular circumstances, a party may be ruined by too low rates; and that leads me to warn you, gentlemen, that no legislature can soundly legislate, and no man can soundly judge by an examination of instances. You must legislate upon aggregates—upon the whole. You must make your measures of traffic with reference to aggregates—to the whole, or you will fail. The course of proof on the other side, and in behalf of these petitions, has been proofs of instances, calculated to mislead those who hear and consider them. I ask if this be not true? Does it prove that a railroad has lost money because a single consignment has been carried below cost? Does it prove that a traffic is ruinous because one of its attempts has been a failure? Is that enterprise badly managed which loses money once? Just look at the invoice of traffic that fills twenty or thirty cars, of ten tons each, at a remunerative rate, it is passing on a route; it meets with a snow storm. This involves the necessity of clearing the road; it pressing into service a hundred Greeks and numerous auxiliary engines, and an expenditure of means equal to three or four times the value of the freight to clear away the snow and to get the train through. That trip proves a fearful loss. Yet is that business badly managed because it has lost money in an instance, by circumstances existing in a particular case? This fault and this fallacy underlies the whole of the proof in behalf of these petitioners. Our proof goes by aggregates and general principles, and on them all sound commercial men must stand and to them all sound legislators must look.

Look at the evidence adduced on behalf of the New York and Erie Railroad, with its statement of through traffic for four years, including the last, and with fierce competition and low prices prevailing during that time. We gave you the number of tons and the number of dollars, eight millions and over, received for that transportation, and by arithmetical calculation it shows that they received one and three quarters of a cent per ton per mile on the whole! Is not that a remunerative rate? There were plenty of instances during that time, where the road lost money on particular operations. If they were prevented from doing this because they lost money in those instances, they could not have recorded the many instances where they made money. I take that as an instance to show that evidence based upon particular cases is a falacy that will mislead every man, and put him on his way towards ruin who thus does his business, and every legislator at fault who is guided by it.

I will quote one more particular instance, to show the fallacy of depending upon proof of particular instances, and that is the argument of Mr. Cobb, in his last speech, based upon the transportation of the sugar from New York to New Orleans, at an exceedingly low rate.

Mr. COBB—From New York to St. Louis.

Mr. HAWLEY—I am obliged to you for the correction. There were 600 hogsheads of sugar carried at a rate which seemed to be very low, and the illustration was given to prove that the railroad had taken a traffic that belonged to the canal, by the unusually low rate. Let us see how it was. Belcher & Co., of St. Louis, have a great sugar refinery—an immense establishment—the running of which requires a vast consumption of crude sugar daily, and the stopping of which would cost him $500 each day it remained still. They were running low in material, and could not get a supply by river from New Orleans, by reason of low water. They telegraphed to New York to purchase so many hogsheads of sugar, and to send it by rail, as they must have it in a certain specified time. That order came to New York, and came to the knowledge of the transportation lines. They began competing for it. The competition was between the New York and Erie and Baltimore and Ohio roads. The rates ran down to that low figure complained of by the gentleman. The New York and Erie took the sugar and carried it forward to St. Louis. Perhaps they lost money upon it, perhaps not—they thought not. If it had not been carried by them, it would have been carried by the Pennsylvania Central or Baltimore and Ohio roads, for it could not wait for the canal. This particular instance shows the fallacy of pretending that railroads must necessarily be confined to a specific class of articles and specific rates, to do its business well.

And while I am on that subject, I want to call your attention to this classification of canal and rail freights. There is no line that will separate and divide freights uniformly—one article always on one side of the line, and another article always on the other. In some places, all articles are canal freights, and in others, all are railroad freights. As, for instance, at Port Jervis, on the New York and Erie railroad, everything there is railroad freight, because it cannot go to or from that place by canal. And so, too, there are places where freight cannot be reached by railroad. Then we come to a class of articles which belong to the rail, if they can get to the rail, by reason of their great value and the short time in which the carrying must be accomplished. There is another class of articles that belong to the railroad sometimes, and to the canal sometimes, growing out of the situation of their owner. If the owner of beef. pork or flour cannot afford to wait for returns the time that would be required to have them transported by canal, he sends them by railroad; but if he can afford to wait, he sends by canal, and gets lower rates of freight. There is no line that can be drawn that is sure and certain to discriminate in every case. Each man's judgment is his guide in the particular case, and he will send his goods by that means which will best subserve his interest. That is the explanation on that point.

We go a little further, and let us see what is really the question—the difficulty complained of here. It is that the roads charge a different rate per mile per ton for different distances. They call it a discrimination against the people of this state. I will not criticise any further than to say that they give it a wrong name. It is not discriminating against the people of this state at the cost of our citizens. They will allow the citizens of this state to carry at the same rate they will allow the citizens of other states to carry, from between all points on their road and over all their western connections. When they show these low freights from Chicago east are they not for the benefit of the New York citizen? Is not the citizen of New York interested as purchaser and consumer? Is it not for his benefit in three cases out of four? It is often his property as soon as it is consigned and started from Chicago? Is it not the New York citizen who owns and controlsthe property from the point of competition in the extreme west to the State of New York? But there is no discrimination against the citizen of this state because he happens to live in this state. He has the same advantage in these long freights as any body else; and the people of the State of New York have more interest than all the rest, because they are interested in the largest proportion of freight when it starts, and all of it when it arrives.

Then they say further, that it operates injuriously upon particular localities of the State of New York. At Buffalo, for instance, they complain that this has been the cause of driving Buffalo out of the wholesale trade. I beg to say that in point of fact this is a mistake, as well as a mistake in theory. Since when did Buffalo cease to be a place of wholesale merchandising? Since the competition and low rates there has been just as many wholesale establishments in Buffalo as there were three years ago when the competition commenced, and before it commenced. The wholesaling had ceased at Buffalo long before the rival lines were opened and the competition commenced, and the change of their trade is not because of these things. There are now in Buffalo as large wholesale establishments as there ever was, but not so many of them. The reason is because Buffalo is not the right place for them. It is not due to the prices of freight on canal and railroad and much less to a discrimination in those prices as to distance. It is due to other causes. When Buffalo was engaged in the wholesale trade, the merchants west had not the money to buy wholesale stocks to sell. They came to Buffalo because it was only by tedious stage rides that they could reach New York, consuming the valuable time of the merchants. They found at Buffalo stocks that accommodated them. There were wholesale establishments but very small ones when compared to those of this day. Then a hundred thousand dollars in a wholesale business made it a very large establishment, but that amount makes no sort of a wholesale establishment now. As the tide of emigration and wealth and production and capital went west, Chicago came to be the place which held the relation to the west that Buffalo had once held, in the purchasing and selling of merchandise between the west and the New York market. Then Buffalo was so far from New York that there was some object to be gained by purchasing a stock there and not going to the Metropolis for it. But now the merchant on arriving at Buffalo, he finds himself only 18 hours from the Metropolis, which he can reach at a cost of nine dollars, and as he prefers to go where stocks are large and credits most desirable, and where the attentions of the city are the most considerable, to New York he goes. Not only is that true of the general course of trade but in the tendency of things for the people of Buffalo even go to New York to make their retail purchases.

I ask, is it possible that the Board of Directors of the New York Central Railroad, making a discrimination in the prices of freight in favor of long distances, has had anything to do with that? These remarks are true of all the changes. The "whirligig of time brings about many changes"—changes the footsteps of commerce—alters the capacities of a community, and destroys the relative value of localities. No statutes can stop the movement. That brings me to say that the laws of trade extend over all civilized communities. They are as delicate and subtle as a telegraphic wire, and as strong as the Atlantic cable. Those laws pay no attention to sovereignties, or state lines or political divisions! Nor can they be made to; and until you find a legislature that has power and jurisdiction as broad as the field of commerce itself, you cannot regulate the laws of commerce by legislation. If you undertake to do it in the State of New York and put up your adamantine statutes—making laws like the Medes and Persians, unchangeable, the effect will only be to separate ourselves from the whole commercial world by the establishment of a different code that does not affiliate with and cannot control the code of the commercial world outside the state. Trade with the world and not against it. Let me bring this down to a practical point. Let us see if the remedy for this competition is at all adequate to the pretended disease—is the plaster as large as the wound? What, is it claimed, has brought about this competition—this terrible thing of competition, which in the year 1859 has come, for the first time to be considered a crime, though lauded and blessed through all time hitherto. Competition has done all this. We used to bless competition as the means that swept down the barriers of monopoly. But now we come to the time when it is charged that it is an act of oppressive monopoly for a railroad to compete by reducing prices. The competition has been how and where? Why, between Baltimore and Ohio, the Pennsylvania Central, the New York and Erie, the New York Central, the Erie Canal and the Grand Trunk railroads. The last I have mentioned is not by any means the least. Can you stop that competition? Not until you have a power that shall extend over and control all these lines. Your jurisdiction is limited to those within this state. Where the others exist, you have no legislative control. The course of trade is between the northwest, the west, the southwest and the eastern cites, which last are the gates of the commerce to Europe. What is wanted? You want the commerce to go forward in such a way as to be relieved of burdens, instead of putting it where they will be imposed upon it. Competition enters the field of commerce, and the rates go down, benefiting the consumer at the east, who gets his produce and provisions at cheaper rate, while the producer at the west gets a larger compensation because the cost of carrying is less. I do not care how you may speculate about it. The consumer and producer are benefited just in proportion as you reduce the cost of transportation, and the total amount of reduction is added to the wealth of the people.

The competition goes on and prices run down. You propose by your statute to tax these lines of railroad so that they cannot compete. Will that stop the competition? It takes from the gains of two of your own lines of communication, and built for that purpose, and only the Erie canal remains. But the struggle between the Pennsylvania Central, the Baltimore and Ohio, and the Grand Trunk still goes on; and unless the Erie canal has the power, the capacity and facility of carrying all freights lower and quicker than they, diversion will continue to go on. Have you done anything towards a remedy? Will not that freight at the west find the eastern marts and be sold there in the same kind of competition with Rochester and Western New York products that it otherwise would? I take the special instance complained of, that of the Rochester miller. He buys his grain in Michigan, pays freight on it to Rochester, grinds it there and then has to pay for the flour as much freight as they pay from Detroit to New York. Let us see the result of the proposal for remedy—the measure which is to effect a cure of this difficulty. Notwithstanding your prohibition on the New York roads, the flour of Detroit still finds its way to the New York market just as cheaply as before, and your pro rata law raises the prices of freight on the Rochester miller, and makes the margin against him by so much the worse. I ask if that is not the effect? Have we not proved that that is the tendency? I am not going to say we have proved that it costs twice as much to carry way freight; I am only contending that the proof shows that it costs decidedly more. I am not going to say that all that has been alleged is a mistake; but I do say that unless you can show that your act will compel the Detroit man to pay more for carrying his produce to New York, it will not have the effect you call for; and if you do succeed in that, I then say that you have made the great radical mistake by your statute of increasing the price of transportation between the west and the city of New York.

I come now to another cause of complaint, namely, that the producer in Western New York is damaged by the competition of the producers of the far west monopolising his market in New York. You propose a pro rata regulation as a remedy. I say it is no remedy, for the reason that notwithstanding the pro rata, the produce of the far west would find its way to the eastern seaboard at the same low rate while the producer in Central New York is taxed a higher rate, by reason of that pro rata regulation—and the margin is made even worse. That is true whether the produce goes to New York and Philadelphia by the Pennsylvania Central, or to Boston by the Grand Trunk road. It is not necessary to produce that effect that it should go to the city of New York, because a hundred thousand barrels of flour in Philadelphia or Boston rules the price in New York just as well as though it were in the city of New York, with the exception of the difference in the transportation, which is not more than five cents a barrel. Flour can not be scarce and dear in New York and plenty and cheap in Philadelphia or Boston. So that if you stop up the channel of trade to the city of New York and divert this rich traffic to Philadelphia, nevertheless the evil to remedy, which you unwisely undertook to apply the pro rata regulation, not only exists, but is increased. I ask if these positions are not tenable—if there is any reply to them? I do not mean to measure that effect by exactly so many cents and so many dollars. I show that such is the tendency; and I say that you cannot afford to encounter that tendency.

Since when was it that New York outstripped Philadelphia in growth and commercial prosperity? It dates from the time the Erie canal afforded it better facilities for interior traffic. It has made our city the Metropolis and our state the Empire. Within two years, the enterprise of these cities has challenged our supremacy; and they mean if they can to win it for themselves. They have afforded facilities that seem now to be as good as ours, and we begin to doubt whether we hold that superior position that we held before. The struggle has commenced, and it is a war of giants. There are 150 millions of dollars of capital invested in the railroads of the State of New York, and there are forty miliions in the canals of the State of New York, and these rival routes have a much larger investment than that. Here are between 300 and 400 millions of dollars invested in the interprises that are entered for this struggle for supremacy in the traffic between the East and the West! and it is not yet decided who will hold it. It is a war of giants; put no shackles, I pray, on the limbs of our champion. You hold the shears of Delilah, beware how you pass the glittering steel across his locks of strength. With entire satisfaction, my learned friend, Mr. Cobb, produced statistics of the tonnage and transportation on these great competing lines, showing that the New York Central had its reasonable per cent of the aggregate amount, that the New York and Erie had its reasonable per cent, that the Pennsylvania Central and Baltimore and Ohio had each its per cent of this traffic, and he triumphantly concluded that notwithstanding all that had been done by other states, the roads of New York had maintained their position. So they did after a hard fight, without much profit. But that was done without any existing pro rata. It was done because of low rates in competition, which you are to stop by passing this law, and render it impossible for a New York road to go into the market and take freights at low rates. Pass this bill, and wait another year, and when you come to take statistics, you will find that there is no such division of the tonnage; the long freights will have left us, won from us by low rates. I am afraid that your pro rata will take away the capacity of the New York roads to carry cheap. I am not going into a detail of this subject. All that has been done by the witnesses better than I could do it. They understand the railroad business, as well as our experienced friends understand the canal business. If I wanted advice about canals I would consult canal men, if about railroads I would consult railroad men. On both sides they have been at school and often to the school of adversity, the best of all schools. They have studied with all possible inducements to learn, and to learn correct.

Gentlemen, you may say that I exaggerate the consequences of this crisis. But when you consider that the smallest amount of established advantage of one route over another, on the whole, will change the course of any amount of traffic that can be enumerated, you may well reflect that I do not overestimate the importance of the crisis. Cities are built in this age by commerce alone, and by commerce they are destroyed. New York and London may be destroyed by fire or by war, and New York and London will be rebuilt by the same causes that created them. But if you change the laws that built them up so that contribution which built them up does not go on, but is withdrawn, they are sure to moulder and decay, and take their rank among the ruined cities of the past. They and their institutions will become ruined monuments of a mistaken policy. There was a time when Bristol was the chief exporting and trading town of England. Liverpool then was nothing. Where it now is was nothing but uninhabited marshes surrounded by a few fishermen. But Bristol had a large number of little vexatious charges or tonnage taxes on vessels entering that port, not expensive, but expressed in shillings and pence. Liverpool opened her port without the shillings and pence tax, and soon the coasters resorted thither; the large vessels followed, and in time it became a great maritime port, built by the difference of a little wharfage charges and tonnage duties of those two towns. Bristol is nowhere. Liverpool, by the laws of growth and circumstances surrounding its position, has grown up to be a great market, chiefly because it has been the cheapest and most favorable port in the trade with America. The same laws are still in operation; and they are very likely to change the relation of Liverpool to other towns in England. The lines of steamers between New York and Liverpool have the trade of England alone at that end of the voyage to rely upon for profit. Farsighted men, whose policy is lower rates and larger business have, with admirable judgment and foresight, established other lines of steamers. They run to and from the continent, touching at Southampton. Starting from the continent with a compensating cargo they can underbid Liverpool by a considerable figure. But for the government subsidy the Cunard line, like the Collins' line, would before this have ceased to run to Liverpool, and now, even now there are more steamers touching at Southampton than at Liverpool. Wait a few years and the laws of trade will exhibit to our children a Southampton more than a rival to Liverpool. Why is this? These changes have resulted and still continue to result from the progress of ideas; from the ingenuity of men; from the accumulation of capital; from improvements in science; from low rates; finally from the unshackled laws of trade. Therefore let no city boast that it standeth lest it fall.

I have been a Buffalonian. For 20 years I lived in that city, and during all those years no argument could satisfy a citizen of Buffalo that anything could stand in the way of its prosperity. But it has lost its wholesale trade; and that is not all of its losses. It made mistakes in its policy, just such as are proposed to be made here. Twenty years ago, on this floor, a repre sentative of that city, by exertions which he plumed himself secured the termination of the New York and Erie railroad at Dunkirk. Some eighteen years ago, the Canada railroad, then about to be commenced, sent its Directors to Buffalo, proposing its citizens to subscribe for a little of its stock, and aid in its construction, in return for which they would make Buffalo its eastern terminus. A meeting was held at the American Hotel, which I attended. A leading counselor of the town made a speech against the enterprise, and the aid sought was refused. By those two mistakes, Buffalo ceased to be a point where the great railroads cross. They forced from themselves those advantages which carry commerce with them, and trade has gone from that town. The effect of the slighest mistake of this kind may be felt for years to come, and a citizen of New York may live to see the day when there is another city as prosperous and as great as she. If by any means whatever the great portion of the western products should be directed to the seaboard at Philadelphia, instead of New York, it is as inevitable as that men are wise and cupidity exists as an element in human transactions, that the ships will go after that produce. And if they do that, it is just as inevitable that the imports brought in these ships will go to Philadelphia. I do not say that these things are going to happen, but I say it is the tendency, and the exact and only tendency of the measure here proposed.

It will do to speak slightingly of rivals. We ought to keep our courage up. We ought to fight on thinking as little of them as is wise, but not *too* little. The Grand Trunk railway is an institution intended to compete for the western traffic. It has invested in it sixty millions of dollars, under circumstances that no return of that capital is expected, and by the ruling powers is not looked for. It has entered for trade, and England will make such sacrifices for trade as have never been thought of in this country. What has England not done for trade? Can any man look and find a motive for England carrying on a twenty years' war against the first Napoleon, that is not based upon a desire for the trade of the Continent? England did not care one rush for legitimacy. This is proven by the fact that she now is in alliance with the descendant of that usurping Napoleon, now sitting on the throne of the Empire. That war was carried on because Napoleon excluded from Europe the traffic of England. She carried it on with no care for the balance of power in Europe, but solely in order that her people might trade. England will spend any sums of money to secure a large trade. Why? In self-defence she must have it, and must have constantly increasing in quantity. The Grand Trunk railway is more than a railroad, it is a political institution wielded for political purposes. The company is reaching out for traffic, and whether they make money or not, is of no account to us, provided they do the trade and continue to do it. Does it help us that they sink money by underbidding our railroads in this market? Not at all. But, the gentlemen say, they will back down. Well, I think they will back down, but they certainly will not, unless we keep up the competition. If we withdraw this competition by shutting up two of our lines, the Grand Trunk will get our trade and retain it, at remunerative prices, and will grow stronger and stronger with its successes.

Do you advise us to withdraw this competition? Is it not fortunate that some men have invested a hundred and fifty millions of dollars in these railroads, to fight out this battle for the State of New York? Are you going to prohibit this contest, and drive them into a corner where it is posible they may be broken down?

I was sorry to hear the argument made by the gentleman who first addressed you in behalf of these petitioners, Dr. Hunt of Buffalo. I was sorry it was made—its tone was so despairing of the enterprise of this State. It amounted to this: that it was of no use, we cou'd not get the trade, or if we did, we should get it only by carrying it around three sides of a square, and the line on the remaining side would beat us; and it was of no use! The Grand Trunk railway would break down; that the Pennsylvania would not make money, and the Baltimore and Ohio could not compete with us, and therefore we should resign, and in order to make it sure that we shall resign, the Legislature is asked to pass a statute which makes it indispensable we should resign. Is it true that the State of New York is to give up its trade. Only think what an admission this is; that the State of New York has ceased to be the empire of commerce; that our avenues cannot do the carrying trade between the west and the east as well as other roads, and that this large expenditure shall be given up.

It is claimed that the whole amount which these railroads receive on through freight is lost by them in expenses. Where does it go? It goes for the citizens of this state. Five thousand—yes almost six thousand men are employed in the New York and Erie road, and four thousand and more on the New York Central, direct employees. A number very large, but difficult to ascertain with certainty, derive their support by indirect connection with these enterprises. But allowing, for the sake of the argument, that the long freights do not pay much profit to the railroad companies, nevertheless these four or five millions of dollars are spent in the State of New York and paid for by the trade of the west. That vast tonnage is all carried to New York and exchanged for eastern commodities, and a reasonable profit results to the New York merchants. Must it all be resigned? Why? What for? Simply that Oswego may grind, or Rochester may grind, and that Buffalo may sell at wholesale as well as at retail, that a class may be benefited; thus imperiling the trade of the state by interfering with its laws. Are you going to tax the general commerce in order that a locality may thrive?—or that a caste may succeed.

Let us go a little farther, and see whether this

power of discrimination is not common and necessary to all lines of traffic and all kinds of trade. Look at the Erie canal. It is always customary in freights to charge different rates in reference to the distance they are carried. Short distances pay a higher rate than long distances. The very same discrimination on the canals has always existed, and exists now. And provided this law be passed, it will not have the effect on the Erie canal that it is believed. The best you can imagine is, that the canal will retain the same amount of business it has been accustomed to do.

I will now call your attention to the respective interests of Oswego and Buffalo, which are said to be involved in this question. It is the old question which has been debated in this House by the month, that high tolls pro rated would send everything by the lakes to Oswego, and low tolls sends it by Buffalo. The contest between Buffalo and Oswego, as such, are immaterial; but the principle illustrated is the same as proposed in the pro rata law. Let me illustrate it. Pro rata will compel a fixed rate per ton per mile between the lakes and the Hudson. It is (say) 300 miles from Buffalo to Albany, and say 200 from Oswego to Albany. The lake will bring freights from Chicago or Detroit to Oswego about as cheap as to Buffalo. Oswego has always claimed that they could freight just as cheap, adding the trifling toll of the Welland canal. The rail rates being pro rata and high, the freights would of course seek the shortest rail line because it would be cheaper. Suppose, for example, that the pro rata tariff on any quantity were $1.00 from Buffalo to Albany by rail, it would be but 66 cents from Oswego to Albany, a difference sufficient to change the course of every ton of freight on the lakes.

It is proper for me to add, that the proof shows us that the pro rata measure would lose us a portion or all of the traffic from beyond the border of the state. That loss we cannot afford to encounter. That it would increase largely the charges upon transportation within this state. That increase would be a great misfortune. That it would strike down and destroy great interests under the mistaken idea that it would build up small interests. It would reverse the policy that has made us great, and in fact be an act of voluntary abdication of the empire of commerce ot which we are now so greatly proud. You, gentlemen of the committee, may have a potential voice in deciding this momentous question. There is much more which I could wish to say, but after thanking you for the patient hearing you have afforded me, I will conclude by saying, that the measure under consideration is one of proposed legislative interference with the laws of trade which will not produce the effects desired by the petitioners, but rather aggrevate the mischiefs from which they ask relief. That the evils of which they complain are in fact a public benefit, for which we ought to be thankful.

If the railroads can indeed transport cheaper than the canals, we are unfortunate, and I am glad of it; and the State of New York could adopt no worse policy than to so hamper them by statutes as to destroy that capacity.

All taxes are burdens, and there could be nothing more unwise than for this state to tax, in any degree, that great western commerce upon which her prosperity so completely depends.

Mr. FLAGLER inquired, if all the statements had been made adverse to the petitioners.

Mr. THOMPSON—I was about to state, that I read to the Committee the names of several other experts in railroad transportation, whom I expected to examine on this case. But the course of examination has been so rapidly pursued and has been so clear and decisive and uncontradicted in all the points we deem material to the question, I shall forbear, in behalf of the three roads whom I represent, pressing upon the Committee the examination of any further witnesses on these points at this time. It seems to me, that if anything was ever proven before a Committee, or in a court of justice, beyond contradiction, it is the facts which have been testified to, to-day by Mr. Brooks, and which have been confirmed by the evidence of every other witness that has come upon the stand. We have brought gentlemen from cities in the west, from cities in the east, from cities at the south, and from points where these converging lines come together, and all testify to one uniform state of facts,—they all confirm the testimony of Mr. Brooks, given in a clear and intelligent manner; and I therefore deem it unnecessary to further trouble the Committee, or waste its time, if they deem it such, to examine the other witnesses announced to be examined. They have been in attendance during the day, while the testimony already in was being elicited.

Now, I do not propose to trouble the Committee with a summing up on the evidence of this case. It has been rather pleasantly objected, that I have made three speeches before the Committee already. I felt it necessary, in the opening of this proceeding, both for my own convenience and the enlightenment of the Committee, that you should have line upon line and precept upon precept—here a little and there a little. I knew this well; where great efforts had been made to prejudice the mind of the Committee, and the mind of this House and the minds of the people at large, upon this most important subject, I knew that members of the Committee might come here, as members of the House had come, with their minds made up in reference to this matter, upon the false and fraudulent allegations which are contained in these petitions, every one of which have turned out to be untrue in fact, and unfounded, so far as their deductions and reasonings are concerned.

I mean, therefore, to occupy the attention of the Committee but for a few moments, by way stating what I deem we have proven beyond all question and equivocation, so that if your Honors were sitting as jurors in a court of justice to determine upon the truth or falsity of these allegations, you would not be obliged to leave the jury box before saying that the allegations in these petitions are not made out—that the indictment is false and fraudulent, and that the defendants are not guilty of the offense which the petitioners have laid to their charge. Now, Mr. Brooks states to you, after showing what his opportunities have been for judging—the time he has spent in the operation of railroads, the attention which he has given to the business—he states that the cost of operating railroads in the transportation of through freights is different from the cost of their operation in the transportation of way freights;—that the cost of moving through freights is less by nearly half on the average than the cost of moving way freights. This is one proposition which I submitted in the opening remarks which I made. We have proved that by Mr. Brooks, by Mr. Hubbie, by Mr. Phillips, by Mr. Stone, and by the testimony of every single witness who has been examined in behalf of the interests adverse to the petitioners; and all the ingenuity which our ingenious friends on the other side have displayed in the cross-examination of our witnesses, for the purpose of contradicting, limiting or modifying the testimony which has been given, has signally failed in its aim, for not a witness has varied in his testimony one iota. And what is remarkable, is that these gentlemen, after 20 years experience on most of the principal railroads of the United States, unite in stating to you, as men upon their honor, that the relative cost of through and way freights differs in the precise ratio of one to two.

Now, is this committee, in the knowledge of its members—which certainly is not as extensive as the knowledge of the gentlemen who have been examined—will this committee, I say, on the *ipse dixit* of the gentlemen on the other side, say that these statements are not to be relied upon; that they are fallacious; that they are made up by railroad men, and therefore not to be regarded? Certainly not! Great interests of this description are not to be trifled with in this way. When we have proved this beyond all question, beyond all alliteration, by the examination and cross-examination of experienced and intelligent witnesses, I put down their statements as evidence of fixed fact, which the committee will regard as proved. in making up their report, either *pro* or *con* in this matter.

Now, we have proved, in the second place, that the cost of transporting freight in the winter is double the cost of transporting it in the summer. We have given you the reasons for all this: first, on account of the frost hardening the track, throwing up the track and bending the rails, fringing the locomotive with icicles, and filling up the track with snow, so that three or four locomotives are frequently employed in clearing the track, with all the available force of the railroad company, to get it in a condition so that freight and passenger trains may proceed on their course. On this, as well as on various other accounts, which have been testified to before the committee, and certified to as if upon oath, winter transportation costs more than summer by from one-third to one-half; and that, secondly, the roads through the State of New York have all this disadvantage to cope with in their conflict and contest for the through business with the Pennsylvania Central and Baltimore and Ohio roads, in the south; and that this disadvantage on the Grand Trunk line is compensated to some extent by the fact that that road has a wider bed, is thrown up considerably above the water ways, so that the snow blows off from the track, and that it is a long line, constructed over a country which gives it every advantage it can; which has been fostered by government, and which has endeavored to take care of the road from its inception up to the present moment. So that this second fact I have substantiated beyond all question, namely, that winter transportation costs far more than summer transportation.

Then, we have proven a third fact, and that is, that a pro rata tariff, such as is contemplated and drawn up by these petitioners, and is presented to the House, would operate only as a notification to rival lines that our rates were fixed, and they would only have to drop their rates a cent or two lower than ours to take away, inevitably, all the through business of the road; and if this through business was taken from us, one important source of emolument and compensation, these roads would be deprived of, because two-thirds, in the estimation of some of the witnesses, of the cost and equipment of the road, is in consequence of the way business, and that the way business is the principal business contemplated by the road. Take any of these roads in the State of New York, and the principal business of it is the way business. Witnesses state that two-thirds of all the cost of construction is properly chargeable to way business; and you can operate a road with new or through business, without taking into consideration the two-thirds of the construction account chargeable to way and freight business, only one-third being the cost of the through business; and therefore all these calculations on the other side are utterly fallacious, because it is the only business they can do in addition to their ordinary rates of compensation—in the ordinary business they are called upon to perform.

We have proved, further, by the judgment of these witnesses, that such would not only be the inevitable result of a fixed tarriff which could not be altered for a month, but we have proved also, that such has been the result on rival lines in two instances. Prior to 1858, when these southern lines had not completed their connection with the extreme west, the Central and Erie Railroads maintained something like arbitrary rates for transporting through freights. The result was, that the moment the rival lines in the south were completed, they commenced underbidding, and the competition of 1858 at once ensued, which resulted, after a severe struggle, lasting some time, in these roads coming to their senses, and asking a remunerative rate for the carriage and transportation of freight along the lines. That compact was violated again the next year, and in April, 1859, commenced another unprecedented struggle between these rival lines for supremacy. And that struggle continued unti, the 15th of July, 1859, and I may here remarkl that almost every instance of extreme low rates, for freights, which is contained in this publication of the Clinton League, is covered by the time between March 15th, and July 15th, 1859;—taken and instanced falsely and unfairly, so far as these operations upon general principle is concerned. Although they may be facts standing by themselves, yet in the relation in which they are put, they are false, and unfair, and incorrect, and are instanced for the purpose of showing what has been the usual practice of railroad companies in reference to this through transportation. These low rates were made at a time when these rival lines were struggling for supremacy, and are brought in here by the agents of the Clinton League and the petitioners for the purpose of prejudicing the committee, and have been sown broadcast over the country during the last political campaign, and have been put into the hands of every candidate for office for the purpose of warping his judgment in the case. Gentlemen have told me over and over again, that they have been utterly surprised at the fallacy of the allegations contained in these papers upon which they gave pledges. Nay, more, they come here, some of them, pledged that if this state of facts was true they might feel called upon to interpose some mode of legislation for the purpose of correcting it. But they find that it is not true; that it is the exception and not the rule, and that the only salvation of the New York lines is that they shall have the privilege of putting down rates on their through freights provided rival lines undertake to bid below them, and that the moment the Legislature undertakes to tie them hand and foot and make their rates at a precise figure, no more and no less, that moment they put a knife to the throat of every road in the state of New York, and though it is done to benefit the canals, yet the only benefit to any one is to these rival lines of railroads in the north and south. It is an utter piece of suicide, without any compensating advantage whatever.

We find, further, from the testimony of these witnesses that these rival lines, which gentlemen on the other side say there is no danger of competing with us, we find them active and energetic in all the cities on the seaboard; that they have three or four offices in Broadway, New York, offices in Boston, and agencies in all the western states and cities on western thoroughfares, soliciting this through freight. And yet gentlemen pretend here that there is no danger that it will be diverted from the lines of the State of New York; that it is certain to flow into the canal if it does not go on the railroads under these adamantine rates of freight. It would be amusing, the manner these gentlemen trifle with these great interests, were it not so serious a subject—to see the manner in which these gentlemen come here and assume against the interests of these railroad companies to act for the stockholders—self-constituted guardians of those who are in the clutches of these unwise directors whom they have chosen to take care of their interests; stockholders and bondholders who are clamoring at the doors of this legislature, according to the assumption of these modest gentlemen, for protection against their own agents! I repudiate the assumption on the part of those gentlemen. I appear here for the Central Railroad to represent its interests, by virtue of an appointment; have the legal power to make that representation. I represent the Hudson River Railroad by virtue of the request of its President. I represent the Boston Branch, running from Chatham Four Corners to Hudson, at the request of Mr. Powers, its officer. I represent these several personal and private interests, and I object to the gentlemen on the other side, and who are opposed to these interests, assuming to represent them, and if they still claim to represent them, I call for the power of attorney.

Now, sir, let me state further what we have proven. We have proven that it is impossible for lines of unequal length to run from a common centre and receive the same amount pro rata for the freight they carry. It is an utter impossibility, the witnesses say, the long lines will not consent to it. And here are some peculiarities in reference to the Hudson River Railroad which I think ought to be mentioned. In the first place we compete with the river during eight months of the year. We are compelled, therefore, to make a through tariff which will give us this through business. In the next place we carry large quantities of milk. It is started at a time which is convenient for the transportation of that kind of merchandise, runs at a high rate of speed, stopping at Castleton and taking on milk, and so at every station to New York. Our agent tells you that it is worth as much and that the company has uniformly received as much for the transmission of that freight from the lowest station as from the highest station, within 20 miles of the city of Albany—that the reason is, it requires the same handling of cans, taking them on and putting them off, and is attended with the same responsibility, is conveyed on the same train which takes the milk on the whole line on the way down. Now it is precisely the same with reference to the very last can put on within 20 miles of New York, as if the train had started from Albany, for the sole purpose of putting on that can. And the can of milk within 20 miles of the city of New York has just as much right to be pro rated, in reference to the whole amount of milk carried from Castleton to the city of New York, as these gentlemen have to beseech the powers of this legislature, and its committee, to pro rate (which I believe means give to the rats in good Latin) freights along the line of the Central and Erie Railroads, between stations this side of Buffalo or Rochester, and the cities of Albany or New York.

We have proved another thing. incidentally, which is a tender point with my friend on the other side.

Mr. COBB—Don't spare me.

Mr THOMPSON—The excellent gentleman our Secretary of the Clinton League (Mr. Cobb), that mysterious body which has spread its ramifications throughout all the State of New York, and into every manufacturing, mechanical and political department, that gentleman seemed not to comprehend the facts which were testified to by one of the witnesses with reference to the difference in favor of the transportation which would go down the lakes and land at Oswego, and the same property landed at the city of Rochester. It was shown that there was some 15 or 20 cents in favor of flour, and a like proportion in favor of wheat taken to New York via Oswego from the west, than that taken by Buffalo. And the gentlemen have requested me very tenderly not to get up any difficulty between the cities of Buffalo and Oswego. But I cannot bear, as a citizen of this State, that any unwise or injudicious discrimination should be made in favor of Oswego against Buffalo. Buffalo has builded her warehouses in days of greater prosperity than those in which she has now fallen. She has had her lines of steamers and propellers, and many of them are now lying high and dry without business; and the rats are running through some of the storehouses. For one, as a citizen of New York, I should be reluctant to deplete Buffalo for the benefit of Oswego. Oswego is a young, beautiful and flourishing town; growing more and more prosperous, and from the enterprise and intelligence of her politicians and her forwarders—gentlemen who are here, quick and alert to look out for her interests, she will be well cared for. But I do protest against this pro rata legislation sustained by Oswego men for the purpose of cutting off Buffalo and giving to their own city an undue and improper advantage.

I think we have proved another thing. I think we have proved that this allegation which has been so often rung in the ears of the committee, and in the ears of the assembly through all the papers, of an unjust discrimination against the citizens of this State, is untrue and falls to the ground. It is a piece of clap-trap—one of those popular humbugs which men make use of for political, personal party purposes; but the moment you test it by the facts it ceases to be of any influence. Against whom do you discriminate in carrying through freights on our railroads for such a compensation as is adequate to the carrying of it? Against none, unless it can be shown that as the prices of through freight falls way freight rises. Has it not been proved that these two modes of transportation are upon entirely different footings—that one is carried on by agencies and influences which do not belong to and are not necessarily employed by the other? This has been testified to by every witness produced by us, and we might have proved it by 50 more—men connected with railroad transportation. We have shown, as to this matter of discrimination between long and short routes, that it is a principle applicable to ocean navigation, to all river navigation, canal navigation (and even on the canals of our own State it is held to), and railroad transportation. It has become a law of commerce. It has been pursued from the beginning—is unchanged and unchangeable. It is not in the power of the committee, without destroying every interest which they are called upon here to protect, to make any such iron rule as will interfere with this natural mode of conducting this transportation business. It cannot be made remunerative upon any other principle than those upon which it is now conducted. A gentleman getting into a stage-coach at the foot of the Alleganies, where a double team has to be put on, and is drawn up an ascent of three or four miles to the top of the hill, might just as well get out of the coach and demand to pro rate his fare on the basis of the passenger's fare who traveled 400 miles, as the shipper of way freight on these railroads.

But it is said that these unequal rates do not give to persons the same benefits. I reply, that no mode of transportation ever did. Second, the property would increase instead of diminishing in value, especially for all light, valuable goods. Even classification cannot remedy the evil, and it has never done so. It was further said, that the manufacturers have moved out of the state to get lower freights. I think gentlemen have been mistaken on this subject. I think no man could be so unwise as to move out of the State of New York from either along the line of the canal or either of our railroads into some distant point beyond the line of all of them for the purpose of getting his goods to market at a cheaper rate than he could get it from his former location. I think such cannot be true. Our people are a migrating people. The fact that a man has moved from this state into Wisconsin, Michigan or Illinois, is no evidence that he has moved out to get lower local freights, for the testimony is, that on those western lines he would be compelled to pay higher local rates than he would on our own roads. So where is the gain? His gain is a loss. If he has expatriated himself for such a foolish reason, he had better get back again to his own home as quickly as he can. It is said further, that it has depreciated the price of lands and made the west our rivals; in other words, that it cheapens breadstuffs and prevents speculation. I desire to know if there is any natural or political right in a person living nearest market to have the greatest advantage; on the contrary, all our modes of transportation and communication, whether by steamboat or railroad, have been lauded and approved, over and over again for the last 20 years, because they brought those furthest from the market into competition with those who were near; thus benefiting the consumer by cheapening the cost of the breadstuffs for the poor man to sustain his wife and children. I call that a benefit, not an evil. But by the tables which have been put in here this afternoon, the fact is apparent that the lines in the western part of the State of New York, through which the canals and railroads run, have been increasing in value constantly for the last 25 or 30 years.

But the gentlemen say, they are here benevolently to prevent the railroads carrying freight for less than they can afford. Is there any proof of that? Is there any proof that it is carried for less than the roads can afford to carry it? I deny that there is any proof. All that is speculation. They have no data on the other side, no proof; they are not practical railroad men; and unless this Committee is to take allegation and clamor for proof, then the evidence is conclusive on the side of the company that they carry at remunerative rates. But a single witness testified that freight had been carried for less than could be afforded: Mr. Briggs, who speaks of some cattle, flour and a few articles which were carried by the Hudson River Railroad. He admitted that they were compelled to carry them down at less than remunerative rates, and that the reason was, they should otherwise gone down empty for the freights which were brought back by the train on its return, so that it was profitable to the company to take the freights even at these low rates under the circumstances; and besides they came in competition with river navigation and were compelled to accept low rates.

We have shown further, that passengers follow freight, and that they are an important item in these modes of transportation; and that if they are taken off—taken away from these roads, it is a loss considerably more in the ratio as to the cost of their transportion than even the loss of freight.

We have proved further, beyond all question, that the commerce of the city of New York, has increased by the amount of freight which has poured into her. And for one, I have always had great pride in the Empire city of the Empire State. I have loved to see her wharves crowded with commerce; to see her streets thronged with a busy population; to see her hundred thousand chimneys smoking with the evidences of industry, thrift and mechanic arts; and I desire to enter my protest here once and forever against any policy that shall cripple her strength, that shall drive away the commerce from her, that shall cut off those arteries of communication that are pouring this life-blood into and through her, by an insane experimenting upon how much she may be depleted and yet survive. New York has a deep interest in this question.

It is there that these great thoroughfares carry the commerce which passes over them, and which they are struggling for not only for their own benefit, but for the purpose of benefiting the commerce and trade of the State of New York, and in our state, remember it well, that when one member suffers all the members suffer with it. If New York is injured or depleted, and her commerce destroyed, there is no business interest in the whole Empire State that is not jeopardised and injured.

Now I shall go over the various other grounds which have been occupied by the witnesses, because I find I am already taking too much time.

I find, gentlemen of the committee, in the course of this examination that there are three classes of persons who are signing these petitions. In the first place, I find more politicians who want revenue. They think it popular to cry up the canals and cry down the railroads, with the view of setting these two interests in antagonism one to the other. This has been one of the occupations of the Clinton League for a year or two past—to poison the public mind and give to this matter a political turn. For one, I desire that there shall be no influence of that kind brought to bear upon this committee. I believe they have the manliness and courage, and honor, to stand up and look this question full in the face; look at it from the facts which have transpired, and not from false and fraudulent allegations which have been sown broadcast over the country.

I find another party interested and aiding in this cry—the forwarding interest—who contend that this competition is turning away the bulk of the canal transportation. But the difficulty is, with these gentlemen, they are not in a condition to look at the matter intelligently because their craft is in danger. They suppose the canal craft to be in danger. They suppose that this measure is to pour the tide of transportation through the canals, and, therefore, their interests are concerned in breaking down railroads. But I think these gentlemen are mistaken. I think they must be convinced by this investigation that they are a little mistaken—that there is no reason why the canal should be deemed antagonistic to the railroad interest. But, as I intimated when I opened this case to the committee, if that were the fact, what are the ominous forebodings for the future of a new mode of transportation as contrasted with the old? What are the forebodings of history? We have evidence that canals have been abandoned and railroads constructed on their borders. But I don't mean to say here that unless the canal is protected by undue legislation—unless you put railroad tariffs upon all competing lines that canals cannot live. I do not believe it. For one I suppose that when the canal is enlarged—when it is "speedily enlarged," in the language of some of the democratic papers—it will fulfill the hopes of those who have always been in favor of the canal and of the canal policy. But I say now, as I said before, if the canal cannot live on its own merits by the freight which naturally comes to it when enlarged to its full capacity, and when steam is the power used to propel its boats, then I say let it go down, and the quicker the better. It can never live by taxing railroad lines for its support. No interest ever ought to live any more than the old scows ought to live on the Hudson if they cannot do so except by taxing the railroad on its borders.

Then, a third class who advocate this measure, I find to be the millers, merchants and mechanics along the line of the roads, who want to enjoy cheap freights, who are restive under advanced rates in the winter, and are anxious that this bill should pass. I have to say, on this point, that all merchandise and freight sells higher in winter than in summer. That, I think, is the general rule. Then, in the winter, but little freight passes over the line, except flour, and the increased price of the commodity secures a profit, even at the enhanced expense. But, aside from this consolation, we have proved that the 25 per cent advance contemplated by this bill is altogether too low as a winter tariff. All our witnesses put the increased expense at 50 per cent.

So far as I am concerned, I return my thanks to the committee for listening to my four speeches. All I can say, I had not time to make them shorter in the opening of the case. We had two objects in view—one was to enlighten ourselves and the committee, and the second was to occupy the time until we got our witnesses here. The second speech, which my honorable friend, Mr. Smith, complains of as communicating nothing new, seemed to be necessary, because the witnesses I desired to examine did not happen to be here on the stand. However, we have got through this matter very pleasantly; and I have no doubt that when the committee come to make up their report, there will not be a single man who will put his name to a report in favor of a pro rata, and that we may regard it as a subject dead and buried for the future.

STATE OF NEW YORK.

No. 47.

IN ASSEMBLY, FEB. 1, 1860.

REPORT

Of a Majority of the Select Committee on Petitions for regulating freights on Railroads in this State.

Mr. Flagler in behalf of said committee, respectfully submits the following

REPORT:

The subject referred to your committee is universally admitted to be of the first importance, and has agitated the public mind for several years past. During the last Legislature, especially, numerous and earnest petitions from the people invoked the interposition of law to protect them from the alleged injurious discriminations in rates of freights imposed by railroad corporations of this State. Protracted examinations and discussions before three several committees of the last Assembly, to whom the subject was successively referred, delayed the introduction of a bill for the relief of the petitioners until a period so near the close of the session that the friends of the measure were unable to obtain a decision upon it before the final adjournment. This opportunity afforded the opponents of the pro rata measure during the last session, while it accomplished the defeat of the law, has not been without its advantages, since it has admonished your Committee against unduly yielding to similar calls for delay, and has aided in the return of the question to the Assembly in ample time for its adjudication.

Another important result flowed from the investigations and discussions before the committees of the Assembly at the last session. We refer to the able and elaborate report (Assembly document, No. 178,) submitted to the Assembly by Messrs. H. A.

Lyon, L. Ranney and S. A. Law, a majority of a select committee on that subject. That report established by its startling array of facts the existence and magnitude of the discriminations against our citizens in the railroad management of this State, and the urgent necessity of restraint and correction. Your committee adopt as conclusive the statements and arguments of that report in regard to the propositions therein discussed. The publication of several thousand copies by the Assembly, and its extensive republication in newspaper and pamphlet form has brought its statistics and cogent reasonings in contact with the public mind throughout the State.

By these and kindred means the attention of the community has been arrested, and a public sentiment—quite too long dormant, while high-handed abuses of privileges granted to railroad corporations were continued and multiplied—came at last to be almost universally and intensely aroused ; so that from all quarters of the State—east, west, north and south, from canal counties and railroad counties, from localities long and richly favored with public improvements and from those also hitherto sequestered and now soliciting some proportionate share of public benefit—from these, and all of these, the people as with one united and earnest voice plead with us, their representatives, for protection against improper and ruinous railroad management. They as of right demand of us, their servants, to compel those corporations to recognize our citizens as the equal of the citizen of other States, and that we shall secure to the former, under legal sanctions and penalties, the use of those roads on as favorable terms as they grant to all the world besides. This mandate of the people it will be the height of wisdom for us to obey, unless indeed we come to the conclusion that we are wiser than those who have laid upon us the responsibilities of legislation, and can give safe and ample reasons for our disobedience. Impressed with these considerations, your committee entered upon the duty assigned to them by the Assembly. Their sessions were frequent and protracted. The principal railroad of this State was promptly notified that the subject was before the committee. Officers and counsel of that road, and also in succession, representatives of other railroads in this State, presented themselves with their explanations and arguments. Managers of confederate railroads in other States, were present, also, with their statements in behalf of their associate corporations.

The time of your committee has been chiefly engrossed in

listening to these pleas, in denials or extenuation of the practices charged by the memorialists upon railroad management in this State, and the novel and extraordinary course of its apologists before your committee is referred to in explanation of the delay in reporting the conclusions of the committee to the Assembly.

In behalf of the petitioners, several citizens of our State appeared with ample proofs, confirming the convictions of your committee that the petitioners do not err in their statements as to the improper practices charged upon the railroads of this state or exaggerate the mischiefs thereby entailed upon the people.

PROPOSITIONS ON WHICH THE QUESTION RESTS.

Several distinct methods are instanced in which the railroads of this State abuse their privileges and oppress our citizens, viz:

1. Property of citizens of other States is allowed transportation on them for less—much less—proportionably than the products of our own citizens.
2. Citizens of given localities in this State are compelled to pay unequal rates of transportation as compared with other localities.
3. Citizens of our State are at times entirely debarred from sending their products by New York railroads, while the entire force of these roads is given for long periods to moving the preferred property of the citizens of other states.
4. Losses on freights carried for citizens of other states are not only made up, but large profits in the aggregate are secured by extravagant rates charged our citizens.

These propositions your committee regard as established beyond all cavil or contradiction. Not only have those practices obtained in former years, but they are continued to the present time.

SPECIMENS OF DISCRIMINATION IN RATES OF 1859.

Specimens of comparative freight tariffs were exhibited to your committee in the presence of the representatives of railroads implicated, and the literal correctness of them not denied.

A few of these are adduced as proving the continuance and extent of discrimination.

March (previous to opening of canals), New York Central Railroad carried flour, Sandusky to New York at 65c. per bbl. Tariff price, Buffalo to New York, 70c.

April, New York Central Railroad: Pork, Chicago to New York, at $1 per bbl. Tariff price, Buffalo to New York, 75c. Flour, Chicago to New York, at 50c. per bbl. Tariff price, Rochester to New York, 40c.

April, New York and Erie Railroad: Flour, Chicago to New York, at 50c. per bbl. Tariff price, Portageville to New York, 65c.

April, New York and Erie Railroad: Flour, Buffalo to New York, at 40c. per bbl. Tariff price, Owego to New York, 50c.

April, New York Central Railroad: Furniture in boxes, New York to Cleveland, at 60c. per 100. Tariff price, Troy to Buffalo, 70c.

May, New York Central Railroad: Flour, Toledo to New York, at 35c. per bbl. Tariff price, from Buffalo, Lockport, Bloomfield, &c., 40c.

May, New York Central Railroad: Merchandize, New York to Buffalo, 1st class, 40c.; 2d, 30c.; 3d, 30c.; 4th, 20c. New York to Chicago, Ill., all classes, 25c. per 100 lbs.

May, New York and Erie Railroad: Hides, Chicago, Ill., to New York, at 28c. per 100 lbs. Tariff, Buffalo to New York, 35c.

May, New York and Erie Railroad: Merchandize, New York to Milwaukee, Wis., 1st, 2d, 3d and 4th classes, at 20c. per 100 lbs. New York to Binghamton, 1st class, 50c.; 2d, 40c.; 3d, 30c.; 4th, 20c. per 100 lbs. New York to Owego, 1st class, 55c.; 2d, 47c.; 3d, 35c.; 4th, 27c. per 100. Owego to Dunkirk, 1st class, 63c.; 2d, 47c.; 3d, 35c.; 4th, 27c. per 100.

May, New York and Erie Railroad: Provisions, 1,000 bbls., Toledo to New York, at 17½c. per 100 lbs. Tariff price, Buffalo to New York, 20c.

May, New York Central Railroad: Stock hogs, Chicago to New York, 40c. per 100 lbs. Tariff price, Buffalo to Canastota, N. Y., 65c.

May, New York Central Railroad: Flour was carried from Indianapolis, Ind., to New York, at 67c. per bbl. Tariff, Indianapolis to Buffalo, 60c.; tariff, Buffalo to New York, 40c.=$1.

May, New York Central Railroad: Oil (Linseed), New York to Buffalo, at 20c. per 100. Tariff, Albany to Buffalo, 35c.

May, New York Central Railroad: Flour, St. Louis, Mo., to New York, at 62c. per bbl. Tariff, East Bloomfield to New York, 40c.

May, New York Central Railroad (all rail): Merchandize, New York to Cincinnati, O., 1st class, 80c.; 2d, 60c.; 3d, 40c.; 4th, 30c. per 100 lbs. Tariff price, New York to East Bloomfield, N. Y., 1st class. 72c.; 2d, 44c.; 3d, 38c.; 4th, 32c. per 100 lbs.

May, New York Central R. R.: Knock-down furniture, New York or Boston to Urbana, Ill., at 30c. per 100 lbs. Tariff price, Buffalo to Urbana, 57c.

May, New York and Erie R. R.: Flour, Chicago, Ill., to New York, at 42c. per bbl. Tariff price, Buffalo to Corning, 35c.; Elmira, 40c.; Owego, 45c.; Great Bend, 50c.; Deposit, 55c.; Hancock Station, 55c.; Narrowsburgh, 65c.; Pt. Jervis, 67c.

June, New York Central R. R.: Pork, Louisville, Ky., to New York, at 15c per 100 lbs., out of which the road paid 5c. lake freight, leaving 10c. per 100 lbs. to be pro-rated between 800 miles of railroad. Tariff, Buffalo to Auburn, 124 miles, is 15c. per 100 lbs. Tariff, Auburn to Syracuse, 26 miles, is 10c. per 100 lbs.

June, New York Central R. R.: Carried wheat, in bags, from Louisville, Ky., to New York, at 25c per 100 lbs.=15c. per bushel. Tariff on wheat, East Bloomfield to New York, is 25c. per 100.

June, New York Central R. R.: Flour, Louisville, Ky., to New-York, at 40. per bbl. Tariff, Louisville to Buffalo, was 60c. Tariff, Buffalo to New York was 40c.=$1.00. Tariff, Rochester, Lockport and Bloomfield, 40 c.

July, New York and Erie R. R.: Carried flour, Detroit to New York, at 45c. per bbl. Tariff from Addison Station to New York, 60c.

June, New York Central R. R.: Carried cattle from Sandusky, O., to New York, at $35 per car. Tariff, East Bloomfield to Albany, $57 per car. Tariff, sheep and swine to Albany, $69 per car.

June, New York and Erie R. R.: Cattle, Chicago, Ill., to New York, at $35 per car. Tariff, Springwater, to New York, $85 per car.

June, New York and Erie R. R.: Cattle, Toledo, O., to New York, at $35 per car. Tariff, Binghamton to New York, $60 per car. Tariff, sheep and swine, $70 per car.

December, New York Central R. R.: Dressed Hogs, Cleveland, O., to New York, at 65c. per 100. Tariff, Buffalo to New York, 60c. Tariff, Batavia to New York, 65c. Tariff, Cleveland to Buffalo, 22c. per 100.

Your committee are of opinion that no extended remarks are needful to impress the minds of all with a sense of the palpable injustice of the railroad freighting system of this State.

The facts speak trumpet-tongued, proclaiming that our citizens have urgent cause to present themselves before this Legislature for relief.

EXCLUSION OF OUR CITIZENS FROM RAILROAD TRANSPORTATION.

There is another mode, as already stated, in which citizens of this State are deprived of the benefits contemplated in the construction of railroads within our borders. It is their exclusion, at times, from railroad transportation while citizens of other states extensively enjoy it. This system of embargo laid upon the property of our citizens, has been in operation, it appears, for several years and was never more rigorous or severe in its effects than during the fall of 1859.

The short crops in 1858 limited freights by canals until the movement of the crop of 1859. Scarcity of canal freights and unremunerative prices had driven a large portion of the boatmen navigating our canals to the laying up of their boats, so that there was an inadequate supply to move the property suddenly and unexpectedly thrown upon them about the middle of October. As appears by bills of lading shown to your committee, these bills for Buffalo shippers, even of through property, came back from the freight offices with the endorsement upon them "to be forwarded at the companies' convenience." Way freights were totally declined, and soon after through freights offered at Buffalo were excluded also, while fleets of vessels with western freights, were received with the usual endorsement, "Received and paid freights and charges," and promptly forwarded to destination.

Your committee quote from statements read in their hearing, statements not denied by railroad representatives who were present at the time and also listened to them.

The New York Central Railroad received at Buffalo, consigned to it direct, during the period from October 20th to November 20th, during which time its doors were closed to citizens of this State, as follows:

Alcohol,	717	bbls.
Ashes,	558	casks.
Bacon,	65,400	lbs.
Butter,	128,500	lbs.
Cotton,	420	bales.
Flour,	300,020	bbls.
Machinery,	462	pack's.
Peas,	1,900	bush.
Seed,	2,518	bags.
Grindstones,	384	pieces.
Tallow,	76,200	lbs.
Whiskey,	2,695	bbls.
Beef,	26,564	bbls.
Broom corn,	967	bales.
Bones,	483	sacks.
Cheese,	1,969	boxes.
Eggs,	773	bbls.
Leather,	727	rolls.
Oil cake,	461	sacks.
Pork,	1,355	bbls.
Glue,	332	bbls.
Hides,	11,000	pcs.
Wheat,	53,094	bush.
Wool,	589	bales.

besides several thousand packages of sundries.

The tariffs of freight offered the citizen of this State during this interregnum, are unimportant, since, whatever they might have been, the citizen could not procure transportation for his property; but on the twentieth of November, flour was charged from Buffalo to New York 70c. per bbl., and on the first of December, advanced to 80c. per bbl., an advance of more than one hundred per cent. upon ruling rates during the season of canal navigation, according to the invariable practice of former years.

The contract rates at which the New York Central Railroad transported this property so consigned to it direct, while closing its doors to the citizen of this state, is of deep interest, because another illustration of the uniform discriminating policy practiced by the railroads against the citizen of this state, while in this case this road did not stop at its usual severe discriminations, but went further in denying to the citizen all participation in the public benefits it was intended to create, by denying him transportation for his property at any price, while devoting its total facilities to strangers.

Beginning with October 20th, and running forward to November 20th, the following examples, which comprise highest as well as lowest contract rates there appearing, viz:

Flour.—Joliet, Ill., to N. Y., at................$0 80 per bbl.
Divided, namely: Joliet, Ill., to Detroit, Mich., rail, ...$0 27
Lake, Detroit to Buffalo,................ 0 10
N. Y. Central and Hudson River R. R's,.. 0 43 = $0 80 "

Flour.—Joliet, Ill., to Albany, at...............$0 75 per bbl.
Divided, viz: Joliet to Detroit, Michigan Central R. R., ...$0 29
Lake, Detroit to Buffalo,................ 0 12
New York Central R. R.,................ 0 34 = $0 75 "

Flour.—Joliet, Ill., to Boston, Mass.,............$0 90 per bbl.
Divided, viz., Joliet to Detroit, Michigan Central R. R.,...........................$0 28
Lake, Detroit to Buffalo,................ 0 10
N. Y. Central R. R., to Albany,.......... 0 30
Western R. R., Albany to Boston,........ 0 22 = $0 90 "

Flour.—Joliet, Ill., to Pittsfield, Mass,, at........$1 00 per bbl.
Divided, viz: Joliet to Detroit, rail,.....$0 26
Lake, Detroit to Buffalo,................ 0 12
N. Y. Central R. R., Buffalo to Albany,... 0 34
Western R. R., Albany to Pittsfield, ... 0 28 = $1 00 "

Beef.—Joliet, Ill., to Boston, Mass., at.......$0 44 per 100 lbs.
Divided, viz: Joliet to Detroit, Michigan Central R. R.,...................$0 14
Lake, Detroit to Buffalo,............. 0 05
N. Y. Central R. R., to Albany,...... 0 15
Western R. R., Albany to Boston,.... 0 10 = $0 44 "

Beef.—Chicago, Ill., to New York, at.........$0 39 per 100 lbs.
Divided, viz: Chicago to Detroit, Michigan Central R. R.,....................$0 13
Lake, Detroit to Buffalo,... .... 0 05
N. Y. C. and Hudson River R. R's,... 0 21 = $0 39 "

Beef.—Cleveland, O., to New York, at........$0 32 per 100 lbs.
Divided, viz: Lake, Clevel'd to Buffalo, $0 12
N. Y. Central and Hudson River R. R., 0 20 = $0 32 "

Flour.—Chicago, Ill., to New York, at...........$0 80 per bbl.
Divided, viz: Chicago to Detroit,........$0 27
Lake, Detroit to Buffalo,................ 0 10
N. Y. Central and Hudson River R. R's,.. 0 43 = $0 80 "

Flour.—Detroit, Mich., to New York, at.........$0 53 per bbl.
Divided, viz: Lake, Detroit to Buffalo,...$0 10
N. Y. Central and Hudson River R. R's,.. 0 43 = $0 53 "

Beef.—Chicago, Ill., to Boston, Mass., at.......$0 44 per 100 lbs.
Divided, viz: Chicago to Detroit, rail,.$0 14
Lake, Detroit to Buffalo,.............. 0 05
N. Y. Central R. R., Buffalo to Albany, 0 15
Western R. R., Albany to Boston,..... 0 10 = $0 44 "

We might multiply extracts from these bills of lading without finding a solitary instance of higher rates, unless it may be to some point short of Boston or New York, like the one herein cited from Joliet to Pittsfield, Mass., which, although 107 miles shorter than Boston, is charged 10c. per 100 lbs. on same commodity dearer than to Boston; and it is observable that while the New York Central railroad was transporting this property at above rate, viz: on the 23d day of November, the citizens of Buffalo (for a month excluded entirely, and on the 20th of November again graciously permitted to offer his property in sparing quantities,) was charged 70c. per barrel on flour and 35c. per 100 on beef and pork.

Mark the contrast:

Flour.—Detroit to New York,..................$0 53 per bbl.
Buffalo to New York,........................ 0 70 "

Beef.—Cleveland, O., to New York,..........$0 32 per 100 lbs.
Buffalo to New York,..................... 0 35 "

Beef.—Chicago, Ill., to New York,............$0 39 per 100 lbs.
Buffalo to New York,..................... 0 35 "

Beef.—Joliet, Ill., to Boston,.................$0 44 per 100 lbs.
Buffalo to Boston,....................... 0 45 "

The rates from which the above parallels are given was upon no stinted quantity—no isolated case, but for such quantities as 300,000 bbls. flour, 26,000 bbls. beef, 65,000 lbs. bacon, 76,000 lbs., tallow, &c.

The question may suggest itself, did the Legislature chartering the railroads of this State intend to create a vast forwarding line between the seaboard and the western States, from which the citizen should be excluded at pleasure, donating to the corporators eminent domain, a free gift, to enable them to construct their track? What entitled this few to such distinguished consideration over the many? Did the Legislature intend thus to create a power over the people, or an opponent to itself? Has the State expended its millions in canal construction, at the same time with lavish bounty of privileges created a power within its own boundary to destroy them? Has the State invited its citizens to navigate its canals and invest their means in that pursuit but to furnish victims to another portion of its citizens, and to this purpose endowed them with extraordinary privileges, and even a portion of its sovereignty? Can any other conclusions be drawn than the affirmative of the foregoing propositions, if the practices of the railroads of this State as herein related are to any degree justifiable, and to be reconciled with the object and intent of the Legislature in creating them?

There are several objections urged by the opponents of the measures of relief prayed for by the petitioners, which your committee cannot forbear to notice.

ARE RAILROAD CORPORATIONS UNDER LEGISLATIVE CONTROL?

The novel and dangerous doctrine was advanced by railroad counsel before your committee, that railroad corporations are not amenable to Legislative control in the management of their business. The claim seems to rest upon the idea that these corporations having paid the appraised value of their right of way to the citizen, the franchise ceases forever, and the corporation possesses exclusive rights in the property, &c. In the opinion of your committee the wish that this were true is parent to the assertion. Should no corrective remedy by Legislation be applied to the present practices of railroads, practically the same may become so.

We find by reference to the books, the following definitions of the origin and the relations of these corporations to the people: "The right to construct a railroad is a public franchise, granted to the company for the public benefit. The company in accepting it undertakes on its part to use it in such a manner as will best accomplish the object for which the Legislature designed it. A departure from that design in its use would work a forfeiture of its franchise, and the Legislature, from the nature of the grant, would have the right to interfere and direct the management and use of the franchise in such a manner as would best subserve the public interest."

The right of private corporations to take property is the right of the State, the right of eminent domain, and can only be justified and sustained on the ground that the lands are taken for public use. Railroads are clearly constructed for the public benefit. They are not mere private enterprises built and operated exclusively for the benefit of the stockholders.

The Legislature may, when any such railroad shall be opened for use, from time to time alter or reduce the rate of freight or fare or other profits upon such road, &c.

The Legislature may alter, amend or repeal, &c. Every such corporation shall start and run their cars for the transportation of passengers and property at regular times, to be fixed by public notice, and shall furnish sufficient accommodations for the transportation of all such passengers and property as shall within reasonable time previous thereto be offered for transportation at the place of starting, and the junction of other roads, and at usual stopping places established for receiving and discharging way passengers and freight for that train, and shall take, transport and discharge such passengers and property at, from and to such places, on the due payment of the freight for fare legally authorized therefor, and shall be liable to the party aggrieved in any action for damages for any neglect or refusal in the premises.

RAILROAD COMPANIES PRO RATE WITH EACH OTHER.

In the hearing before the committee it was held by railroad counsel that it was impracticable to apply the principle of pro rata in fixing rates of railroad freights in this State. The same opinion was expressed by parties called in behalf of those corporations, and yet these same railroad officials acknowledge that different roads pro rate with each other, and numerous instances were brought to the notice of your committee, showing the practice to be very extensive. Your committee give a few illustrations:

May 24, New York Central R. R.
Carried tobacco from Louisville, Ky., to New York, at 20c. per 100 lbs.
Pro rated between the several lines over which it was carried, as follows:

Louisville ferriage, and Jeffersonville R. R., 108 miles, at	02 4-100c.	per 100 lbs.
Bellefontaine and Cleveland, O., 206 miles, at	06	do
Propeller, Lake Erie, from Cleveland, 180 miles, at	05	do
N. Y. C. and Hudson River railroads, 442 miles, at	06 96-100	do
	20c	do

November 23, New York Central R. R.
Beef, from Chicago to Boston, Mass., at 44c. per 100 lbs.

Chicago to Detroit, Michigan Central railroad, 283 miles, at	14c.	per 100 lbs.
Lake Erie, Detroit to Buffalo, 350 miles, at	05	do
New York Central railroad to Albany, 298 miles, at	15	do
Albany to Boston, Western railroad, 156 miles, at	10	do
	44c.	do

November 23, New York Central railroad.
Beef, Chicago, Ill., to New York, at 39c. per 100 lbs.

Chicago to Detroit, Michigan Central railroad, 383 miles, at	13c.	per 100 lbs.
Lake Erie, Detroit to Buffalo, 350 miles at	05	do
New York Central and Hudson River railroads, 500 miles at	21	do
	39c.	do

May: New York Central railroad contracted with a St. Louis (Mo.) operator in flour to convey 10,000 bbls. from St. Louis to New York, at $0.62½ per bbl. which was pro rated between the several links in that transportation as follows:

St. Louis to Peoria, Ill., by river, at	$0 12½	per bbl.
Peoria to Chicago, by railroad, at	0 10	do
Lake, Chicago to Buffalo, at	0 15	do
New York Central and Hudson River R., at	0 25	do
	$0 62½	

To the canals the following rates would have been charged, viz:

St. Louis to Chicago,	38 and 40c.
Lake,	25
	63c.

Leaving to be paid ½c per bbl. as a premium for the privilege of carrying the same for nothing from Buffalo to New York!!!

An instance was in May last published in a respectable Albany paper, as follows: "A lot of flour passed through this city destined for New York, Tuesday, which was delivered from the interior of Indiana to Albany, for twenty-nine cents per barrel, of which the New York Central railroad's share was ten cents and a fraction per barrel. The tow boat's share was two cents per bbl."

During the early part of September the following instances of western contracts are compared with prices charged the people of this State.

Wheat in bags, from Louisville, Kentucky, to New York, at $0.47 per 100=28 2-10 per bush.

Tariff price from Louisville to Buffalo was 38½c. per 100 lbs.= 23 1-10c. per bush.

Leaving to New York Central railroad 8½c. per 100=5 1-10c. per bush.

Also several thousand bbls. of flour contracted at Davenport, Iowa, to New York, at......	90c.	per bbl.	
Tariff rate, Davenport to Chicago, at........	44c.	"	
Lake freight, Chicago to Buffalo, at..........	30c.	"	
	74c.		
Leaving to New York Central and Hudson R.,	16c.	per bbl.=90.	
At same time charged citizens of Buffalo to New York, ...	45c.		
Also several thousand barrels of flour contracted at Quincy, Ill., to New York, at....	90c.	per bbl.	
Tariff rate, Quincy to Chicago, at...........	45c.	"	
Chicago to Buffalo, Lake, at................	30c.	"	
	75c.		
Leaving New York Central and Hudson River,	15c.	per bbl.=90	
Tariff price Buffalo to N. Y., at.............	45c.	"	
Also several thousand barrels of flour contracted from St. Louis, Mo., to New York, at	90c.	"	
Tariff rate, St. Louis to Chicago, at..........	40c.	"	
Chicage to Buffalo, Lake, at................	30c.	"	
	70c.		
Leaving for N. Y. Central and Hudson River..	20c.	per bbl.=90.	
Also several thousand barrels of flour, contracted to St. Louis, Mo., to Boston, Mass., at	95c.	"	
Tariff rate St. Louis to Chicago, at..........	40c.	"	
Chicago to Buffalo, Lake, at................	30c.	"	
Western Railroad, Albany to Boston, at......	25c.	"	
	95c.	"	
Leaving for New York Central Railroad,.....	00	"	$0 95.

It is not likely the New York Central Railroad actually transported this St. Louis flour from Buffalo to Albany, for $0.00, (while actually costing it $47.29-100 per bbl., as appears by their sworn reports, provided, to move a ton of flour, costs as much as the average cost of moving tonnage), but that through its various appliances it compels every road and lake line in the chain of transportation to pro rate with it, in any contract its agents see fit to make, while to the canal shipper or Buffalo commission merchant, full local rates are inflexibly adhered to.

We find no instance in which western railroads pro rate or divide the freight obtained with the canals, but on the other hand, insist upon full rates. The canals, consequently, in such cases, would be compelled to carry such property for the excess over local western tariffs, which in some cases would be less than the State tolls charged upon it, and in others actually nothing at all!!! Is it marvellous that under such a system the revenues of this State from canal tolls diminish, and State taxes are piled up mountain high?

WILL THE PRO RATA LAW DIVERT TRADE?

It is strenuously urged as an objection to interference with the present practices of railroad corporations, that it would divert trade to other routes north and south of this State. Your Committee believe the objection to be entirely fallacious, as a candid examination of the question will demonstrate.

The bill under consideration of your committee does not prescribe the rate of freight to any railroad. It is framed upon the hypothesis that railroad managers themselves can best determine the rates at which they can afford to transport property, and that sufficient roads are now constructed to keep exorbitant rates in check by competition, each working upon its merits. Were there but one road, it would be proper to prescribe a maximum rate, but the bill only requires that whatever rates they may see fit to make, shall be upon a scale of equality to all. It invites the commerce of other States to pass over our railroads upon the same terms extended to our own citizens, but the objection would seem to imply that the roads must be permitted to continue a system of discrimination against the citizen to enable them to secure the property of strangers. Further, it would seem to imply that to secure the property of the stranger, non-remunerative rates must be offered, and the deficiency taxed upon the property of the citizen. If otherwise, there could be no reason (other than for extortion) to discriminate, since fair remuneration is all any corporation should be entitled to demand. Were there any principle of good policy in permitting this practice, it would become the imperative duty of the Legislature to provide a disinterested tribunal to which to refer complaints, that the self-interest of railroad directors had over-valued their services, to the unnecessary hardship of the citizen. In other words, railroad directors are not the proper tribunal before which to adjudicate questions between themselves and the people.

But as to the question of diversion to southern or northern routes. It is premised by your Committee that in the long run, trade, like water, must flow in natural channels. While diversion for a time may be produced by artificial means, the effort contains within itself the element of its own destruction, and the movement of property between the seaboard and the western States must, in the end, fall into the cheapest route.

If New York does not possess that route, it is in vain to protract the struggle to retain it. If on the other hand, New York does possess a plateau of ground extending from tide water to the great inland seas, over which property may be transported at less cost to the carrier than any other, all other routes become proportionably inferior, and however long they may protract the warfare the result in favor of New York is inevitable.

It may not be improper to allude to some of our advantages. The Western States are drained upon the north by the great inland seas to some part of which tends every canal and railroad penetrating these States.

These seas form the outlet to 3500 miles of immediate coast, and bounded by the richest producing land upon the continent.

The cost of transportation upon these seas for eight, and frequently nine months of the year, is second only to ocean cheapness. The State of New York is the isthmus between these seas and tide water. She possesses also the metropolis of the nation to which the surplus products of the whole country will finally concentrate, whether transported over natural or unnatural routes, whether lifted over the peaks of the Allegany and Cumberland mountains upon the south, or along the borders of perpetual frosts upon the north, or floated down the Mississippi and along the ocean coast. Across this isthmus, connecting the inland seas with tide water, we have a canal unparalleled upon the face of the earth for direct lines and freedom from lockages, with resources for supply o water equal to any emergency. Upon this canal, transportation is third only to the ocean in cheapness; and upon the eve of a still greater development in that direction, without exhausting re sources, in the way of improving and cheapening.

The inland seas and tide water are also connected by a railroad 298 miles in length, of nearly air line and water level. Upqn the south 2700 feet of higher grades must be overcome, together with sharp curves. Upon the north a circuitous eleven hundred miles of railroad located through a latitude of intensity of frost and snows unknown to our favored isthmus. This allusion to the general merits of the routes between the western states and the seaboard is deemed by your committee sufficient, and beg to refer to Document No. 178, of the Legislature of 1859, for the full and statistical proofs of the position assumed by your committee in the above general terms, with the allusion only to the testimony of those several railroad companies, as given in their annual reports, as to the percentages of cost to themselves respectively, in performing the traffic, viz:

1. New York Central, 53 per cent of gross freight earnings.
2. New York and Erie, 58 do do do
3. Pennsylvania Central RR., 59 do do do
4. Baltimore and Ohio, RR., 66 do do do

Of the Grand Trunk we have no reports; but if quoted instances are any indications of the character of its through traffic, it would appear at present that it is paying a premium for the privilege of transporting through property.

Before leaving the subject of the relative merits of the railroads within and out of this State to control the movement of property between the western States and seaboard, the impression remains with your committee that but three routes among all the railroads named before your committee can upon their merits be esteemed competitors, viz., New York Central, New York and Erie, and the Pennsylvania Central. The relative cost of movement of these three lines, we find by reference to the reports of these roads, respectively, to be as follows, viz:

New York Central. Per ton per mile.			New York and Erie. Per ton per mile.			Pennsylvania Central. Per ton per mile.		
1854,....	1c.	6m.	1853,....	1c.	1m.	1854,....	2c.	1m.
1855,....	1	5	1854,....	1	5	1855,....	1	6
1856,....	1	4	1855,....	1	2	1856,....	1	6
1857,....	1	5	1856,....	1	2	1857,....	1	6
1858,....	1	3	1857,....	1	6	1858,....	1	4
1859,....	1	2	1858,....	1	5			
6 yrs. av.	1c.	$4\frac{1}{10}$m.		1c.	$3\frac{2}{10}$m.	5 yrs. av.	1c.	$6\frac{6}{10}$m.

By the foregoing it will appear that the greater cost of movement of the Pennsylvania Central over either the New York Central or New York and Erie, more than counterbalances the few miles difference in her favor as between New York and Chicago. As for the rivalries between the cities of New York and Philadelphia for the western trade, the fact that of flour and other western produce passing over that road, 50 per cent is destined directly to New York, Boston and Providence, would seem a conclusive answer. If we required more, we might quote the language of Pennsylvania merchants while speaking of the present position of Philadelphia compared with her position before the construction of the Pennsylvania Central railroad: "*She has come to be but merely a large manufacturing town on the route to New York.*" The contest, therefore, seems to be not between our own and other railroads, but between the combined railroad interests and the Erie canal, and that every reduction of tolls upon the canal, and every additional inch of water has been followed by the New York Central railroad in more than equal reductions upon such traffic as legitimately belongs to the canals, because it may be carried by canals profitably, but not by the railroads in competition, except at a loss; and every witness introduced on the part of the railroads upon the subject of the commerce of the country, has stated while upon the stand that the ERIE CANAL REGULATED PRICES TO THE WHOLE RAILROAD SYSTEM, and the reductions in tariffs occur at the period of its opening, and the advance at the period of its close. All concur in the statement that the present winter tariffs of all the roads are restored to paying rates, and the inference is inevitable—*the Erie canal is closed by ice!!*

It has been repeatedly testified to before your committee, that the total construction, expenses of the railroad, machinery and repairs, are charged to the local business of the road, while foreign business, or business arising beyond the terminus, is not charged with any portion of these expenses, consequently foreign business is regarded as that which costs comparatively nothing, and the price for its transportation nearly nett gain. To your committee this seems erroneous and unjust towards the legitimate or local business, while this improper mode of apportionment of expenses attendant upon freight traffic seems largely to have modified the statements made by the witnesses as to the relative cost of through and way business. Your committee beg to adopt the language of Chancellor Walworth in the case of Beekman vs. Saratoga & Schenectady railroad:

"If a mode of conveyance has been discovered by which the farmer can procure his produce to be transported to market at half the expense which it would cost him to carry it with his own wagon and horses, there is no reason why the public should not enjoy the benefit of the discovery."

In speaking of these discoveries (railroads,) he says: "It must charge one uniform price," &c. "It is not sufficient that he can procure his property to be transported as cheaply as he previously could have done, but he is entitled to the BEST USE of the discovery," &c. How, therefore, has the citizen the benefit of this newly discovered mode of transportation if the expenses of construction and the bulk of those attendant and necessary to its operation are charged upon him, while the facilities thus produced are extended to a foreign business without being to the remuneration of anything beyond merely the operating expenses attendant upon each specific movement of such property?

To do the business of the citizen for a fair compensation, without oppression and exorbitant charge, would seem to be the undertaking assumed by the railroads in accepting the franchise, and should any discovery be made, or additional traffic arise which may tend to cheapen the operations of these roads, such benefits should not be the exclusive property of the railroad corporations and be appropriated to their advantage only, but be equitably divided with the citizen in cheapening the value of the services to be performed for him. The obligations imposed upon railroads to transport the property of the citizen under what circumstances soever it may be offered, may be regarded as a portion of the outlay necessarily to be incurred in building railroads, since to refuse to perform such service would amount to a *misuse* of privilege, and work a forfeiture of the charter. The performance, therefore, of such service becomes a necessary element in estimating the cost at which these facilities can be extended to the general community. If this mode of estimating the cost at which the facilities of our railroads might with propriety be extended beyond our domestic to a foreign traffic, may it not also be the proper rule for estimating the services between different localities within our own community? If so, the uniformity of rate predicated upon aggregate distances and aggregate value of services prayed for by the petitioners, and provided for in the bill, would be clearly demonstrated.

Your committee therefore arrive at the conclusion that across the State of New York lies the natural track for commerce between the east and the west, and that it may be performed at fairly compensating rates to the carrier without any fear of diversion, and the theory so pertinaciously urged and reiterated, that these competing routes are built and will be run at whatever loss, we think is a fallacy. Everything in nature is recuperative. The mightiest lakes or oceans would be drained of the last drop of water but for the return of their losses in rains. A self-sustaining channel, or one sustained by natural laws, would be perpetual, and more or less navigated to all time, but an artificial channel requires frequent and total reconstruction, and unless recuperative in profits, in the end must come to disuse and decay. But the real question for your committee's consideration, is the duty owed by our corporations to the people of this State, for we believe the prime motive in permitting their construction and endowing them with privileges, was to promote the prosperity of the people of this State, at the same time afford to these corporations such remuneration from the undertaking as they should be susceptible of without detriment to the main objects of the Legislature in creating them.

THE TRUE POLICY OF RAILROADS.

We cannot perhaps better express this duty, both to the people and the permanent good of these corporations, than by using the very language of an author high in authority among railroad circles upon the other side of the Atlantic. We quote from "Scrivenor's Railways of the United Kingdom." He says:

"It is gratifying to observe that every year for nine years in succession an increase of receipts are visible. This is a cheering fact, giving promise to the long expectant shareholders that a better time is dawning. . . . This should revive within him faith and hope in the system he has founded, while it should rouse and stimulate the executive bodies to renewed exertions to increase yet more these receipts by a fuller development of the mighty resources of the railways over which they preside. But sure I am this annual increase cannot be maintained by unscrupulous competition. Such proceedings will certainly diminish the *total traffic.*

"The best policy for a company to pursue is to cease striving after *non natural traffic*, and diligently to cultivate and improve the *natural traffic* arising in their own district. To this end, it is of the first importance to secure a manager thoroughly competent to his work, who shall discover the wants and requirements of the provinces through which his line extends, making it his business to develop, foster and encourage every species of traffic to be found in that district. His highest aim should be to open up new springs in his own locality, the fresh streams of which will enrich the proprietors and cannot be taken from them.

The competition between company and company will not aid the progress of the railways viewed in their combined aspect. The companies who seem so eager to enter upon strife with their neighbors will rue the day they entered upon this warfare. An *unnatural traffic* can never be made to pay; it is liable to ruinous competiti n from the party working the cheaper course, and is certain to receive ultimate defeat, for traffic like water will only flow through natural channels, and can never be diverted from its course except at ruinous sacrifice of money and labor.

"It is of infinite importance to us as a nation," he continues, "to encourage the companies to develop their own traffic, and to discourage their attempts at plundering each other, because the first named policy adds to their general utility, whilst the latter policy is suicidal in character with reference to themselves, and destructive of progression in a national sense. And never can the rail thoroughly prosper until the great majority of the community, those connected directly or indirectly with land-owners along their lines, shall regard it as their legitimate road. A rail without farms on it, is like a river without landing places, a street without houses, a crane without chains or tackle, a steamboat without an engine, an engine without a boiler, a spinning mill without cotton or flax. Only by the interests of the borderers on railways being united with those of the railway owners can railroads prosper; and the largest proportion of their difficulties arises from the belief that their customers are a race of people indefinitely squeezable in purse, while the customers regard the railway owners as a mere crew of extortioners.

"I wish from my heart to see English farmers and English railways prosper. It is the duty of the former to exert *themselves*,—it is the duty of the latter to encourage the public of all classes to build houses, locate farms, erect factories, &c., &c., near the line; then shall the railways grow up into streets of a value greater than the most sanguine imaginations have yet calculated on.

"It is a hopeful practice," continues this writer, "that railways can be adapted to the wants, and draw tributes from the multitude, without exciting their indignation!"

Such, in the opinion of your committee, is an outline of correct railway management, and if adopted by the roads of this State in hearty earnest, would have little or no occasion to appeal to legislation for corrective remedy.

ASPECTS AND MOVEMENTS IN OTHER STATES.

In our sister State, Pennsylvania, the people are suffering similar discriminations and exactions imposed by her leading railroad corporation, the Pa. Central; and her citizens, like our own, are indicating, in unmistakable terms, their determination to redress these wrongs. The history of that State in regard to internal improvements, is replete with instruction and warning to our citizens. At an early day she constructed her main line of canal, connecting Philadelphia and Pittsburgh, and thence inviting the trade of the vast region bordering upon the Ohio river. The cost of this important public work was about $20,000,000.

Its salutary effects in developing the resources and promoting the general prosperity of that commonwealth, are beyond all computation.

It yielded also very handsome returns for the investment in the revenue which it contributed to the treasury of the State. For five years, ending with 1856, inclusive, the receipts from that source are estimated to have averaged about $1,500,000 per year. Meanwhile, the Pennsylvania Central railroad, authorized in 1846, had been constructed, holding the same relation to the main line of canal in that State, which the New York Central railroad bears to the Erie canal. That powerful corporation, like its twin monopoly of the Empire State, cast a covetous eye upon the business of the canal by its side. In that State, as here, men were found ready to decry canal transportation as belonging to a past age, and destined to be superseded by the speedier and more advantageous railroad movement. In an evil hour for Pennsylvania, her Legislature, in 1857, was seduced into passing a law under which her main line of canal, costing $20,000,000, and yielding a revenue averaging $1,500,000 per year, passed from the ownership of the Commonwealth, into the hands of its rival, the Pa. Central railroad, for the beggarly pittance of $7,500,000! In our State, unfair and suicidal competition, combined with artful and systematic efforts to depreciate the intrinsic value of our canals, have not been crowned with the same success as in Pennsylvania; for here, most fortunately, our canals are still the property of the people. Pennsylvania well may, and does envy us the possession of what she has lost—the control of the canals of the State. Her citizens now loudly affirm that in the sale of her public works "the interests of all concerned were sacrificed, and that instead of the wholesome competition intended to be *reserved*, the citizens of that State are left to the tender mercies of a corporation which may and does oppress them." The manner in which the Pennsylvania Central railroad has requited the privileges granted it, is strikingly exhibited in a report of the Pittsburgh Board of Trade, adopted in September, 1858. Your committee, quote from it a few only of the illustrations of the system of railroad discriminations and exactions levied upon the people of that State by its overshadowing railroad power.

"The distance from Cincinnati to New York, via. Pennsylvania Central, Ft. Wayne, and C. C. & Cin. roads, is 826 miles. Distance from Pittsburgh to Philadelphia, 352 miles.

"The charge between the two latter places, if proportional to that between Cincinnati and New York, would be 27, 69-100 cents per 100 lbs., or $5.53 8-10 per ton. The actual charge from Pittsburgh to Philadelphia, per card rates, on fourth class goods, is 50 cents per 100 lbs., or $10 per ton.

"A wholesale grocer in this city was charged by the railroad the same freight on a large lot of sugar as was paid by a Cincinnati house at the same time. He succeeded in getting a reclamation, by which he paid two-thirds as much as the Cincinnati house, though his goods were only carried half the distance.

"A merchant in a town on the Mississippi river was charged the same price for freight on bales of brown muslins, bought in this city, as he paid on the same goods from New York, via Pittsburgh.

"The full extent of discrimination against us by private contracts, we have no means of ascertaining, but occasional accidental developments, such as these, render it probable that it is very extensive.

"The farmer whose railroad station is Greensburg, Pa., pays 40 cents per 100 lbs., or 24 cents per bushel, for carrying his wheat 329 miles.

"The farmer whose station is Cincinnati, Ohio, pays only 58 cents per 100 lbs., or 34 cents per bushel, to carry his wheat 734 miles.

"The merchant at Johnstown or Blairsville, pays the same freight on his goods as if he resided in Pittsburgh.

"The manufacturer of axes in Lewistown, pays the same freight to Pittsburgh, from that place, 173 miles west of Philadelphia, as his competitors in the latter city.

"A maker of an article of hardware in Shrewsbury, York county, shipped goods to Pittsburgh, by way of Harrisburgh and the Pennsylvania railroad, at 77 cents per 100 lbs., at the same time by way of Baltimore, Harrisburgh and Pennsylvania railroad at 45 cents."

These practices bear their appropriate fruit in Pennsylvania as in our own State. In depicting the deplorable results which have fallen upon their citizens, the same report vividly daguerreotypes scenes, the counterpart of which are but too familiar within our own borders. It says:

"These discriminations operate injuriously not only to the city of Pittsburgh, but also against every station along the line of the Pennsylvania railroad; every merchant of Pennsylvania whose goods move on its cars; every farmer or manufacturer, the product of whose industry is borne upon it to an eastern or western market. * * * *

"Pittsburgh houses, engaged in the wholesale dry goods or grocery and other branches of business, have been compelled, by the force of these discriminations, to change their location to western, and in some cases eastern cities. * * * *

"The permanent interests of the State of Pennsylvania, and especially her chief cities, are being sacrificed to the aggrandizement of the managers of the Pennsylvania railroad, and the apparent present advantage of the stockholders. * * * * * The Pennsylvania railroad becomes what the Legislature never meant it to be, an oppressor of the citizens—wronging the home shipper, by making him pay double as much as the foreign, and the whole of a tax which ought to be paid out of the gross profits of the Company's business. . . . .

"To prove that the discriminations charged, in their baleful effects were not imaginary, we refer . . . . to the decaying engine shops, the silent and deserted boat yards, the idle steamers and ruined millers, the produce business banished to western points, the shipping business monopolized by a corporation, and merchants and manufacturers of all kinds leaving Pennsylvania for other States."

"As when in times past, the wise Legislature of Pennsylvania made each of her two principal cities, the terminus of her great public works, many flocked to avail themselves of the advantage—so now enterprising people hurry off to establish themselves in the distant towns to which, by the selfish policy of an ungrateful corporation, these advantages have been transferred."

Your committee forbear multiplying these extracts. Not only

are the people of Pennsylvania suffering with us from a kindred cause, but they are demanding of their representatives the application of the same remedy asked by our constituents at the hands of this Legislature. The following is a summary of what Pennsylvania asks:

SEC. 1. All railroad companies in the State of Pennsylvania shall so regulate their tolls and charges for motive power and transportation, that the said charges shall at no time be greater per passenger, or per ton, per mile, on passengers or freight, destined to or from any port or place in this Commonwealth, either by railroad or canal, than may be charged per passenger or per ton, per mile, for the same description of goods or merchandize transported over an equal distance on said road, coming from, or destined to, any port or place in any other State.

SEC. 2. The rate of charge per ton, per mile, on pig iron, blooms, ore, coal, lumber, fire-brick, and all other articles, the product of this State, not commonly carried to or from points in other States, shall at no time bear a higher relative proportion of charge to other goods or freight than they now bear, according to the tariff of the Pennsylvania railroad company.

The subject was before the Legislature of that State at the last session, and a bill embracing the above provisions passed the Senate but remained unacted upon in the Assembly. Your committee are advised that the reform will be passed upon by the Legislature of that State at its present session, and the action of this body in granting the relief so loudly demanded by our constituents will not only redress our own wrongs, but will strengthen the hands of those who, in our sister State, are endeavoring there to inaugurate a similar reform, and emancipate them from their thraldom under railroad corporations.

In Ohio, as your committee are advised, a bill has been recently introduced into her legislature, and is before the committee on finance, with strong expectations of a report in favor of the Pro Rata reform. A leading journal of that state of a recent date, says, "that all the evils complained of in New York are suffered in Ohio to the fullest extent."

In Maryland, also, the question of railroad discrimination is before her legislature. The House of Delegates, in response to numerous petitions, recently passed the following order:

"*Ordered*, That the Presidents of the North Central and the Baltimore and Ohio railroads be requested to inform the House of Delegates whether their companies have not discriminated against the city of Baltimore in their rates of freight."

The inquiry thus set on foot will not be allowed to rest until the evils complained of are adequately redressed.

In this reform New York proudly leads the way. When she utters her potential voice, the battles of the railroad kings on our western prairies will cease, for Pennsylvania, Ohio and Maryland will join her in declaring that they shall no longer replenish their mutual losses by foraging upon the citizens of their respective states.

The conclusions of your committee may be summarily stated in the following propositions.

1. The law calls railroad corporations into being on the ground that their construction and use will promote the public good. To this public good or general welfare the pecuniary interests of the stockholders must be secondary.

2. This public good involves the right of the citizen to the BEST USE of the railroad.

3. Whenever any railroad corporation, in its management, makes the presumed or even real interest of the stockholder paramount to the public good, or when it grants its use to transport the property of the citizen of other States in priority or on better terms than it concedes to our citizens, there is an abuse of its franchise which demands either a forfeiture or an ample remedy.

4. It is demonstrated that railroad corporations in this State are systematically managed in a way which makes the public good subservient to the caprice or supposed interest of their controlling officers, and renders nugatory the right of our citizens to the *best use* of those roads.

The bill submitted to your committee, and reported by them favorably to the Assembly, rests upon the following considerations:

1. It rests upon a principle in the law of trade, that service rendered and compensation paid, shall be *pro rata*, or in proportion.

2. It rests upon the belief that the regulations and restrictions it imposes will be of incalculable benefit to the citizens of our State—restoring to them the advantages promised them in the construction of railroads, and which have been audaciously wrested from them to be conferred largely upon strangers, to whom they are under no obligations.

3. It rests also upon the opinion that under it railroads instead of being ruined or even crippled, in any legitimate use of their franchise, will receive uniform and remunerative returns for the transportation of freight, and consequently larger yields of dividends to their stockholders.

4. It relies upon the Erie canal, acknowledged by railroad competitors to be the great regulator, to prevent any diversion of trade from the city of New York, or the State at large.

5. It contemplates compelling railroads to recognize the great principle they have so generally and so grievously departed from, viz., that the public good was the par amount consideration which gave them being, and that to the promotion of the public welfare, the supposed interest of the stockholders is, and of right ought to be, secondary or subservient.

The undersigned agreeing in these facts, arguments, and conclusions, unite in reporting the bill referred to the committee, with sundry amendments, to the Assembly, and respectfully ask its concurrence in the same. Signed.

T. T. FLAGLER, HIRAM SMITH, 2d.
JEREMIAH EMERICK, J. FULTON,
E. G. MOULTON.

STATE OF NEW YORK.

No. 60.

IN ASSEMBLY, FEB 8, 1860

REPORT

Of the Minority of the Select Committee on the Pro-rata Freight Bill.

Mr. VARIAN, in behalf of the minority, submitted the following:

REPORT:

That they have given a patient and candid consideration to the subject of a pro rata freight bill, embraced in the numerous petitions prsented to the Legislature at its present session, and have endeavored, by all the light to be derived from so much investigation as the majority of the committee have permitted, to arrive at a safe and satisfactory result. No measure for years past, proposed for legislative action, involves such vital interests to the integrity of public faith, the safety and remunerative value of private property, the growth and prosperity of our commerce, and especially in the city of New York, as this: and we may well pause at the threshold and inquire what evils are complained of, and what wrongs are sought to be redressed by legislation, and whether *this* is the appropriate remedy for the oscilliations of trade, and the inequalities incident to the great and growing commerce which the empires rising west and northwest of us, are now pouring through our thoroughfares into the seaboard city of New York.

THE PETITIONS.

The peculiar character of the petitions read before us, is the subject of remark; many of them highly inflammatory and unfair on their face, comparing the *entire receipts* of the N. Y. Central R. R. for a year, with the *tolls* received, during the *same period*, by the canals (omitting entirely the amount of freight received by forwarders,) and on this statement, predicating the great gains of this company, designating it as a "grinding monopoly" over the rival enterprise of the "people," and warning us of grevious taxation to come, unless the railroads are at once compelled to carry way freight at *lower rates*, while with singular inconsistency the same petitions aver that they are now transporting through freight for *less* than they can afford! One of these petitions is headed as follows:

TAX PAYERS!

Look at these figures and calculate upon the COSTS *and* RECEIPTS *of our State Canals and Railroads.* WITNESS, that while our citizens are laboring under an annually, *increasing* canal debt, a powerful Railroad monopoly has grown up, at one time dividing among its stockholders *profits* to the *enormous* amount of $8,894,500—a sum *greater* than the *original cost* of the ERIE CANAL, and has ever since paid FAT *dividends* at the *expense* of our *canal revenue.*

The cost of our *State Canals*, as per report of 1858, was $54,250,655. The cost of the *New York Central Railroad* when *consolidated*, and State tolls taken from her freight (in 1853) was $24,154,860. The annual *gross* receipts of these two institutions, for the past seven years, have been as follows:—

Compare the Railroad *freight* column with the Canal business: that explains the whole matter.

	Erie and Champlain canals.	New York Central Railroad.			
	Total.	Passengers.	Freight.	Oth. sources.	Total.
1853,	$2,928,663	$2,829,609	$1,835,572	$122,279	$4,787,458
1854,	2,754,376	3,151,519	2,479,821	287,000	5,918,340
1855,	2,436,519	3,242,229	3,187,603	131,749	6,561,581
1856,	2,498,628	3,207,378	4,328,041	171,929	7,707,348
1857,	2,310,536	3,147,637	4,559,276	320,337	8,027,250
1858,	1,882,014	2,532,647	3,700,270	295,496	6,528,413
1859, (estimated,)	1,480,000	2,566,370	3,337,270	279,331	6,200,971
	$16,290,376		☞$23,427,853☜		$45,731,361

Shall we continue to be taxed for the support of Railroad monoplies? If not, sign this petition, and forward to the member from your district.

It is apparent, therefore, that while these petitions emanate from the same source, they combine the names of persons actuated by divers, and dissimilar views, and whose objects in urging legislation are not alike, and that some, if not all, of them are in error.

The MODE OF PROCEDURE adopted by the majority of the committee, was not as satisfactory as could have been wished. Assuming all the divers allegations strewn through the petitions to be *prima facie* true, until *disproved* by the railroad companies, thereby exalting them into evidence, and requiring *no proof of the truth of the* facts alleged.

Indeed, the most singular feature of these investigations is, that although the companies urged and insisted that witnesses should be examined *under oath*, it was declined by the committee, and a report has been made of certain allegations, as facts, not only against the statements of many witnesses, but *without one particle of proof to support them.*

The Legislature will therefore attach little weight to petitions so contradictory on their face, and so unsupported by proof, and will safely look beyond them for any reliable facts on which to act in the premises.

The subject of a pro rata freight bill, as applicable to railroads, is not entirely new in this State, (although no other State or government has adopted any such policy,) it was urged upon the last Legislature, but was wisely left to regulate itself, within the limits of existing statutes, which contain as many and as stringent regulations as are consistent with the public interest, on the one hand, and the safety and protection of private property and enterprise on the other.

It has been the cherished purpose of the State for years to discontinue *special* legislation, and adopt such *general statutes*, as might enable individuals to unite their capital, and transact their business in a corporate capacity, free from the inconvenience of partnership, and at their own election to create a bank, or construct a railroad, or pursue mechanical or manufacturing enterprises, it is a privilege *common to all* citizens alike, and when accepted, involves equitably and fairly only such future legislative interference with the legitimate affairs of such corporation as the general charter reserved, or pressing public exigencies call for, and then only in a manner infringing no rights, venturing upon no experiment, jeapordizing no interest or property invested on the faith of the State, and the ordinary course of business.

Whether existing railroads act under special or general charter, they are to be regarded in view of these principles, and are not to be sacrificed by the reserved power "to alter or amend," exercised in an arbitrary way, and without reasons of the most pressing urgency.

The third section of the consolidation act of 1853, subjects the last named road to the provisions of the general railroad act of 1850, in all important particulars.

A grave constitutional question meets us here: it is *whether the State has the power to dictate the prices of passing the commerce of other states through our borders to market!* If it may do this, then the exclusive power conferred upon Congress to regulate commerce with foreign nations and among the several states is a nullity. Indeed this interference with the commerce of one State passing through another by land or water, by such State, was the very thing the Congress designed to prevent. It is mere evasion to say that the State does not fix a price, but only requires the company to do it under certain pains and penalties. What a company or a person does under State dictation, is done by the State itself, otherwise this entire limitation of State power, in its action upon commerce, might be nullified by deputing it to others; the warrant of the individual is the authority of the State. How can this be effective without direct interference with commerce "among the several states?"

While the *power* may thus be doubted and denied, the impolicy of its exercise is beyond all question as it relates to the commerce of other states. If the State becomes a "common carrier" by the ownership of a canal or railway, she may regulate her charges as such carrier, but not by the exercise of State sovereignty or general legislation.

The railway interest of this State has become one of its most important elements of prosperity. It has invested capital to the extent of about 150 millions of dollars. The amount of its investment is *one-tenth* the value of the entire taxable property of the State, and seven times as great as the entire cost of the Erie canal up to this date.

This large sum paying its proportion of our taxes has the right to look to the State for its safety, for on the pledge of State faith it has been advanced and invested in railways. Hundreds and thousands rely upon the regular income of these investments in stock or bonds for their daily support. To destroy or impair this would be ruinous and unjust; to cripple the usefulness or injure the income of our railways would subject us to the reproach of unfair dealing with important interests, which State policy and State faith require us to protect. The examination of witnesses before the committee elicited the following facts:

1. That the railways of New York, in the prosecution of their freight business, run two separate trains of cars. One confined to the way business, taking on and delivering freight along their respective lines; and the other confined to their through business, receiving merchandize from other connecting roads and lines, and transporting it to its destination on other roads, or at the seaboard. That this way and through business are entirely distinct, employing each its separate agencies, and being conducted on different principles, the one but slightly dependent on, or influencing the other.

2. That different rates or prices for transportation were charged on way freight from those charged on through freight: a large part of the petitioners' showing being made to substantiate this difference in price.

3. That the rates of *winter* transportation are increased over those demanded in the *summer*.

The Minority refer to the published statements made before the committee, herewith submitted, in the entire confidence, that they will show that the above constitute the only charges made out in this investigation, and this honorable body will look in vain for any management on the part of these companies, not referable to the foregoing heads.

Let us see whether these corporations infringe *any law*, or violate *any duty*, in conducting their freighting department on the principles above stated.

1. It was proved before the committee, that from the nature of the carrying trade, this distinction between through and way business was inevitable; that the one related only to the termini, and the other affected every station: that the one passed on the road in bulk, without delay, and without handling, and in large quantities of about 300 tons, while the other, employing nearly the entire force of the road, was carried in small quantities for short distances; nor was it proved that in a single instance the way freight was ever delayed a moment in consequence of any interference by freight carried through the whole line.

What authority or reason the Legislature has for interfering with this course of business, applicable alike to all railways in the United States, it is difficult to see. The same reason would compel the State to dictate to all persons their course of dealing, and their method of doing business,—a tyranny to which no private individual would for a moment submit.

2. That different prices were demanded for carrying way freight, or

freight from station to station along the line, from those at which the roads contracted through freight; and upon this it is insisted, by the majority of the committee, that an "*unjust discrimination*" is made "against" the citizens of our own, and in favor of the citizens of other States, and that only the same rate per ton per mile should be demanded on *all* freight, without regard to where it comes from, at what point it is delivered, or at what cost it is moved.

The first point insisted on, is on its face specious and plausible; yet on inspection will be found to be utterly unsound. It assumes the very point in dispute, viz: that the discrimination or difference in price is "unjust," and is "against" the citizens of our own State.

The question whether the roads are "unjust" in the prices they demand of our citizens, depends not upon what they do for others, but whether the prices demanded of them are exhorbitant.

On the subject of the cost to the companies of transporting way as compared with through freight, Mr. Minot, of the New York and Erie railroad, stated as follows:

Q. I come now to the subject of the comparative cost of through and way freights. What, in your judgment, after all your opportunities for observation, is the difference in the cost of transporting through freights and way freight?

A. It would be different on different parts of the road; on some parts of the road the cost would not be 25 per cent more; on others, it would be 50 per cent, and on some portions of the road, say the Delaware division, it would be double.

Q. With reference to the whole of the business you have done, what is the difference between the through business and the way business—what per cent?

A. That is susceptible of an accurate answer, which I am not able to give without an examination of the figures.

Q. I mean an approximate amount, not the actual?

A. I should think that the cost of the way freight was 50 per cent greater than the through; but there are a great many elements that enter into the calculation, and it might vary somewhat; I do not propose that the committee should understand me as saying that it would cost exactly so much more or so much less, but that the tendency is larger because of these elements, which they can see as well as we.

Q. State those elements of increased cost on way freight, chargeable to it, and not chargeable to through freight?

A. The elements are the diminished work done by the motive power, the additional cost of labor, the additional cost of fuel, the additional cost of station expenses, additional track expenses, track repairs, station-houses, side-tracks and their maintenance, and the interest on the additional capital required to do it; these are some of the main items.

Q. Can you give an approximate estimate or statement of what way stations and fixtures have cost on that road, which would not be needed if you did a through business only; I speak of an investment, not of current expenses?

A. I understand your question to be this: How much more has been expended on the road to enable it to give facilities for doing a way business than would have been expended if the object had been to do a through business only?

Q. Yes, sir, as an investment?

A. I should think from six to eight millions of dollars.

Q. Then the interest on the capital would be chargeable as current expenses on that account, in addition to other items you have mentioned, wages, &c.?

A. Yes sir.

Mr. Brooks, President of the Michigan Central railroad, gave the following testimony:

Q. As a manager of a road I ask you this question: what is the difference in the cost of railroad transportation of through freight as compared with way freight?

A. Almost every road would present a somewhat new case. But there is no doubt that upon all roads it costs a good deal more to transport the local than the through freight. On some roads the difference in the two classes would be very much greater than on the others. There are so many causes that affect it more in some cases and less than in others, one can hardly fix a stated per cent difference. The cars in the one case do not run as full as in the other, nor do the trains take as many cars. The maximum number of cars of a full train is about thirty. The local train takes one or two on and picks others up on the route; as it picks up and drops cars on the route, the average will differ from station to station. I have generally supposed that more money could be made at two cents per mile per ton on long business, than at three cents on local. That must make a difference of fifty per cent. Some roads will make that figure smaller. There are cases where it might be larger. There is entering into that question a phase that is not always thought of. New business is generally long business. New business can be done somewhat cheaper than old business. If you will allow me to go into an explanation, I will try to make myself understood in that regard. The fixed business, for which the road is built, has fairly charged upon it the whole expense of the operation of the road. The fixed business, which may be regarded as legitimately belonging to the line, is that which the public depends upon it to perform, and for which it was built. There are certain classes of expenses connected with the management, not incidental to the increase of business; as, if you please, the decay of the perishable materials connected with its structure. The roadway, the ties, the care of its bridges, its culverts, its drainage, ditches, the sliding of its banks, the wooden material connected with its rolling stock. The decay of that goes on as much in a smaller as in a larger business. There is a certain class of agencies connected with it, not influenced by he greater or less quantity of business. All the principal agents at the extremities of the line, these are not influenced in any appreciable degree by new business brought upon the line. I have generally supposed that perhaps nearly one-third of the expenses of railway management was not increased by the increase of business. Therefore, I would say that if the total cost of working the road or business was a cent a ton per mile, (I state that not as representing the cost, but as a mere example,) then new business could be done for two-thirds of a cent, and the other trade would not be affected by increased tonnage. It will follow from that that if new business is taken at the exact cost of the current business of the line, there is a profit incident to that business, while, if you take the whole business at that cost, your line is worthless. In my own judgment I have always regarded that theory, and have sought new business as the exigency of trade seemed to make it expedient. If we had current trade one way and empty cars the other, we would take freight at a very low rate to fill up the empty cars. There are seasons of the year when our rolling stock is unemployed, that we would enter it upon any business at these low rates to make something out of it. The new business thus sought, not being legitimate business belonging to the road, and for which the road was not constructed, has been almost always taken at rates which are near the cost of movement. It is that element which I have endeavored to describe, which generally rendered it desirable for long lines to seek distant business.

This same distinction between the cost of through and local freights was shown to exist in all modes of transportation, whether by stage, canal, railway, rivers, lakes or ocean craft, as will be seen by the following statements of testimony:

Mr. Powers, of the Hudson and Boston railroad, who, for many years, was engaged in forwarding on the river, and is now interested in river transportation, states that "it is and has been the invariable custom to charge a way-business between Albany to New York, fully up to the through rates;" that "the rates between Albany and Catskill, or any place between, on a barrel of flour, had invariably been 12½ cents, while from Albany to New York it was sometimes 5 or 6 cents."

Mr. Drullard, general freight agent of the New York Central road, who was, previously to his connection with the road, engaged for many years in canal forwarding, states that the practice has always been to charge higher rates, in proportion to distance, on way freight, than on through freight, and he gives the following instances: "Discriminations against New York producers, and in favor of western producers," which occurred during the past season.

May, 1859. New York to Buffalo, 514 miles, 10 cents per 100 lbs. New York to Rochester, 415 miles, 12 cents per 100 lbs. At pro rata, it should have been 8 4-100 cents per 100 lbs., or one-third less than was charged to Buffalo.

June, 1859. New York to Lockport, 483 miles, 16 cents per 100 lbs. New York to Cleveland, 700 miles, 12 cents per 100 lbs. A pro-rata to

Lockport would be 7 87-100 per 100 lbs., or less than half the amount charged.

June, 1859. New York to Lockport, 16 cents per 100 lbs., 483 miles. Brockport to Medina, 10 cents per 100 lbs. At pro rata, the rate between Brockport and Medina would be nine mills, or less than one-tenth that was charged.

July, 1859. New York to Syracuse, 8 cents per 100 lbs., 366 miles. Syracuse to Manlius, 10 miles, 8 cents per 100 lbs. At pro rata, the rate between Syracuse and Manlius would have been three mills per 100 lbs., instead of 8 cents.

July, 1859. Albany to Syracuse, 166 miles, 12 cents per 100 lbs. New York to Syracuse, 316 miles, 8 cents per 100 lbs. At pro rata, between Albany and Syracuse, would be 4 1-5 cents, or about one-third the amount charged.

July, 1859. Albany to Rochester, 269 miles, 14 cents per 100 lbs. New York to Rochester, 419 miles, 10 cents per 100 lbs. At pro rata, from Albany to Rochester, would be 6 42-100 per 100 lbs.

July, 1859. Albany to Rome, 125 miles, 10 cents per 100 lbs. New York to Syracuse, 316 miles, 8 cents per 100 lbs. At pro rata, from Albany to Rome, it should have been 3 27-100 cents per 100 lbs.

July, 1859. Albany to Utica, 100 miles, 10 cents per 100 lbs. New York to Detroit, 12 cents per 100 lbs. A pro rata would be, from Albany to Utica, 1 96-100 cents per 100 lbs., or less than one-quarter the price charged.

August, 1859. Albany to Amsterdam, 47 miles, 10 cents per 100 lbs. New York to Cleveland, 12 cents per 100 lbs. A pro rata from Albany to Amsterdam, would have been 8 mills per 100 lbs.

August, 1859. New York to Brockport, 17 cents per 100 lbs. New York to Sandusky, more than double the distance, 12 cents per 100 lbs.

August, 1859. New York to Chicago, 1,400 miles, 18 cents per 100 lbs. New York to Rochester, 415 miles, 12 cents per 100 lbs. A pro rata would have been, from New York to Rochester, 5 14-100 cents per 100 lbs.

August, 1859. New York to Detroit, via Oswego, 14 cents per 100 lbs. Syracuse to Canastota, 20 miles, 10 cents per 100 lbs. A pro rata, from Syracuse to Canastota, would have been 4⅔ mills, or less than half a cent per 100 lbs.

September 1, 1859. On the day the Canal Convention was held in Rochester, the freight on flour was 35 cents per barrel, by canal, both from Buffalo and Rochester to New York, one 514 miles, and the other 415 miles. At pro rata rate, it should have been only 29 64-100 cents per barrel from Rochester. Difference against Rochester millers, nearly 6 cents per barrel.

October 21, 1859. Buffalo to New York, 50 cents per barrel for flour. New York to Cleveland, 12 cents per 100 lbs. A pro rata on flour, from

Buffalo to New York, would be 19 cents per barrel, or considerable less than one-half charged.

In conclusion, Mr. Drullard says: These cases have all occurred within the present year, and they might be multiplied to fill up as many books as have been published by the Clinton League. They are of every day occurrence, and show quite as glaring a difference as can be found on any of the railroads of the State. They show one prominent feature in the carrying trade—that short distances pay higher rates than long ones, by the same mode of transit.

Mr. Spaulding, of New York, for twenty-five years a forwarder, confirms the statement of the existence of the difference in the rates between through and way freight on all modes of transportation.

These statements, made by gentlemen of long and large experience in the cost of railway transportation, fortified by the reasons and uncontradicted by a single witness, are to be taken as true, and as establishing the fact beyond question, that the cost of carrying way freight bears no comparison with and is not affected by the cost of freight carried through the entire line, and *the only question to be considered is whether the freights from any given point on the line are too high or more than remunerative to the company!* Unless this can be shown, and no attempt was made to show it before the committee, the complaint of the petitioners, that they do not get "the best use of the road, and that unjust discriminations are made," and other vague and general charges of like character, are unjust to the railroad companies, unless we adopt the principle which runs through most of the petitions, that private property invested in railways, becomes the prey of personal cupidity and public plunder, and may be confiscated whenever local interests or popular opinion becomes corrupt enough to demand it.

Local Tariffs on different Railroads.

But in respect to the local rates and their alleged exorbitancy on the New York roads, the point was completely met and contradicted by the testimony of witnesses who appeared before your committee. An examination of the local tariffs by Mr. Spaulding, of fourteen of the principal freighting lines, disclosed the fact that while only one of the number was as low as the local rates on the New York Central railroad, the others were from 25 to 50 per cent higher.

Mr. Hubbie, president of the Cleveland and Columbus railroad, testified that he had examined the local tariffs of eighteen railroads; and on four of them only were the rates as low as on the New York Central. Mr. Drullard also gave similar testimony.

These tariffs on way freight are not uniform, and from the nature of the case, cannot be. Take as a specimen, the article of milk, carried on the Hudson river railroad. It was stated by Mr. Briggs, the freight agent of the Hudson river railroad at East Albany, that a train was run for the special purpose, and the same price per can of ten gallons was charged all along the line. Without explanation, this might have seemed unequitable, but when it was stated that a train had to be started from East Albany, run with high speed, stopping at every station, and that the cost of handling was the same everywhere, and that the return cars brought up the empty cans and little or no freight, it was evident that the cost on the shorter routes did no more than pay, and that if they were advanced in proportion to the distance carried, it would exclude from market all above a point forty or fifty miles from New York. These same reasons were shown to be applicable to most of the way freight. *The majority of the committee, in their reported bill, have excepted milk and some other articles, thus admitting the force of the principle, which is as applicable to all other articles as those excepted.*

The allegation that these local freights were compelled to await the convenience of through merchandize, repeated again and again in the petitions, and reiterated in the same language by the majority of the committee in their report, was not sustained by proof, on the statement of any one having any knowledge of the fact, and the subscriber is therefore compelled to consider the charge as entirely groundless. Indeed, it is hardly possible, that anything of the kind could occur, except in rare instances, at the termini of the road, and then only in the event of the equipment being deficient, no instance of which was brought to the attention of the committee. On the contrary, Mr. Drullard, superintendent of freight department on the Central railroad, says, to his knowledge, the allegation is untrue. His language is as follows: "Mr. Cobb is very much mistaken in his statemant before the committee, that no property was shipped for the citizens of Buffalo between Oct. 20th and Nov. 20th, on the Central railroad. They had, it is true, large quantities of freight to be forwarded at that time, but it did not prevent shipments of Buffalo freights between the dates just mentioned. It frequently occurs in the fall, when the canal has more than it can do, that forwarders are desirous of making large shipments on the railroad on short notice, at a time when there is a large quantity of property in the railroad freight houses, which has been previously received. This delays property of the Buffalo forwarders for a few days, as property must be dispatched in the order it is received. But this state of things never lasts but a few days at a time."

Contrary to the allegation of a majority of the committee, the undersigned is informed by Mr. Drullard, that from October 20th, to November 20th, 100 car loads of flour, wool, and other freight, equal to 1,000 tons, were shipped from Buffalo, for people there, to the East, during the period which the committee claim Buffalo was excluded from a participation of the benefits of the railroads.

2. How is it proved that this difference in prices operates "*against*" citizens of our own State? This claim can only be justified by the same course of reasoning that would sustain the farmer in Westchester county in complaining that the railroad discriminated "against" him, because the farmer of Rensselaer or Columbia was not charged more on his ship-

ments for a longer distance. The gain of his neighbor is not his loss, unless he can also prove that what is so carried and sold is of quantity sufficient to affect the price of the article in the general market. This was not pretended in respect either of milk or flour. The surplus products of our State, passing on these lines to market, are not of sufficient amount to increase or diminish their market value at the point of final disposal or consumption. It was said that our citizens had moved out of the State, and gone farther from market, to get to it at cheaper rates; but not only was there no proof of this, but the local rates of transportation on all western connecting roads, from local to central points, was proved to be higher than on the New York lines, so that no motive could exist to compel such expatriation.

The wealth of the State, as affected by railroads, obtained from the official records of the Comptroller's office.

The following table exhibits the value of the real and personal property in the State of New York, for the years 1828, 1838, 1848 and 1858:

	1828.	1838.	1848.	1858.
Real,	$260,438,875	$504,230,837	$526,624,883	$795,403,134
Personal,	68,978,191	126,564,164	125,663,318	306,449,115
Total,	$329,417,066	$630,795,001	$652,228,201	$1,101,852,249

The Erie canal was completed and put in operation in the year 1824, and by 1828 may be said to have fairly commenced its work in developing the resources of the State. Its influence, in this regard, became manifest by the assessment of 1838, which shows an increase in the valuation of the property in ten years, of $301,377,935, or 91½ per cent.

During the succeeding ten years was the beginning of our railroad system. But up to 1848, its extent was limited; its means and equipment incomplete, and was without connections beyond the State, and was yet too imperfect in all its aspects to be felt as a means of State prosperity. But during the period the canals were in the full tide of success, business had rallied from the revulsion of 1837, and the inland commerce of the State was thriving; but it had increased the wealth of the State to the full measure of its power during the ten years preceding, and thenceforth for this purpose was without influence, for the table shows that the increase of the value of the property from 1838 to 1848, was only $22,433,200, equal to only 3½ per cent against 91½ per cent of the previous decade. It was during the ten years following, from 1848 to 1858, that the railroad system became perfected—improved machinery, tracks and rolling stock, and other facilities came into general use. The New York and Erie, and Hudson River railroads were completed, and numerous branch roads penetrated every portion of the State, making lands available, which, until the completion of these ways had remained unimproved, and almost valueless, and finally with the extension and completion of its connections with the far west and south west, the system was so far advanced as to be able to exhibit its influence in unfolding and adding to the wealth of the State. It should be borne in mind too, that the system was not complete during the whole of this period, but its powers during the time that it was in successful operation in advancing the prosperity of the State, are to be seen in the increase of the valuation of the real and personal property during the ten years ending 1858, of $449,624,048, equal to 69 per cent against the 3½ per cent of the previous ten years, when the canals, during the whole period, were in the full fruition of their success.

Many statements were made, showing that the railroads *carried through* freight, at a less price per ton per mile, than they demanded for way freight; this, in the opinion of the subscribers, is justifiable for the following, among other reasons:

1st. The road, rolling stock and equipment being in order, and used principally for the crrrying trade along its line, can take on and accommodate its through business in addition, without materially increasing its expenses, and at a cost therefore much less than the average of its ordinary business; whether a train of through cars passes along the line, in no way affects those who use the road from way stations, unless, indeed, as several gentlemen stated, the profits so made *serve to keep down the prices of local freight*, which would be largely increased if compelled to bear the entire cost of running the trains. The charge that the roads carry through freight at less than cost is not sustained by any proof.

2d. The amount of through freight thus carried goes into the consumption of our population, increases largely the supply of articles of prime necessity, such as flour, beef, pork, &c., preventing the monopoly, as in former years, of those necessaries. It might assist speculation if these articles from the Western States were excluded from the New York market, but would operate disastrously both upon the producer and consumer, by surrendering the monopoly of the markets into the hands of those who always thrive best where the necessaries of life are held at stationary prices.

3d. It secures to the New York railroads the carrying trade of the west, which, at fixed prices of highest rates, would pass off on rival routes south of us—on the Pennsylvania Central and Baltimore and Ohio roads—thus building up the cities of Philadelphia and Baltimore at the expense of New York, and destroying our State commerce for the benefit of competing routes and cities; and north of us, to Portland, Boston, over the Grand Trunk railway. The majority of the committee seem to feel no successful rivalry in this respect; but how presumptuous this confidence is, will appear from the following statement.

Mr. Stone, president of the Cleveland and Erie railroad, states that a pro-rata measure, "similar in its provisions to the one now proposed in this State, was proposed in the Ohio Legislature in the years 1852 and '53. It was regarded as impracticable, and it did not pass the Legislature," He "thought it would be impracticable to put such a law in force, particularly on through freights, * * * as the least embarrassment in trade over any one competing line would throw the trade on the other lines." * * * "If such a tariff were published, and fixed without change, if it were at or below cost, the line might do a proportion of the business; but if it afforded a profit, to any extent, the competing lines would take it at enough below to entirely control the trade. Ten cents a ton would change it from one route to another." * * * He thought "if any one line was restricted from the Mississippi valley to the Atlantic cities, and all the rest left free, it would practically annihilate its value." Mr. Minot, superintendent of the New York and Erie railroad, says that "a very small difference in the rate for carrying freight, say twenty cents a ton, with the same time, would turn the freight of the country to other lines."

A pro rata tariff, to remain fixed for a month, "would be very injurious, for we could not meet the competitions of other roads by coming down as low as they, and we should lose a great deal of business: they would have it in their power to fix their tariff so that we could not get any through business, or very little, if any; the other roads, knowing our tariff, would arrange theirs so as to get the whole of it." * * * He thought "the New York and Erie would give up their through business beyond all doubt." * * * "The ability to fix rates from day to day for long freight, was a very great element of power in a railroad, to enable it to keep up prices by its being able to meet its competitors, if they were taking a course that it thought injurious.

Mr. Marsh, for fifteen years Secretary, and at present Receiver of the New York and Erie Railroad, states that, "under a pro rata, the New York roads would have no power to compete in the western markets for through traffic," that "a small reduction by the competing lines would take away the freight, and would continue to do so until the rates were fixed below cost, when the competing roads would give it to us;" that under such a statute, the through business could not be retained, and would not be attempted to be."

Mr. Brooks, President of the Michigan Central road, states that, "in the centers of trade in the West, if any one of the several lines should put out its rates as fixed and unchangeable for a month, the others would certainly do the business, unless the rate was fixed at a point where no profit could be made; then the line having the fixed rates would do the business." * * * "Ability to change rates operated to keep rates steady." Mr. Brooks stated certain experiences of his own, both in passenger and freight traffic, which justified this conclusion: "While passengers would leave a line gradually, under such a restriction, freight would leave it *en masse* at once." * * * "If the rate on the New York roads was fixed at so much per ton per mile for thirty days, the effect would be to give the freight to the other lines for twenty-nine days out of that month, unless the rate was so low as to afford no profit." Mr. Phillips, Superintendent of the Boston and Worcester Railroad, states, "that the effect of pro rata on the Boston road would be such, that unless they put their prices of freight very low per mile, so as to leave no profit, the business would go to other routes, which, in competing for it, would put their rates a little lower. The only safety that roads had in competition, was to be able to follow the reductions of others at once. If, on the completion of the Southern roads to

Chicago and the West, the New York roads had not been able to reduce their rates at the same time with their competitors, the latter would have taken the through business.

Mr. Hubbie, president of the Cleveland, Columbus and Cincinnati railroad, states, that in case of a stated tariff for a month, the New York roads, if their tariff was so low that no profit could be made, might retain their shares of the business, but if it left any margin for profit, the other routes would bid enough lower to get the business.

The New York roads gave the western roads fixed tariffs up to 1858, but the competition of the southern roads, just completed, compelled a deviation in order to retain the through freighting bnsiness.

Mr. Hammond, superintendent of the Chicago and Quiucy and Burlington railroad, states, that under the proposed pro rata bill, the New York lines could not take a pound of the through freight from Chicago. The first, second and third classes would go round, and the fourth class would be divided.

Mr. Boody, president of the Toledo and Wabash Valley railroad, Mr. Briggs, freight agent of the Hudson River railroad, Mr. Powers, superintendent of the Hudson and Boston railroads, and other persons whose statements were received, all gave testimony similar to the foregoing. Still the majority, in their report, as if conscious of the presence of this evidence, advise that if New York cannot carry below all others at fixed rates, "it is in vain to protract the struggle," and that she should give it up.

It is humiliating to contemplate this language, and the results which would inevitably follow its adoption. Our State pride—the conciousness of our ability by greater enterprise to compete with our rivals, to overcome shorter routes, and cheaper transportation—advantage of markets, and the prestige of past achievements, all call upon us to retain what we have, and secure more if possible, and to "give up" nothing in the race of honorable competition.

What advantage is to accrue to our citizens or our railways by this exclusion of the through freight, under *the fixed tariff*, *unalterable for a month*, no one can perceive; while its loss will operate disastrously upon all concerned, and divert from our State sources of wealth which once lost can never be regained.

It is stated by the majority of the committee that a movement is already on foot in Pennsylvania and the western states, with the prospect of success, designed to apply the pro rata principle to their roads. In that event they leave us to infer that our New York roads would still retain their relative position with respect to their formidable southern rivals.

We will not pause here to question the propriety of speculating upon any such action on the part of other legislatures, but on the supposition that they should adopt the pro rata system, it would give Philadelphia and Baltimore a decided advantage over the city of New York.

If we allow but one cent per ton per mile for the transportation of freight, the *shortest* distance from central points at the west would give Philadelphia the advantage over New York, the latter taking her own roads, of

$12 30	per car of	10 tons from	Cleveland.
13 60	"	"	Chicago.
16 10	"	"	St. Louis.
18 90	"	"	Columbus.
18 90	"	"	Cincinnati.

Baltimore being 298 miles nearer to Cincinnati than New York is by her roads, would have the large advantage under a pro rata system of $29.80 per car of ten tons! The correctness of this statement may be easily ascertained by any one who will estimate the relative distances.

It will also be seen that, under a general pro rata system, our New York roads could not compete with their southern rivals for freight to New York. The latter would deliver to, and take from New York, at a less rate by from $3 to $10, per car of ten tons. By what process of reasoning, therefore, can the majority of the committee urge that our State or our roads are to be benefited by the general adoption of the pro rata principle ?

It would inevitably deprive them of every pound of through freight, and involve them in certain ruin, unless by an increase of their *local* rates they could make up their loss.

But that would add to the burthens of our people, and our State would lose the benefits of a commerce which has thus far been the chief element of her prosperity.

Have our farmers contemplated the results upon themselves of the loss of the supremacy of our markets, which would follow the recommendation of the majority of the committee, and the surrender, by New York, of her commercial prestige ? How it would depress, instead of increase, the value of the commodities in the seaboard, which, while selling for less in the market, would have to bear an increased cost of transportation by all the difference of the sums now realized for the freight to be permanently lost, if the bill now reported is passed as a law.

It has been urged that in case the railways cease to carry through freights, some of it will find its way to market on the canal, and thus the State will receive the benefit in tolls, which will be lost by the owners of the road.

It is clear that no such result could enure in respect of any freight of the 1st, 2d, and 3d class, and only to a very limited extent on those of the 4th class; for *all freights*, as well as *passengers*, follow the principal lines of transit. If three classes of merchandize pass on the southern lines, to and from the seaboard, the fourth will follow, and the State will strangle private enterprise without any benefit to herself. And besides, no State, has the moral right to saddle upon new and cheaper modes of conveyance, the burdens of the old and obsolete. No such policy can stand; it will break down those who sustain it, and sooner or later bring its advocates to ruin. The seizure of private property by the State, to avoid taxation on its enterprises, which are not self-supporting, cannot be justified by honesty or fair dealing, and is too monstrous for consideration.

Advance of Winter Prices.

3. It was further shown that the average cost of winter, over that of summer, on the northern roads, was at least 50 per cent as much as the advance of freight, on account of frost, snow, breakage, and the wear and tear incident to high latitudes and inclement seasons. The statements were full and complete on this point, and uncontradicted; yet the majority, by a strange oversight, attribute this advance to the absence of canal competition during the winter months. If this were so, it would be difficult to perceive why our railroads should be united in the amount of their prices by a cause which has no *existence*, as in the winter months *there are no canals!* It is the same as if they never existed; they might as well be filled with rock as ice for five months; and having no power of completion, ought not to be considered as regulators any more than a turnpike. The advanced cost of winter transportation was, however, the reason most satisfactorily proved to justify higher rates, experts stating that the winter rates were no more profitable to the railways than summer rates.

It is also proper to state that the most of the freight tariffs read before the committee were for the purpose of showing,

1. The difference in price between through and way freights, and

2. The low tariff charged on through merchandize, which the petitioners claimed was not remunerative to the companies.

This last charge, as hereinbefore stated, was not sustained by proof; and, moreover, those freight bills were principally taken from periods within the past two years, when rival roads were engaged in a struggle of ruinous competition for this trade, which was retained by our lines only from their ability to carry as low as the southern roads; and when, had a pro rata freight bill existed, with no power in the companies to alter it for a month, they would have swept the whole transportation of freight from their lines to Philadelphia and Baltimore, and left our State prostrate and powerless in the contest.

It was thus evident that this whole warfare on our railroad interests is founded in prejudice, interest, or mistake; and that, no legislation can correct these differences in freights; and that the ability of the roads to command western freights at all, lies in their power at any moment to alter their tariffs, so as to meet their rivals in western cities on terms of equality. It is this *ability to fall* that keeps competing roads in check, and is *the only means* of coercing them into terms; and so evident is this, that no greater boon could be proffered to other roads than such a bill as the majority recommend, to tie our own roads hand and foot, and surrender them to the mercy of their foes. It is at once false, unjust, and suicidal! The undersigned does not deem it necessary to examine at length the false principles of political science, and the unsound logic which have crept into the report of the majority. They are so apparent as to correct themselves.

Much is said by them about "natural traffic," and "non-natural traffic." It is not quite certain in what sense the committee use these terms; but all modes of transportation are non-natural, or artificial. Our noblest rivers are useless without art, to invent and construct boats and vessels. Our canals and railways are but triumphs of art over nature. that which is cheapest and best will conquer in the end, and will draw to itself the public use and regard. There is no such thing as "natural traffic," any more than "natural locomotives," or "natural canal boats."

The summary of principles, at the end of their report, is equally, in the judgment of the undersigned, unsound.

It is said the law *calls* railroads into being for the public good, primarily, and only *secondarily* for the interest of the stockholders. It is not perceptible how the law calls them into being at all, or why the public good is primary in their creation, in any other sense than a partnership, or transportation company is called into being by the law, and is organized for the public good first, and for the interest of the partners in a secondary sense. If the principle reaches beyond this, it is rank agrarianism. Railroads are the property of those who build and pay for them, as really as anythirg else. The State may levy taxes on private property in any shape, upon principles of uniformity, but it has no right to seize what is embarked in the carrying trade, any more than what is employed in banking or agriculture. This is an outrage no civilized government has ever before attempted. If allowed as to railways, it is justified on canals, rivers, lakes, turnpikes, carriage by land or by water. If a citizen claims that common carriers owe him the "*best use*" of their mode of transportation, and that he is to judge what that "best use" is, he may claim exemption from the payment of all fares, and make himself master of all he covets, on the principles advocated in the report of the majority.

The principles which they assert, as embodied in the bill, are equally subversive of all public honor and private right. It is assumed that the "public" (used as a canal phrase) own the railways, that the stockholders interest is "secondary," and that the public are to be restored to the advantages promised them in the construction of railroads, which have been "audaciously wrested from them." This is most extraordinary language to apply to their great interests, and is premonitory of violence and spoliation. It can mean nothing else, being totally subversive not only of private right, but of sound morals.

Penalties.

Under the law as reported, if an overcharge shall occur for a single pound, whether by mistake or in consequence of wastage, shrinkage, or other cause, the company so offending is subjected to a fine of $1,000, which sum "shall belong to the plaintiff" or complainant. Errors in bills of lading received from connecting lines, become the errors of the company; for unless it shall detect and correct such errors before it receives the freight, it incurs the penalty imposed. Thus is the company placed, to a great extent, in the power of the informer, whose restless cupidity will ever be on the alert to find occasion for prosecution.

Forty cents per ton for handling, &c.

As an offset to the increased cost of carrying *local*, as compared with *through* freights, the majority of the committee propose to allow the companies 40 per cent per ton for handling, and in the same proportion for fractional parts of a ton. But they seem to overlook the fact that this very provision imposes additional labor, and hence additional cost upon the companies. Thousands of parcels and packages are daily brought to them, ranging from a few pounds up to two thousand pounds. In order to comply with the law, each parcel must be carefully weighed, the fractional proportion per ton per mile estimated, and the fractional proportion of the 40 cents per ton apportioned to each parcel so weighed and estimated. The cost of the additional labor thus required, would more than counterbalance the compensation allowed. And here let it be borne in mind, that shipments in parcels are almost invariably composed of articles which do not and never will go by canal.

The undersigned would call the particular attention of the House to one important fact, that the proposed measure has not the merit of being the source or means of revenue to the State ; on the contrary, if any weight is to be attached to the testimony of the numerous and intelligent witnesses examined before the committee, its practical effects will be to injure the general business of the State, and thereby diminish its sources of revenue.

The subject is of the first importance; and from the fact that much prejudice has been created, and many false views are entertained in respect to it, the undersigned has thought proper to append the evidence, taken by a stenographer, to his report, that this honorable body may take such action in the premises as may be just, believing that the whole matter is more wisely left to regulate itself without legislative control.

GEO. W. VARIAN.

STATE OF NEW YORK.

No. 59.

IN ASSEMBLY, FEB. 6, 1860.

REMONSTRANCE

Of the Chamber of Commerce, against the passage of "An act in relation to the transportation of freight on the several railroad of this State," &c.

CHAMBER OF COMMERCE,
NEW YORK, *February* 2, 1860.

To the Hon. the Legislature of the State of New York:
In Senate and Assembly convened:

The remonstrance of the Chamber of Commerce of the State of New York, against the passage of "An act in relation to the transportation of freight on the several railroads of this State," and "An act imposing tolls on railroads," respectfully represents:

That the first named act, commonly called the pro-rata freight bill, is grounded on false principles of legislation, tyrannical in its provisions, and subversive of the best interests of the State. It provides that all the railroads in this State shall carry freight at the same rate per mile for a short distance, that they charge for a long distance. This arbitrary interference with the natural laws of trade, is justified by the friends of the bill on the ground that the producers of this State need protection from western competition, and that the State canals need protection from railroad competition. Will its passage secure these ends? If it *does*, it must necessarily be at the expense of the railroad and commercial interests of the State. And your remonstrants would respectfully ask, what right has the State to legislate in favor of one interest, at the cost of others? Why unjustly interfere with the chartered rights of railroad companies, and diminish their profits, when they are already seriously depressed? Why aim a deadly blow at the commercial supremacy of the State, when that supremacy is known to be the element which has enabled her to outstrip her sister States in population and wealth? Justice and sound policy alike forbid such legislation, even if other interests should receive commensurate benefits. But your remonstrants aver, and will endeavor to show, that such cannot be the case with this bill. If it becomes a law, it cannot fail to mar every interest it affects, including those it is specially designed to aid.

The railroads of this State now carry through freight at cheaper rates per mile than they charge on local freight. The *pro-rata freight bill* demands their equalization. How shall this be done? A careful analysis of the question will show that it cannot be done at all; or, rather, that compliance with the law will be impracticable on any other basis than a total abandonment of the through freight. The prices charged for the carriage of that class of freight are governed by a competition which embraces numerous lines of transportation, in other States and in Canada. Therefore, these prices cannot be enchanced by the roads of this State, without diverting the whole carrying trade of the west to those of other States, which are now successfully competing for portions of it. Any advance, however small, would be certain to produce this result. If any doubt exist on this point, it will be removed by considering that the bill requires the New York roads to publish their rates, and forbids their alteration for at least thirty days. The competing lines of other States, thus enlightened on the subject, will not fail to take advantage of our folly, by placing their rates slightly below those established here, to monopolize the western business. Nor, on the other hand, can local freights be carried at present through rates. An attempt to do so, would deprive the roads of a large share of their profits. They would soon become bankrupt, deteriorate in quality, be unsafe for travel, and finally lost to their owners, and the people of the State deprived of their use.

Thus the railroads cannot bring about the equalization in their charges, which the bill requires, without producing one of two consequences:—the loss of their through business, or the loss of most of their profits on local business. If they attempt to increase their charges on through freight, they lose it, and it goes into the hands of competitors from other States; if they abate the difference now charged on local freight, they are ruined. Which will they do? The answer is obvious. They will do neither. They will not attempt to bring about the required equalization, but will proceed to comply with the arbitrary provisions of the bill by abandoning through freight altogether, and, as a compensation for its loss, and the loss of the through travel that accompanies it, they will enhance their charges on local freights. They must necessarily adopt this course, for the bill compels them to choose between this alternative and the utter prostration of their business. And what must be its effects on the interests of the State?

It is evident, in the first place, that it must impose heavy burdens on those residing in the interior and in the western sections of the State. It will increase the expenses of sending their surplus products to market; it will add to the cost of their supplies, diminish railroad disbursements in their midst, and paralyze their commerce.

These are the bitter fruits it must yield to those whose interests it is intended to promote. In the next place, the railroads of the State, representing a capital of $160,000,000, must be seriously injured, if not utterly prostrated, by the loss of all their through freight and a share of their through travel.

But these consequences, much as they are to be deplored, are quite harmless in comparison with the blighting effects that this ill advised measure is calculated to produce on the commercial interests of the whole State. By depriving our railroads of the power to carry through freights, it will necessarily turn them into other channels, and send them to other commercial marts. We shall thus lose a large share of that valuable western commerce which now centres here. This loss will be felt in every city and town on the lines of the railroads, as well as in the city of New York. In fact any injury inflicted on the commerce of the State must be felt in every country, town and hamlet, for it is the chief element of her prosperity.

Your remonstrants cannot believe it possible that your enlightened bodies will favorably entertain a measure so fraught with evil as this. Instead of obstructing our means of transport and communication with the great and growing west, the State should do everything in its power to increase these facilities. Our commercial supremacy is not so secure for the future as we are prone to believe. A single act of madness and folly, like the one before you, might transfer our commercial scepter to other hands. We have active and vigilant rivals on every side, and they are exerting every effort to draw off our trade. The Grand Trunk railroad especially, is likely to attract the commerce of the west to a large extent. It is mainly owned by British capitalists, who are content with $2\frac{1}{2}$ and 3 per cent per annum on their investments, especially when, as in this case, it tends to gratify their strong national feelings by giving their own country an advantage over a dreaded rival. It is already attracting freight from the confluence of the Ohio and Mississippi rivers, and it is constantly increasing its powers by securing control of different railroad lines in the western States. Nor should this State be unmindful of the rapid increase in the commerce between western States and Europe by way of the St. Lawrence river. In 1857, the first and only vessel of that year, cleared from the upper lakes direct for Europe. In 1859, the number reach one hundred. At this rate of increase it would require but a very few years for that channel to absorb the whole carrying trade of the west.

These significant and alarming facts demonstrate the urgent necessity, not merely of refraining from unfriendly commercial legislation, but of united and vigorous efforts to increase the facilities of trade with other States. To this end, the canal enlargement should, in the opinion of your remonstrants, be speedily completed and fitted for steam navigation, with the tolls reduced to rates that will insure to it a fair portion of the western freight; and the railroads should be left perfectly free to exercise their full capacity in the same direction. It is only by a liberal and enlightened policy of this character that the State can hope to retain her present commercial supremacy. She must not shut her eyes to the fact that railroads are about to supersede canals in the transportation of goods, as they long since superseded both stages and canals in the carrying of passengers. The older and less perfect methods of intercommunication should not be permitted to stand in their way, and impede their progress and usefulness. The canals and other interests may be injured by them, just as the value of hand looms were injured by the introduction of power looms, but in both cases society is greatly benefited by the change. In truth, the arts of civilized society never take a step in advance without injuring some of its members. But this is no sufficient reason against their adoption. They constitute the advancing steps by which a higher civilization is attained.

Most of the objections urged against the *pro-rata freight bill* will apply to the proposition to toll the railroads. The two bills are the same in principle, differing only in degree. The latter would seriously interfere with the western commerce of this State, but it would not, like the former, utterly destroy it. But the policy of tolling the railroads is mainly urged on financial grounds.

Its friends say it will put money in the State treasury. True, this must be its direct effect: but its ultimate consequences must be to protect the trade and commerce of other States against the competition of New York. In effect, it offers a bounty to Philadelphia and Baltimore on the south, and to Portland and Quebec on the north, for taking trade which would otherwise come to this city. Your remonstrants do not envy the commercial prosperity of those cities: but they do protest against an act of self-destruction, on the part of our representatives, for the benefit of our rivals.

Another effect of the special tax propesed would be to enhance the prices of food brought from the west to the population of our crowded cities and villages, while it would at the same time tend to diminish the employment, and reduce the compensation of labor.

For these, and many other reasons that might be advanced, your remonstrants respectfully, but most earnestly, urge the rejection of both bills.

By order of the Chamber of Commerce.

P. PERIT, *President.*

Attest, J. SMITH HOMANS, *Secretary.*

STATE OF NEW YORK.

No. 35.

IN SENATE, FEB. 8, 1860.

REPORT

Of the Minority of the Select Committee, on the petitions and bills for imposing Tolls on certain Railroads.

The question of taxing some of the principal lines of railroads in our State, is again pressed upon the Legislature, and the attention of the undersigned has been given to a careful consideration of the measure, and of the bearing of the same upon the general interests of the State, and upon localities, as well as upon the property invested in these works. A matter of such grave importance, deserves careful examination, and a wise reflection upon its justice, necessity, and consequences. This matter has, for many years, been considered, and discussed, and as it has been examined, in its various bearings, the same conclusion has been reached by the Legislature. And that has been, that it ought not to be adopted. The first thought that naturally arises in this: Are there now, any different reasons why the railroads should be specially taxed, than have heretofore existed? Are they any more independent of competition? As the canal approaches completion, and its capacity is about to be tested, after having been in a transition state for twenty years, have we learned what it will be capable of, when thus finished, and whether it will be necessary to adopt a measure for its protection, that has always heretofore been regarded as of such doubtful propriety, as to induce all previous Legislatures, since 1851, to reject it?

In the year 1851, the question was settled, and the broad and distinct ground taken by the Legislature, that thereafter no tolls or charges should be levied or charged by the people of this State, upon our railroads. They were left to be regulated, in respect to their charges upon the transportation of property, by the salutary control which the laws of trade will always exercise. There are some very interesting facts in respect to the business of transportation that year, which may be usefully presented and considered. The tolls upon the canals that year amounted to the sum of $3,700,000, with a tonnage of 3,582,000, or about $1.00 toll per ton. The tolls on the canals were reduced, and this at once lessened their revenue. In 1858, the tonnage on the canals had increased to 3,655,000, or an addition of 80,000 tons upon the aggregate tonnage of 1851; but the revenues, in 1858, were $2,047,000, or a reduction of $1,600,000.

Why was this course of reducing the canal tolls resorted to? While this process of reduction was going on, the tonnage kept up, or was increased, as is shown from '51 to '58. In no year was it reduced, except in 1857, during the pecuniary revulsion. It would seem clear, that there must have been some cause for reducing tolls, some sound and controlling reasons. The reason undoubtedly was, that it was deemed necessary so to reduce the canal tolls to meet competition, for that was the ground taken and pressed by the forwarders on the canals. The largest amount of canal tolls ever received (except in 1847) was in 1851. Then the tolls were reduced, and the revenue fell off over half a million of dollars the first year.

Before this period, we had enjoyed almost the whole of the western trade, through our canals. Two years later, in 1853, in order to render our lines of railroads most efficient, to enter upon the competition of this western trade, the various companies owning and occupying the route which is now the New York Central, were consolidated into one company, the objects, design, and reason for which, was to give to this line the most efficient organization, and the best capacity to continue the great business of transportation through our State, and to bring the products of the west to our market. This was most wise and provident legislation, as the event has shown. For had this line been left in the disjointed state in which it then was, the growing strength of other routes, which will be alluded to, would have diverted the trade from our State.

In thus preparing the New York Central railroad to enter upon the course of competing for the western business, freed from taxation, one most important condition was required or imposed upon it. The rate of way passenger fare was limited to two cents per mile. And this is now the rate of passenger fare on that road. It is supposed that this low rate is confined to our State, and that nowhere else can there be found a rate as low. This rate, in first class express trains, is just about equal to the lowest rate in open cars, at slow speed, in other countries. A large local, or way passenger business, is transported by this road, and those traveling upon it, have the benefit of this low rate of fare, which was thus imposed as a condition.

In 1858, the competition in the carrying trade, at the great grain points at the west, had become severe and sharp. These points are far beyond our State. Property designed for market there, at the outset, takes its course and direction to its destination. In order that the owners may use our canal, as an avenue of trasportation, we reduce our tolls, so that, by reduced charges, we may invite such property through our State. These reductions have been so large, that upon an increased business, or tonnage, we actually find our canal revenues lessened $1,600,000, in the year 1858, below what they were in 1851. This reduction of tolls has enabled the canal to keep up its tonnage, but it gets less pay for it. Now the question arises, can it get any higher rate of tolls? Can the revenue be increased, by such higher rates? If such increase can be sustained, then all that is necessary, is to raise the tolls. The same rate of tolls charged in 1858, as in 1851, would have very largely increased the revenue of that year, if the tonnage could have been kept up. While the greatest amount of canal tolls was in 1851, under the process of reduction, the tonnage has kept up. During this period, the great lines of railroad, south and north of us, have sprung up, and entered into competition with us for this great western trade. To meet *them*, we have been compelled to reduce the tolls on our canals. To meet *them* our two railroads have been compelled to carry at *their* prices, or lose the trade. If the canal tolls have been necessarily reduced, so that *it* may share in the western business, so have our railroads equally been compelled to reduce *their* rates, so as to share in the same business. If we cannot raise the tolls on the canals, neither can our railroads raise their rates, because the same consequence would follow to each. They would lose the trade. The two great southern lines, the Baltimore and Ohio, and the Pennsylvania Central, and the Grand Trunk on the north, would at once take the trade. The primary object of very many who press for tolls on our railroads, is to raise their rates. That is, so to burthen them, as to drive them out of the competition. This is why the various measures are pressed against the railroads. The course is justified, because it is supposed that then the business would take the canal. But there is the same power left that has forced down the tolls on the canals, and the rates on our railroads. The imposing a burthen on our railroads, while it deprives our own lines of the power to compete for the business, only strengthens the great lines south and north of us. It cripples our own railroads. It turns the tide and the bulk of the western trade, through other avenues, and to other markets. Our canals will lose, instead of gain, because it will grow up other markets, will turn western business from us. It is vastly more important to our canals, that our own railroads should carry the western property, rather than that it should be transported by the southern or northern routes, because they take the trade *from* our State, and other States and cities grow and profit, at our expense. These rival lines will thus be directly strengthened, and benefited, by the imposition of tolls on the railroads of this State. The object of those engaged upon the canals, who press this measure, is to compel our railroads to raise their rates.

Those engaged in transportation on the canals, may not be good advisers as to State policy, though they have always pressed for the reduction of State tolls, and have exerted the main force that has produced such reduction from time to time. The tolls are but a part of the whole cost of transportation, and if the State reduces, the forwarder gets the benefit, for he may not be forced correspondingly to reduce his share. The interest of the forwarder is always against that of the State; for he wishes force, or induce the State to reduce *its* share, that is, the tolls, while he may not follow the same policy. It is his interest to keep up his share of the whole charge. He finds the Central and the Erie railroads carrying at low rates, because the rates are fixed for them, by the offers of the Pennsylvania Central and the Grand Trunk, and he seeks legislation to force the Central and the Erie railroads to raise their rates, which he calculates drives *them* out of the competition. This result produced, he considers that the canal, as he denominates it, (but really himself), has disposed of all the power of competition for all the property, that *must* come through this State, and so it must come by the canal, that is, by his craft thereon. All this time, while producing this result, he will not consent to raise tolls on the canals, because that would lessen his share. Now is not this a plain and practical solution of the position of the parties. It is the interest of the railroads to raise the rates if they could, and should they turn round and apply to raise the tolls on the canal, they would in fact be occupying the same position that those engaged in transportation on the canal are pursuing in respect to the railroads. If we look at all these matters in an enlarged point of view, it will be found that these suggestions are practical and plain common sense.

It is the interest of the producer, consumer and of every locality to have rates of transportation at the lowest attainable point. But the interest of the forwarder on the canal is to have high rates. Hence he is not a good adviser. It is also the interest of the railroads to get the highest attainable rates, but that point is forced down by the competition of the rival routes, and then they are complained of for carrying so low, and it is even charged upon them that they are carrying lower than they can afford to.

The charges of transportation go to increase the cost of the article carried. These charges are a tax on the producer or consumer, and it is a common interest that they should be fixed at the lowest remunerating point. Those only are interested to raise them, who wish to drive others out of business. Now any effort of this State to drive foreign lines to raise rates or retire from the competition, is utterly powerless. We may injure ourselves and benefit other lines and other cities at our expense, but we can only match them and sustain ourselves by the freeest competition of our own works. The laws of trade are far above the power of any enactments that we may adopt. We may put just such burthens on our railroads as to destroy their business, but we shall only inflict a great injury thereby upon our State and our great city. That city has grown by reason of its lines of transportation to the interior. Impede, embarrass, or obstruct them, and we shall see in our waning trade, too late, that we have bound down our own energies, and unwisely deprived ourselves of a boon that we might have enjoyed.

The railroad has stretched all over the country. It has carried markets into every neighborhood. It has thereby raised the value of lands. Has encouraged agricultural industry, because it has made markets for the surplus. Its power of diffusing trade, of affecting the exchanges of property, is beyond all former knowledge. It has spread over States, where canals were before in use. Look at Pennsylvania, at Ohio, at Indiana and Illinois with their canals and their railroads. Each has had much experience. Each has constructed and owned canals. Each now gives to its railroads full power to compete for business, unembarrassed by State restrictions and controlled only by that law which will govern,—the law of trade.

The means of transportation are now largely in excess of the business, and property must be carried at low rates, because of such excess. Chicago, Milwaukie and Toledo are the great grain points at the west. In each of these may be found the offices and agents of the great railroad lines of the country. Those agents contract for the transportation of the property by their respective lines. They are skilled in the business. They control the charges, and the agents of the New York Central and the Erie, must make as low rates as the Pennsylvania Central, the Baltimore and Ohio and the Grand Trunk, or loose the business. Just so must those who do business upon the canals. Prices at these great points are fixed through, and must be so contracted. Those who seek to embarrass the railroads desire thereby to drive them out of the competition for the through business. Would it not operate most disastrously to the city of New York to have it understood in the great grain points alluded to, that the State of New York had taxed the lines of trade between them and the seaboard? The feeling towards such a measure would not be conciliated by its mistaken character, or its folly, but it would most certainly embarrass the unobstructed intercourse which we wish to maintain with those great centers of trade.

Our canal is just upon the point of completion. Next year or next season, we may see it completed, and it then will be ascertained how its capacity and power of transportation will compare with other lines. It is most earnestly hoped that it may be a better line of transportation than the railroads, and that we shall find the benefit of the great amount which it has cost in its completion. If however, it cannot overmatch the railroads, we cannot mend the matter by legislation. It will only make it worse to tax our railroads. On the contrary, we shall find it our interest to sustain them, to aid them in competing for the trade which we have enjoyed and which is so essential to our prosperity and success. Internal commerce, by means of our canals and railroads, is our great State interest. These lines in free and unobstructed action have made the city of New York the great commercial center of the whole country. All parts of the State have an interest in the prosperity of that city. It is a great mistake to suppose that we can have any interest in obstructing the longest possible lines of communication with our city. At the outset of the canal, it was looked upon with an unfriendly feeling by the inhabitants of the river counties, because the effect was to bring the western part of the State in competition with them. But this was a narrow view, and has given place to more sound conclusions there. Equally unsound is it, for any section of our State to consider that there can be any true interest to tax, or embarrass the railroads, because they bring property from the western States to our markets. The railroads, by so doing, are advancing the common property, in which all cannot but share.

All parties and interests, except the carrier himself, are directly interested in favor of low rates of charge. The railroads are forced to carry low, and for that they are complained of. Disguise it as we will, the plain truth is, that this is the very essence and point, and force of their offending, *that they carry at low rates.* The canal forwarder wishes to tax the railroads, to embarrass them by difficult and burthensome regulations, so as to force them to impose higher rates, and to drive them from competition for the through business. This very plain statement seems to be really the whole of the matter of complaint. It is claimed by our railroad companies, and it is supposed truly, that they transport property at lower rates than any other lines in this country or elsewhere. Conceding this to be true, what is there to complain of? Who is injured thereby? Are not the railroads by thus carrying at the lowest rates, fulfilling, in the very best faith the object for which they are authorized, constructed and sustained? Ought we not to look with distrust upon any person or interest which complains of such low rates? It would certainly seem that the lower they are able to carry property the better for all. There certainly must be a great delusion, to suppose that this great State, can so legislate in respect to its own railroads, as to force them to higher rates of charge, as to drive them from all power of competition for through business ; to make them at the great grain points at the west, entirely and wholly dependent upon the railroads of other States, and other markets, for a trifling share in a great trade that should be free to all.

This question has been thus far treated, in the plain and practical view which would strike the unprejudiced examiner as correct. Allusion has been made to other lines, and it is proper that they should be presented, so that a just estimate may be formed of their relative capacity.

In our State, we have the Hudson River railroad to Albany, the New York Central to Buffalo, the Lake Shore road to Toledo, and the Michigan Southern to Chicago. There is another route by the Suspension Bridge, by the Great Western in Canada and by the Michigan Central to Chicago.

We have the Erie railroad to Buffalo and to Dunkirk, and thence by the Lake Shore and Michigan Southern to Chicago. From Cleveland on the Lake Shore roads connect across the State of Ohio with Cincinnati. By way of Cleveland, also of Toledo and of Chicago, they connect with St. Louis.

The Pennsylvania Central extends from Philadelphia to Pittsburg, and there connects with the Pittsburgh and Fort Wayne road direct to Chicago, and is the shortest and most direct line of rails. It connects directly with Cincinnati and St. Louis.

The Baltimore and Ohio railroad has its first great connection with the Ohio river. It connects also direct by rail with all the other great points at the west.

The city of Philadelphia has a large interest in the Pennsylvania Central, and that interest is an active one for the benefit of that city.

The city of Baltimore has a large interest in the Baltimore and Ohio railroad, and uses most efficiently for the benefit of that city all the power which such an interest gives.

The Grand Trunk extends from the city of Quebec and also from the city of Portland by a single route to Port Sarnia at the foot of lake Huron, and thence by rail to Detroit. At Detroit, it connects with both the Michigan Central and the Michigan Southern to Chicago, and with the Detroit and Milwaukee to the latter named city. It thus reaches all the great grain points at the west.

It is matter very proper to be considered here, that the connection of the New York Central with Chicago is through Canada, and through Pennsylvania and the Erie railroad only connects with the west through the last named State. The legislation of that State has been most severe upon the Lake Shore line, and if in protection of its own railroads, it should follow our example in taxing or embarrassing the line across that State, the whole loss would fall on us, just as it would if we tax our own roads.

It is also proper to say, the Sunbury road from Erie to Philadelphia is in rapid progress, and then our whole trade from the west on the south side of lake Erie is to come across Pennsylvania, though the borough of Erie. If we set the example to tax, embarrass and obstruct roads, how effectually can Pennsylvania close up the matter by a similar course; only we may be sure she will not tax the Sunbury, but will wisely leave the business untaxed and unobstructed to flow over her own road to Philadelphia. This may be no fanciful view, if we commence by taxing and obstructing the trade of the States west of Philadelphia. They might make common cause to urge that State to cut us off. There is not a conceivable aspect of this whole question that is not fraught with difficulty and danger, and we ought not to take a course so contrary to experience and a sound understanding of the course of trade.

The distance from Philadelphia by the Pennsylvania Central, is nearer to the following named places than New York is by her roads, as follows;

To Cleveland by 123 miles.
Chicago " 136 "
St. Louis " 160 "
Cincinnati " 190 "

From New York to the western towns, the distance is less by way of the Pennsylvania Central than by either of our New York roads. It is actually 47 miles less from New York to Chicago by the Pennsylvania road than by our roads. So it is 100 miles less to Cincinnati. The Pennsylvania Central is a most thoroughly constructed road, and in 1858 it largely exceeded the New York Central in tonnage. It has then abundant capacity for business. It has a most central connection in Chicago with all the western and northern roads entering that city. In the event of taxation or embarrassment upon our lines, that will be the most eligible rail connection between New York and Chicago and the great western points. Though the trade first reaches Philadelphia, still that will be the preferable route. If our roads can only sustain themselves at present, what will they do with taxes and embarrassment?

The Baltimore and Ohio railroad is a powerful competitor for the western trade. In its shorter length of line to the Ohio river, it has immense advantages. It was at first supposed that its high grades were a draw-back upon its power; but it has an abundant compensation in cheap fuel. The coal costs so little, that it crosses the mountains without difficulty. The increased power produced by the cheap fuel, levels the mountion.

The Grank Trunk is a new and powerful line. Already it has under-bid the other roads, in the western markets. It is seeking the connection and control of one of the Michigan roads, in its line to Chicago. It has a powerful regular line of steamers upon the ocean connected with it. It takes property direct from Chicago to Liverpool. It receives property on the continent of Europe, and delivers at all the various points of our country west, wherever there is a rail connection. It delivers property in Portland, Boston, or New York. It receives at St. Louis, and all the western cities. It is altogether the greatest work of the kind in this country, and, in some respects, in the world. This great work is sustained by the provincial government, and by the States through which it extends; and this, as well as the two southern roads, are encouraged by their respective legislation, to enter into the fullest competition for the western business. They are rivals in such trade, conducting their business on a large scale, and if fully understood and appreciated, it would certainly seem that we should encourage, rather than obstruct and embarrass our lines.

While the railroad interest has been growing up, and extending all over our country, a most important change has been wrought thereby, in distributing trade through the whole year. Formerly all the surplus productions of the western country were purchased during the winter, on the credit of large commission houses, and was held over for the opening of interior navigation in the spring. The value *then*, of course, regulated the success or failure of the speculation of purchasing during the winter. It was, though necessary, always an uncertain mode of conducting the business. The property must be held, and so held on the credit of some parties. If the value rose, it was maintained; then acceptances were met, and all went well, only the producer, who sold long before the property was marketed, in the reduced price which he received, really paid a large share of the interest and charges. If the value fell, on the opening of navigation, then the commission house failed, and often the ruin extended widely into the interior. All this is now changed. The difference in value, between the wheat of the farmer, in his barns, and at the seaport, is only that of the low rate of transportation, which competition has fixed. The telegraph tells him daily, the eastern prices. His grain, his pork, his cattle, are sold for cash, and the only time between the payment of the value to him in the country, and the realization of value at the place of sale, is the time required for transportation to market. It is the substitution of cash for credit; it is the realization of actual value to the farmer. It is the saving of interest. It is the practical working of actual correct business, for the slow and uncertain working of the old system. It is a great reform. It will never go back. Business is, and will be sounder than it has been. All this is of most benign influence. Precisely the same benefits are derived in transportation westward on goods and fabrics. Values are more uniform. Interest is saved. Large capital or large credit is less necessary. Now, who is to deny that very much of this has resulted from the railroad ? The length of time calculated for the transit from St. Louis, Chicago, &c., to New York, by the various avenues, is correctly understood, and the quick route has been adopted for valuable property. In the uncertain and unfinished state of the canal, for many years back, the time of transit upon it has largely increased, and has been uncertain. This has forced property on to the railroad, and, beyond all question, has stimulated the construction of them. The great cities at the east, have seen the necessity of direct and extended connection with the interior. They have felt the value of their railroads, and they encourage and sustain them. All these reasons have grown up the railroad interest to a position of necessity and conceded strength. Their position and their strength is beyond our power of control, except that only we can cripple our own roads, and thus retire from the competition.

The completion of the canal, now so near at hand, is most earnestly desired. We shall then, with our two railroads, have a strong position to enable us to preserve the western trade. It has been the opinion of men of large experience, of intimate connection with commerce, and the best powers of forming sound opinions, that our railroads, strengthened to meet the competition of other lines, would draw business to the canals, which would otherwise leave our State, and seek other markets.

We cannot monopolize trade any longer, but we can invite, and the spirit and effort with which that is done, will have its influence.

For some time after the Reciprocity treaty with England, we had a considerable business in the carrying of English bonded goods through our State. Now they have left our ports, and our lines, and taken the northern route. There is obviously a tendency, in the ports of the great western lakes, to get up a direct trade with England, and, accordingly, we begin to see such measures in progress. These, while they divert trade from our city, strengthen other lines, which are under the power of interests entirely antagonistic to New York. We can't afford to add to the charges on our lines, when so little turns the property. The small amount, derived from tolls on the railroads, will be a poor compensation for the loss of business, and the depreciation of property in our State. The city of New York may far better be taxed an equivalent amount, and have trade left free, than to have tolls put upon the railroads. She cannot have her trade through foreign routes, and through rival cities.

There should be no feeling of jealousy towards our railroads, because they have grown up a large business. Their profits have been very limited, and by no means such as to excite any apprehension. It is far better for every man in the State, that they should be prosperous and remunerative, rather than that they should be taxed, depressed, and by the same course, pursued towards them, destroyed. They have fulfilled precisely the course that we should have asked of them. Had they fixed rates so high, under a mistaken policy, as to allow the trade to be diverted, which they otherwise could have controlled, then we should have justly complained of their managers, for pursuing a selfish and unmanly course. Then we should have said that they were allowing a great boon to pass out of our hands, that they were depriving us, by their mistake or supineness, of that which, from their position, we had a right to demand that they should preserve to us.

Under all these circumstances, is it good faith to tax them? Where is the limit of taxation? The slightest, it is believed, will turn the trade. A little more will ruin them, and destroy the property. They have not been able to derive the rate of profit on their investment, which is guaranteed by the Legislature, in the fundamental law, in respect to railroads. This law points out the mode of examining this matter. The 33d section of the General Railroad law of the State is as follows:

"The Legislature may, when any such railroad shall be opened for use, from time to time, alter or reduce the rate of freight, fare, or other profits upon such road; but the same shall not, without the consent of the corporation, be so reduced as to produce, with said profit, less than ten per centum per annum on the capital actually expended; nor unless, on an examination of the amounts received and expended, to be made by the State Engineer and Surveyor and Comptroller, they shall ascertain that the net income derived by the company, from all sources, for the year then last past, shall have exceeded an annual income of ten per cent upon the capital of the corporation actually expended."

The plain meaning of this provision is very obvious, and at once raises the question, how can we alter or reduce their profits without their consent, so long as they do no wrong, and do not, and cannot make a profit of ten per cent. Have we not made a fair bargain with the railroad companies, that they, building and properly using the roads, may ask protection, and may claim it against any application to reduce their business below ten per cent. They never will realize that profit, it is very clear, but it by no means follows that we can deprive them of any profit. There are great principles involved in this matter. The character of the State is involved. The imagined popularity of every cry against corporations, and against property, will not allow us to overlook grave questions of interest, to the solemn faith of the State. Now, to a plain understanding, this 33d section is a pledge not to reduce profits. The railroad companies may claim what is certainly sound, that we cannot do indirectly that which we cannot do directly; that the imposing tolls will reduce their profits, and therefore that it is not right to tax them, to force them to abandon a legitimate business which certainly it is for the benefit of the great mass of the State that they should continue.

The right to alter or repeal the charters of these companies when there has been an *abuse* of privilege or *fraud* is clear, but it has not been exercised without cause, and our State has not as yet interposed to reduce or impair the pecuniary value of such investments, made and held in good faith.

It is due to the great interests involved, that this question should be examined in every aspect, with a view to a wise conclusion, because the action invoked, may be so disastrous.

There is still another view of this question. Though our railroads are within our own State, yet they so connect with other States, both east and west, as to make them directly connected with our works, and the comity which properly exists between the States, should indicate to us the propriety of duly considering their interests. It is very obvious, that beyond the bounds of our State, both east and west, this matter of taxing our roads, is not regarded with favor. Of course it will not be so regarded. Property passes over our railroads, consigned from Boston to Chicago, to St. Louis, to Cincinnati, &c., and vice versa. We tax our railroads for this transit. There is no corresponding tax in Massachusetts, in Pennsylvania, Ohio, or any western State. This tax, by the amount thereof, lessens the realized value to the eastern manufacturer, and the western producer. It at once raises the question as to the course of the State of New York. The measure is canvassed *first* in respect to its bearing upon the question of comity, and fair dealing in a common trade, on our part; and *second*, in respect to its essential and legal propriety. Now as to the *first*, if it is a violation of fairness on our part, if it is in appearance, like taking an advantage of our position, and levying a charge on the trade between the States through ours, we should hesitate to adopt it; because States cannot even so well adopt such measures as individuals, and *they* always fail in the end in this line of management. It would be regarded as unfair, and illiberal, and unbusiness-like by us, and means would be found to thwart our aims, to get rid of the burthen, and it would be a lasting charge, and sore complaint against us, that we should be compelled to yield to and give up. We know how we regarded the action of Pennsylvania when she sought by a change of gauge to stop the property in passing through that State, It was here, and in Ohio, considered as an act unworthy of a great State, and this sentiment forced a repeal of the provision. Precisely so Massachusetts and Ohio would justly consider our taxing measure, and we could not hold the position, which we should there assume. This is just as certain as the tax amounts to anything for it is the most natural feeling in our nature, to resist and countervail anything that is not fair. The course of New Jersey in respect to the trade and travel, through that State, between New York and Philadelphia, is another example upon this view of the matter. We have only to see what is the sentiment of our people in respect to that line, and we shall hesitate to place our State in a similar position.

There is another or *second* view of this matter, in respect to the rights of other States, which deserves our careful consideration.

Can we tax the transportation of the property of other States on its transit through our State on railroads without violating the provisions of the Constitution of the United States, which have been held by the Supreme Court thereof, to give to Congress the exclusive power to regulate commerce among the States, and which provide that no State can, without the consent of Congress, lay any impost or duties, on imports, or exports, or any duty of tonnage.

Now the very presentment of the proposition, will convince any unprejudiced or disinterested person, that there is much to be considered. We seek to tax the property of citizens of Massachusetts, on its way through our State, to Ohio, for the benefit of our treasury. This tax is to be paid by the producer or consumer, and is no part of the cost of transportation, and no benefit to the party who does not furnish the transportation, but on the contrary, a burthen. It is not like the tolls on the canal, which are a part of the proper cost of transportation, because they are what the State is entitled.to, by virtue of its having constructed, and owning the canal. The tolls are not a tax on the transportation on the canal. The tolls on the railroad are nothing else but a tax, entirely unnecessary as a means of aiding, procuring or sustaining the transportation. The transportation on the railroads would be just the amount of the tax less to the producer or consumer of the property, if there was no toll, and all the cost, expenses, and profit of the business, would be fully paid. Not so on works owned by the State. If there could be no tolls for the use of the State's canal, then the canal would not have been made.

We can't refuse this right of passage, if it is paid for. There is not in our organization any principle upon which we can make citizens of other States pay tolls, or head money on themselves, or taxes on their property, in passing through our State, or on coming in to it. The whole has been fully paid for to the railroad up to this time, without any tax, and will continue to be so paid. If we attempt to tax the transportation, and thereby increase the cost, that excess is no more, and no less, than demanding from citizens of Ohio and Massachusetts, payment for a license to pass through our State. Upon this subject, and as presenting it in the plainest and most forcible manner, reference is made to a report in this Senate made by the late Charles A. Mann, which may be found as Senate Document, No. 38, for 1851. The whole question in that report, is presented with a clearness and breadth which always marked the acts of the distinguished author, and as it was fully sustained by the Legislature, it will well repay, as it deserves, a careful and thoughtful reading. Nothing since that day has changed its force or application; on the contrary, the course of trade has strengthened and confirmed everything then presented. The following extract from that report is here presented as bearing directly upon that branch of the question:

"The State governments hold the right of way, through their jurisdiction, in trust for the use and benefit of the public; and in the reason and nature of things, they possess no more power to obstruct the use of the rights of way thus held, or to monopolize their use, than they do to obstruct or monopolize the natural highways—the navigable water-courses of the country. Commerce among the States, is doubtless, by the provisions of the Constitution of the United States, to be as free and unrestrained on land as on water. No one would probably claim or insist that this State could, by prohibitory laws, exclude from our borders the property of citizens of other States or countries, brought here for the legitimate purposes of commerce, or prevent our own citizens from carrying their property to other States or countries for market. Such regulations would be a direct interference with the powers of Congress, "*to regulate commerce with foreign nations and among the several States.*" Nor will it be claimed that the State government has the power to tax for the sole purpose of filling its treasury, the transportation of property of citizens of other States through or over any part of our jurisdiction, or the property of our own citizens on its way to market in other States, in case the same is transported on our common public highways. If the citizen of Ohio comes to the line of our jurisdiction with his wagon load of wheat destined to market, the State government has no power to meet him, as he enters our borders, and demand of him the payment of a toll or tax on each bushel of wheat in his wagon, for the privilege or right of passing with his load over our common public highways or through our jurisdiction. The Constitution of the United States has given to the citizens of all the States *the free right of way* into and through the several States. It is expressly adjudged by the Supreme Court of the United States, in the emigrant passenger cases, (7 Howard's U. S. Reports, page 464,) 'that Congress has regulated commerce and intercourse with foreign nations and between the several States by *willing that it shall be free;* and it is therefore not left to the discretion of each State in the Union either to refuse a right of passing to persons or property through her territory, or to exact a duty for permission to exercise it.' The court also, in the same case, say: "A right to exclude is a power to tax; and the converse of the proposition is also true, that a power to tax is a power to exclude.'

"Mr. Justice McLean, giving the opinion of the court, holds the following language: 'If persons migrating to the Western States may be compelled to contribute to the revenue of Massachusetts, of New York, or Louisiana, whether for the support of paupers or penitentiaries, they may with equal justice be subjected to the same exactions in every other city or State through which they are compelled to pass, and thus the unfortunate immigrant, before he arrives at his destined home, may by made a pauper by oppressive duties on his transit. Besides, if a State may exercise this right of taxation or exclusion of a foreigner, on a pretext that he may become a pauper, the same doctrine will apply to the citizens of other States of this Union, and thus the citizens of the interior States, who have no ports on the ocean, may be made tributary to those who hold the gates of exit and entrance to commerce.'

"In the steamboat case of Ogden vs. Gibbons, (9 Wheaton, 200,) Chief Justice Marshall says, in speaking of the extent of the power to regulate commerce among the States: 'It is almost laboring to prove a self-evident proposition, since the sense of mankind, the practice of the world, the contemporaneous assumption and continued exercise of the power, and universal acquiescence, have so clearly established the right of Congress over navigation and *the transportation of both men and their goods*, as not only incidental to, but actually of the essence of the power to regulate commerce.'

"If a State government has no power to tax commerce or transportation carried on within her borders on the common public highways, and navigable rivers within its jurisdiction, does the power exist to tax the same commerce or trade when carried on our railroads, plank roads and turnpikes, constructed for the public use by the government; or in other words, does the state, by authorising the right of way over its soil, to be improved by private capital and enterprise, for the purpose of facilitating the operations of commerce and intercourse, acquire a monopoly of the right of way thus improved? for "a power to tax is a power to exclude;" and a power to exclude confers the power of making the right of way a monopoly, and thus subjecting the right to use rail, plank, and turnpike roads, so far as they are the instruments of carrying on or regulating commerce between the states, to the absolute and unrestricted control of the State governments.

"Railroads are a new and improved mode of land transportation, not unlike in their effect upon the trade and business of the country, to the application of steam power to the propelling of vessels on water. When this state granted the right to the exclusive use of steam power for propelling vessels on the Hudson river, to Fulton and Livingston, it did not take away, impair, or in terms, interfere with the rights of navigation, which existed prior to the invention of steamboats in the methods theretofore used. Yet the Supreme Court held, in the case of Ogden *vs.* Gibbons, (9 *Wheaton*, 200,) that the grant to Fulton and Livingston, of the exclusive right of transporting persons or property by steam power, was an interference with commerce between the states, and was therefore unauthorised by law, and void.

Chief Justice Taney, in the case before referred to, (7 *Howard*, 492,) says: "We are all citizens of the United States, and as members of the same community, must have the right to pass and re-pass through every part of it, without interruption, as freely as in our own State; and a tax imposed by a State for entering its territories or harbors, is inconsistent with the rights which belong to citizens of other states, as members of the Union, and with the objects which that Union was intended to attain. Such a power in the States could produce nothing but discord and mutual irritation, and they very clearly do not possess it."

The citizens of other states who use the long lines of transportation, are deeply interested in the legislation of states and municipalities through which they pass, and they scrutinize them with a sharpness equal to their interest. The citizen of Ohio, or of Illinois, is often more affected by the facilities of the obstructions of our railroads, than are the majority of our own citizens, because they are valuable to him as the way to market, by and over which he sells and buys his wares. He feels directly any burthen imposed upon the line of trade, and such feeling will as-surely be followed by the most natural and common impulse, to resist what he deems imposition and unlawful, or to seek another line, rather than to submit to what he deems wrong.

The undersigned has endeavored to present this question in a plain light, under the conviction that it is entirely contrary to the interests of the State, that it is unwarranted by authority, that its consequences will be disastrous, that it will bring us into disrespect and collision with other States, and finally, that it is contrary to the spirit of the age.

RICHARD B. CONNOLLY.

THE PRO RATA QUESTION.

WHAT IS THE TRUE POLICY

OF THE

STATE OF NEW YORK?

DISCUSSED BY

J. W. BROOKS, ESQ.

ALBANY:
WEED, PARSONS & COMPANY.
1860.

PREFACE.

To the Public:

In anticipation of the contest which is now taking place before the Legislature of the State of New York, in regard to the imposition of restrictions upon the carrying trade of our railways, the undersigned addressed a letter to John W. Brooks, Esq., of Boston, asking his views on the subject. The following reply, though written in December last, is remarkably pertinent to the present state of the discussion, and will throw much valuable light on all the questions involved.

It is worthy of the careful attention, both of those who enact our laws and those whose interests are to be affected by them.

GEORGE H. THACHER.

Albany, *Jan.* 28, 1860.

DISCUSSION

ON THE

PRO RATA FREIGHT LAW.

In considering what the effect would be upon the New York Railroads, and upon the State of New York, to have her roads embarrassed in their efforts to procure business from the West, their geographical position and that of their rival lines must be examined.

The business of the Western States has several centres, to and from, or through which, the traffic of the various districts passes. The order in which these are geographically situated, most favorable to the New York Central Road, are somewhat as follows:

1st. *Detroit*, through which passes most of the traffic of the State of Michigan, including that of Lake Superior.

2d. *Cleveland*, through which passes the business of the northern portion of Ohio, the most of Indiana, the southerly half of Illinois, a portion of north Missouri and of southern Iowa.

3d. *Chicago,* to which converges the business of the northern part of Illinois, Wisconsin, Minnesota, part of Iowa and a part of north Missouri.

4th. *St. Louis,* through which passes a large portion of the business of Missouri, a portion of Kansas, and much of the lower Mississippi valley generally.

5th. *Cincinnati,* through which passes much of the business of the southern part of Ohio, the Ohio valley below Cincinnati, and a portion of the business of the lower Mississippi valley.

The distances of these various points, through which the business of the respective districts is drained, to New York, are as follows:

I.—DETROIT TO NEW YORK:

	Route	Miles.
1.	Via Great Western, N. Y. Central and Hudson River,..	676
2.	" Toledo, Lake Shore and Erie,..................	776
3.	" Steamer to Cleveland, Pittsburgh and Philadelphia,	681
4.	" Steamer to Dunkirk and New York and Erie, ...	680
5.	" Toledo, Cleveland, Pittsburgh and Philadelphia, ..	765
6.	" Toledo, Cleveland, Wheeling and Baltimore and Ohio,..............................	881

II.—CLEVELAND TO NEW YORK:

	Route	Miles
1.	Via Lake Shore, N. Y. Central and Hudson River,....	624
2.	" Lake Shore and New York and Erie, ...	602
3.	" Pittsburgh and Philadelphia,....................	591
4.	" Cleveland and Pittsburgh to Wheeling and Baltimore and Ohio,........................	707

III.—CHICAGO TO NEW YORK:

	Route	Miles
1.	Via Michigan Central, Great Western, N. Y. Central and Hudson River,......................	960

	Miles.
2. Via Michigan Southern, Lake Shore and New York and Erie,	957
3. " Michigan Southern, Cleveland, Pittsburgh and Philadelphia,	947
4. " Pittsburgh and Fort Wayne and Pennsylvania Central,	908
5. " Pittsburgh and Fort Wayne to Alliance, Cleveland and Pittsburgh to Wheeling and Baltimore and Ohio,	1031

IV.—St. Louis to New York:

1. Via Chicago, Michigan Central, Great Western, New York Central and Hudson River,	1341
2. " Terre Haute, Alton and St. Louis, Wabash Valley, Toledo, Cleveland, Buffalo and Albany,	1197
3. " Terre Haute, Alton and St. Louis, Bellefontaine and Crestline, Cleveland, Lake Shore, New York and Erie,	1133
4. " Crestline, Cleveland, Pittsburgh and Philadelphia,	1122
5. " Ohio and Mississippi to Cincinnati, Marietta, N. W. Virginia and Baltimore and Ohio,	1116

V.—Cincinnati to New York:

1. Via Cleveland, Columbus and Cincinnati, Lake Shore, New York Central and Hudson River,	879
2. " Cleveland, Lake Shore, New York and Erie,	857
3. " Columbus, Pittsburgh and Philadelphia,	711
4. " Columbus, Central Ohio to Wheeling, Baltimore and Ohio,	826
5. " Marietta, North Western Virginia and Baltimore and Ohio,	776

From these distances, it appears that the New York roads can never, under any circumstances, be anything but co-workers with the more southern lines, in the transportation business between the West and the city of New York. They cannot monopolize it, nor can they even participate in it, except at low rates of transportation.

From those districts, which, from their age, wealth, and the magnitude of their business, have made the city of New York what it is, the New York Central is so much longer than the more southern routes, that it must work at a much less rate per mile than they do, or it would lose the traffic altogether.

A well-established and popular passenger route will continue, at a moderately higher rate of charge, to carry a decreasing proportion of the passenger business; but even in this class of traffic, if a difference is long allowed, it will finally prove fatal to the interest of the road charging the higher rate, while in the transportation of freight, the line charging a higher rate than another, between the same points, at once loses the business. It is, therefore, clear, that the New York Central cannot make a rate of charge independently of the other lines competing for the same business. Should it charge more, it would get none of the traffic; should it charge less, the trade of the other lines would at once be diverted, and they forced to adopt the same rates.

Much bitter and expensive experience has settled the principle, that the rates between all competing points must be alike over all the routes, which would share in the carrying trade, irrespective of their length.

As no two of these routes are of the same length, the prices charged upon any articles of freight between two competing points, must be at a different rate per mile upon each of the routes—less per mile upon the longer, and more per mile upon the shorter line.

From Chicago to New York, by the shortest route, in connection with the New York Central Road, is 960 miles; by the Baltimore and Ohio it is 1050 miles. The former would get about 7 per cent more per mile than the latter for the same business.

From Cincinnati to New York, by the shortest route in connection with the New York Central Road, is 879 miles; the same via Pittsburgh and Philadelphia, is 711 miles. The former must, consequently, carry for about 23 per cent less per mile than the latter.

Each road will, therefore, get more per mile upon some of its long traffic than its rival lines, and less upon other of its long traffic.

It has been found in practice, that the only equitable, as well as practicable method of dividing the price received for the transportation of freight between competing points, over a route composed of several separate roads, is, by the distance carried upon each road, a pro rata per mile, with such moderate allowances for ferries, &c., as may be equitable to the parties who support them for the common benefit.

Any road which would not recognize this principle, and should insist upon a uniform rate upon freight from all sources, would soon lose a large portion of its long traffic. If, for example, the New York Central would not take its pro rata portion of the through rates with the roads west and south of Cleveland, those lines would send their business from all of Ohio, Kentucky, Indiana, Illinois, Wisconsin, Iowa, Minnesota, Missouri, in fact the business of the whole of the Ohio and Mississippi valley, by the more southern routes to New York. Any other plan of division would take from one road a portion of its earnings to give to another. It inevitably results, that every line participating in the long business, must carry the same kinds of freight at different rates of charges, when coming from different competing points, at lower rates when the road forms a part of the longer line, and at higher rates when it forms part of the shorter line, between the competing points.

It may be suggested, that the through rates are lower than is necessary; this may well be left to those whose daily business is but a continued experience, qualifying them as judges in this matter. Except in cases of unsettled competition, when the public gets all the advantage, the interest of the companies will lead them to procure as high rates as the business will bear.

Before the great increase of railroads in the Western States, the business of each district of that great region had but one general way to get to and from a market. The trade of the Ohio and Mississippi valleys proper went via New Orleans, and that of the lakes by the Erie canal. Rates of freight could then be changed without so sensibly affecting the course of the traffic, and without very materially reducing the area drained in any particular direction. Moderate changes would, in those days, rather have affected the production, than changed the current of traffic. The multitude of railroads which now lattice the Western States, have rendered all the natural, as well as the artificial channels of trade, accessible throughout every part of that region.

Facilities for transportation have increased upon all the outlets for Western freight, methods of management have been simplified, the cost reduced, certainty, dispatch and safety very much enhanced, not only upon the Ohio and Mississippi, in efforts to take business via New Orleans, but as well upon the northern artificial avenues to the seaboard.

If the rate of freight between St. Louis and New York be raised but a little too high, a large proportion of it will go via New Orleans; and that requiring a more speedy route to market, will take the river via Cincinnati and Wheeling, reaching the seaboard by the Baltimore and Ohio and Pennsylvania Central Roads. The same may be said of the rate from Cincinnati; and whatever changes the route of freight from these points, will also change that of two-thirds of the whole West, and other kindred causes will alike affect the rest. It is, therefore, wholly out of the power of the railroad lines to control the price of the long freight; they must take it at the rates at which it is moving through other channels, or lose it altogether.

A large proportion of the long freight, between Boston, New York, and other eastern cities, and the Mississippi valley, as high up as west of Chicago, now goes round via New Orleans, and, but for the low inland rates of the past two years, the increased facilities in coasting and river transportation would have made serious inroads upon the business of the northern lines, which run eastward and westward.

The margin for profit upon all produce transactions and mercantile business generally, in the Western States, has been reduced by the extended use of the magnetic telegraph and the increased facilities for transportation, thereby rendering all holders of property for transportation very sensitive to small changes in the rates, which would not, in years past, have been noticed. These and other causes have rendered the tenure, by which the East and West lines hold a portion of the traffic of the West, such as to require constant and watchful care. A very moderate increase of rates, especially while the Ohio and Mississippi are free from ice, would largely reduce the area of country drained to the eastward.

Within the year, another natural avenue of trade with the West has been opened to use. A considerable number of vessels are now loaded at ports upon the lakes for a direct European trade ; and the St. Lawrence outlet will be rendered a still more formidable competitor by the now opened Grand Trunk Railway, which can transfer produce directly from its cars into vessels bound for Europe, at Montreal or Portland, and will be likely to reap a large return traffic, in merchandise, with the West.

New York city has been made what she now is, by the trade of the West. She once held the only avenue to that source of wealth, and was the sole market for a vast region. Within two years, three new and powerful routes have been opened from all this region to the seaboard, all adverse to the interests of New York; the Pennsylvania Central and Baltimore and Ohio upon the south, and the Grand Trunk upon the north.

The increasing disposition to embark in a direct trade between the lake ports and Europe, renders the present a time when great prudence and foresight should be brought to a consideration of all matters calculated to affect the current of trade passing through the State of New York.

It may be urged, that as the trade of the West can reach New York as well by the more southern routes, as those of New York State, the experiment of a light toll might be put upon the latter without proving eminently hazardous to the western business.

The answer to this would be, that, although the other lines are as short, and in many cases shorter, to New York, than the New York routes, yet they are controlled and managed by an interest wholly adverse to that of the State of New York.

With all these avenues opened from rival cities to the source of trade which has created New York, her every effort should be exerted to add to and not reduce her facilities for trade with the West. Is it wise for New York to be indebted to rival interests for her trade with the West? Is it prudent to allow her traffic to pass through rival cities before reaching her?

It is well worth while to inquire into the relative distances between the great centres of Western trade and the cities of New York, Philadelphia and Baltimore. They are as follows:

	Miles.
From Detroit to New York,	676
From Detroit to Philadelphia,	677
From Detroit to Baltimore,	695
From Cleveland to New York,	624
From Cleveland to Philadelphia,	503
From Cleveland to Baltimore,	521
From Chicago to New York,	960
From Chicago to Philadelphia,	820
From Chicago to Baltimore,	845
From St. Louis to New York,	1,197
From St. Louis to Philadelphia,	1,034
From St. Louis to Baltimore,	930
From Cincinnati to New York,	879
From Cincinnati to Philadelphia,	623
From Cincinnati to Baltimore,	640

From this it appears, that very large portions of the West are much nearer to Philadelphia and to Baltimore than to New York, via the New York roads, and some of the most wealthy and populous districts are more than two hundred miles nearer. During the year 1858, by an arrangement between the four trunk lines reaching to New York, Philadelphia and Baltimore, the rates of freight from Boston and New York to the West were fixed at a price somewhat less when, forwarded via Philadelphia and Baltimore, than when sent directly inland from Boston or New York. This, of course, made the rates from Philadelphia and Baltimore considerably lower than from

New York, and the injury to the lines through the State of New York was immediately felt. Under this arrangement, goods were taken from New York to Baltimore and Philadelphia, thence west to the Ohio and Mississippi rivers, then north as far as Galena, and thence east to the interior of Illinois. The western importing merchants directed their importations to the more southern cities, thus diverting from and depriving New York of the advantages of their importing business, and its roads of their carrying trade.

In view of the fact, that the western importer is likely to make his home purchases in the city where his imports arrive, it is of eminent importance to New York that the passage of their imports through her city should be retained. This clearly cannot be done, excepting the rate of freight to the West be as low as from the other cities.

These more southern cities are but just entering upon the advantages of their position. Want of communication has heretofore excluded them from participating in a trade built up and until now monopolized by New York.

Philadelphia's population has increased to nearly half a million without these advantages, and her progress with them will certainly be greatly accelerated.

Both the Pennsylvania Central and Baltimore and Ohio railroads, were built from motives of state and city policy. A profitable investment for capital was not the moving cause for the construction of either: they were constructed for the promotion of the interests of their respective States and the cities where they terminate.

Their destiny cannot be fulfilled, excepting by taking to their cities a large share of the trade of the West.

The means of defence possessed by New York, to counteract the effect produced by these new rivals for a trade heretofore her own, are simply the New York Central and New York and Erie railroads. If there is a way by which these lines can better facilitate the long traffic, or by which it can be done at a still more moderate rate of compensation, it is greatly for the interest of the State of New York that such a method should be devised. The canal can carry the heavy goods, but the freight which goes by rail, will find its way over some one of the railway lines. It is therefore for the interest of New York to enable her roads to carry all freight which the most liberal policy and well devised system can obtain, and as the rate is the prime moving cause to direct the current, every possible accommodation should be given to business from competing points, and the most liberal policy towards the New York roads is absolutely essential to enable them to do and retain this business. Not only does much of the present trade of New York with the West depend upon this, but also that of all its future increase.

It has been suggested, that it was unfair to charge rates for local business, materially higher for the distances carried than those for through business. A little consideration will exhibit the fallacy of this view. The especial advantages resulting from the Central Road to the traffic along its line and to the long or foreign traffic, are largely in favor of the business upon its line. By its construction and its vast equipment, it has provided an avenue and market for the business upon its line throughout the whole year, whereas but a few years ago, this whole business was at a stand-still for five or six months in the whole year, excepting so much of it as was done by teaming. From it, this community has received all the advantages derived from the difference between railroad charges and the cost of teaming, or all the advantages arising from a business of twelve months in each year, instead of six or seven months only.

The simple question bearing upon the rate for local charges, should be, are they in amount just and proper? They most certainly are if about equal to the usual charge of other railroads and will then no more than yield a fair income upon the capital invested in the enterprise. It is neither wrong nor unjust to the people along the line, that the foreign traffic should be done at lower rates, provided that it is not done at less than cost. In the latter case the company would be rendered less able to do the local business at a fair rate, but as long as the through business paid any profit at all, it would, to just the extent of that profit, render the company able to modify its local charges, and still act justly as trustees to its stockholders.

All thinking men concede that unprofitable railroads do not satisfactorily respond to the just expectation of their patrons. It is for the interest of all parties that every enterprise of public utility, should be remunerative to those who engage in it, and especially is it for the interest of the community, directly reaping the advantages of a good, safe, well-managed railroad, or rather reaping the inconveniences and discomfort of an unsafe, unreliable one for the transaction of their daily business.

These positions being true, it is for the interest of all concerned that the New York road should do all the through business it can procure, from which any profit can be gleaned, even if the rate be very low indeed.

The cost of doing contingent business is not as great as that of the original or fixed business; there are certain very large expenses not influenced by the amount of business, such as the decay of all perishable materials, in the track, bridges, stations, wooden portions of cars, &c., a great variety of expenditures which, in the aggregate, would probably amount to one-third of the whole. The expenses which should be regarded as properly attachable to any new business, procured from abroad by competition, are but about two-thirds as much as those chargeable to the business already done. With this just view of the cost of new business, as compared with that already being performed, it is clear that new business can be sought at pretty low rates and still yield a profit.

I have said that parties interested in the local business should not complain unless the long business should be done at less than cost, and the company thus be rendered less able to do the local business at a fair rate. There may be exceptional cases; if, from any causes of competition, connected with the foreign traffic, the road is liable to lose its hold upon that traffic, it is for the local interest that every method should be taken to retain it, even should it be carried for a time below cost. Better suffer this for a time than risk the permanent loss of a profitable business.

In this matter, it seems to me that the interests of the company and of its local patrons are the same; there can no possible harm result to the local patrons from any rate yielding a profit, at which the long business may be done, but rather good in proportion to the profit obtained upon it.

Nothing can be clearer, than that the New York roads could not keep their local charges as low as they now are, should they lose the through business. They would assuredly lose it at a higher rate of charge, for it must be evident that being carried, as it is obliged to be carried, at a low figure, yet it is the highest that can be obtained.

There is only left for consideration, whether the profits realized are exorbitant; whether they yield such dividends as may justly subject them to the complaint of the community; the reverse of this latter proposition would seem to be the case, as exemplified by the low rate at which the stock may be purchased in the market.

The foregoing considerations, lead to the following general results:

1st. The increase of railroads throughout the whole West has been so great that every part of that region, which was once solely tributary to New York, has now several avenues to other and rival markets.

2d. The number and character of the new outlets from the West, decide by the natural laws of trade what goods shall go by canal and what by more expeditious routes, and no power rests with the State of New York, or her railroads, to change it, and any abridgment of the freedom or ability of the New York railroads to compete for the long business, will only throw that business upon other lines and send it to other markets.

3d. The cities lying to the south of New York, having just been brought as near to all, and much nearer to large portions of the West than New York, the prosperity of the latter city requires that the railroads of New York should carry the long business at the lowest possible rates of charge, consistent with their being kept in a requisite state of efficiency.

4th. But about two-thirds of the operating expenses are directly increased with the increase of business, and therefore the cost properly to be estimated against new business, which has other outlets as rivals to the road, is but about two-thirds the average cost of the whole, and thus it is fair to estimate that a profit may be obtained on such business, though the price received for it be only equal to the average cost of the whole; but if the local business be done at the same rate, it is clear that the entire capital of the company would be lost.

5th. All that portion of the State drained by the road, and to the city of New York, is equally interested with the company in having all the business done upon it, which can be procured and which will yield any profit whatever, as it all tends to increase the ability of the company to charge moderate local rates, and benefit the State at large by inducing business through its territory.

6th. As the business done against the competition of rival routes, though taken at rates below a fair price, is charged as high as those routes will carry for, the pecuniary advantages rendered to the people who furnish it, are far less than those rendered to interior localities, where the railroad charges during much of the year, are greatly lower than any other means of transportation, and all through the year it furnishes extensive facilities not otherwise attainable.

7th. The city and State of New York having just lost their monopoly of the trade of the West, must look to their two great railroads in their effort to retain a fair share of it, and happily in this the interests of the State, fairly understood, are entirely identical with those of the roads.

J. W. BROOKS.